THE GR

The figure of the grateful slave, devoted to his or her master in thanks for kind treatment, is ubiquitous in eighteenth-century writing on slavery and in literary works from Daniel Defoe's *Colonel Jack* (1722) to Maria Edgeworth's "The Grateful Negro" (1804). Yet this important trope, linked with discourses that tried to justify racial oppression, slavery, and colonialism, has been overlooked in eighteenth-century literary research. Challenging previous accounts of the relationship between sentiment and slavery, George Boulukos shows how the image of the grateful slave contributed to colonial practices of white supremacy in the later eighteenth century. Seemingly sympathetic to slaves, the trope actually undermines their cause and denies their humanity by showing African slaves as willingly accepting their condition. Taking in literary sources as well as texts on colonialism and slavery, Boulukos offers a fresh account of the development of racial difference, and of its transatlantic dissemination, in the eighteenth-century English-speaking world.

GEORGE BOULUKOS is Assistant Professor of English at Southern Illinois University, Carbondale.

THE GRATEFUL SLAVE

*The emergence of race in eighteenth-century
British and American culture*

GEORGE BOULUKOS

CAMBRIDGE
UNIVERSITY PRESS

CAMBRIDGE UNIVERSITY PRESS
Cambridge, New York, Melbourne, Madrid, Cape Town, Singapore, São Paulo, Delhi

Cambridge University Press
The Edinburgh Building, Cambridge CB2 8RU, UK

Published in the United States of America by Cambridge University Press, New York

www.cambridge.org
Information on this title: www.cambridge.org/9780521885713

First published 2008

Printed in the United Kingdom at the University Press, Cambridge

A catalogue record for this publication is available from the British Library

ISBN 978-0-521-88571-3 hardback

Cambridge University Press has no responsibility for the persistence or
accuracy of URLs for external or third-party internet websites referred to
in this book, and does not guarantee that any content on such
websites is, or will remain, accurate or appropriate.

Contents

Illustrations

Acknowledgments

Much thoroughly deserved gratitude is due from the author for contributions to this project during its fifteen-odd years. I cannot praise enough my dissertation co-supervisors at the University of Texas at Austin, Drs. Lance Bertelsen and Lisa Moore, ever reliable and ever enthusiastic. The other members of my committee all helped greatly: Dr. Helena Woodard taught the seminar that framed my topic, Dr. Ann Cvetkovich helped me focus in on it, Dr. Jim Sidbury offered the uncompromising perspective of an historian, and Dr. Jim Garrison found time despite all his duties. Dr. Leah Marcus, although not officially on the committee, read many drafts and offered her inexhaustible resources as an intellectual mentor. My dissertation group – Scarlett Bowen and Jenneken Van Keppel – provided an intellectual community and delightful lunches. Matthew Goldstein read and proofread many drafts, only to have his work undone by a further decade of revisions. Stephanie Buchanan helped me work through the thorniest points as we strolled through Austin's Clarksville neighborhood. Beyond UT, many colleagues made key contributions. Among them, Roxann Wheeler and Brycchan Carey, as well as establishing the lay of the land in their excellent books, offered the enthusiasm that inspired me to believe that the project was viable and perhaps even valuable. At Oberlin College, my "Transatlantic Studies" group – Anu Needham, Gillian Johns, and Sandy Zagarell – helped me situate my project intellectually, Wendy Motooka made a few small, if revolutionary, suggestions, and Kate and Bethany helped me think – and eat – well. At Southern Illinois University Carbondale, Ryan Netzley, David Anthony, and John Downing read drafts and proposals thoughtfully; Anne Chandler offered insights and books; Zoltan Markus, Jonathan Weisen, and Natasha Zaretsky talked me through crises of confidence; and Scott McEathron, Ken Collins, Michael Molino, Kevin Dettmar, and Michael Humphries gave my research full departmental support. My brother, Manolis, and my father, Athanasios, tracked down key texts for me in Austin and in Cambridge; my mother, Carol, gave an early version a most attentive reading. John Plotz provided timely advice and reassurance; Sam Baker, his insights and digital copies of otherwise inaccessible texts. Working with Linda Bree and Maartje Sheltens at Cambridge University Press has been a pleasure. Peter Kitson and my other anonymous reader for the press deserve thanks for their scrupulous readings and excellent suggestions. My childhood friend Ivan Kreilkamp has been the academic equivalent of a godfather to this book. Without his vigilant attention, it would have died an early death. Of course, all remaining errors are my own.

Institutional thanks are due to the University of Texas at Austin for a Dissertation fellowship, to the Mellon foundation for my post-doc at Oberlin, to the Office of Research Development and Administration at SIUC for a research seed grant, and to SIUC's Cola Dean's office and English Department for financial support. Many libraries and librarians have contributed much, among them: UT's Perry-Castañeda Library especially the Interlibrary Loan office; Harvard's Houghton Library, the New York Public Library, the New-York Historical Society, the Schomberg collection, the Regenstein library, the Oberlin College library, OhioLink, I-Share, and SIUC's Morris Library, especially Marti Kallal and Stephanie Graves. An earlier version of chapter 3 first appeared in *Eighteenth-Century Novel*, of chapter 2 in *ELH*.

Many students at Oberlin and SIUC have also contributed to the development of the project. At Oberlin, one student's insistent questions led to my reading of Equiano; my graduate students at SIUC have inspired me and subjected my readings to profitable questioning. Many other friends, students, and colleagues have contributed moral, material, and intellectual support: Patrick Amory, Mary Helen McMurran, Dave Mazella, Jon Bing, Doug Eklund, Edward Lewine, Laura Ruberto, John Smylie, Jonathan Ayers, Mary Grover, Chris Stribakos, Carol McCarthy, and Ash Corea. A special, if unfortunately vague, thanks is due to the many members of the listserv C18-L, and to the collective wisdom of the list itself, for contributions to this book too numerous to specify. In closing, I dedicate this book to Laura, Eleni, and Thea, and thank them for their love and patience.

Introduction

THE SIGNIFICANCE OF THE GRATEFUL SLAVE

Before the abolition movement brought sustained attention to the "problem of slavery" in British culture, slavery was nonetheless a problem.[1] Slavery is an inherently paradoxical institution, depending on laborers who are valuable precisely for their human abilities – their ability to learn continuously and to perform complex, demanding tasks – but at the same time systematically, and symbolically, denying them the expression of their humanity.[2] And, of course, enslaving and dehumanizing human beings inevitably provokes their resistance.[3] Peter Hulme, in his reading of the meaning of slavery in *Robinson*

---

[1] David Brion Davis's two classic studies, *The Problem of Slavery in Western Culture* (New York: Oxford University Press, 1966) and *The Problem of Slavery in the Age of Revolution, 1770–1828* (Ithaca: Cornell University Press, 1974), referred to below as *Western Culture* and *Age of Revolution*, examine the contradiction of slavery in an age claiming to value liberty. Christopher Leslie Brown offers a brilliant rethinking of the meaning and effects of this "problem" in eighteenth-century British culture in *Moral Capital: Foundations of British Abolitionism* (Chapel Hill: University of North Carolina Press, 2006).

[2] See Ira Berlin, *Many Thousands Gone: The First Two Centuries of Slavery in North America* (Cambridge, MA: Harvard University Press, 1998), 2–3; Philip D. Morgan, *Slave Counterpoint: Black Culture in the Eighteenth-Century Chesapeake and Low Country* (Chapel Hill: University of North Carolina Press, 1998), 257–8; Eugene Genovese, *Roll Jordan Roll: The World the Slaves Made* (New York: Vintage, 1976), 16 and *passim*; David Brion Davis, *Inhuman Bondage: The Rise and Fall of Slavery in the New World* (New York: Oxford University Press, 2006), 3; and Orlando Patterson, *Slavery and Social Death: A Comparative Study* (Cambridge, MA: Harvard University Press, 1982). That slaves were valued for their human abilities was noted from the seventeenth century: see Morgan Godwyn, *The Negro's and Indians Advocate* (London: The Author, 1680), 13–14, and Colonel Samuel Martin, *Essay on Plantership*, 7th edn (Antigua: Robert Mearns, 1785), 2, 4.

[3] Stanley Elkins' controversial *Slavery: A Problem in American Institutional and Intellectual Life* (Chicago: University of Chicago Press, 1959), arguing that slaves became docile "Sambos," galvanized scholarly interest in slave culture and slave resistance. Two key studies were John Blasingame, *The Slave Community: Plantation Life in the Antebellum South* (New York: Oxford University Press, 1972), and Genovese, *Roll Jordan Roll*. For studies of the eighteenth century, see David Barry Gaspar, *Bondmen and Rebels: A Study of Master–Slave Relations in Antigua with Implications for Colonial British America* (Baltimore: Johns Hopkins University Press, 1985); Morgan, *Slave Counterpoint*; Robert Olwell, *Masters, Slaves, and Subjects: The Culture of Power in the South Carolina Low Country, 1740–1790* (Ithaca: Cornell University Press, 1998); and James Sidbury, *Ploughshares into Swords: Race Rebellion and Identity in Gabriel's Virginia, 1730–1810* (Cambridge: Cambridge University Press,

Crusoe, gives pithy expression to the dilemma this creates: "the problem with slavery is that slaves are dangerous because forced to labor against their will; the danger is removed if their 'enslavement' is voluntary and therefore not slavery at all."[4] How can such a paradoxical state of voluntary slavery be achieved? Eighteenth-century fiction suggests that it can be done through an emotional relationship, a relationship of gratitude. Friday sets Crusoe's foot on his own head, eagerly offering himself as a slave. Friday is grateful, devoted to Crusoe, for having saved his life, happy, even eager, to be his slave.[5] Strikingly, Defoe both presents this relationship as "realistic" within the terms of his novel and also as a form of wish fulfillment, as Crusoe dreams of the arrival of just such a slave before it actually takes place.[6]

Although Friday is an Amerindian, Hulme contends that his enslavement is meant as a negotiation of the issues of African slavery.[7] Furthermore, the relationship of mastery through gratitude is so satisfying to Crusoe that he uses it as the model for all his subsequent social relationships on the island.[8] Still, Hulme concludes in his reading, the relationship between Crusoe and Friday represents "a final step that, historically, was never taken," because, of course, "slavery was never founded on the gratitude of the slave."[9] The actual practice of slavery could not be based on gratitude; such slavery remains a master's fantasy, a dream.[10] However, in the eighteenth-century British Atlantic world, the central literary image of plantation slavery – one which came to have a profound impact on views of real slavery and, indeed, on imagining the possibility of racial difference – was of grateful slaves.

The grateful slave, in fact, was the dominant trope in eighteenth-century fictions about slavery.[11] The trope describes the successful reform of slave

---

1997). For slave revolts, see Michael Craton, *Testing the Chains: Resistance to Slavery in the British West Indies* (Ithaca: Cornell University Press, 1982) and Richard Hart, *Slaves Who Abolished Slavery: Blacks in Rebellion*, 1985 (Kingston: University of West Indies Press, 2002).

[4] *Colonial Encounters: Europe and the Native Caribbean 1492–1797* (New York: Routledge, 1986), 205.

[5] As Hulme points out, Friday is not called a slave, ibid., 205.   [6] Ibid., 206.

[7] See ibid., 205. Roxann Wheeler, "Christians, Savages, and Slaves: From the Mediterranean to the Atlantic," in *The Complexion of Race: Categories of Difference in Eighteenth-Century British Culture* (Philadelphia: University of Pennsylvania Press, 2000), 49–89, critiques those who take Friday unproblematically as African.

[8] Hulme, *Colonial Encounters*, 216.   [9] Ibid., 205.

[10] Gaspar describes eighteenth-century masters demanding "gratitude" from their slaves for humane treatment (*Bondmen*, 130–1).

[11] Those critics who have identified the grateful slave as a recurrent trope have done so in asides. See Claudia Johnson, *Jane Austen: Women, Politics, and the Novel* (Chicago: University of Chicago Press, 1988), 107–8; Katie Trumpener, *Bardic Nationalism: The Romantic Novel and the British Empire* (Princeton: Princeton University Press, 1997); and Moira Ferguson, "*Mansfield Park*: Slavery, Colonialism, and Gender," *Oxford Literary Review*, 13 (1991), 124. The books devoted to slavery in eighteenth-century literature are: Wylie Sypher, *Guinea's Captive Kings: British Anti-Slavery Literature of the XVIIIth Century*, 1942 (New York: Octagon, 1969); Moira Ferguson, *Subject to*

plantations through the ameliorative efforts of a sentimental planter or overseer; the reforms end brutal punishment of slaves, and the slaves become
personally devoted to the reformer in gratitude for his kindness. Their
devotion results in highly productive labor under the new, humane regime
of discipline. The key to this regime of discipline is the threat that non-
compliant – "intractable" – slaves will be sold away to new, presumably
less humane, masters. The first instance of this trope appeared in Daniel
Defoe's 1722 picaresque novel, *Colonel Jack*; versions continued to be
written throughout the century, and into the nineteenth century, with
the majority of eighteenth-century examples coming in the 1780s and
1790s, at the height of the abolition debate.

When examples of this trope have been analyzed, they have often been
understood as part of (or as foreshadowing) the anti-slavery movement,
because they begin with sentimental attention to the suffering of slaves.[12]
Less often have scholars noticed that the trope depends for its success on
two key assumptions: first, that plantation slavery will continue in a brutal
form that makes the humane reformers' efforts remarkable, and second,
that Africans can be induced not just to accept slavery, but to embrace it, to
be overwhelmed by ecstatic gratitude toward someone who continues to
claim mastery over them.[13] As if to underline the difference implied in
the second point, "white" characters in grateful slave novels reject the

---

Others: British Women Writers and Colonial Slavery, 1670–1834 (New York: Routledge, 1992); and Eva
Beatrice Dykes, *The Negro in English Romantic Thought, Or a Study of Sympathy for the Oppressed*
(Washington: Associated Publishers, 1942). The following books deal extensively with eighteenth-
century representations of slavery: Markman Ellis, *The Politics of Sensibility: Race, Gender and
Commerce in the Sentimental Novel* (Cambridge: Cambridge University Press, 1996); Srinivas
Aravamudan, *Tropicopolitans: Colonialism and Agency, 1688–1804* (Durham, NC: Duke University
Press, 1999); Keith A. Sandiford, *The Cultural Politics of Sugar: Caribbean Slavery and Narratives of
Colonialism* (Cambridge: Cambridge University Press, 2000); Charlotte Sussman, *Consuming
Anxieties: Consumer Protest, Gender, and British Slavery, 1713–1833* (Stanford: Stanford University
Press, 2000); Marcus Wood, *Slavery, Empathy and Pornography* (Oxford: Oxford University Press,
2002); Felicity A. Nussbaum, *The Limits of the Human: Fictions of Anomaly, Race, and Gender in the
Long Eighteenth Century* (Cambridge: Cambridge University Press, 2003); Philip Gould, *Barbaric
Traffic: Commerce and Antislavery in the Eighteenth-Century Atlantic World* (Cambridge, MA:
Harvard University Press, 2003); Deirdre Coleman, *Romantic Colonization and British Anti-
Slavery* (Cambridge: Cambridge University Press, 2005); and Brycchan Carey, *British Abolitionism
and the Rhetoric of Sensibility: Writing, Sentiment, and Slavery, 1760–1807* (New York: Palgrave, 2005).
Those works centrally concerned with slave narratives are discussed in chapter 5 below.
[12] See Ellis, *Politics*, 87; Ferguson, *Subject to Others, passim*; and Sypher, *Guinea's Captive Kings*, 257–317.
[13] Ellis (*Politics*, 100) acknowledges these contradictions, but sees grateful slave fictions as progressive;
Carey (*British Abolitionism*, 52, 67) reviews the debates, ultimately agreeing with Ellis. Ferguson,
Subject to Others, sees the limits of some of these fictions, but wholeheartedly views others as anti-
slavery. For more insistently critical positions, see Nussbaum, *Limits*, 143, and Alfred Lutz,
"Commercial Capitalism, Classical Republicanism, and the Man of Sensibility in *The History of
Sir George Ellison*," *SEL*, 39:9 (1999), 557–74.

constraints of gratitude, not only for themselves, but also for their white servants. In Defoe's novel, for instance, Colonel Jack's master, Smith, disdains Jack's offer to show "as much Gratitude as a *Negro*."

Recognition of the importance of this trope – which also appeared, if less pervasively, in drama and poetry, and in non-fictional writings, including travel writing and polemical essays – carries implications for three important and interrelated issues in studies of the British Atlantic world of the eighteenth century: slavery, sentiment, and racial difference. One of the key ambitions of this study is to place these issues in the context of the emerging transatlantic culture of eighteenth-century Britain.[14] As explored in the Epilogue below, the ongoing cultural power of the "grateful slave" trope can be gauged by the influence of such fictions on nineteenth-century US culture, for instance on key sections of *Uncle Tom's Cabin*: the forced sale of Uncle Tom (who could be seen as a "grateful slave" himself) to pay Mr. Selby's debts, a scenario previously envisioned by Maria Edgeworth in "The Grateful Negro" (1804), and the martyrdom of Uncle Tom, anticipated closely in Dr. John Moore's *Zeluco* (1789).

The grateful slave trope, most importantly, when contrasted with the concepts of race underlying polemical discussions of African slavery throughout the century, offers a case study in the transatlantic negotiation of concepts of human difference in the eighteenth century. The trope begins with a nod to human similarity, in the sentimental attention to slave suffering, but ends with the suggestion of meaningful difference, as the slaves are so overwhelmed by passionate, irrational gratitude that they enthusiastically accept their state of slavery. This implies distinctions from the rationality, desire for independence, and rejection of slavery expected from whites.

These racial implications of the grateful slave trope mark a striking departure from the consensus views of race and slavery in eighteenth-century Anglophone culture. Only in response to the watershed moment of Lord Mansfield's 1772 decision to free a petitioning slave in the Somerset case were ideas of difference tentatively brought into the mainstream of debates on slavery. A fascinating example of the consensus views from which the grateful slave trope departs is Edward Trelawny's *Essay Concerning Slavery* (1746). Trelawny was the sitting governor of Jamaica as he wrote. His primary

---

[14] This study is intended as a contribution to the "transatlantic" studies following the path-breaking works of Paul Gilroy and Bernard Bailyn: Gilroy, *The Black Atlantic: Modernity and Double Consciousness* (Cambridge, MA: Harvard University Press, 1993); Bailyn, "The Idea of Atlantic History," *Itinerario*, 20 (1996), 19–44, and *Atlantic History* (Cambridge, MA: Harvard University Press, 2005).

concern was maintaining white supremacy, in the ability to control and exploit the labor of slaves; "our Danger," as he explains, "being plainly owing to the too great number of Negroes in Proportion to white Persons."[15] Trelawny is not exclusively committed to using whites to keep slaves in their place; he acknowledges that "Freemen" of "one Colour or another, white, black or yellow" will serve the purposes of maintaining a "due Proportion" to slaves.[16] To help reach this proportion Trelawny makes two proposals: to stop importing "Negroes" to Jamaica and to exclude them from skilled jobs, in order to lessen the need for their labor. He never suggests that blacks are inferior or incapable, only that they, in sufficient numbers, represent an unanswerable threat.

Trelawny states matter-of-factly that slavery is immoral, and that he wishes for its abolition, but sees that as unfair and impractical.[17] But he frankly recognizes the slaves' humanity, even in his fear of them. He quite cleverly answers the philosophical arguments of Locke and Hobbes that sparing the life of a conquered enemy justifies demanding his service in perpetuity, pointing out that once the demand can be made, the state of war between the two combatants is actually over, in which case killing the captive is no longer morally valid.[18] Further, Trelawny argues, even if the state of war is assumed to continue into captivity, this implies that the captive also has a continuous right to kill his captor and free himself (8–11). Although he treats it as a grudging concession to philosophical views of slavery, this idea of slave and master in a continued state of war seems best to explain his own imagining of Jamaica's slaves, and his motive in writing the essay, which is to plead the case for strong measures to keep whites in a position to enforce their dominance over slaves.

Trelawny is explicit that his fear of slaves is based on their humanity. Noting the large number of plantations shown by the poll tax of 1740 to

[15] London: Charles Corbett, [1746]. This quotation (and the following) is from the third page of the unnumbered introduction. Trelawny published the essay anonymously. For the attribution to him, see Peter C. Hogg's invaluable bibliography, *The African Slave Trade and its Suppression: A Classified and Annotated Bibliography of Books Pamphlets and Periodical Articles* (London: Cass, 1973), 140.
[16] Trelawny here offers an illustration of Theodore Allen's thesis in *The Invention of The White Race* vol. I: *Racial Oppression and Social Control* (London: Verso, 1994) and *The Invention of the White Race* vol. II: *Origin of Racial Oppression in Anglo-America* (London: Verso, 1997) that white privilege in the mainland colonies served the purpose of creating allies for the ruling class against their slaves, and that other intermediary classes, defined in other terms, could serve the same purpose.
[17] Unnumbered Introduction, 3–4, 14.
[18] See Thomas Hobbes, *Leviathan*, 1651, ed. C. B. MacPherson (Baltimore: Penguin, 1968), 255–6 (Part II, chap. 20), and John Locke, *The Second Treatise of Government*, 1690, ed. Thomas P. Peardon (Indianapolis: Bobbs-Merrill, 1952), 14. For analysis of Hobbes and Locke on slavery, see Carole Pateman, "Contract, The Individual, and Slavery," in *The Sexual Contract* (Stanford: Stanford University Press, 1988), 39–76, esp. 44–5, and Davis, *Western Culture*, 116–21.

operate at ratios of thirty black slaves to one white man, he asks worriedly,
"what must this come to in the Course of a few Years?" (18). His answer is
left implicit, as he goes on to mock the ill-preparedness, and the self-
deception, of the planters:

> One would imagine that the Planters really think the *Negroes* are not the same
> species with us, but that being of a different Mold and Nature, as well as Colour,
> they were made entirely for our Use, with Instincts proper for that Purpose, having
> as great a Propensity for Subjection, as we have to command, and loving Slavery as
> naturally as we do Liberty; and that there is no need of any Art or Discipline to
> subject ten Men or more, to one, no need of any Management, but that of
> themselves they will most pleasantly submit to hard Labour, hard Usages of all
> kind, Cruelties and Injustice at the Caprice of one white Man – such, one would
> imagine, is the Planter's Way of Thinking. (19)

Trelawny makes no bones about it: his goal is the subjection of his fellow
men. Although Trelawny publishes only a few years after Hume's notorious footnote suggesting the serious possibility of racial inferiority, such a
way of imagining slaves is intended by Trelawny to register as utterly
absurd.[19] The moment in which he wrote would not allow his readers to
miss the irony: Jamaica in the late 1730s and early 1740s had been racked by
continuous warfare with groups of Maroons – runaways organized into a
guerilla force – and by several revolts.[20] His argument, then, is for a need
for a more thorough, more carefully regulated system of white supremacy
that will keep the slaves' inevitable human urge for freedom in check. The
type of "management" Trelawny imagines is very different from that of the
grateful slave trope.

Trelawny's view typifies two tendencies of the discourse on slavery and
racial difference before the watershed moment of the Somerset case in 1772,
neither of which has been recognized by scholars. Firstly, it captures the
rhetorical state of play, in which the possibility of racial inferiority is mentioned – but only to be mocked, and often to be attributed to one's antagonists
in argument as means of discrediting them. Only a fool who believes this,
suggests Trelawny, would reject my proposal. Secondly, Trelawny illustrates a
mentality in which slavery is to be regretted and African humanity cannot be

---

[19] He does make denigrating comments, for instance about the failure of slave women to be chaste (35).
[20] See Craton, *Testing the Chains*, 81–96. Peter Linebaugh and Marcus Rediker, *The Many-Headed
Hydra: Sailors, Slaves, Commoners, and the Hidden History of the Revolutionary Atlantic* (Boston:
Beacon, 2000), 193–5, argue that serious insurrection seemed imminent in the 1730s and 1740s.
James G. Basker shows that the London press frequently reported slave uprisings from 1737 on: "'To
the Next Insurrection of the Negroes': Johnson, Race and Rebellion," *The Age of Johnson*, 11 (2000),
37–51.

denied but, as slavery entails a virtual state of war, the use of force to keep slaves in place is, if not exactly justified, nonetheless necessary.[21] This attitude was not confined to colonial politicians, but also can be found in the writings of planters, English journalists and indentured servants, as we will see in chapter 3 below. The Somerset case, in which James Somerset sued to avoid being returned to colonial slavery by a master who had previously abandoned him, was viewed as challenging the legality of slavery not only in England itself, but potentially in the colonies as well.[22] This changed the rhetorical situation for discussions of slavery, leading defenders of the planters, such as Edward Long and Samuel Estwick, to suggest, for the first time, the possibility of substantial difference as a justification of racialized slavery.[23]

Given this rhetorical state of play – in which accepting Africans' full humanity is the default position – the image of the grateful slave enabled the transition, at its most dramatic between 1770 and 1790, to a raced view of humanity throughout the British Atlantic world in the wake of the racialization of colonial slavery itself. The grateful slave trope marked the movement away from the assumption of humanity,[24] based on the Christian orthodoxy of monogenesis (the unity of mankind due to a single act of creation by God) to the serious consideration of meaningful racial difference, through theories introduced into metropolitan discourse in response to the perceived threat of the Somerset case.[25] The ambiguity of the grateful slave – its simultaneous affirmation and circumscription of

---

[21] As governor Trelawny was expected to defeat Cudjoe's Maroons, but instead made peace with them. They agreed to return runaways, helping address the threats outlined in the *Essay*; see Hart, *Slaves*, 98–105, and Craton, *Testing the Chains*, 87–9.

[22] Although Somerset won the case, the belief among both eighteenth-century Britons and some later scholars that the decision freed all slaves in England is mistaken. For the definitive account, see F. O. Shyllon, *Black Slaves in Britain* (London: Oxford University Press, 1974), 76–140. On the impact of the decision for blacks in the colonies, see Simon Schama, *Rough Crossings: Britain, the Slaves, and the American Revolution* (New York: Ecco, 2006), 18, 222, 380.

[23] See chapter 3 below.

[24] On the development from this position, monogenesis, to the nineteenth-century racist position of polygenesis, see Stephen J. Gould, *The Mismeasure of Man* (New York: Norton, 1981), 39–42 and *passim*; Nancy L. Stepan, *The Idea of Race in Science: Great Britain, 1800–1960* (Hamden, CT: Archon, 1982), 1–5 and *passim*; Londa Schiebinger, *Nature's Body: Gender in the Making of Modern Science* (Boston: Beacon, 1993), 136–42; Hannah F. Augstein, "Introduction," in *Race: The Origins of an Idea* (London: Thoemmes, 1996), ix–xxxiii; Ivan Hannaford, *Race: The History of an Idea in the West* (Baltimore: Johns Hopkins University Press, 1996), 257–71; and Roxann Wheeler, *Complexion*, 37, 296–9. George Fredrickson argues that scientific polygenism, because un-Christian, remained unpopular even in the antebellum South: *The Black Image in the White Mind: The Debate on Afro-American Character and Destiny, 1817–1914* (New York: Harper, 1971).

[25] Winthrop Jordan, who argues that prejudice preceded racial slavery, acknowledges that spiritual equality was taken for granted in the eighteenth century even by colonists: *White Over Black: American Attitudes Toward the Negro, 1550–1812* (Baltimore: Penguin, 1969), 215.

African humanity, of African capacities for reason and emotion – enabled this transitional role. To engage a metropolitan audience, the trope begins with deference to human unity, before developing strong implications of significant differences. The sentimental, reformist scenario of the grateful slave, presented in fictional narrative, was far more engaging to the values of its metropolitan audience than were the explicit arguments put forth in the polemics of apologists for slavery like Long and Estwick.

The rhetoric of Trelawny – who states "I cou'd wish with all my Heart, that Slavery was abolish'd entirely, and I hope in Time it may be so" – and other early-century commentators on African slavery calls another key scholarly assumption into question.[26] Adam Hochschild, in his lively account of the abolition movement, takes a typical view in claiming that, as late as 1787, if "you had stood on a London street corner and insisted that slavery was morally wrong, nine out of ten listeners would have laughed you off as a crackpot. The tenth might have agreed with you in principle, but assured you that ending slavery was wildly impractical."[27] However, scholars looking directly at the early century have documented that attitudes toward slavery were consistently negative (or apologetic) whenever the topic came up.[28] Well before the watershed moments of the Somerset case (1772) and the beginning of the parliamentary campaign against slavery (1787) – and well after them, too – even the most ardent supporters of colonial slavery made sure to position themselves, like Edward Trelawny, as understanding that slavery was wrong and that all right-thinking men would at least regret its existence.[29] What changed at the end of the century, then, was not the simple acknowledgment of the immorality of slavery, but the sense that the English were in a position to do something about this.[30] Previously, slavery was just another front in an all-out war to establish oneself and one's country in a position of power adequate to ensure survival.

---

[26] Trelawny, unnumbered Introduction, 4.
[27] Adam Hochschild, *Bury the Chains: Prophets and Rebels in the Fight to Free an Empire's Slaves* (Boston: Houghton Mifflin, 2005), 7.
[28] See Brown, "Antislavery Without Abolitionism," in *Moral Capital*, 33–101, and John Richardson, "The English and Slavery," in *Slavery and Augustan Literature: Swift, Pope, Gay* (New York: Routledge, 2004), 13–37. See also Suvir Kaul, *Poems of Nation, Anthems of Empire: English Verse in the Long Eighteenth Century* (Charlottesville University of Virginia Press, 2000), 2–6.
[29] Even Edward Long did this: *Candid Reflections*, 73. For further examples see Brown, *Moral Capital*, 369.
[30] Indeed, anti-slavery was a cause that was taken up by conservatives, not only radicals: Nicholas Hudson, "'Britons Never Will be Slaves': National Myth, Conservatism, and the Beginnings of British Antislavery," *Eighteenth-Century Studies*, 34 (2001), 559–76, and Brown, *Moral Capital*, 333–88.

No one can dispute that "slavery" had strongly negative political con-notations throughout the period.[31] And it was long into the century, too, that the term "slave" continued to be applied to those whom we would now classify as colonial indentured servants. White Englishmen could easily imagine themselves becoming slaves,[32] especially through Barbary slavery and galley slavery to Catholic powers, but also through plantation slavery and even naval impressment.[33] This added, at once, to their willingness to call slavery immoral, and to their willingness to see life as a war-like struggle in which it was indubitably better to become a master than a slave. Hence, the idea in the grateful slave trope of African slaves coming to accept their state of slavery is strikingly new in eighteenth-century discourse. Their acceptance of slavery becomes more emphatic later in the century as "free labor" becomes increasingly central to British ideology. The possibility that enslaved Africans could become free laborers is confronted, and rejected, in a complex move within grateful slave fictions. The ameliorationist reformer invokes free labor as an ideal and models his reforms on it, while nonetheless concluding that the slaves are incapable of becoming free.

This history of attitudes to slavery is of great importance in understanding images of the grateful slave. For, if the default rhetorical approach to slavery, even for planters, is to regret it, the fact that grateful slave narratives question slavery's cruelty is much less remarkable than it may at first seem. Indeed, the grateful slave embodies an aspect of the eighteenth-century politics of slavery

[31] See Michael Guasco, "Encounters, Identities, and Human Bondage: The Foundations of Racial Slavery in the Anglo-Atlantic World" (Ph.D. diss., College of William and Mary, 2000), 12–128; Davis, *Western World*, 3–28, 91–121; J. C. D. Clark, *The Language of Liberty 1660–1832: Political Discourse and Social Dynamics in the Anglo-American World* (Cambridge: Cambridge University Press, 1994); and Jill Lepore, *New York Burning: Liberty, Slavery and Conspiracy in Eighteenth-Century Manhattan* (New York: Knopf, 2005), xi–xii.
[32] As Linda Colley hints in *Captives* (New York: Pantheon, 2002), 47, James Thomson's words "Britons never, never, never shall be slaves" do not reflect the impossibility of such a fate, especially in reference to Barbary captivity. Nicholas Rogers, "Vagrancy, Impressment and the Regulation of Labour in Eighteenth-Century Britain," *Slavery & Abolition*, 15:2 (1994), 102–13, argues that the emergence of "free labour" was in fact slow and torturous; Michael J. Rozbicki documents that new projects to enslave the poorest Britons were dreamt up into the mid-eighteenth century: "To Save Them From Themselves: Proposals to Enslave the British Poor; 1698–1755," *Slavery & Abolition*, 22:2 (2001), 29–50. And some Scottish miners were held as unfree laborers even in the eighteenth century.
[33] These specific forms of slavery for whites were invoked in the Somerset case; people we classify as "indentured servants" were often called slaves in the eighteenth century; both of these issues are discussed in chapter 3, below. For the pervasiveness of narratives of Britons as captives, see Joe Snader, *Caught Between Worlds: British Captivity Narratives in Fact and Fiction* (Lexington: University Press of Kentucky, 2000) and Colley, *Captives*; on impressments, see Daniel James Ennis, *Enter the Press-Gang: Naval Impressment in Eighteenth-Century British Literature* (Cranbury, NJ: University of Delaware Press, 2002), and Vincent Carretta, *Equiano, The African: Biography of a Self-Made Man* (Athens, GA: University of Georgia Press, 2005), 49–51.

that has been neglected in scholarship: amelioration. Amelioration seems to recognize slavery as a problem, but seeks to solve this problem through reform rather than more extreme measures such as emancipation. The solution it offers, in fact, denies that slavery is inherently problematic by imagining that it can be made acceptable, or that Africans can be understood as suited to it. In the final quarter of the century, with the rise of the abolition movement and of revolutionary rights discourse, amelioration only became more pervasive as the meeting ground between planters and opponents of the slave trade. In 1787 the London Abolition Committee in essence endorsed a concept of amelioration when it voted to make the ending of the African slave trade, rather than emancipation, its political goal. Part of the argument against the trade became that eliminating the supply of fresh slaves would force planters to ameliorate the condition of those remaining. Planters, too, argued that they were changing their own laws and practices to ameliorate slavery – that they had recognized doing so as being in their own best interests – and therefore that further intervention by parliament was unnecessary.

The significance of the grateful slave trope's indirect but insistent account of racial difference is that it challenges the standing consensus on race and slavery from within the rhetorical norms of the time. Throughout the seventeenth century and up until the 1770s, positive articulations of racial difference, and suggestions that slavery could be made palatable, were extremely rare. A consensus backed by standard interpretations of scripture – which Trelawny takes for granted – held that God had created all men in his image and therefore they all participated in a common humanity. Challenges to this consensus took the form of brief, elliptical suggestions of the possibility of polygenesis – multiple, separate creations by God which would then lead to distinct natures for different human groups.[34] The most notorious hypothesis of difference in the entire century came in Hume's 1742 essay "Of National Characters." Notably, even Hume took this position in a footnote. Hume's iconoclastic comment did attract notice, but did not attract adherents until after the Somerset case increased the stakes of debate in the 1770s. Indeed, as late as 1774, an apologist for slavery used Hume and his view of race as a bogeyman,

---

[34] For two early and isolated suggestions of polygenesis, see John Atkins, *A Voyage to Guinea, Brazil and the West Indies in His Majesty's Ships, the "Swallow" and "Weymouth,"* 1735 (London: Cass, 1970), 39; and Davis, *Western Culture*, 340 n.17 and 452–3 on Peter Heylen; Godwyn scornfully invoked Heylen's suggestion (*Negroes and Indians*, 18).

accusing his anti-slavery opponent, John Wesley, of Hume-like (and therefore un-Christian) implications of racial difference.

Simultaneous to these developments in discourse, however, colonial practices of racial oppression and white supremacy developed from their beginnings into a familiar system, backed by social expectations and positive law. Several historians of plantation slavery and race take Bacon's rebellion of 1676 in Virginia as the originary moment for institutionalizing colonial practices of race.[35] Since Eric Williams' *Capitalism and Slavery* (1944), social constructionist historians have hewed to his line that "slavery produced race." I follow Williams in believing racialized plantation slavery precedes, and produces, the practices of race, in the sense of the colonial system of racial oppression.[36] But the colonial system and vocabulary of race did not immediately create a theoretical framework.[37] So key questions remain unanswered: how do these colonial practices come to affect metropolitan discourse? How did they bring about colonial racism? Colonial practices, according to this timeline, are established about 100 years before their impact registers on metropolitan conceptions and discourse. Historians have not addressed this question, as work on the colonial practice and the metropolitan intellectual history of race have been pursued on separate tracks, and have yet to be synthesized together.

Despite the inclination of literary scholars toward historically minded social constructionism in the last few decades, it has been the intellectual

---

[35] Allen, *Invention*, and Edmund S. Morgan, *American Slavery, American Freedom: The Ordeal of Colonial Virginia* (New York: Norton, 1975).

[36] Allen offers a polemical overview of "the origins debate," "Introduction" to vol. I, 1–24. For a moderate view see "Race and Slavery: Considerations on the Williams Thesis," in *British Capitalism and Caribbean Slavery: The Legacy of Eric Williams*, ed. Barbara L. Solow and Stanley L. Engerman (Cambridge: Cambridge University Press, 1987), 25–49. For work following and developing Williams, see Morgan, *American Slavery*; T. H. Breen and Stephen Innes, *"Myne Owne Ground": Race and Freedom on Virginia's Eastern Shore* (New York: Oxford University Press, 1980); J. Douglas Deal, *Race and Class in Colonial Virginia: Indians, Englishmen, and Africans on the Eastern Shore During the Seventeenth Century* (New York: Garland, 1993); and Anthony S. Parent, Jr., *Foul Means: The Formation of a Slave Society in Virginia 1660–1740* (Chapel Hill: University of North Carolina Press, 2003). For a contrary view, see Alden T. Vaughan, "Blacks in Virginia: Evidence from the First Decade" and "The Origins Debate: Slavery and Race in Seventeenth-Century Virginia," in *Roots of American Racism: Essays on the Colonial Experience* (New York: Oxford, 1995), 136–74. For arguments that the Williams' model understates Iberian influences, see James H. Sweet, "The Iberian Roots of American Racist Thought," *William and Mary Quarterly*, 54:1 (1997), 143–66, and Guasco, "Encounters."

[37] Williams adds the important caveat that "slavery in no way implied in any scientific sense, the inferiority of the Negro" (*Capitalism and Slavery*, 29). Barbara J. Fields supports Williams and warns against proceeding "as though the chief business of slavery were the production of white supremacy rather than the production of cotton, sugar, rice, and indigo": "Slavery, Race and Ideology in the United States of America," *New Left Review*, 181 (1990), 99.

historians, rather than the historians of social practices, who have been most influential on literary-critical models of race. Winthrop Jordan's 1968 book *White Over Black* has remained tremendously influential, particularly for scholars of sixteenth- and seventeenth-century literature, despite Theodore Allen's searing critique of it in his 1994 *Invention of the White Race*. Allen contends that Jordan's view of racial slavery as an "unthinking decision" borne of a pre-existing prejudice on the part of Englishmen against the color black, and hence against Africans, in effect naturalizes racial difference, reading it as inevitable rather than the product of specific historical practices.[38] Allen opposes to Jordan's view his own, in which racial oppression is a policy consciously deployed by the upper classes of Virginia to win the loyalty of lower-class whites and to guarantee their aid in maintaining a system of labor exploitation capable of supporting the plantation system.

The assumption of the present study is that racial distinctions must not be taken for granted as a reflection of obvious physical differences, or as indicating any meaningfully correlated sets of characteristics, but must be seen instead as simply the results of historical and cultural developments.[39] While my model of race is social constructionist, built on the assumption that both belief in racial difference and the practice of racial domination are cultural systems with specific histories, I depart from the work of Williams, Edmund Morgan, and Allen, in using the evidence of the rhetorical norms of the eighteenth century to bring into relief what I call the "transatlantic

[38] See "Introduction," I: 1–24.

[39] The anthology *"Race," Writing and Difference* has made central to literary studies the concept that race is a fiction: see Gates' introduction, "Writing, 'Race' and the Difference it Makes" (1–20) and Anthony Appiah's "The Uncompleted Argument: DuBois and the Illusion of Race" (21–37); Appiah develops his position in *Color Conscious: The Political Morality of Race* (Princeton: Princeton University Press, 1996), 30–105. The premise that the racial distinctions are the result of social practices, and determined by power relations, is the basis of the "Invention of the White Race." Theodore Allen is a founder of this school of thought; other important works include David Roediger, *The Wages of Whiteness: Race and the Making of the American Working Class* (New York: Verso, 1991) and Noel Ignatiev, *How the Irish Became White* (New York: Routledge, 1995). John Garvey and Noel Ignatiev, eds., *Race Traitor* (New York: Routledge, 1996) and Paul Gilroy, *Against Race: Imagining Political Culture Past the Color Line* (Cambridge, MA: Harvard University Press, 2000), 15, call for the abolition of race as a social practice. Appiah has taken the position that "if we are going to move beyond racism, we shall have to move, in the end, beyond current racial identities" (*Color Conscious*, 32). David Theo Goldberg, on the other hand, reasserts the distinction between "racial identification" and "racism" in *Racial Subjects: Writing on Race in America* (New York: Routledge, 1997), 10, and, in *Racist Culture: Philosophy and the Politics of Meaning* (Cambridge: Blackwell, 1993), takes a pragmatic stand rejecting essentialism but allowing for a culturally defined racial identity for policies such as affirmative action. Cornel West, *Race Matters* (New York: Vintage, 1994), 39, insists that race is an oppressive fiction, but one which makes the black community possible.

gap" in practices and conceptions of race. However much we may regard Williams' argument that slavery produces race as a bedrock truth, then, we still have to explain how the colonial practices of race produced by slavery got translated into a theory of difference, and into metropolitan beliefs and discourses. Indeed, as Trelawny's essay suggests, colonial practices of racial oppression do not appear to have led directly to concepts of racial inferiority even in the colonies themselves.

My argument against any stable concept of natural or essential human difference before the eighteenth century depends on an analysis of representations of Africa. These are the representations on which Jordan's interpretation of pre-existing prejudice depends. I argue, drawing on the position of historian of Africa P. E. H. Hair, that these representations clearly show xenophobia, but fail to indicate any concept of essential difference.[40] Indeed, seventeenth-century travel writing about West Africa is obsessively concerned with specifically cultural forms of difference, especially religion, commerce and the aristocratic bearing, or lack of it, of African kings and potentates. Winthrop Jordan himself argues that the categories of "nature" and "nurture" are far less stable in seventeenth- and eighteenth-century discourse than twentieth-century scholars have expected them to be.[41] This is true, and therefore it is important both to broaden the sense of what cultural difference may mean in the eighteenth century, and to be careful not to impose anachronistic distinctions on eighteenth-century texts.

The fact that the grateful slave trope supports an ameliorative vision undermines an assumption of many studies of slavery and abolition. Sentimental sympathy has often been seen as a driving force of the abolition movement.[42] But if such sentimental sympathy can support amelioration as

---

[40] P. E. H. Hair, "Attitudes to Africans in English Primary Sources on Guinea up to 1650," *History in Africa*, 26 (1999), 43–68.

[41] See chapter 3, pp. 104–5 below.

[42] For the key statement, see Davis, *Western Culture*, 333–7, and *Age of Revolution*, 46. No one in *Anti-Slavery Debate: Capitalism and Abolitionism as a Problem in Historical Interpretation*, ed. Thomas Bender, (Berkeley: University of California Press, 1992) questions this, although the debate is about the linkage of sentiment, abolition, and capitalism: see especially Thomas L. Haskell, "Capitalism and the Origins of Humanitarian Sensibility, Part I & Part II," *American Historical Review*, 90 (1985), 339–61, 547–67 (rpt. in *The Slavery Debate*). Literary scholars have followed Sypher, *Guinea's Captive Kings*, 105 and *passim*. R. B. Heilman describes "humanitarianism" as "the alma mater of emancipation," *America in English Fiction: 1760–1800* (Baton Rouge: Louisiana State University Press, 1937), 29. Jordan, *White Over Black*, 368–9, endorses the linkage, offering the caveat that humanitarian amelioration could work against abolition by making slavery seem acceptable. See also James Walvin, *England Slaves and Freedom* (Jackson: University Press of Mississippi, 1986), 100; Paul Langford, *A Polite and Commercial People* (New York: Oxford University Press, 1992), 514; Chris Jones, *Radical Sensibility: Literature and Ideas in the 1790s* (New York: Routledge, 1993), 2; and

well as emancipation, the association between sentimental sympathy and the ending of slavery becomes much more complex. The sudden, unexpected, unprecedented emergence of a new type of feeling – sympathy for those at the very bottom of society – has been framed as a kind of humanitarian miracle of the eighteenth century. While the disinterested commitment of abolitionists is wonderful and admirable, however, this version of events leads to a quite distorted understanding of sentimentalism. The grateful slave is a case study in the use of sentiment to support slavery (while demanding its reform) and to imagine racial difference as a powerful reality (if within certain conceptual bounds). Sentiment, on close inspection, turns out to be a cultural form without a predetermined content. This is a noteworthy point, because scholars, directly and indirectly, have linked sentiment, anti-slavery and the novel together, seeing all three as technologies of bourgeois power, and thus as ultimately sharing a single political agenda.[43]

It is my argument, instead, that the sentimental aspect of the grateful slave trope engages an established tradition – familiar from the late seventeenth century – of using emotional response to oppression and torture as a way of distancing oneself from responsibility for such aspects of the colonial enterprise. Indeed, I contend that such evasive sentimental posturing relates to emerging models of British identity, cast in opposition to the "black legend" of Spanish cruelty, and through identification with the martyr-victims of Foxe's *Book of Martyrs*. However, this is only one strand of sentiment, a plastic cultural posture that could be used to defend slavery and to attack radical politics, even while being otherwise deployed to undermine the hegemony of the aristocracy.

Like sentimentalism more broadly, the grateful slave trope was also, to a lesser degree, plastic. By the last decades of the eighteenth century, the grateful slave was familiar enough that it did not register as belonging to a specific party or position, and could be embraced by ardent supporters of the slave trade, ameliorationist reformers who disliked the trade but feared emancipation, and even by advocates of violent slave uprisings. Still, it always contained two central elements: an ameliorative view of slavery, and suggestion of racial difference. This rise to universality coincided with the

Phillip Fisher, "Making a Thing into a Man: The Sentimental Novel and Slavery," in *Hard Facts: Setting and Form in the American Novel* (New York: Oxford University Press, 1985), 87–127. For recent dissent, see Amit S. Rai, *Rule of Sympathy: Sentiment, Race and Power 1750–1850* (New York: Palgrave, 2002), 1, 6 and *passim*; Nussbaum, *Limits*, 142–50; Carey, *British Abolitionism*, 11; and Brown, *Moral Capital*.

[43] An influential example is G. J. Barker-Benfield, *The Culture of Sensibility: Sex and Society in Eighteenth-Century Britain* (Chicago: University of Chicago Press, 1992), 224–5.

philosophical ascendancy of theories of racial difference. The philosophers Kant, Jefferson, and Raynal shared a consensus on the irrational, passionate nature of Africans that amounted to a more explicit version of the difference implied by grateful slave novelists. Black Atlantic writers Ignatius Sancho, Olaudah Equiano and Ottobah Cugoano were alone in resisting the racial implications of the grateful slave, despite the numberless anti-slavery texts of the abolition debate. Equiano, for instance, confirms the effectiveness of one master's management strategy of backing up kindness with the threat of being sold for "bad" behavior, explaining that slaves work harder for him because they are "afraid of disobliging him," not out of gratitude.[44] But even Equiano and Sancho saw amelioration as, on the whole, desirable.

In sum, the grateful slave trope seems to call attention to the suffering and humanity of slaves, but it nonetheless works to imagine the problem of slavery solved by showing African slaves as capable of becoming devoted to their masters and even as embracing their condition. Furthermore, once gratitude makes certain forms of slavery acceptable, deeper differences between master and slave begin to be implied. Indeed, after 1787, those who protest vigorously against the abuse of slaves, but accept the view of blacks as irrationally passionate, are likely the most effective at establishing the conceptual possibility of racial difference for their metropolitan readers. This account of the dissemination of racial difference challenges the positions of Winthrop Jordan and David Brion Davis, who argued influentially in the late 1960s that the belief in racial difference originated with the first contacts between English and Africans. Jordan and Davis hold that the concept of difference emerged out of pre-existing prejudice against blackness in European culture, and was well established (if not clearly articulated) in the eighteenth-century Anglophone world.

The Grateful Slave, although committed to the idea that texts can work to change culture, nonetheless breaks with the methodology of the literary Foucauldians of the 1980s and 1990s. It breaks with the New Historicism by insisting on viewing cultural categories in a diachronic frame. By demonstrating that representations cannot be said to generate the social category of race without reference to the history of social practices, it also breaks from the methodology of Foucauldian literary historians like Nancy Armstrong, who insist that representations precede, rather than reflect, social realities.

---

[44] Olaudah Equiano, *The Interesting Narrative and Other Writings*, ed. Vincent Carretta (New York: Penguin, 1995), 100.

Instead, *The Grateful Slave* attempts to account for the interplay between discourses and social practices of race, through which race as a primary category of identity was developed and disseminated unevenly across the Atlantic world. This approach allows a fresh synthesis of work on race in previously unreconciled fields, especially social histories of race in the colonies emphasizing the practice of whiteness, and intellectual histories of the conceptualization of race in the metropole focused on science and the nineteenth-century change from monogenesis to polygenesis.

The purview of the present study is limited to prose works, offering a detailed history of the development of the grateful slave trope in fiction, with contextualized comparisons to polemical writing and travel writing. My claims for the importance of representations of slave gratitude depend most heavily on the specific history of the trope in fictional works. Nonetheless, grateful slaves played a role – if a less emphatic one – throughout literary and visual culture. In poetry, other tropes – particularly tragic stories deriving from the "Inkle and Yarico" story and Thomas Day's "Dying Negro" – were more dominant, but grateful slaves appeared, as they did in drama.[45] In visual culture, the pervasive image of the prayerful, kneeling slave of the famous Wedgwood medal can be taken in the spirit of the trope (see Figure 1), offering those who would labor for abolition reassurance that ex-slaves would be submissive and grateful to them for their efforts.[46] Similar black figures, kneeling at the feet of such icons as Ben Franklin and Lady Liberty, were used in both England and America to celebrate abolition and emancipation acts and to imply that freed slaves

---

[45] Many poems touch on the possibilities of ameliorative kindness and resulting slave gratitude. Notable examples are excerpted in James G. Basker, ed., *Amazing Grace: An Anthology of Poems about Slavery, 1660–1810* (New Haven: Yale University Press, 2002): "The Planter's Charity," 1704, attributed to Bernard Mandeville) (45) James Grainger, book 4 of "the Sugar Cane" 1764 (158) William Cowper's "Charity," 1782 (295) anonymous hymns attributed to a Lady, published by Phillip Gibbes, 1797 (512–13) and David Humphreys on the reception of General Washington by his slaves after he wrote their manumission into his will, 1800 (549). In drama see Thomas Bellamy's *The Benevolent Planters* (1789), reprinted in Jeffery N. Cox, ed., *Slavery, Abolition and Emancipation: Writings in the British Romantic Period*, vol. V, *Drama* (London: Pickering and Chatto, 1999), 109–28; slaves promise gratitude for kindness, without it being a major plot element, in Archibald Maclaren, *The Negro Slaves* (London, 1799), 10, 12, 17; John Fawcett's *Obi, or Three-Fingered Jack*, in Cox, *Slavery*, 204; and William Hutchinson, *The Princess of Zanfara* (London: Wilkie, 1789), 5. Elizabeth Inchbald's *Such Things Are* (London: J. Robinson, 1788), 73, offers a contrasting view of gratitude in India.

[46] See Jan Nederveen Pieterse, *White on Black: Images of Africa and Blacks in Western Popular Culture* (New Haven: Yale University Press, 1992), 58–60; Barbara E. Lacey, "Visual Images of Blacks in Early American Imprints," *William and Mary Quarterly*, 53:1 (1996), 155; and Marcus Wood, *Blind Memory: Visual Representations of Slavery in England and America 1780–1865* (New York: Routledge, 2000), 21–3.

1. *The Kneeling Slave, "Am I not a Man and a Brother,"* Oil on canvas after Wedgwood Medallion; English School, eighteenth century. Copyright Wilberforce House, Hull City Museums and Art Galleries, UK. Courtesy of The Bridgeman Art Library International.

2. Samuel Jennings, *Liberty Displaying the Arts and Sciences*, 1792, Courtesy of
Winterthur Museum, Delaware.

would, in their thankfulness, remain devoted, even subservient, to whites
(see Figures 2 and 3).[47] Of course, other images of blacks, particularly the
orientalized image of the young black servant, were also very common in
the British eighteenth century.[48]

[47] Such pictures include Samuel Jennings, *Liberty Displaying the Arts and Sciences*, 1792, Library
Company of Philadelphia, in Albert Boime, *The Art of Exclusion: Representing Blacks in the
Nineteenth Century* (Washington: Smithsonian Institution, 1990), figs. 2–8; Christian August
Lorentzen, *Homage to Ben Franklin*, 1790s, in Hugh Honour, *The Image of the Black in Western
Art*, vol. IV, *From The American Revolution to World War I*, pt. 1, *Slaves and Liberators* (Cambridge,
MA: Harvard University Press, 1989), 76; an illustration engraved by William Henry Worthington
after Robert Smirke for the volume *Poems on the Abolition of the Slave Trade* in Honour, *Image*, 97,
and Richard Westmarcott's Funerary Monument for Charles James Fox, 1812–22, in Honour,
Image, 99–100.
[48] See David Dabydeen, *Hogarth's Blacks: Images of Blacks in Eighteenth-Century English Art* (Athens,
GA: University of Georgia Press, 1987); in addition to those studies listed in notes 46–7, see Debbie
Lee, "Intimacy as Imitation: Monkeys in Blake's Engravings for Stedman's *Narrative*," in *Slavery
and the Romantic Imagination*, 66–119, and Peter Erickson, "Representations of Blacks and Blackness
in the Renaissance," *Criticism*, 35:4 (1993), 499–527.

3. Robert Smirke, illustration for James Montgomery, "The West Indies, a Poem in 4 Parts," in James Montgomery, James Grahame, and E. Benger, *Poems on the Abolition of the Slave Trade*, 1809, engraved by William Henry Worthington. Courtesy of Morris Library, Southern Illinois University Carbondale.

The Grateful Slave, despite its focus on prose writing, attempts to provide a thick description of the cultural context of images of slave gratitude. The next section of this introduction establishes a comparative framework, relevant to all the subsequent chapters, by establishing the cultural status of gratitude in the Anglophone eighteenth century beyond representations of African slaves, including a consideration of gratitude in narratives of white Barbary slaves.

WHITE SLAVERY, WHITE GRATITUDE:
COMPARATIVE FRAMEWORK

Outside of the context of colonial slavery, gratitude was an oft-invoked value in the transatlantic eighteenth century.[49] "Gratitude" was, in the seventeenth century, the proper mode of feeling in a large number of hierarchical relationships, at least for the person defined as occupying the inferior power position. Christians were to feel grateful to God for their creation and for the providence guiding their lives. Children were to feel grateful to their parents for their lives. Both of these relationships were beyond question, outside of rational assessment or ongoing reevaluation. God, and parents, were both understood to deserve gratitude not for specific acts of kindness or benevolence, not for opportunities provided, but simply for one's creation, one's very existence.[50] Slave gratitude appears to follow the same logic, but, as we will see in the chapters below, white characters in grateful slave fictions make it clear that the obligations of gratitude are not appropriate determinants of their behavior.

In English politics, the civil war was accompanied by a rethinking of the relationship between the people and the sovereign. As the king was often understood as a "master" and a "father," these rethinkings affect the understanding of these other relationships as well. In the view of Filmer and Hobbes, the king should be obeyed without question, much like God or the father of the family; the Lockean contractarian view of the king's ongoing responsibility to the people implies the need for rational assessment to determine when gratitude is owed. In line with the patriarchal views of Filmer and Hobbes, gratitude began the period as the default expectation for women's attitudes toward their lovers in courtship, and for servants toward their masters – in a world in which any relationship between an employer

---

[49] See Jay Fliegelman, *Prodigals and Pilgrims: The American Revolution Against Patriarchal Authority 1750–1800* (Cambridge: Cambridge University Press, 1982); Maaja Stewart, "Ingratitude in *Tom Jones*," *Journal of English and Germanic Philology*, 89 (1990), 512–32; and William Gosnell Sayres, "The Discourse of Gratitude in the Novels of Jane Austen" (Ph.D. diss., University of New Hampshire, 1995).

[50] See Stewart, "Ingratitude"; Fliegelman, *Prodigals*; Gordon J. Schochet, *The Authoritarian Family and Political Attitudes in 17th-Century England: Patriarchalism in Political Thought*, 1975 (New Brunswick: Transaction, 1988); and Anthony Fletcher, *Gender, Sex and Subordination in England 1500–1800* (New Haven: Yale University Press, 1995), 99–279.

and an employee could be understood as a "master/servant" relationship.[51] By the end of the eighteenth century, key changes had come about in all these relationships, and (except perhaps for the relationship to God) they had all been redefined as subject to negotiation and to ongoing reassessment.[52] Thus according to Jay Fliegelman, the American colonists justified their rejection of England, and even their war for independence, by making an analogy between England and an unreasonable, tyrannical parent, a parent who inhibits its children from maturing beyond their nonage and attaining independence. Similarly, by the end of the eighteenth century, "benevo- lence" had become an ideal by which to judge those in positions of power, from kings and parents to suitors and masters of servants and slaves. What had been taken for granted as an inherent aspect of power was redefined as a virtue, and even a rare virtue, in the culture of sentimentalism.

Given this brief history of the relationship between gratitude and benev- olence in the transatlantic long eighteenth century, the scenario of the grateful slave is hardly an unexpected one. Slaves, like servants, children, wives, predictably are expected to be grateful. The key questions are, first, whether or not slave gratitude is understood as an inevitable debt, or as being earned by the master's active benevolence; second, whether or not slave gratitude differs from that of children, wives, servants, and subjects; and, finally, whether slave gratitude undergoes the same process of reevaluation, or instead takes a unique – and therefore especially revealing – course.

My argument is that African slaves in particular are consistently repre- sented to be grateful in ways that exceed the expectations for whites. Gratitude continues to be expected to produce binding obligation for slaves even as it is increasingly understood as needing to be subordinated to independence for Europeans, whether gentlemen or laborers. English masters – if they are "kind" – are treated like fathers, kings, or gods in relation to their slaves, and the slaves actively accept this relationship. The seemingly rational and contractual relationships for which the Africans express gratitude are uncomfortably circumscribed, and have the feeling of bad faith about them. Indeed, novels representing the grateful slave do follow the broad parameters of the paradigm that I have outlined, as they show the reformer actively earning the slaves' gratitude through benevo- lence, with an increasing tendency to present the debt of gratitude in

---

[51] Daniel Defoe, *The Great Law of Subordination Consider'd* (London: S. Harding *et al.*, 1726).

[52] See J. J. Hecht, *The Domestic Servant Class in Eighteenth-Century England* (London: RKP, 1956) and Scarlett Bowen, "'A Sawce-Box and Boldface Indeed': Refiguring the Female Servant in the Pamela–Antipamela Debate," *Studies in Eighteenth-Century Culture*, 28 (1999), 257–85.

pseudo-contractual terms, and a decreasing tendency to show him as intentionally imposing, or mystifying, his authority. But unlike the protagonists of English novels (Crusoe and Clarissa being classic examples), or the English colonists in the Americas, or indeed representations of servants in English households, the slaves in this scenario never chafe against their masters' demands, never try to assert their own independence or maturity, and never seek to renegotiate their contract of gratitude.

This gap between black and white versions of gratitude grows increasingly pronounced at the end of the century, as white protagonists emphasize their maturity, rationality, and independence. Hence, the slaves' gratitude at once connects to a dearly held value, represents a desire for a return to the patriarchal worker/employer relations of a pre-contractual era, and serves as a marker of difference in the present moment. Slave gratitude, in its excess, its failure to be trammeled by reason, marks Africans as different from the British. Furthermore, slave gratitude is the opposite side of the coin from bloody vengeance, which is sometimes presented as equally natural to Africans. The idea that Africans could be grateful for slavery marks them as excluded from the values of liberty and independence which were already established as part of, but nonetheless increasingly central to, the definition of Englishness. British readers of grateful slave fictions, then, were asked to accept that Africans' capacity to control emotion through reason, and their self-conception and expectations, were radically different from their own.

Not unexpectedly, then, comparing slave gratitude with "gratitude" as experienced by European characters, expressed in autobiographical writings, and codified in moral philosophy, reveals a great disparity. The gratitude of sentimental protagonists, or gentlemen, must be unsolicited to be genuine and to influence their behavior. Indeed, sentimental feeling depends on reason and on the ability to maintain integrity and independence, or else even the sympathy it promotes ceases to be meaningful. Rousseau (often considered a key advocate of sentimentalism) once haughtily broke off his friendship with a benefactress, Madame d'Epinay. Under pressure to accompany her on a trip to Geneva, Rousseau denied that he owed a debt of gratitude, and invoked the chains of slavery in an instance much less famous than the opening of the *Social Contract*. In a 1757 letter to d'Epinay's lover, Grimm, he wrote:

As for kindnesses, I do not like them, I do not want them, and I do not feel grateful to those who force me to accept them, as I explained to Mme d'Epinay before I received any from her. It is not that I object any more than anyone else to the sweet chains of friendship – but once the chain is pulled too tight, it breaks, and I am free.[53]

While Rousseau's behavior may not adhere precisely to the canons of gentlemanly conduct, nonetheless, he emphasizes the need for emotion to be spontaneous and genuine in order to be compelling. "Kindnesses" one is "forced to accept" will not elicit gratitude. The very act of demanding gratitude negates the obligation felt.

Two British writers considering ethics from a philosophical perspective in the second half of the eighteenth century take approaches to gratitude that, while emphasizing its moral importance, nonetheless resonate with the limits that Rousseau places on the demand for the performance of obligations. In Robert Dodsley's extremely popular pseudo-Hindu text, *The Oeconomy of Human Life* (1750), "gratitude" is one of the entries in the section on "social duties."[54] Dodsley begins the section by effusively praising the moral force and social value of gratitude, and concentrating specifically on the joys of gratitude for those receiving favors: "the heart of a grateful man delighteth in returning a benefit received."[55] Strikingly for a text written by an ex-servant and presented as a document conveyed to Europe from the colonial endeavors of the East, Dodsley ends the section with an emphasis on the uncomfortable effects of disparities of power in relationships of gratitude:[56]

Envy not thy benefactor; neither strive to conceal the benefit, he hath conferr'd: for, though to oblige is better than to be obliged, though the act of generosity commandeth admiration, yet the humility of gratitude toucheth the heart; and is amiable in the sight both of God and man.

But receive not a favour from the hand of the proud; to the selfish and avaricious have no obligation: the vanity of Pride shall expose thee to shame; the greediness of Avarice shall never be satisfy'd. (83)

---

[53] Maurice Cranston, *The Noble Savage: Jean-Jacques Rousseau 1754–1762* (Chicago: University of Chicago Press, 1991), 86.

[54] Despite occasional attribution to Lord Chesterfield, Dodsley is almost certainly the author; see Ralph Straus, *Robert Dodsley: Poet, Publisher, and Playwright*, 1910 (New York: Burt Franklin, 1968), 169–81; Donald D. Eddy, "Dodsley's 'Oeconomy of Human Life,' 1750–1751," *Modern Philology*, 85:4 (1988), 462; and Harry M. Solomon, *The Rise of Robert Dodsley: Creating the New Age of Print* (Carbondale, IL: Southern Illinois University Carbondale Press, 1996), 300 n. 69. Solomon, documenting its popularity, notes that "No book published in the eighteenth century was issued in more separate Printings" (*ibid.*, 139).

[55] Robert Dodsley, *The Oeconomy of Human Life*, 9th edn, vol I (London: Dodsley, 1758), 82.

[56] Dodsley had been a footman; his first book was entitled "The Muse in Livery." The first edition of "The Oeconomy" was presented as a translation of a "Bramin" text. For detailed discussion of Dodsley's career and the history of "The Oeconomy," see Straus, *Dodsley*, and Solomon, *The Rise of Robert Dodsley*.

Although Dodsley's point that "to oblige is better than to be obliged" is a truism of sentimental fiction, such fiction rarely insists on the possibility of exploitative abuse. Dodsley's somber warnings to "receive not a favour from the hand of the proud" and that "the greediness of Avarice shall never be satisfy'd" are particularly apropos to the "grateful slave" trope.

In 1785, William Paley offered a consideration of gratitude, capturing its eighteenth-century contradictions, in a section on social duties in his *Principles of Moral and Political Philosophy*. He sets the stage by defining gratitude as conveying to a benefactor an "imperfect right": "A benefactor has the right to returns of gratitude from the person he has obliged," but such an "imperfect right" cannot "be asserted by force . . . or course of law"; interestingly, Paley lists as similarly imperfect "the poor neighbour['s] . . . right to relief."[57] Paley notes that the possible expressions of gratitude, and relationships of "person obliged" to "benefactor" are of a "variety which admits of no bounds," and subsequently addresses the limits on, and failures of, gratitude in human relationships:

> gratitude can never oblige a man to do what is wrong, and what by consequence he is previously obliged not to do. It is no ingratitude to refuse to do, what we cannot reconcile to any apprehensions of our duty; but it is ingratitude and hypocrisy together, to pretend to this reason, when it is not the real one: and the frequency of such pretences has brought this apology for non-compliance with the will of a benefactor into unmerited disgrace. (163)

Paley's convoluted parsing of potentially conflicting duties, the need not to allow obligation to bring us to violate "the apprehensions of our duty" on one hand and the need to avoid "non-compliance with the will of the benefactor" on the other, and his further implication that the obligations of gratitude are burdensome enough to produce frequent evasions, demonstrates how vexed they are. Notably, for Paley, "duty" appears to be "duty" to self, as he opposes it to obligation. Remembering too that the obligation of gratitude is unenforceable, it begins to seem singularly hopeless as the basis for a system of social organization.

Even more relevant to the dynamic of the grateful slave are the restrictions Paley places on the demands a benefactor should make on persons obliged:

---

[57] William Paley, *The Principles of Moral and Political Philosophy*, foreword by D. L. Le Mahieu (Indianapolis: Liberty Fund, 2002), 53. Further citations are given parenthetically in the text. In *The Principles*, 137, Paley denounces the African slave trade as immoral and unjustified, but argues for gradually allowing Christian conversion to replace slavery for Africans in the colonies.

It has long been accounted a violation of delicacy and generosity to upbraid men with the favours they have received: but it argues a total destitution of both these qualities, as well as of moral probity, to take advantage of that ascendancy which the conferring of benefits justly creates, to draw or drive those whom we have obliged into mean or dishonest compliances. (163)

While "dishonest compliances" are presumably covered by the idea of conflicting duties, the benefactor's demands for "mean" acts are not explicitly addressed from the point of view of the "obliged." While Paley is clear that no such demands can be enforced, he leaves the basis of valid excuses vague. One wonders to what degree one's "apprehensions of duty" can be invoked to protect oneself from descending to "meanness"; clearly, however, Paley views the making of such demands on the part of the benefactor as unethical.

Dodsley and Paley both provide evidence supporting Maaja Stewart's contention that gratitude was undergoing a dramatic reconceptualization by the mid-eighteenth century, under the pressure of changing economic relationships. "In the Renaissance ideal," Stewart explains, gratitude was an all-encompassing relationship, like that from which Paley seems to begin: "the servant was grateful to his master for protection and nurture and the master was grateful to his master for service, and all – masters and servants – were grateful to God for his bountiful and unpayable gifts."[58] In the eighteenth century, by contrast, man's relation to God no longer functioned as a model for all social relationships. People began to believe that "obligation marks inferiority" once economic relationships became primarily contractual (523). Stewart concludes:

Grateful heroines, and some grateful children, will abound in later eighteenth- and nineteenth-century literature, but manliness will be defined by virtues other than gratitude. In a society where "the first of earthly blessings" is defined as "independence," manly virtues flow out of possession and self-possession. (531–2)

For Stewart, then, as masculinity and economic agency are redefined in terms of "independence," gratitude goes into decline. To apply her argument to slavery, Africans are denied the possibility of any such masculinity and slotted into the position of permanent children. Still, fictional Africans' version of gratitude is quite different than that of British heroines, even if heroines' experience of gratitude differs in turn from that of their heroes.[59]

[58] See Stewart, "Ingratitude," 523.
[59] See Gillian Skinner, "'The mild lustre of modest independence': Economies of Obligation in Novels of the 1790s," in *Sensibility and Economics in the Novel, 1740–1800: The Price of a Tear* (New York: St. Martins, 1998), 154–86.

While late-century heroines may often be grateful, their gratitude is not unproblematic. In Ann Radcliffe's gothic novel, *The Italian* (1796), the hero, Vivaldi, is incensed when the heroine, Ellena, defines her commitment to him by saying "I will obey the dictates of gratitude." "This assurance," he complains, "feebly as it sustains my hopes, is extorted; you see my misery, and from pity, from *gratitude*, not affection, would assuage it."[60] A similar scenario plays out in the denouement of Maria Edgeworth's *Belinda* (1801). Once Clarence Hervey, insisting that "I make no claim upon your gratitude," determines that Virginia, the young woman he is expecting to marry, is attached to him out of obligation rather than love, he is freed from his engagement to her and they can both marry more happily.[61] In Jane Austen's *Mansfield Park*, Fanny Price is pressed to marry Henry Crawford out of the gratitude she is expected to feel for his proposal. But she resists heroically, preferring a genuine emotion of love, and some critics have seen her as being placed in the position of a slave in these scenes.[62] These heroines are put in the position of falsifying their emotions due to the obligations of gratitude, which are explicitly contrasted to deeply felt, genuine forms of emotion. In other words, the untrammeled feelings of grateful slaves contrast with the rational independence of white men, but also with the deeper, more genuine feelings, the much more complex psychic interiority, of white women in late-century fiction.[63]

In *Emile*, Rousseau articulates through a paradox the complexity of the discourse on familial gratitude in the sentimental era of the late eighteenth century. The decline of the family, he contends, originates in the refusal of "fashionable" women to put aside their own amusements and nurse their children. Fathers follow the lead of these failed mothers: "let us not be surprised that a man whose wife did not deign to nurse the fruit of their union does not deign to raise him."[64] This parental neglect is repaid through the loss of children's love: "the children, sent away, dispersed in boarding schools, convents, colleges, will take the love belonging to the paternal home elsewhere, or to put it better, they will bring back to the

---

[60] Ann Radcliffe, *The Italian, Or The Confessional of the Black Penitents: A Romance*, ed. Robert Miles (London: Penguin, 2000), 178.

[61] Maria Edgeworth, *Belinda*, 1801, ed. Eiléan Ni Chuilleanain (London: Dent, 1993), 439.

[62] For examples see Ferguson, "*Mansfield Park*," 118–39; Maggie Malone, "Patriarchy and Slavery in *Mansfield Park*," *Essays in Poetics*, 18:2 (1993), 28–41; and Susan Fraiman, "Jane Austen and Edward Said: Gender, Culture, and Empire," *Critical Inquiry*, 21 (1995), 805–21.

[63] On such interiority, see Nancy Armstrong, *Desire and Domestic Fiction: A Political History of the Novel* (New York: Oxford University Press, 1987).

[64] Jean-Jacques Rousseau, *Emile: Or On Education*, ed. and trans. Allan Bloom (New York: Basic, 1979), 49. Further citations are given parenthetically in the text.

paternal home the habit of having no attachments" (49). Rousseau here seems to embrace what Stewart describes as the Renaissance model of unquestioned, non-contingent love for, and gratitude to, parents – "the love belonging to the paternal home" – and even to view it with nostalgia. And yet, Rousseau does expect parents to be evaluated for their specific behavior, seeing alienation of the child's love as a natural and appropriate judgment on their failings. The very possibility of a child's forming "the habit of having no attachments" suggests that the old ideal of automatic gratitude to parents is impossible in human experience. Instead, love for parents is a conditioned response, the result of an ongoing relationship, not at all a given. Rousseau rephrases his point and, in so doing, moves from the Renaissance model to the Enlightenment contractual model of gratitude, quite as Stewart's and Fliegelman's studies would suggest.

Rousseau then repeats this equivocation in even more revealing terms: "Emile is an orphan. It makes no difference whether he has his father and mother. Charged with their duties, I inherit all their rights. He ought to honor his parents, but he ought to obey only me" (52–3). Again, he invokes the old model ("he ought to honor his parents") only to strongly affirm an underlying change. The "ought" becomes ambiguous in its repetition. How can Emile "honor" his parents, when "honor" has been completely severed from "obey"? Furthermore, in this account, parental rights and duties have become alienable, exchangeable. Indeed, when Rousseau concludes, "that is my first or, rather, my sole condition," he shows a complete reconception of parental rights and duties; they are now entirely negotiable, even assignable to a third party with no necessary or natural claim on them whatsoever.

More radical still than Rousseau in articulating the eighteenth-century reconception of gratitude was the philosopher William Godwin, who, in his 1793 opus *An Enquiry into Political Justice* concludes that "Gratitude, therefore, if by gratitude we understand a sentiment of preference which I entertain towards another, upon the ground of my having been the subject of his benefits, is not part of either justice or virtue."[65] Godwin sees such personal gratitude as both irrational and anti-social. We should honor the love of humanity in general exhibited in benevolent acts, not the benefit conveyed to ourselves. Interestingly, Godwin cites the American preacher Jonathan Edwards as a source for the argument that gratitude is not a virtue.[66]

[65] William Godwin, *Enquiry Concerning Political Justice*, 3 vols., ed. F. E. L. Priestley (Toronto: University of Toronto Press, 1946), I:129.
[66] See Jonathan Edwards, "The Nature of True Virtue," in *Basic Writings*, ed. Ola Winslow (New York: Signet, 1966), 241–9.

Godwin's stark rejection of gratitude, of course, made in the context of the debates about the French Revolution, found a reply in Edmund Burke's denouncing of "ingratitude" as at the core of revolutionary values: "Ingratitude to benefactors is the first of revolutionary virtues. Ingratitude is indeed their four cardinal virtues compacted and amalgamated into one."[67] Despite his defense of gratitude, and his ease with a vision of a hierarchical society linked by chains of individual relationships, Burke himself was very skeptical of the image of British colonialism as a benevolent enterprise, at least in the contexts of India and Ireland.[68]

It could be objected that the comparison of Rousseau, of British moral philosophies, or of protagonists of British novels, to African slaves would never have been understood as valid in the eighteenth century, due to the importance of hierarchical distinctions in the period, and that comparison between the European poor and African slaves would be more apt. And indeed, there is evidence that the meaning of gratitude was changing even for the British poor who were being supported by the poor law. Donna T. Andrew argues convincingly that the understanding, and goals, of charity offered to the poor evolved throughout the eighteenth century. Andrew contends that the conception of charitable giving changed dramatically in the eighteenth century, moving from a desire to elicit gratitude and affirm the social structure, by illustrating the dependence of the lower classes on their betters in the 1740s, to a desire to impart a sense of "independence" and economic agency, achieved in part through reforms of the adminis-tration of the poor laws that would put an emphasis on temporal limits for support of the poor.[69] Hence, the role of gratitude in the lives of African slaves and the British poor took very different courses. Some of the very same progressive writers – Maria Edgeworth for instance – who, while generally paternalist, felt the need for the self-sufficiency of the poor, were unable to conceive of Africans as ever being safely trusted without the direct control of their masters.[70] Understandings of African slaves and British

---

[67] Edmund Burke, *A Letter from the Right Honorable Edmund Burke to a Noble Lord* (London: J. Owen and F. and C. Rivington, 1796), 55. For discussion of gratitude in this debate – framed in terms of Mary Shelley's novel *Frankenstein* – see William G. Sayres, "Compounding the Crime: Ingratitude and the Murder Conviction of Justine Moritz in Frankenstein," *English Language Notes*, 31:4 (1994), 48–54, and Johanna M. Smith, "'Cooped Up': Feminine Domesticity in Frankenstein," in *Frankenstein*, ed. Johanna Smith, 2nd edn (Boston: Bedford, 2000), 313–34, esp. 319–23.

[68] Jennifer Pitts, "Edmund Burke's Peculiar Universalism," in *A Turn to Empire: The Rise of Imperial Liberalism in England and France* (Princeton: Princeton University Press, 2005), 59–100.

[69] Donna T. Andrew, *Philanthropy and Police: London Charity in the Eighteenth Century* (Princeton: Princeton University Press, 1989).

[70] See my essay, "Maria Edgeworth's 'Grateful Negro' and the Sentimental Argument for Slavery," *Eighteenth-Century Life*, 23 (1999), 12–29.

workers were not univocal, of course, at the close of the century. Slavery's apologists argued that the condition of the British poor was worse than that of slaves precisely because slaves could count on their masters' obligation to care for them,[71] attempting to exploit nostalgia in a time of disturbing and disruptive changes to the ideology of benevolence and gratitude in the domestic economy.

One of the simplest and most direct ways of establishing that representations of African slave gratitude introduce a sense of difference between Africans and Europeans is to compare them to narratives of Europeans held in Barbary captivity. This point of comparison likely would have been apparent to English-speakers in the seventeenth- and eighteenth-century transatlantic world; Linda Colley and Joe Snader convincingly argue for the cultural importance of such narratives in Britain, and Paul Baepler and Philip Gould show their familiarity in early American culture.[72] Most such seventeenth-century narratives conceive of Barbary slavery as a natural extension of a world divided between "Christian" and "Mohametan" beliefs and identities, while some place that division in a secondary position in order to give all the more emphasis to the split between Catholics and Protestants. And most of the narratives are presented in deeply providential terms, suggesting a need for continual consciousness of gratitude to God, and presenting their personal escapes as direct evidence of God's favor.[73]

William Okeley's 1675 Barbary narrative is centrally concerned with recording, and properly expressing, gratitude for the interventions of providence, and as a result, his decision to escape becomes troubling. Okeley emphasizes his concern that proper gratitude be shown for God's interventions in a lengthy prefatory letter to the reader, in which he warns against "the reader's great danger [which] lies in running over some of God's works and yet not seeing God in His works."[74] Okeley is even concerned that his own adventures (culminating in an escape in a canvas

---

[71] For examples see James Tobin, *Cursory Remarks upon the Reverend Mr. Ramsay's Essay* (London: G. and T. Wilkie, 1785), 60–1; Gilbert Francklyn, *An Answer to the Rev. Mr. Clarkson's Essay* (London: Logographic, 1789), 199–204; and James Makittrick Adair, *Unanswerable Arguments against the Abolition of the Slave Trade* (London: J. P. Bateman, [1790]), 177.

[72] Paul Baepler, "The Barbary Captivity Narrative in Early America," *Early American Literature*, 30 (1995), 95–120, and *White Slaves, African Masters: An Anthology of American Barbary Captivity* (Chicago: University of Chicago Press, 1999); Philip Gould, "American Slaves in North Africa," in *Barbaric Traffic*, 86–121.

[73] For an excellent collection of these narratives, see Daniel J. Vitkus, ed., *Piracy, Slavery, and Redemption: Barbary Captivity Narratives from Early Modern England* (New York: Columbia University Press, 2001).

[74] I quote from "Ebenezer, or, A Small Monument of Great Mercy, Appearing in the Miraculous Deliverance of William Okeley," in Vitkus, *Piracy*, 124–92; this quotation is from 134.

boat) might distract readers from their more mundane but no less pressing debt of gratitude to the almighty:

Let those who would not abuse this narrative beware, lest while they are admiring providence in this instance of our preservation, they do not overlook those eminent appearances of God toward themselves every moment … Consider, God has kept thee many days and many years, and every minute of those many days and years, when there was but a hair's breath between thee and death: dost thou then admire God preserved us alive in a vessel of cloth? (138)

This escape is at once a heightened instance of, and a potential distraction from, the simple fact that God is directly responsible for preserving every human life every day.

Okeley further uses his prefatory letter to attempt to define "Turkish slavery" by contrast to Christian goodness: "Perhaps thou art a servant to a Christian: dost thou murmur? It shows thou little knowest what it is to be a slave to an imperious Turk" (139–40). Furthermore, he contends that "The Christian religion is surely the most excellent religion in the world because it holds the balance so easy between superiors and inferiors" (140). While this invokes a basic distinction between "Christian" and "Turkish" identity positions, Okeley's claims as to why one is preferable to the other are not actually borne out in his text. His escape is enabled in part by the kindness and trust shown him by his final Muslim master. In his constant search for signs of God's goodness to him, Okeley is compelled to praise this Muslim "patron," invoking gratitude:

And if I should be silent here, I should be the most ungrateful wretch living. I found not only pity and compassion but love and friendship from my new patron. Had I been his son, I could not have met with more respect nor been treated with more tenderness. I could not wish a friend a better condition than I was then in, excepting my bonds. (168)

Here, Okeley neglects his promised distinction between Christian and Turkish slavery, and instead raises the question of exactly where he draws the line between God's providential goodness and his master's voluntary kindness.

And, as one might expect given his emphatic providentialism, Okeley is troubled by escaping from such a good master: "There arose a scruple; nay, it amounted to a question: whether to escape from my patron, one that so dearly loved me, so courteously treated me, had fairly bought me, were justifiable before God and men" (170). Part of his concern is that he had prayed to God to be given a kind master. Is it a denial of providence to be dissatisfied after the granting of this prayer? Despite the theoretical overlap between gratitude to masters and gratitude to God, Okeley sidesteps this question, instead reasoning that his happiness with his good master could never be permanent, because "he might die and leave me to another or live to sell me to another who might be of another character" (171). Okeley goes on to argue that "Man is too noble a creature to be made subject to a deed of bargain and sale, and my consent was never asked to all their bargains, which is essential to create a right of dominion over a rational creature where he was not born a subject" (171). Although Okeley sees gratitude to God as the basic approach to each moment of life, and to interpreting minute daily events, he cannot be bound even to an excellent master – one he believes God provided him in response to a prayer – by gratitude human or divine. Despite this eloquent rejection of slavery for humankind in general, Muslim merchant seaman who fell into British hands ran the risk of being falsely accused of piracy so they could be sold for slaves.[75]

In sum these sixteenth- and seventeenth-century Barbary narratives contrast with eighteenth-century African grateful slaves in two key ways. First, they articulate the desire for escape from slavery as basic to human nature, but only after weighing and rejecting gratitude, even gratitude to God, as an insufficient reason to remain enslaved; and second, they give a clear sense of a world in which the primary categories of identity are still religious, whether Christian vs. Muslim or Protestant vs. Catholic; they repeatedly identify people and the expectations of their behavior by religious affiliation, almost never by physical characteristics. "Renegades," the liminal figures of Barbary captivity, like mulattoes in nineteenth-century American fiction, may seem ambiguous but only serve to confirm the binary structure of identity in the period. Renegades, although treated with scorn, nonetheless return easily to their original, deep-seated Christian identity; the narrators of Barbary narratives take it for granted that renegades will rally to the side of Christian compatriots at any opportunity, and – in their own writings, at least – are rarely disappointed.[76] On the one hand, this is simply a fantasy that denies the disturbing realities; on the other, Christian birth comes to trump the renegades, adopted, professed identity; and therefore, religious identity begins to seem more essential than cultural, and thereby hints at later conceptions of national (and even racial) identity.

[75] Nabil Matar, *Turks, Moors, and Englishmen in the Age of Discovery* (New York: Columbia University Press, 1999), 32. See also Colley, *Captives*, 82.
[76] For an example, see John Rawlins, "The Famous and Wonderful Recovery of a Ship of Bristol, Called the Exchange, from the Turkish Pirates of Argier," in Vitkus, *Piracy*, 117–18.

The disparity between conceptions of gratitude for African slaves and for the British – even British Barbary slaves – is, to a degree, simply a variation on the classic paradox addressed by David Brion Davis in his books on *The Problem of Slavery* and typified in Johnson's famous quotation about Americans: "How is it that we hear the loudest yelps for liberty among the drivers of negroes?"[77] The question is how slavery for Africans could be accepted in a culture which used "slavery" as the term for unacceptable exploitation, often to protest abuse, or arbitrary constraints on "liberty," and placed an increasing value on independence, individual economic agency, and contractual relationships.[78] My answer is that it was through the dissemination of a sense of difference – which only arrived in its final, concrete form in the concept of race as understood and practiced in the nineteenth century – that the British came to believe that different standards could be applied to Africans.

Representations of Africans as grateful even for their state of slavery were one cultural aspect of the dissemination of this sense of difference. While there was not a widely shared concept of race that could be taken for granted until the end of the period I am studying, nonetheless, ideas of "difference" that fell short of "race" itself were becoming increasingly familiar. The role that gratitude played in making this difference a familiar concept was highly complex. It helped bring to the metropole the new categories of identity on the ascendant in the colonies. The theoretical implications of this claim are, perhaps, a small step back from the bold, Foucauldian thesis that representations generate and shape culture, but not all the way back to the theory that texts passively reflect the culture they come from.[79] Instead, I am conceiving of "grateful slave" texts as bridges between differing cultural situations, and between beliefs and practices, within the English-speaking transatlantic world, and therefore as opening up – or perhaps unleashing – new possibilities for imagining race and slavery in colony and metropole alike.

---

[77] From "Taxation No Tyranny," in *The Works of Samuel Johnson, LL. D.: Together with His Life . . .* vol x, ed. John Hawkins (London: J. Buckland *et al.*, 1787), 142. The infrequently noted context of the quotation is to argue that "slavery" apparently is not "fatally contagious," and so the English need not fear that the "subjection" of the colonists will "tend to the diminution of our own liberties."

[78] In addition to the works cited in n. 31 above, see Catherine Gallagher, "Workers and Slaves: The Rhetoric of Freedom in the Debate over Industrialism," in *The Industrial Reformation of English Fiction 1832–1867* (Chicago: University of Chicago Press, 1985), 3–35, and Alan Macfarlane, *The Origins of English Individualism* (Oxford: Blackwell, 1978).

[79] Armstrong's theoretical model in *Desire and Domestic Fiction* is perhaps the clearest expression of this concept.

The first chapter of *The Grateful Slave*, "The prehistory of the grateful slave," begins by examining key seventeenth-century English-language accounts of West Africa, contending, against Winthrop Jordan and the scholars of the English Renaissance who follow him, that the discourse on Africans was then marked by xenophobia rather than race. Such texts reflect a situation in which European travelers, including slave traders, were at the mercy of local potentates; scholarly assumptions that Europeans were already in the position of imperial mastery are mistaken. Representations of African kings vary from demeaning mockery to extravagant praise, depending on how generous and welcoming they are to the writer in question. Only at the very end of the century, in his account of a 1693–4 voyage, does slaver Captain Thomas Phillips covertly hint at the possibility of essential racial difference. Phillips follows the classic formula of the long eighteenth century, invoking ideas of racial difference – and practices of racial oppression – only to strenuously disclaim them both. He tells of having refused to allow the brutal practices of his underlings. Nonetheless, he naturalizes racial slavery – complaining of the "slavery" of the tasks incumbent upon his crew – and he even hints at the reality of biological differences illustrated by immunities to disease, and by the different reactions of caged tigers to blacks and whites. In contrast, Captain William Snelgrave, in his 1734 book, is the first travel writer to represent slaves as grateful to him – he contends that he rescues them from their depraved religion and brutal kings – but is also the first to explicitly embrace racial subjugation, justifying the execution of rebellious slaves as necessary to convince them of the sanctity of white men. Both Phillips and Snelgrave, however, use sentimental language to package their accounts of racial oppression and racial difference in terms palatable to their metropolitan audience.

The second section of this chapter establishes that the lack of a strong concept of racial difference is not the only difficulty confronting seventeenth-century British writers representing the colonial project to a metropolitan audience. Because scenes of colonial mutilation, torture, and execution could remind readers of similar scenes in Foxe's *Book of Martyrs*, such representations of colonial violence present a challenge to the basis of English Protestant identity. Foxe's work offers identification with the tortured martyr as an invitation into Protestantism, positioning the torturer as specifically Catholic. Hence, when the English represent the mutilation and execution of enslaved Africans, they must distance themselves from responsibility for torture, and present themselves as humane, sentimental, and passive. The English impulse to identify in sentimental terms with suffering and to disavow individual responsibility for colonial violence, thereby glossing over its systemic nature, originates a cultural dynamic that the trope of the grateful slave will continue to develop.

Chapter 2, "The origin of the grateful slave, 1722" is devoted to analysis of Daniel Defoe's *Colonel Jack* (1722), the earliest novel offering a scene of plantation reform. The argument is that *Colonel Jack* narrates the emergence of racialized slavery for a metropolitan audience not accustomed to the notion. Indeed, Jack arrives on the plantation as a "slave" himself and, paradoxically, uses his sympathy with African slaves to institute white privilege and racialized slavery on the plantation. When he becomes an overseer, Jack cannot bring himself to whip his charges due to having been himself a slave. Frustrated with this inability to use violence, Jack instead threatens slaves with brutal punishments only to pardon them at the last moment. Jack succeeds by eliciting the slaves' gratitude, transforming them into devoted and productive workers. But Defoe draws a distinction between the gratitude of "Negroes" and whites: the owner of Jack's plantation dismisses Jack's offer to prove that he has "as much Gratitude as a *Negro*" as inappropriate for a white man. *Colonel Jack* has two notable differences from other versions of the grateful slave trope: first, Jack indulges in a momentary outburst of racist theorizing, which he then abandons to turn to his project of sentimental manipulation; second, he treats his sentimental connection with the slaves not as natural, but as the result of the shared experience of slavery, and as valuable not in itself, but as a tool for manipulating his African charges.

"The evolution of the grateful slave," my third chapter, begins with an illustration of the gap between theories and practices of race in the British transatlantic world, through the example of the Somerset case of 1772, in order to establish how innovative were the racial implications of the grateful slave trope. The pamphleteer Samuel Estwick, for instance, defending the planter interest, enters the debate over Somerset to suggest that black and white differ not in possessing the capacity of moral sense, but in their ability to exercise of that capacity. Estwick bows to rhetorical norms by framing his concept of difference as marginal and novel. The chapter then charts the plantation reform scenes in novels by Edward Kimber (1754), Sarah Scott (1766), and Henry Mackenzie (1777) that together raise the "grateful slave" to the status of a recognizable trope in fiction, and reveals the parallel between the implications of these novels and Estwick's position.

Reflecting changes in metropolitan consciousness since *Colonel Jack*, each novel takes for granted both sentimental sympathy and the racial basis of slavery. The reformer succeeds by taking slave self-interest as the foundation of efficient production. As a result, each of these novels resorts to a pseudo-empirical account of racial difference – although one rhetorically contained within monogenesis – to reject the possibility of making African slaves into free laborers. The reformer, aware of the norm of monogenesis, introduces the possibility of racial difference as if it were a hypothesis to be disproved. Ultimately, however, the contrast between the rational benevolence of the reformer and the irrational, excessive gratitude of the slaves demonstrates that Africans must depend on the guidance of their white masters. Unlike Estwick, who was too bluntly invested in difference to challenge successfully the established consensus on race, these novels are subtle enough to be acceptable to a metropolitan audience.

The emergence of the abolition debate into cultural centrality, I argue in chapter 4, "The 1780s: transition," leads to conceptual instability, as the earlier Christian consensus on shared humanity falls apart, and new models of difference are not yet established and familiar. Furthermore, ameliorationist views of slavery are increasingly influential, but also subject to stern criticism, as both emancipation and abolition of the trade are still bandied about by anti-slavery activists. A more explicit version of the racial difference implied by the earlier grateful slave novelists, although not yet mainstream, became a tacit consensus among philosophers. Despite their strongly differing responses to slavery, Kant, Jefferson, and the Abbé Raynal all hold that Africans are a passionate, emotional, and irrational "race." The central components of the grateful slave trope – its dependence on ameliorationist politics and commitment to the reality of difference – undergo their most serious scrutiny of the century in fictional treatments.

Lucy Peacock, in her story "The Creole" (1786), offers the apotheosis of the paradigm, representing slaves who insist on supporting their mistress despite having been emancipated. Thomas Day, on the other hand, in *Sandford and Merton* (1783–9) takes a radical turn, imagining a plantation owner's son cured of his domineering arrogance by being forced to acknowledge his dependence on, and gratitude toward, others. Dr. John Moore, in *Zeluco* (1789), also reverses familiar roles, having the devout slave Hanno attempt to educate the sentiments of his cruel master, Zeluco. Instead of breaking from the racial consensus underlying the grateful slave, however, Moore makes Hanno's passionate irrationality the basis of his stoic devotion to his savior. Moore anticipates the "romantic racialism" of antebellum abolitionists, making Hanno a grateful slave to Christ despite his master's cruelty. Indeed, Hanno's martyrdom anticipates Uncle Tom's.

I turn to black Atlantic writers in chapter 5 "Gratitude in the black Atlantic: Equiano writes back, 1789." They – unlike their white anti-slavery colleagues – challenge the racial message underlying the grateful slave paradigm. Ignatius Sancho prefers kindness to cruelty in slave management, but engages in complex, playful evasions when called upon to express gratitude himself. Ottobah Cugoano rejects outright charges of African irrationality, views slavery as inherently cruel, and dismisses masters' claims of relative kindness as mere quibbles. Olaudah Equiano exposes the coercion, and the self-interest, behind masters' claims of kindness, and yet suggests that any kindness is more desirable than brutality. He also demonstrates that gratitude becomes the official face of the oppressive system of whiteness in the colonies, a system that oppresses him even after he is nominally free. Indeed, Equiano insistently appeals to the prior metropolitan value of universal, impartial justice against established colonial practices of white privilege and enforced gratitude.

The grateful slave fictions of the 1790s, as I explore in chapter 6 "The 1790s: ameliorationist convergence" are unlike their ambiguous predecessors of the 1780s. They demonstrate the dashing of Equiano's hopes for deploying the previously dominant consensus on human similarity against colonial racial oppression. As abolitionists deemphasize the issue of emancipation, and planters defend themselves as committed to humane reform, amelioration becomes a shared goal. Nonetheless, in the wake of the Haitian Revolution, and Equiano's *Interesting Narrative*, novels of the 1790s take the seemingly radical step of featuring African protagonists or narrators critical of slavery. These African characters, however, are either themselves excessively grateful to kind whites, or are exceptional, noble leaders who control non-aristocratic Africans by eliciting their gratitude. Thus, even the most seemingly radical works collapse back into a strong implication of African irrationality. The only real challenge to the grateful slave paradigm in the decade comes in its racist, pro-slavery rejection. Hector MacNeill's *Memoirs of the Life and Travels of the Late Charles Macpherson* (1800) parodies grateful slavery, making the sentimental reformer a comic martyr to his good intentions, at the hands of his own, emphatically ungrateful, slaves. *Macpherson* draws the moral that only relentless discipline can control Africans' inherent depravity, and therefore that slavery is the ideal state for such sub-humans. But even *Macpherson* ends with the redemption of a version of amelioration, premised on cultivating family values in the "best" and most tractable slaves. Mary Pilkington, in her 1798 story for children, "The Faithful Slave," by contrast, resets a grateful slave story to England, beginning the process of adapting the trope to reassure audiences that blacks will remain grateful and submissive even after abolition and emancipation.

The Epilogue, pointing to the continued use of the grateful slave in British writings of the early nineteenth century, including Maria Edgeworth's popular 1804 short story "The Grateful Negro," traces the transatlantic afterlife of the grateful slave in antebellum US imaginings of slavery, freedom, and racial difference. The grateful slave became a staple of nineteenth-century US children's fiction, thereby shaping white citizens' attitudes to race. Its legacy can be seen in the "romantic racialism" of abolitionists like Harriet Beecher Stowe and Lydia Maria Child, who were directly influenced by Edgeworth and Dr. Moore to depict "negroes" as a gentle, loving, inherently Christian race, unlike whites primarily in their inability to pursue rational self-interest. The grateful slave, however, also underlies the pro-slavery vision of a familial relationship between benevolent paternalist masters and faithful dependant slaves. Black anti-slavery activist Frederick Douglass, in a striking rhetorical reversal, insists on his master's "base ingratitude to my poor old grandmother" who "had peopled his plantation with slaves."[80] A report in *The Atlantic*, intending to illustrate the un-Christian hypocrisy of Southerners, tells of a "Faithful slave" who protected his master during Nat Turner's rebellion, and then, informing the master "he could not live a slave any longer, and requesting him either to free him or shoot him on the spot" was immediately executed, a martyr to humanity and freedom.[81]

---

[80] Frederick Douglass, *Narrative of the Life of Frederick Douglass*, ed. Benjamin Quarles (Cambridge, MA: Harvard University Press, 1960), 76.
[81] T. W. Higginson, "Nat Turner's Insurrection," *The Atlantic Monthly*, 8:46 (1861), 181.

CHAPTER I

The prehistory of the grateful slave

This chapter works to establish two intertwined aspects of the prehistory of the eighteenth-century grateful slave trope in late seventeenth-century British culture, particularly in travel writing and colonial reportage: the complexity of conceptions of racial difference and the sentimental self-positioning of reporters of colonial violence. The first section, arguing against scholarly claims that anti-black prejudice was well established in the seventeenth century, examines the dominance of cultural difference, or xenophobia, over essential difference, or race, in seventeenth-century travel accounts of West Africa. Although the influential travel accounts of West Africa available in English do contain denigrating views of black Africans, these views are defined in cultural terms and do not exceed the xenophobia applied to other groups. Travel writers created an "Oroonoko effect" by holding up African "kings" to a European standard. While some were ridiculed for falling short of this standard, others were lavishly praised (as Aphra Behn praises the fictional Oroonoko) for meeting it. These judgments reflect not racist disgust, but the writer's success, or lack of it, in cultivating an African potentate as a trading partner.

By the end of the century, slave-trading captains (who wrote many of the accounts of West Africa from 1680 to 1740) writing for a metropolitan audience were in a difficult position. They had to represent practices of racial oppression to metropolitan readers who still saw difference in cultural and religious, rather than essential, terms. The serious possibility of racial difference in their texts emerges, paradoxically, from attempts to acknowledge and assess the "humanity" of Africans. Their accounts, in complex ways, document the emergence of a transatlantic gap in racial consciousness, between the practice of white supremacy in the middle passage and the colonies and the metropolitan discourse insisting on the unity of humankind. This gap has the immediate effect of making useful sentimental representations of African slaves and of colonial violence. The rhetorical desire of these authors to appear "humane" – or sentimentally engaged – to their metropolitan readers is often at odds with the treatment of the enslaved that they record: here we see an attempt to negotiate this transatlantic gap in terms that anticipate the fictional grateful slave trope.

The second section of this chapter provides a deeper context for understanding the desire for sentimental self-positioning in texts representing colonial violence and torture in the late seventeenth and early eighteenth centuries. It does so by addressing the conceptions of racial difference, the colonial project, and Protestant community that produced the need for the British to claim both sentimental identification with, and concrete difference from, enslaved Africans.[1] How do such representations position the Englishman engaged in the colonial project? Furthermore, how do such representations draw on, or respond to, the discourse, and the complex politics, of torture and martyrdom made almost ubiquitous in early modern British culture by Foxe's *Book of Martyrs* (also known as the *Acts and Monuments*) and its derivatives and analogues? My argument, in brief, will be that scenes of colonial torture are particularly complex for the British at this time, challenging their sense of identity by undermining both the negative model of the Spanish and the positive model offered by Foxe's martyrs. As Linda Colley has argued in *Britons*, Anglican Protestantism was a cornerstone of the British national identity under formation following the 1707 Act of Union.[2] Both sections of this chapter are case studies in the transatlantic dissemination of racial, religious, and colonial identities, and the problems such identities entail.

XENOPHOBIA AND RACE

This section is concerned with explaining the significance of the dramatic shift in British representations of West Africa from Behn's *Oroonoko* (1688) to Defoe's novels *Robinson Crusoe* (1719) and *Captain Singleton* (1720).

---

[1] Laura Brown, *Ends of Empire: Women and Ideology in Early Eighteenth-Century English Literature* (Ithaca: Cornell University Press, 1993), 19 and 44–5, reads women as symbolic scapegoats for empire in this period. And yet, in the late seventeenth century, the British could still understand themselves as provincials rather than imperial masters: see Alok Yadav, *Before the Empire of English: Literature, Provinciality, and Nationalism in Eighteenth-Century Britain* (New York: Palgrave, 2004). Perhaps because they felt vulnerable, the British public supported colonial endeavors vociferously well into the eighteenth century; see Kathleen Wilson, *The Sense of the People: Politics, Culture, and Imperialism in England, 1715–1785* (Cambridge: Cambridge University Press, 1995) and *The Island Race: Englishness, Empire and Gender in the Eighteenth Century* (New York: Routledge, 2003). My model of the sentimental approach to colonial violence develops from Mary Louise Pratt, *Imperial Eyes: Travel Writing and Transculturation* (New York: Routledge, 1992) and Jill Lepore, *The Name of War: King Philip's War and the Origins of American Identity* (New York: Knopf, 1998).

[2] "Protestantism," in *Britons: Forging the Nation 1707–1837* (New Haven: Yale University Press, 1992), 11–54. Colley invokes Foxe as a centerpiece of this process (*ibid.*, 25–8). I use the term "British" in application to the late seventeenth century for clarity despite the risk of anachronism.

Behn's hero lives in a lavish court, like any hero of romance, although the
trappings are distinctly oriental; Defoe's Africans by contrast are nameless,
naked savages in a bleak, empty landscape.[3] My focus here is not on reading
these novels specifically, but rather on the changing conceptions of Africa
and Africans that take place in the three decades between them. It is at this
very time that the idea of racial difference between "white" Britons and
"black" Africans first appears in English writing, specifically in travelers'
accounts of West Africa. It is a period of transition, in which many texts
(particularly but not exclusively those written earlier in the period) such as
Behn's *Oroonoko*, do not evince a clearly "racialized" consciousness about
Africans, while others do, although in extremely inchoate form.

   Travelers' accounts of Africa in this period confront scholars with a
definitional problem. What does the emergence of a concept of "race" that
produces a strong sense of difference look like? How do we distinguish it
from a xenophobic emphasis on cultural and religious difference? Race
only becomes distinct from xenophobia when it is systematic, a primary
category of identity, and when it allows for systematic denigration of a
given group or groups. In fact, in these texts, "race" becomes meaningful
through raising the possibility of, and *rejecting*, the exclusion of Africans
from the category of the human. The aftermath of this consideration of
total African inferiority, however, is not as simple as it has seemed to most
scholars who have addressed it. Texts that raise and reject the possibility of
African inferiority cannot be understood simply as "rejecting" race or
racism, because the discourse of race was not yet stable and such "rejec-
tions" could not be read at the time – as they often are now by scholars – as
opposing a familiar or even dominant position.[4] Indeed, opening up the
possibility, or introducing the hypothesis, of sub-human status for Africans
allows the hypothesizer to settle on a seemingly more reasonable position
that takes for granted a subtler difference between African and European,
while nonetheless claiming that both can still be included within the
category of the human. "Dehumanization" works in the late seventeenth-
and early eighteenth-century discourse on West Africa through posing, not

[3] See Roxann Wheeler's reading of *Captain Singleton* in *Complexion*, 104–36.
[4] For arguments that "race" was still open-ended and under formation into the last decades of the
   eighteenth century, see Wheeler, *Complexion*, and Dror Wahrman, *The Making of the Modern Self:
   Identity and Culture in Eighteenth-Century England* (New Haven: Yale University Press, 2004),
   83–126. See also Derek Hughes' polemic against the anachronistic use of race: "Race, Gender, and
   Scholarly Practice: Aphra Behn's *Oroonoko*," *Essays in Criticism*, 52:1 (2002), 1–22. Joanna Brooks,
   American Lazarus: Religion and the Rise of African-American and Native Literatures (New York:
   Oxford University Press, 2003), 16, warns against taking the instability of race in the period to
   mean that "race was not a major determinant of lived experience."

through definitively answering, the question of black Africans' humanity: in other words, it works by creating meaningful difference within the category of the human. Certainly nothing like the nineteenth-century "scientific" view of polygenesis yet existed.

I have discussed Winthrop Jordan's position in the debate on the origins of racial slavery in Anglo-American culture in the Introduction, noting Theodore Allen's criticisms of Jordan's account of an "unthinking decision" in opposition to the "socio-economic" analysis of C. L. R. James, Eric Williams, and Edmund Morgan, who see "racism" as arising out of the social and economic conditions of slavery. Despite seeing race as being born of Europeans' "inherent" prejudice against blackness and hence Africans, Jordan has been influential on literary critics engaging with race, particular those concerned with Shakespeare and the English seventeenth century.[5] Jordan is particularly relevant to this chapter, because he begins his famous book, *White Over Black*, with readings that present the "prejudice" against blacks and black skin as already apparent in accounts of West Africa circulating during the English Renaissance.[6] P. E. H. Hair, a historian who has made a specialty of gleaning historical information about West Africa from early modern European travelers' texts, offers a nuanced alternative to Jordan's position. Hair contends that scholars err in "tearing out what they see as a 'racist' stereotype from the context of English cultural relationships in the period, which, in the time-honored and universal way of cultural self-protection, inevitably tend to discriminate against all non-English ways and manners, overtly or covertly."[7] Hair treats Jordan with

---

[5] See Anthony J. Barker, *The African Link: British Attitudes to the Negro in the Era of the Atlantic Slave Trade, 1550–1807* (London: Cass, 1978), x, 16, 44; Anthony Barthelemy, *Black Face Maligned Race: The Representation of Blacks in English Drama from Shakespeare to Southerne* (Baton Rouge: Louisiana State University Press, 1987); Elliot Tokson, *Popular Image of the Black Man in English Drama, 1550–1688* (Boston: G. K. Hall, 1982); and esp. Alden T. Vaughan and Virginia Mason Vaughan, "Before *Othello*: Elizabethan Representations of Sub-Saharan Africa," *William and Mary Quarterly*, 54:1 (1997), 19–44. Emily C. Bartels, "Before Imperialism: Richard Hakluyt and the Construction of Africa," *Criticism*, 34 (1992), 517–38, and "*Othello* and Africa: Postcolonialism Reconsidered," *William and Mary Quarterly*, 54:1 (1997), 45–64; Linda Boose, "'The Getting of a Lawful Race': Racial Discourse and the Unrepresentable Black Woman," in *Women, "Race," and Writing in The Early Modern Period*, ed. Margo Hendricks and Patricia Parker (New York: Routledge, 1994), 41; and Kim F. Hall, *Things of Darkness: Economies of Race and Gender in Early Modern England* (Ithaca: Cornell University Press, 1995), 2; all follow Jordan while criticizing his inattention to gender. For less favorable accounts of Jordan, see Moira Ferguson, "Juggling the Categories of Race, Class and Gender," in *Women, "Race," and Writing*, 347 n. 4; and Mary Floyd-Wilson, *English Ethnicity and Race in Early Modern Drama* (Cambridge: Cambridge University Press, 2003), 5–6.

[6] Jordan, *White Over Black*, 6–11.

[7] Hair, "Attitudes to Africans," 44. See also April Lee Hatfield, "'A Very Wary People in their Bargaining' or 'Very Good Marchandise': English Traders' Views of Free and Enslaved Africans, 1550–1650," *Slavery & Abolition*, 23:4 (2004), 1–17.

some respect, and means this quotation to apply more particularly to recent literary critics who, Hair believes, tread even less cautiously in Jordan's footsteps. Following Hair, then, in order to locate the emergence of race in the English discourse we have to distinguish carefully between a concept of difference that accords with an habitual xenophobia, and one that clearly exceeds this standard.

Jordan and the scholars following him often consider a passage in the work of Leo Africanus, translated into English from Latin in 1600, as an influence on, or symptom of, English attitudes toward Africans in that time, especially in its highly sexualized vision of black Africans:

> The Negros likewise leade a beastly kinde of life, being utterly destitute of the vse of reason, of dexteritie of wit, and of all artes. Yea they so behaue themselues, as if they had continually liued in a forrest among wilde beasts. They haue great swarmes of harlots among them; whereupon a man may easily coniecture their manner of liuing.[8]

This quotation is often adduced to show that Leo either confirmed or initiated prejudice against the "negro" in England. Leo's text served, from the late sixteenth until the mid-seventeenth century in England, as the primary source of information for English writers on Africa. Jordan suggests that this passage initiates a racial view of blacks as highly sexualized.[9] I dispute that Leo offers a racial judgment here,[10] despite the resonance of the denial of reason, wit, and art, and the suggestion of sexual excess, with later racialized notions of "Negroes."

Indeed, the passage begins with the word "likewise." These "Negroes," then, are similar to the shepherds of Barbary, "neither Mahumetans, Iewes, nor Christians," of whom Leo remarks, "being vtterly estranged from all godly deuotion, they lead a sauage and beastly life" (I:186); to Numidians, who are "most ignorant" and "most slauish" (I:187), and to Libyans who "liue a Brutish kinde of life" (I:187). Furthermore, Leo goes on to qualify his attack on "the Negroes" in particular: "except their conuersation perhaps be somewhat more tolerable, who dwell in the principall townes and cities: for it is like that they are somewhat more addicted to ciuilitie" (I:187). This distinction appears parallel to that dividing the shepherds of Barbary from others in that country,

---

[8] Leo Africanus, *The History and Description of Africa*, 1600, 3 vols., trans. John Pory, ed. Robert Brown (London: Hakluyt Society, 1896), I:187.

[9] Jordan, *White Over Black*, 33–4; Barthelemy, *Black Face*, 5; Tokson, *Popular Image*, 17; Hall, *Things of Darkness*, 34; Vaughan and Vaughan, "Before Othello," 41.

[10] Hair discusses Jordan's use of Leo, "Attitudes to Africans," 43 n. 2, and 44 n. 6. Eldred D. Jones gives a much more balanced account of Leo's Africa than Jordan or his followers: *The Elizabethan Image of Africa* (Charlottesville: University of Virginia Press, 1971), 21–31.

"the most noble and worthie region of all Africa," the inhabitants of which Leo considers "a ciuill people" (I:123).

All the negative quotations come from a section on "what vices the foresaid Africans are subject unto" (I:185). Because the "vices" of the negroes are not represented as unique, or even as notably more excessive than those of other "unciuil" peoples, it is difficult to understand them as being racialized except in retrospect. Leo's caveat on the superior civility of those who dwell in cities, in particular, suggests a cultural rather than an essential distinction. Jordan sees the sexualized representation of the negro as feeding into racialization, but even Leo's allusion to sexual impropriety is not unique to black Africans in the text.[11] The shepherds of Barbary, according to Leo, may not live among "swarmes of harlots," but they are so permissive that fathers fail to preserve their daughters as virgin brides: "yea, the father of the maide most friendly welcommeth her suiter: so I thinke scarce any noble or gentleman among them can chuse a virgine for his spouse" (I:186).

Furthermore, Leo does not except even civil urbanites from his representation of the "inhabitants of Libya," who he claims "liue a brutish kinde of life; who neglecting all kindes of good artes and sciences, do wholy apply their mindes vnto theft and violence. Neuer as yet had they any religion, any lawes, or any good forme of liuing" (I:187). Indeed, Libyans are not unique in these deficiencies: "all the Numidians being most ignorant of naturall, domesticall, & commonwealth-matters, are principally addicted vnto treason, trecherie, murther, theft, and robberie. This nation, because it is most slauish, will right gladly accept of any seruice among the Barbarians, be it neuer so vile or contemptible" (I:187).[12] If ideas of racial difference precede slavery – as many scholars have suggested – it is curious that Leo presents Numidians, rather than negroes, as willing slaves.[13] In the context of this discussion of vices, then, the concession that, for the negroes, "their conversation perhaps be somewhat more tolerable, who dwell in the principall towns and cities; for it is like that they are somewhat more addicted to ciuilitie," for all its hedging, is not minor. Indeed, Leo differentiates the negroes here from Libyans and Numidians only in suggesting that some

[11] Jordan asserts that the English did not distinguish Africans from "Negroes" (*White Over Black*, 5), and Hall follows this (*Things of Darkness*, 30–8). This concept sits uneasily with their emphasis on complexion and Leo's interest in making distinctions between African groups.
[12] This would seem to complicate Sweet's claim that Muslim writers, in particular the fifteenth-century writer Ibn Khaldun, singled out black Africans as slavish ("Iberian Roots," 147).
[13] This is one of the primary differences between what Allen calls the "psycho-cultural" and "socio-economic" schools of interpretation. See Allen's "Introduction," in *Invention*, I: 1–24.

negroes may have greater access to "ciuilitie." Similarly, Hair contends (in a footnote) that in Leo's world, "black Muslims were treated more or less as equals but utter contempt was shown for African 'kaffir' ('heathen')."[14]

It is "Numidia," which Leo describes as lying to the north of "The Land of the Negroes" that he finds "the basest part of all Africa" (I:126), and a place where people live "without all lawe and ciuilitie" (I:151). For Leo, the Numidians are despicable: "they are not onely ignorant of all good learning and liberall sciences; but are likewise altogether careless and destitute of vertue" (I:153). Even the cotton-cloth they wear, Leo notes, is imported from the "Land of Negros" rather than being of their own manufacture (I:151). The Numidians actually depend on the negroes for their clothing, that most basic marker of civilized status.[15]

Throughout his discussion of specific West African countries and groups in book 3 (his longer section on the kingdoms within "The Land of the Negroes"), Leo is very careful to note which groups are "ciuill," "learned," and "rich," which have recognizable religious practices, extensive trade contacts, or impressive military power; and which, by contrast, are "most rusticall and savage," often finding both groups within a single political unit. In other words, Leo's divisions between and within groups are based on a concept of civility that factors in trade, wealth, learning, and religious and sexual practices. The "Arabians," he notes, "are verie rude, forlorne, beggarly, leane and hunger-starued people, having God (no doubt) alwaies displeased against them, by whose vengeance they dayly sustaine such grieuous calamities" (I:161), suggesting a providential rather than an essentialist view of the fate of the various groups he assesses. Leo shows no reliance whatsoever on color as a primary category of division, and his comments on color do not accord with an English preference for paleness. Referring to "Barbaria" (the same region that produces depraved shepherds) he notes, "this is the most noble and worthie region of all Africa, the inhabitants wherof are of a brown or tawnie colour, being a ciuill people, and prescribe wholesome laws and constitutions vnto themselves" (I:123).[16] Indeed, he makes no clear distinction between "brown" and "white" skin, at another point glossing "tawnie" as "white" rather than "brown" or "tan" (I:184).

---

[14] Hair, "Attitudes to Africans," 53 n. 28.
[15] Roxann Wheeler, *Complexion*, 17–21 and 72–3, argues that clothing functions as an aspect of racial identity in the eighteenth century.
[16] Contrast Hall: "Leo seemingly shares with his European audience a disdain for the darkest African peoples" (*Things of Darkness*, 30).

Leo was himself a North African who converted to Christianity in Rome before writing his description of Africa. His book was based on his travels through the known areas of the continent for purposes of trade. Thus, his attitudes are those of Islamic North Africa toward West Africans, inflected by his later conversion and then modified by his English translator, John Pory. It is hardly surprising that a commercial traveler would seek out "civility," or that a Muslim convert to Catholicism would seek out and praise orderly, monotheistic religious practices, while denigrating "kafir" or "pagan" beliefs and distaining "rusticall," uncivilized agricultural groups uninterested in trade. This aspect of Leo's writing – his assessments of the desire and ability to trade, and of the compatibility of local religious practices with his own beliefs – resonates with the writings of English travelers to West Africa in the seventeenth century, not a pre-formed disgust with black skin that is the unconscious beginning of racialization. Leo's view of the difference between African groups should discredit the notion that his derogatory comments about black Africans fit into a "racial" rather than a "xenophobic" worldview.

Leo's concerns as a trader interested primarily in the "civility" and familiarity of those Africans he encounters are similar to those of many seventeenth-century European travelers to West Africa whose writings were available in English. Like Leo, seventeenth- and early eighteenth-century European travelers to West Africa looked at Africans first as potential trading partners, and therefore assessed the black people they encountered in terms of civility, religion, and willingness to trade. In particular, many such travelers were keenly interested in African kings – or those local potentates with the power to tax, regulate, or interfere with trade that they chose to dub kings. Such "kings" were alternately subjected to sarcastic barbs and extravagant praise.

The praising accounts are often strikingly like Behn's depiction of her protagonist in *Oroonoko*, defining African potentates as meeting European standards of nobility.[17] In fact, this representational habit of singling out favored African potentates for praise, and giving it in terms that explicitly invoke comparisons to European nobility, is so pronounced as to create a trope I will call the "Oroonoko effect." Similarly, abuse of recalcitrant trading partners and other frustrating native leaders is often cast in terms of the failure of such African "kings" to behave in accord with European

---

[17] Joanna Lipking, "Confusing Matters: Searching the Backgrounds of *Oroonoko*," in *Aphra Behn Studies*, ed. Janet Todd (Cambridge: Cambridge University Press, 1994), 264, notes this pattern in passing.

norms of regal decorum. Hence, most abuse and denigration of black Africans in these travelers' texts appears to be cultural rather than racial. Nonetheless, it is in these very texts that a "racial" understanding of the differences between Europeans and Africans begins to emerge.

Thomas Phillips, an English captain to whom I will return below, offers a typical example of the ironic attitude Europeans take toward "kings" in Africa:

When we enter'd, the king peep'd upon us from behind a curtain, and beckon'd us to him; whereupon we approached close to his throne, which was of clay, rais'd about two foot from the ground, and about six foot square, surrounded with old dirty curtains, always drawn' tixt him and his cappasheirs, whom he will not allow the sight of his handsome phiz. (216)

Phillips clearly relishes the denigration implied in the detail of the "old dirty curtains" and in the sarcastic reference to "the sight of his handsome phiz." In an age that saw the emergence of the mock heroic as an important poetic mode, readers might be prepared to see the very word "king" as a signal of possible irony and watch for deflation or reversal. Of course, there is also the question of whether the title "king" would be accurate within specific African cultures in application to these specific African leaders, or whether it is merely an inappropriate imposition of European vocabulary and expectation.[18]

Willem Bosman, a Dutch writer much praised, and more often consulted, by English writers on West Africa at the time, is yet blunter:

The Kings in their Dwellings, or, if I may so call them, Courts, do not distinguish themselves by keeping any State. There is no Guard at their Palace Gates, nor any Body to wait on them, . . . and if they are meet in the Streets, they are about as much complimented as a Cobler amongst us. (188)

Indeed, such sneering comparisons might be said to typify Bosman's attitude toward West Africans. These denigrating ironies should not be understood as simple assertions of European superiority, however. They often seem quite the opposite, outbursts of frustration at the extent to which European traders were at the mercy of such native rulers.

Literary scholars looking at seventeenth- and eighteenth-century West Africa sometimes project images like those familiar from Conrad's *Heart of Darkness* backwards in history, imagining the complete subjugation of

---

[18] Robin Law, *The Slave Coast of West Africa 1550–1750: The Impact of the Atlantic Slave Trade on an African Society* (Oxford: Clarendon, 1991), 73–4, sees such usage as accurate; Randy J. Sparks does not: *The Two Princes of Calabar: An Eighteenth-Century Atlantic Journey* (Cambridge, MA: Harvard University Press, 2004), 36, also 1 and 11.

natives well before it was a reality.[19] Of course, the first projects for large-scale British colonialism in Africa did not emerge until the end of the eighteenth century, and most of these projects actually emerge in relation to the slave trade, whether as a buttress to it or as a potential replacement for it.[20] However, one should remember that, even until the middle of the eighteenth century, European factors worked at the sufferance of native authorities. According to historian Hugh Thomas, in 1678, the local chief agent of the Royal African Company recommended that all trading for slaves should be conducted from sloops, offshore: "Once settled ashore, a factor is absolutely under the command of the king where he lives, and is liable for the least displeasure to lose all the goods he has in his possession, with danger also to his life."[21] John Thornton makes it one of the central points of his book *Africa and Africans* that "Africans controlled the nature of their interactions with Europe. Europeans did not possess the military power to force Africans to participate in any type of trade in which they did not wish to engage."[22] Bearing in mind this precarious situation for Europeans in Africa well into the eighteenth century helps explain the relish that European writers take in sneering at African potentates. African leaders enjoyed the power to frustrate the

[19] See Robin Law, "'Here is No Resisting the Country': The Realities of Power in Afro-European Relations on the West African Slave Coast," *Itinerario*, 18:2 (1994), 50–64. Barry Unsworth's *Sacred Hunger* (New York: Doubleday, 1992) and the opening of Alberto J. Rivero's "Aphra Behn's *Oroonoko* and the 'Blank Spaces' of Colonial Fictions," *SEL*, 39:3 (1999), 443–62, take a Conradian view. For the argument that Africa became "the dark continent" in the nineteenth century, see Patrick Brantlinger, "Victorians and Africans: The Genealogy of the Myth of the Dark Continent," in *"Race," Writing, and Difference*, ed. Gates, 185–222, developed further as "The Genealogy of the Myth of the Dark Continent," in *Rule of Darkness: British Literature and Imperialism, 1830–1914* (Ithaca: Cornell University Press, 1988). For objections to the overstatement of British colonial power, see Colley, *Captives*, 9 and *passim*; and Nabil Matar, *Turks, Moors and Englishmen in the Age of Discovery* (New York: Columbia University Press, 1999), 8–12; By contrast, David Armitage in "Introduction: State and Empire in British History," in *The Ideological Origins of the British Empire* (Cambridge: Cambridge University Press, 2000), 1–23, argues that scholars understate the continuity of ideology between the "first, second and third" British empires.

[20] For an earlier example, see Malachy Postlethwayt, "The National and Private Examples of the African Trade Considered" (1746) and "In Honour of the Administration. The Importance of the African Expedition Considered" (1758), both reprinted in *Selected Works*, vol. II (Farnborough: Gregg, 1968), and Brown's account in *Moral Capital*, 269–74. See also Francis Moore, *Travels into the Inland Parts of Africa* (London, 1738) and Anthony Benezet, *Some Historical Account of Guinea* (Philadelphia: Crukshank, 1771).

[21] Hugh Thomas, *The Slave Trade: The Story of the Atlantic Slave Trade, 1440–1870* (New York: Simon & Schuster, 1997), 225–6. Thomas quotes from RAC correspondence.

[22] Thornton, *Africa and Africans*, 7. See also Robin Law, "Here is No Resisting the Country," esp. 60; P. E. H. Hair and Robin Law, "The English in Western Africa to 1700," in *The Origins of Empire: British Overseas Expansion to the Close of the Seventeenth Century*, ed. Nicholas D. Canny (New York: Oxford University Press, 1998); and Basil Davidson, *West Africa Before the Colonial Era: A History to 1850* (New York: Longman, 1998), 188.

European's desires for trade and even to drive them out on a whim. The Europeans exacted revenge not in the colonial encounter itself, but in the arena of their texts, in which these troublesome, frustrating Africans can be laughed at by an European audience, reassuringly cut down to the size of an impertinent cobbler.

Just as sarcastic barbs about the relative puniness of local kings often indicate a frustration with the power of, and impediments to trade offered by, African potentates, lavish, often Europeanizing descriptions of individual leaders – the Oroonoko effect – often appear to be inspired by hopes of, or satisfaction with, a productive alliance.[23] Indeed, for Captain Phillips, the timing of the appearance of an admirable African king seems to have more to do with his problems with the other established local authorities than any-thing else. A King Andreo makes his life difficult, accusing Phillips' English sailors of being thieves. Phillips' initial attempts to placate the king backfire: "At length finding that the more we endeavor'd to appease and convince him, the more insolent he grew, made us resolve to mask ourselves to his humour, and shew him we knew how to huff as well as his majesty" (VI:193). And, just at the moment when this strategic "huff" comes into play, Phillips encounters an inland king, neglected by Andreo, who he admires:

While I was at king *Andreo*'s town, there came one of the inland kings to the side of the council room where we were; he was of a large stature, and had a manly look and good features, and indeed was the most majestick handsome negroe that I ever saw (except the king of *Saboo*).[24]

The admiration directly leads to much more satisfying trade relations: "He presented me with a good leopard's skin, worth 3 or 4 *l.* in *England*, and I him with 3 or 4 bottles of rum, and as many handfuls of cowries, and so we parted very friendly" (193).

Nathaniel Uring, in his 1726 book of travels, writes of a 1701 voyage, describing the *Macundy* of Loango in Angola – "who was absolute sovereign,

---

[23] For related accounts, see Bartels, "Before Imperialism," and Hatfield, "A Very Wary People." On trade as an index of civility in the eighteenth century, see Albert O. Hirschman, *The Passions and the Interests: Political Arguments for Capitalism Before its Triumph* (Princeton: Princeton University Press, 1977), *passim*; J. G. A. Pocock, "The Mobility of Property and the Rise of Eighteenth-Century Sociology," in *Virtue, Commerce and History: Essays on Political Thought and History, Particularly in the Eighteenth Century* (Cambridge: Cambridge University Press, 1985), 103–23; Wheeler, *Complexion*, 109 and *passim*.

[24] Thomas Phillips, "A Journal of a Voyage Made in the Hannibal of London, Ann. 1693, 1694, from England to Cape Monseradoe in Africa and thence Along the Coast of Guiney to Whidaw, The Island of St. Thomas, and so Forward to Barbadoes . . .," in *A Collection of Voyages and Travels*, ed. Awnsham Churchill and John Churchill, vol. VI (London, 1732), 171–239, at 193. Further citations are given parenthetically in the text.

and Sister to the King, who had died some Time before our Arrival" – in *Oroonoko*-like terms: "She was indifferently tall and well shap'd, of a perfect black; had not big Lips nor was she flat Nos'd as most of the Natives are, but well featur'd and comely."[25] Uring approaches the Macundy to appeal to her against some of her "servants" with whom he is dealing for slaves. They insist that an old woman slave belongs to the Macundy, and that Uring must purchase her. When Uring describes her, then, he is looking to her for protection from "injustice." The case ends strangely – the interpreter continues to insist that the Macundy herself wishes Uring to buy the old woman, in translating her response to his petition. But Uring's response is to bribe the translator to take care of the problem, and the translator then promptly gets rid of the "useless" old woman slave. From this, Uring concludes that the translator was imposing on him all along, "that what I had been told was the *Macundy's* Pleasure, there was no truth in" (42). Uring, in other words, persists in seeing her as an embodiment of fairness and justice, and therefore never wavers from his positive and Europeanizing depiction of her.

Uring, giving evidence for the lack of the overwhelming sense of colonial superiority often expected of seventeenth-century Europeans in Africa, also offers a clear picture of the frustrations that the European merchants could encounter in African towns:

> before we were allowed to trade, we were obliged to pay certain duties to the *Macundy, Massuca, Massucambuca, Mallambella* and *Malambanzee*, and several other great Officers of State; and were obliged to threaten to leave the Place, in order to lessen their exorbitant Demands, which at last amounted to the Value of five or six Slaves ... And the Governor of the Town imposed upon us six Servants, which we were obliged to pay a certain Rate *per* Month. (37)

Denigration of Africans, then, follows the form expected of xenophobic representations in general; it is a product of the frustrations entailed by entry into another culture, rather than the expression of a facile assumption of superiority.

François Froger, a French author whose narrative of a 1695–7 journey to West Africa (published in English in 1698) also reveals a denigrating attitude to a local "king" after the French fail to get what they request in a commercial and military negotiation:

---

[25] *A History of the Voyages and Travels of Capt. Nathaniel Uring* (London, 1726); these passages are from 39–40 and 40–1, respectively.

M. *de la Roque* went to desire the King of *Bar* to give us leave to take possession of the Slaves and Oxen, which the *English* had in his Dominions: Whereupon the King reply'd That the Fort being surrender'd, every thing that was left on the Land, of very good right belonged to him.[26]

In the wake of this diplomatic and commercial disappointment, Froger admires the king's physical stature, but otherwise ridicules him for his failure to meet European standards of regal comportment: "The King appear'd a little while after, without any regular Train, in the midst of a great number of Negroes, and attended with some Drummers: He was of a very advantageous Stature, and was cloath'd with a red Doublet beset with the Tails of Wild Beasts, and little Bells" (27). Not only are his attendants inappropriately disorganized, but his dress is an uncomfortable mix of the nearly appropriate (by European standards) – "a red doublet" – and the savage – "Tails of Wild Beasts." Cleverly, then, Froger implies that the king tries and fails to live up to European regal standards. Having set him in this equivocal light, using an apparently objective tone, Froger then begins to emphasize the ludicrous contrast between the lofty expectations of European kingship and this particular African's absurd reality: "The King in this pompous Equipage, holding a Pipe in his Mouth, walk'd with a Majestick Gate under a stately Tree, where he usually gives Audience to the Ambassadors of the neighbouring Princes" (27). Froger's frustration and feelings of impotence underlie his need to assert superiority. In an act of revenge for the impotence of the French to press their demands on this king in his kingdom, Froger uses the king's own words to belittle him: "among other things, this poor King often enquir'd whether he was much talk'd of in *France*" (28). Froger presents his writerly desire to place the king in a European context as the king's own, giving rhetorical substance to his imaginative reversal of cultural power.

The hesitation of commercial travelers to Africa – at least those not primarily interested in slavery – to invoke racial difference may not be surprising, but following the Eric Williams and C. L. R. James hypothesis that slavery produces race, we need to examine when and where the systematic oppression and denigration of black Africans within the slave system began to be disseminated throughout the British Atlantic world. An oft-cited quotation provides useful evidence that those with ambitions for non-slave commerce in West Africa were particularly averse to racialization. In 1623, Richard Jobson, in his optimistic book of propaganda for the potential of trade with West Africa, recalls a telling exchange between

---

[26] François Froger, *A Relation of a Voyage Made in 1695, 1696, and 1697* (London, 1698), 26.

himself and an African trader on the subject of the slave trade. He was offered "certaine young blacke women," and told they were often sold to "white men, who earnestly desired them." He responds by saying: "we were a people, who did not deale in any such commodities, neither did we buy and sell one another, or any that had our owne shapes." Jobson insists on articulating a difference – but it is from the "white" slave traders, whom he calls "another kinde of people different from us."[27] For Jobson, the slave trade is secondary to the pursuit of gold, and therefore the slave trade becomes the occasion for a competitive positioning of the English as the most moral and the most humane trading partners for West Africans. The emphasis on similarity – "any that had our shapes" – seems an almost conscious counter to difference-making implied in the Africans' mention of other "white men." The point here is hardly to differentiate "black" from "white" in a justification of the slave trade, but rather to narrow the perceived gap between Africans and English – for other commercial purposes – at the expense of that very trade; Jobson, in other words, actively resists assimilating himself to the ways – and possibly even into the category – of "white" Europeans. At the very least, Jobson provides evidence of a moment in the seventeenth century when neither race nor African slavery seemed simply natural to a British trader, and offers a notable instance of an Englishman positioning himself as "humane" to advantage.

This "Oroonoko effect" on commercial traders differs markedly from readings of Behn's "Europeanizing" of Oroonoko through the lens of race. Many scholars are quite shocked by the African prince depicted in Oroonoko; indeed, the shock provoked by Behn's novel has made strange bedfellows of early twentieth-century scholars seemingly comfortable with racist assumptions and late twentieth-century proponents of cultural studies. The Africa of Behn's *Oroonoko*, and prince Oroonoko himself have, at least since Wylie Sypher's 1942 book *Guinea's Captive Kings*, been seen as an inaccurate, indeed quite "Europeanized" account of seventeenth-century West Africa.[28] Oroonoko lives in a lavish, if oriental court; much of the action revolves around the king's, his father's, large harem; Oroonoko's beloved, Imoinda, is one of the number of the king's wives and concubines. Oroonoko himself is famously distinguished from other Africans in his physical appearance:

---

[27] Richard Jobson, *The Golden Trade or A Discovery of the River Gambra and the Golden Trade of the Aethiopians*, 1623 (London: Dawsons, 1968), 112.
[28] Sypher begins *Guinea's Captive Kings* by presenting "the noble Negro" as a propaganda tool, and one that is necessarily "illegitimate" (2), because unrealistic.

He was pretty tall, but of a Shape the most exact that can be fansy'd: The most famous Statuary cou'd not form the Figure of a Man more admirably turn'd from Head to Foot. His Face was not of that brown, rusty Black which most of that Nation are, but a perfect Ebony, or polish'd Jett. His Eyes were the most awful that cou'd be seen, and very piercing; the White of 'em being like Snow, as were his Teeth. His Nose was rising and Roman, instead of African and flat. His Mouth, the finest shap'd that cou'd be seen; far from those great turn'd Lips, which are so natural to the rest of the Negroes. The whole Proportion and Air of his Face was so noble, and exactly form'd, that, bating his Colour, there cou'd be nothing in Nature more beautiful, agreeable and handsome.[29]

It is of course noteworthy that Oroonoko's blackness is superior to other Africans' by virtue of being a deeper, rather than a lighter shade. Furthermore, when transferred to a plantation in Surinam as a slave – indeed, even when brutally executed – Oroonoko never loses his aristocratic, even regal bearing. Indeed, the European settlers he comes in contact with perceive and treat him as an aristocrat; his days in Surinam are occupied with conversation and pleasure trips rather than field work.

Behn's Europeanizing depiction of Oroonoko, and of the court in Coromantien, are both held by critics to aid colonial ideology in rather counter-intuitive ways. Some see Behn denigrating the African phenotype – and thus displaying typical British colonial racism – by assimilating Oroonoko to European standards of beauty.[30] This critique is also extended to Behn's depiction of an African court in terms apparently borrowed from the settings of French romance.[31] The subtle implication – in the context of critiques of Oroonoko as a vessel of colonial ideology – is that Behn is uninterested in, and therefore disrespectful of, the real particularity of Oroonoko's Africanness, and of the real conditions of life in Africa.[32] This second position, rather jarringly and as a result of decidedly different

---

[29] Aphra Behn, *Oroonoko, or, The Royal Slave: A True History* (London, 1688), 20–1. Further citations will be to this edition and will be given parenthetically in the text.

[30] Several of the most influential readings of *Oroonoko* make this argument: Laura Brown, "The Romance of Empire: *Oroonoko* and the Trade in Slaves," in *Ends of Empire*, 36–7, and Catherine Gallagher, "*Oroonoko's* Blackness," in *Aphra Behn Studies*, ed. Janet Todd (Cambridge: Cambridge University Press, 1994), 240–1. Brown's argument was first presented in *The New Eighteenth Century*, ed. Laura Brown and Felicity Nussbaum (New York: Methuen, 1987), 41–61. For another instance, see Henry Louis Gates, Jr., *The Signifying Monkey: A Theory of African American Literary Criticism* (New York: Oxford University Press, 1986), 133. For a reading close to mine, see Jacqueline Pearson, "'Slave Princesses and Lady Monsters': Gender and Ethnic Difference in the Work of Aphra Behn," in *Aphra Behn Studies* ed. Todd, 231.

[31] Lipking, "Confusing Matters," 265, sees Behn's scenes of the Coromantien court as "projections into vacant space."

[32] See in particular Moira Ferguson, "*Oroonoko*: Birth of a Paradigm," *New Literary History*, 32:2 (1992), 346–7, and Rivero, "Aphra Behn's *Oroonoko*," 451–2.

motives, verges on repeating the dismissive disgust of Wylie Sypher at the
unreality of the "romantic" notion of "the noble Negro." Joanna Lipking
usefully inquires what the standard is against which Behn's Africans should
be judged.[33] But critics imply that representing an African court as highly
polished and civilized is somehow more conducive to imperialism and
racism than representing Africa as primitive and depraved. In so doing,
such scholars uncritically accept the idea that eighteenth-century Africa truly
was primitive; they take the depravity of pre-colonial Africa as a given.[34]
Catherine Gallagher makes a similar move with her rather circular argument
that representing Oroonoko's body or an African court unproblematically in
European terms actually serves only to remind readers of their already
established assumptions of difference.[35] This excludes the possibility that
Behn and her readers did not assume that Africa was lacking in "civilization"
or that Africans were fundamentally different from them, and thus could
imagine Oroonoko in European terms because they saw him as fundamentally similar to themselves, rather than to imply an unspoken assumption of
his fundamental difference.

Defoe's novels, on the other hand, present an Africa in which no native
would be capable of assuming an aristocratic role once in contact with
Europeans; the coast in *Robinson Crusoe* is populated with primitive cannibals, while the interior in *Singleton* is a blank desert. Indeed, Singleton easily
takes even a local king as a slave, although a certain respect is extended to
him, explicitly in order to facilitate the manipulation of the other slaves. As
Roxann Wheeler puts it, "The novel envisions an Africa emptied of a
commercial infrastructure, including trading and communication net-
works."[36] Furthermore, in contrast to Europe, "Defoe offers a more primitive Africa composed of scantily clad cowherds which places Africa among
the barbaric stages of civilization"[37] – precisely the opposite of commercial
travelers' accounts, which emphasize the differences between African groups
and make efforts to identify the best ways to locate potential partners and
exploit pre-existing economic structures. This Africa, while less remarkable
to twentieth- and twenty-first-century critics than the "romance court" in
Oroonoko, is actually more unusual in late seventeenth-century visions of
Africa, whether in travel accounts or in fiction, despite critical views to the
contrary. This leads to recurring suggestions that specific texts – whether by

---

[33] Lipking, "Confusing Matters," 263.
[34] Ferguson's claim that Behn ignores the historical fact of "warring West African tribes" sits uncomfortably with her charge that Behn's "Europeanized" Coromantien is "uncivilized" ("*Oroonoko*," 347).
[35] Gallagher, "*Oroonoko*'s Blackness," 240 and 244.   [36] Wheeler, *Complexion*, 108.   [37] *Ibid.*, 109.

Michel Adanson, Anthony Benezet, Olaudah Equiano, or Mungo Park – are notable for their strikingly "positive" portrayals of Africa. Certainly, the state of Africa was a polemical issue throughout the century, and became more so with the emergence of the abolition debate. But it is arguably Defoe's totally barren Africa which represents the most uncommon vision. Even Snelgrave, who set in motion many of the central pro-slavery arguments of the late century, represented West Africa as having a fairly stable and complex system of government.

One difference between the actual Oroonoko stories and the traveler's accounts showing an "Oroonoko effect" is that both Behn and Southerne represent Oroonoko as if he were a European prince in blackface rather than a black African. Readings of this representation tend to see it as a "racist" because it translates Oroonoko – a positive, indeed an aristocratic, character – from "black" to "white" terms. This shows not a denial of difference but a cultural failure to conceive of the world in terms of racial identities that correlate primarily with skin color and associated physical differences; it is, then, the culmination of the "Oroonoko effect" first developed in travel writing. Of course, the racial critique of this representation is further complicated by the fact that both Behn and Southerne were playwrights who would be likely to imagine their African character as being portrayed by a British actor in blackface.[38] Their propensity to imagine the character in these terms, and indeed to define Oroonoko as a typical Restoration tragic hero caught between love and honor, may show shades of xenophobia, but nonetheless indicates the lack of a compelling investment at this cultural moment in a familiar concept of "race."

In this context, it may not be surprising that one of the first comments indicating the arrival of the familiar idea of racial difference in this discourse comes, paradoxically but perhaps inevitably, in the form of a denial of such difference. In his account of a 1693–4 voyage (unpublished until 1732), Thomas Phillips considers the violent enforcement of a difference between black and white on board slave ships – he himself is the captain of such a ship – and rejects it in horror:

some commanders have cut off the legs or arms of the most wilful, to terrify the rest, for they believe if they lose a member, they cannot return home again: I was advis'd by some of my officers to do the same, but I could not be perswaded to

---

[38] Robert Hornback, "Emblems of Folly in the First Othello: Renaissance Blackface, Moor's Coat, and 'Muckender'," *Comparative Drama*, 35:1 (2001), 69–99; and Nussbaum, "Black Women: Why Imoinda Turns White," in *Limits of the Human*, 151–88, discuss blackface performance in periods close to Behn's.

entertain the least thoughts of it, much less to put into practice such barbarity and cruelty to poor creatures, who, excepting their want of christianity and true religion, (their misfortune more than fault) are as much the work of God's hands, and no doubt as dear to him as ourselves; nor can I imagine why they should be despis'd for their colour, being what they cannot help, and the effect of the climate it has pleased God to appoint them. (219)

Here, Phillips explicitly evokes the possibility of real racial differences, in the context of the practice of racial violence and subjection.[39] Having raised this possibility, he casts himself in the almost heroic role of the defender of the earlier, more established, and certainly more malleable, system of identity based on religion.[40] He throws the power of his position as captain into the balance, overruling those officers who urge him to mutilate the slaves. Still, even in opposing it, Captain Phillips articulates the emerging system of racial difference, and even its consequences of violence and dehumanization, more clearly than any other seventeenth-century traveler to West Africa. This raises several of the thorniest questions of literary theory in the last two decades: the relationship of textual representations to cultural practices, and the possibility of resistance to established cultural norms. In the indirect pursuit of answers, I will now examine how well Phillips seems to put into practice his stated resistance to the emergence of race in the rest of his journal.

One thing immediately seems clear: Phillips does not believe that enslaving Africans is equivalent to the despising "them for their colour" that he rejects. He is a slave-ship captain, and does not often flinch from what this entails. If slavery produces race as a cultural practice, this implies that slavery precedes race, and thus, theoretically, at some point slavers would not yet have a racial consciousness. Phillips does believe that West Indian slavery is an improvement for West Africans, however much they resist it. He remarks that "They having a more dreadful apprehension of *Barbadoes* than we can have of hell, tho' in reality they live much better there than in their own country" (219).

And beyond this overt endorsement of the trade, the concept of slavery plays a very strange role in Phillips' account. Twice, he complains of "slavery," but both times, Phillips applies the word not to the fate of his human cargo, but instead to unpleasant duties incumbent on his crew. Describing the examination of slaves for venereal disease, Phillips' sympathy is entirely with

---

[39] Contrast the reference to this passage in Jordan (*White Over Black*, 11), Barker (*African Link*, 14), and Gallagher (in her edition of *Oroonoko*), 234.
[40] On religion as an earlier system of identity, see Benedict Anderson, *Imagined Communities: Reflections on the Rise and Spread of Nationalism* rev. edn (London: Verso, 1991).

his ship's surgeon: "our surgeon is forc'd to examine the privities of both men and women with the nicest scrutiny, which is a great slavery, but what can't be omitted" (218). Again, describing the care of slaves dying of the flux, he remarks that

> what the small-pox spar'd, the flux swept off, to our great regret, after all our pains and care to give them their messes in due order and season, keeping their lodgings as clean and sweet as possible, and enduring so much misery and stench so long among a parcel of creatures nastier than swine; and after all our expectations to be defeated by their mortality. No gold-finders can endure so much noisome slavery as they do who carry negroes. (237)

This goes beyond a curious alignment of sympathy. Phillips gestures toward dehumanization with the comment "a parcel of creatures nastier than swine." Further, his comment on the crew's "noisome slavery," describing the very act of enslaving Africans, seems to insist that Europeans' metaphorical slavery is more remarkable than the actual slavery of the Africans. Together with the conflation of negroes and slaves in the last line of the quotation, Phillips here seems to capture the moment in which racial consciousness emerges out of the practice of racial oppression.

   This attitude to slavery begins to erode the sense that Phillips ever genuinely resisted racialization; indeed, refusing to chop off limbs is hardly a commitment to equality. Other than in letting slip the remark about "creatures nastier than swine" – itself ambiguous, as the "nastiness" could refer to racial or cultural difference, or to the disease they are suffering from – what Phillips most clearly resists is attributing the articulation and enforcement of racial difference directly to himself. In the beginning of his discussion of smallpox, Phillips seems to imply a concrete biological difference between cargo and crew, employing an almost wondering tone. Phillips observes "one thing is very surprizing in this distemper among the blacks, that tho' it immediately infests those of their own colour, yet it will never seize a white man" (237), going on to explain that the symptoms are, nonetheless, identical to those in England.

   Phillips goes further towards implying the existence of natural racial distinctions in the description of a caged tiger he kept on board:

> 'Twas strange to me to observe this ravenous wild creature, that he would be as familiar with our white men as a spaniel, letting them play with him, stroak him, take him by the tongue or paw, and would wantonly lick their hands, pat them with his foot like a cat, without offering the least injury; but when he saw a black, tho' at a distance, he would grow raving mad, bounce and leap in his cage as if he would break it to pieces, and his eyes would look like perfect fire, so that I was forced to get a larger and a stronger coop made for him. (231)

Nature makes the concrete reality of difference clear, through the otherwise inexplicable behavior of the tiger. Phillips merely reports the event with wonder, drawing no conclusions himself. This passage can be read as having the same self-contradictory effect as the passage in which Phillips explicitly denies that color is grounds for despising Africans. In each case, Phillips implies the existence of a natural racial order, but he represents himself as humanely deploying his power as captain to contain the violent consequences of this natural order on his ship.[41] In the first instance, his officers are overruled and no limbs are severed; here, he orders the tiger removed to a larger and stronger coop to prevent a mauling.

Phillips, in other words, embodies the transatlantic gap in conceptions and practices of race. He represents not an individual holding out against a new system of identity in favor of an older system, as he implies to his metropolitan readers, but instead occupies the space between two conflicting conceptions of identity. His position as a captain in the slave trade implicates him in the newly emerging practices of white supremacy and racial oppression. However, in returning to England, leaving the trade, and writing his journal, Phillips finds these new ideas and practices in conflict with the older system of understanding identity through religion still dominant there. As a result, Phillips presents race as an unavoidable biological reality, in his discussions of disease and of the tiger, and also as a misguided cultural system, in his discussion of the practice of disciplinary mutilation. Phillips equivocally denies and defends his implication in the emergent process of racialization, invoking the values of his metropolitan audience and yet implicitly bringing to bear those of the slave ship. He uses a posture of passivity to deny personal responsibility, and yet ultimately suggests the truth of the new system.

In a discourse as paradoxical as these travelers' accounts of West Africa, then, it is almost unsurprising that a contentious debate would signal the arrival of a consensus on the reality of racial difference. William Snelgrave, another slave-ship captain, published his *New Account of Some Parts of Guinea and the Slave Trade* in 1734 in order to document his charges of barbarity and cannibalism against West Africans, particularly the King of Dahomey, who had recently conquered swaths of the region. Snelgrave's agenda, if not directly spoken, is nonetheless clear. He wishes to justify the slave trade on the grounds that Africans are better off, indeed rescued,

---

[41] On the connection between passivity and sentiment, see Scott Paul Gordon, *The Power of the Passive Self, 1640–1770* (Cambridge: Cambridge University Press, 2002).

when they are enslaved and taken to British colonial plantations.[42] To this effect, Snelgrave tells sentimental tales of his personal intervention to "save" Africans from the savagery of their own rulers. In the Introduction he sets the tone powerfully by telling the tale of his rescue of an infant from local religious practices at "old Callabar."[43]

Having reported the death of one child in a religious sacrifice, Snelgrave discovers that the king intends another "to be sacrificed that night to his God *Egbo*, for his prosperity" (Introduction 10). Snelgrave grabs the child, and pulls out a pistol to defend his action, "excusing it on the account of my Religion, which, tho' it does not allow of forcibly taking away what belongs to another, yet expressly forbids so horrid a Thing, as the putting a poor innocent Child to death" (Introduction 11). Here Snelgrave implies that, despite being a slaver, he recognizes Africans as fellow humans, apparently to an extent that the Africans themselves do not so recognize each other. Furthermore, Snelgrave tries to show that in his values, humanity comes before trade and property – the horror of "putting an innocent child to death" trumps the rule against "forcibly taking away what belongs to another."

Snelgrave, however, rather easily reconciles the two principles via slavery, purchasing the child to complete the rescue. Snelgrave then discovers the child's mother in the cargo of his slave ship, and, like a grateful slave reformer, reaps the benefits of his humanity:

I think there never was a more moving sight than on this occasion, between the Mother and her little Son, . . . especially when the Linguist told her, "I had saved her child from being sacrificed." Having at that time above 300 Negroes on board my Ship, no sooner was the Story known amongst them, but they expressed their Thankfulness to me, by clapping their Hands, and singing a Song in my praise. This affair proved of great service to us, for it gave them a good Notion of white Men; so that we had no Mutiny in our Ship, during the whole Voyage. (Introduction 13–14)

While the difference between Snelgrave and the King of Old Callabar is articulated as explicitly religious and cultural, a slippage begins: what the slaves learn from Snelgrave's rescue is "a good Notion of white Men," not, say, the blessings of Christianity. Indeed, even when Snelgrave invokes "his

---

[42] This agenda is apparent throughout the book, beginning in the unpaginated Preface. Citations below given parenthetically are to William Snelgrave, *New Account of Some Parts of Guinea and the Slave Trade*, 1734 (London: Cass, 1971).

[43] Barker comments wryly that "Snelgrave had a suspiciously happy knack of finding or thwarting sacrifices" (*African Link*, 136). Wheeler also analyzes the paradox of the sentimental slave trader (*Complexion*, 104).

religion" and "the most high God" to justify his interruption of the child-sacrifice, he defines that God as the one "whom we white Men adored" (Introduction 11). Race operates at the border of the cultural and the natural, and here, religious and racial identity intertwine.

Typically of grateful slave stories, then, Snelgrave's apparently sentimental actions benefit him, instilling a willing obedience in his slaves. Snelgrave also illustrates how a moment of human connection develops a sense of difference. His very sentimental humanity, in contrast to the brutality of African priests and kings, gives his whole cargo "a good notion of white men," leading them to accept their slavery passively. At the same time, by introducing the language of race in reporting the incident to his English audience, Snelgrave disseminates a sense of white privilege, of a natural order in which Africans are grateful to become slaves to white Englishmen, under the cover of a tale explicitly dwelling on his sentimental engagement with African humanity. Snelgrave's account of the slave trade as an effort to "rescue" Africans was extremely influential on slavery's apologists in the abolition debate.[44] Although other pro-slavery writers sometimes made the same point with a different tone – emphasizing African savagery and depravity – Snelgrave's was one of the most influential versions of the "grateful slave" in eighteenth-century thinking about Africa, race, and slavery.

John Atkins, a Royal African Company surgeon, immediately produced a refutation of Snelgrave. His *Voyage to Guinea, Brazil, and the West Indies*, published only one year later, in 1735, casts an effectively skeptical eye on Snelgrave's claims, and his charges of cannibalism in particular.[45] Atkins refutes the charges against Dahomey at some length; in one instance, discussing a local potentate, Cabiceer John Hee of Montzerado, Atkins observes that:

He seemed shy of entering the Ship, apprehending a *Panyarring* [kidnapping]; his Town's People having often suffered by the Treachery of Ships, and they as often returned it, sometimes with Cruelty, which has given rise to the Report of their being Savages and Cannibals at several places. (58)

It is the cruelty and indiscipline of Europeans which has lead to conflict and then to dehumanizing charges against the natives. Here, Atkins does

---

[44] Law's book *The Slave Coast* opens with an anecdote about the presence of Snelgrave's vision of Dahomey in the late-century parliamentary abolition debate, 1–2. J. Robert Constantine, "The African Slave Trade: A Study of Eighteenth-Century Propaganda and Public Controversy" (Ph.D. diss., Indiana University, 1953), 102, documents the usage of Snelgrave in magazine defenses of the slave trade.

[45] *A Voyage to Guinea, Brazil and the West Indies in His Majesty's Ships, the "Swallow" and "Weymouth,"* 1735 (London: Cass, 1970).

his best to expose, rather than to naturalize, what Mary Louise Pratt has termed the "contact zone."[46]

Atkins seems quite aware of the stakes of his dispute with Snelgrave, attacking his opponent's implication that the African slave trade was a kind of divine rescue mission:

When the Nakedness, Poverty and Ignorance of these Species of Men are considered, it would incline one to think it a bettering their Condition, to transport them to the worst of Christian Slavery; but as we find them little mended in those respects at the *West-Indies*, their Patrons respecting them only as Beasts of Burden. (61)

Although he clearly rejects the practice of treating Africans as "beasts," Atkins's rebuttal of Snelgrave does not depend on questioning the implication that slavery is an appropriate destiny for Africans. Indeed, Atkins acknowledges that "the worst of Christian slavery" would be a benefit. His criticism is that British planters exceed this benevolent version of racial subjugation, going too far by leaving any redemptively Christian aspect out of slavery and instead reducing the Africans to mere "beasts of burden."

But does Atkins here employ a racialized concept of African slavery? Apparently, his terminology in the phrase "this species of men" is no accident. Atkins proposes a radical concept of racial difference quite early, as he offers, in passing, the option of polygenesis, preceding Lord Kames' more widely noted suggestion by half a century: "Tho' it be a little Heterodox, I am persuaded that the black and white Race have, *ab origine*, sprung from different-coloured first parents" (39). Atkins rejects Snelgrave's overheated imaginings and strategies of sentimental manipulation. But, as befits an RAC officer, he never rejects slavery itself, and actually tidies up Snelgrave's work, which relied on implication, with a bold, direct hypothesis of natural, original, and unbridgeable racial difference, couched in terms at once scientific and theological.

As we have seen, then, with Phillips, Snelgrave, and his opponent Atkins, in this period, it is those who offer to defend the humanity of Africans who succeed most clearly in raising the possibility of substantial racial difference. The genie of race seems to escape from the bottle when the question is posed, even if the ostensible answer, as in Phillips' case, is a denial of difference. Those who defend Africans' humanity in effect call it into question, or more precisely, create difference and hierarchy within the category of the human. Concluding with Atkins that Africans are not mere beasts, or with Phillips that it is better to avoid chopping off their limbs, or with Snelgrave that they

[46] Pratt, *Imperial Eyes*, 6–7 and *passim*.

ought not to be sacrificed as children, leads not to the dismissal of racial difference but instead to a supposedly "moderate" version of it, in which it is enough that Africans be made slaves. Of course, the moderation of ideas of difference in deference to the dominant orthodoxy of monogenesis is not insignificant. It created the transatlantic gap between the colonial practice of white supremacy and the metropolitan discourse of monogenesis. Indeed, in the late seventeenth century, the hypothesis of polygenesis was advanced, which ultimately proved a useful weapon in Morgan Godwyn's critique of the excesses of slavery in *The Negro's and Indian's Advocate*.[47] Still, such acknowledgments of the limits of metropolitan discourse do not seem to have had any effect as restraints on the extremes to which colonists would go to enforce white supremacy. And yet, the implication that colonists had a more thoroughgoing conception of race which they failed to articulate verges on anachronism. Some evidence – such as Trelawny's example – suggests that colonists did not, indeed could not, deny the humanity of Africans, but justified white supremacy and dehumanization to themselves in material, rather than philosophical, terms.

TORTURE AND SENTIMENT

I would like to return from this point, in which we have seen the transatlantic gap in racial consciousness demonstrated and seen gratitude offered as a solution to slave resistance, to scenes of torture and sentimental response in several of the texts addressed above. Both *Oroonoko* and Phillips' text offer scenes of torture and mutilation of African slaves, and then strive to reassure the audience that not only is the narrator personally incapable of such acts of brutality, but that he feels for the sufferers. Colonial torture and discipline were extremely vexed for seventeenth-century Englishmen. As Jill Lepore argues in her analysis of a scene in which an Englishman describes the torture of one Indian by others – the victim an enemy, the torturers allies of the English colonists – New World torture was something that the English used to differentiate themselves from the Spanish, about whom they promoted the "Black Legend."[48]

---

[47] Godwyn uses the term "Preadamism" to attack what we would call "polygenesis" as heretical (*Advocate*, 18–19).

[48] See Lepore, *Name of War*, chapter 1, esp. 3–5; she connects British identity to rejection of the Spanish, 8. For the definition of Protestant identity in opposition to Catholicism more broadly, see Colin Haydon, *Anti-Catholicism in Eighteenth-century England, c. 1714–80: A Political and Social Study* (Manchester: Manchester University Press, 1993) and Tony Claydon and Ian McBride, eds., *Protestantism and National Identity: Britain and Ireland, c.1650-c.1850* (Cambridge: Cambridge University Press, 1998).

Hence, as Lepore points out, it is crucial for the English to dissociate themselves from such cruelty. In the scene she analyzes from William Hubbard's 1677 text on the *Troubles with the Indians* this process happens in an aside: such "barbarous and unheard of Cruelty, the English were not able to bear, it forcing Tears from their Eyes; yet did not the sufferer ever relent, or shew any Sign of Anguish."[49] This creates a double differentiation suggested but not directly analyzed by Lepore. Not only do the English disclaim the role of torturer, they also disclaim the kind of stoicism – or more precisely, affectlessness – that the victim of torture exhibits.

Victim and torturers, then, are at once made other to the British narrator and observers in one gesture, a gesture that, with tears, confirms the Britons' sympathetic, even sentimental nature as wholly different from that of the Indians. The conflation of tortured and torturers is apparent in the odd wording, in which it is the victim who refuses to "relent." Hubbard ends the scene with an editorial comment that confirms the damning similarity of all the Indians involved in the scene, but also, seemingly unintentionally, calls into question the entire colonial endeavor: "At last they brake the Bones of his Legs, after which he was forced to sit down, which 'tis said he silently did, till they knocked out his Brains. Instances of this Nature should be incentive unto us, to bless the Father of Lights, who hath called us out of the dark Places of the Earth, full of the Habitations of Cruelty" (II:64).[50] Of course, Hubbard is now reporting from just such a "dark place" and, despite the tears, is actually helping to forward the "cruelty" of these habitations.[51] As Lepore reveals, the English had turned

[49] *A Narrative of the Troubles with the Indians in New-England* (Boston, 1677), reprinted in *The History of the Indian Wars in New England*, 2 vols., ed. Samuel Drake (New York: Burt Franklin, 1865), II:64; for more on this scene see Lepore, *Name of War*, 3–5, and John Canup, *Out of the Wilderness: The Emergence of an American Identity in Colonial New England* (Middletown, CT: Wesleyan University Press, 1990), 192–5.

[50] David S. Lovejoy, *Religious Enthusiasm in the New World: Heresy to Revolution* (Cambridge, MA: Harvard University Press, 1985), discusses the "millennial" Protestant belief that the light of the gospel, like the light of the sun, would spread from East to West. The millennium would come at the end of this process (17); some held that the final step would be the conversion of American natives from Catholicism to Protestantism (18).

[51] Karen Ordahl Kupperman, *Indians & English: Facing off in Early America* (Ithaca: Cornell University Press, 2000) and Alfred A. Cave, "Canaanites in a Promised Land: The American Indian and the Providential Theory of Empire," *American Indian Quarterly*, 12 (1988), 277–97, discuss assimilations of Native Americans into Protestant theology and biblical history. Canup (*Out of the Wilderness*, 8–28) by contrast, discusses the effort to present New England as much like England itself. Armitage (*Ideological Origins*, 63–4) calls for more scholarship on the exact role of Protestantism in the development of imperial ideology. Hubbard's understanding of geography, theology, and civilization has resonances, if it does not entirely mesh, with theories of the westward course of civilization (see Eric Cheyfitz, *The Poetics of Empire: Translation and Colonization from The Tempest to Tarzan* (New York: Oxford University Press, 1991) on the "Translatio Imperii") and the four stages or

over the captured victim to his tormentors, and passively, if tearfully, watched as he was tortured.

Hubbard's reference to God's abandonment of certain places connects to a strikingly similar scene of an Englishman who refuses to endorse torture that he nonetheless shows to be ongoing, a scene that includes a similar moment of theological musing. Captain Phillips (in the passage quoted above for its comments on the relation of complexion to race) differentiates himself from those who openly practice racial oppression. He disclaims both the concept of race and the violence of the slave trade, particularly the mutilation of limbs, which "some commanders" use to "terrify the rest" of their cargoes.[52] Although Phillips was "advis'd by some of my officers to do the same," he insists "I could not be perswaded to entertain the least thoughts of it, much less to put into practice such barbarity and cruelty." Here, it is the English themselves – indeed the officers of his ship and his fellow commanders – who are the torturers, and only our narrator refuses to "practice such barbarity." Seen in this context, Phillips is denying his responsibility for the ongoing cruelty of the slave trade even as he explains his participation in it. Perhaps he is using his own sentimental posture – whether or not it is factually accurate – as a way to present the disturbing practices and concepts of race familiar to slave traders to a metropolitan audience more likely to see them as cruel, heretical, and even specifically Catholic. He is much like Hubbard in gesturing toward the systemic violence of his enterprise, and yet invoking personal, immediate feelings as a means of exonerating himself individually. Unlike Hubbard, Phillips is careful not to condemn the whole enterprise: he makes no ultimately self-defeating reference to "habitations of cruelty" that might implicate his own ship. Yet his reliance on his own sentimental affect, on a sympathetic nature that leaves him unpersuaded by his cruel mates, is not quite enough to mask his revelation of the thoroughgoing cruelty of the slave-trading enterprise. This, perhaps, he acknowledges inadvertently in his strangely inverted metaphor of "slavery" to describe the efforts of the surgeon inspecting the slaves which I have analyzed in the previous section.

"stadial" theory of civilization's development (see Wheeler, "Consuming Englishness: On the Margins of Civil Society," chapter 4 of *Complexion*, 176–233) and perhaps most directly with explanations of human difference in biblical or pseudo-biblical terms (see Benjamin Braude, "The Sons of Noah and the Construction of Ethnic and Geographical Identities in the Medieval and Early Modern Periods," *William and Mary Quarterly*, 64:1 (1997), 103–42).

[52] This and all the following quotations are from Churchill, *Voyages and Travels*, 219. The entire passage is quoted above on pp. 54–5.

Phillips' theological aside in this passage – his remark that the "poor creatures ... excepting their want of christianity and true religion, (their misfortune more than fault) are as much the work of God's hands, and no doubt as dear to him as ourselves" appears, like Hubbard and Robinson Crusoe, to regret the merely geographic exclusion of pagans from Christianity.[53] Of course, like both of them, his concept carries, if more subtly, the same resonances of the "dark places" and "habitations of cruelty" of Psalm 74. Indeed, the only differentiation that Phillips explicitly allows between Africans and Englishmen is their "misfortune" in not being Christians. This theological understanding of difference is easy to classify, in the terms of twenty-first-century scholarship, as "cultural" rather than "essential." As such, it is distinct from modern conceptions of race. And yet, such a strict distinction between the cultural and the essential leaves as the excluded middle what seventeenth-century writers clearly experienced as a concrete, if mysterious, difference imposed by God himself. The occasional association of even converted "praying Indians" with Satan is strongly suggestive of a conceptual move toward seeing divinely sanctioned differences as essential.[54] And yet, such positions were far less stable and consistent, and more subject to contextual and polemical uses, than we imagine in describing them as initiating the regime of racial difference. One Puritan observer, Daniel Gookin, went so far as to prefer the martyrological claims of New England Indians to the standard of Foxe's martyrs. Gookin sees John Sassamun, a complex figure whose mysterious killing Lepore considers at length, as "the first Christian martyr of the Indians; for it is evident that he suffered death upon account of his Christian profession, and fidelity to the English."[55] Furthermore, Gookin concludes his history of the Christian Indians calling them: "such as are, through the grace of Christ, the first professors, confessors, If I may not say martyrs, of the Christian religion among the poor Indians in America."[56] Indeed, John Canup reads Gookin as appearing "to strip the colonists of their identity as God's saints and bestow it upon these ruder, but perhaps more deserving 'professors.'"[57]

[53] See Laura Stevens, *The Poor Indians: British Missionaries, Native Americans, and Colonial Sensibility* (Philadelphia: University of Pennsylvania Press, 2004), 1–2, for a consideration of Crusoe's relevant musings.

[54] Lepore, *Name of War*, 45, 112 and *passim*.

[55] Daniel Gookin, *An Historical Account of the Doings and Sufferings of the Christian Indians in New England in the Years 1675, 1676, 1677*, in *Transactions and Collections of the American Antiquarian Society*, II (1836), 440.

[56] *Ibid.*, 523.

[57] Canup, *Out of the Wilderness*, 188; Lepore, *Name of War*, 45, relates such views to the suppression of Gookin's text and his loss of power in the colony.

Why, then, I would like to ask, do torture, sentiment, and God, or better, "true religion," cluster together in these scenes? There is another context, complementary to the Black Legend of Spanish cruelty, in which torture, stoicism, and identification with suffering are constitutive of Englishness and of Protestant identity: the discourse of Protestant martyrology born of Foxe's *Book of Martyrs*.[58] Although there are many, many scenes of torture and execution in Foxe, I will cite one that can serve as typical in this context because it invokes the torture and mutilation of the martyr and also uses a challenge and response structure between torturer and victim.[59] More deeply revealing of the function of such scenes in Foxe's text, however, is its explanation that the victim's apparent stoicism is born specifically of true faith. This points to the function of such scenes of torment in helping to construct a Protestant identity. The example of "An English man Burned at Rome," from the 1684 edition of Foxe, covers the classic elements of a Foxean martyrdom in a more pithy scene than the more deeply detailed – not to say longwinded – accounts of the original Marian martyrs. After the pope himself condemns the unnamed man to be burnt, "some of the Popes Cardinals" decide that he "should be examined by all exquisite Tortures, to make him confess his fellows." But "nothing could be drawn from him, but this speech, *Such was the will of God.*" Subsequently, tormenters "scorched and burned his flesh through all the City of *Rome*" as they drive him in a cart to his place of execution. Then,

Being taken down out of the Cart, and seeing the Post whereunto he was to be fastened with three Chains of Iron; he went of himself to the Post, and falling on his Knees kissed the Chains with which he was there to be bound till the Sacrifice should be ended.

But before the Fire was put to him, he was urged by Friers and Priests to worship an Idol which they presented there before him. From which turning away his face, he shewed unto them his constant resolution to the contrary, holding on to his Christian course unto the end: which he truly testified; for as soon as the

---

[58] See Snader, *Caught Between Worlds*, 3 and Colley, *Britons*, 25–8. Erwin Nicholson, "Eighteenth-Century Foxe: Evidence for the Impact of the *Acts and Monuments* in the 'Long' Eighteenth Century," in *John Foxe and the English Reformation*, ed. David Loades (Aldershot: Scolar, 1997), 143–77, argues that Foxe's influence has been overstated. How important Protestantism was to English national identity in the sixteenth and seventeenth centuries is much debated; see Krishan Kumar, *The Making of English National Identity* (Cambridge: Cambridge University Press, 2003), 95–120.

[59] Knott, *Discourses*, 16, gives a slightly different account of the "pattern" of Foxe's typical scenes. Some of the popular redacted versions of Foxe in the late seventeenth century – for instance the *Martyrologia Alphabetike* (London: R. Butler, 1677), a dictionary-like list of Martyrs with brief biographies – eliminates the dynamics of torture, often remarking only that a martyr was "burnt."

flames of Fire siesed on him, bowing his head he quietly yielded up his Soul into the hands of God.[60]

This scene, like many in *The Book of Martyrs*, develops a dynamic between "stoicism" or, more precisely, faith (on the part of the tortured martyrs), and "sentiment" on the part of the readers, which come together to consolidate an identity position, that of (English) Protestants being defined against papists.[61]

For the reader, the martyr's suffering is a confirmation of the validity of a specifically Protestant faith. Torture, as in this scene, is not only rendered harmless but becomes an occasion for celebrating the power of personal faith and a deeply felt connection to God.[62] Thus, English Protestant readers are asked to identify with the martyrs, not by feeling their pain but rather by feeling the faith which nullifies their pain, and also by joining with the martyr's scorn for the torturer who fails to understand that worldly suffering and worldly ritual are no match for the certainty of redemption. Readers are invited to feel admiration for the martyrs' joyous suffering, to see this "suffering" as a symbol of the power of Protestant belief and thus as a badge of Protestant identity. Slightly complicating this call to identification and possible emulation is the passive role of the witnesses to martyrdoms within Foxe's narrative (as opposed to his readers). Richard Helgerson traces Foxe's insistence on displacing the punishment of the persecutors onto providential interventions of animals, illness, or accident while "the godly remain passive."[63]

---

[60] John Foxe, *Acts and Monuments* (London, 1684), III: 940 (column 2)–941 (column 1). The scenario of an Englishman martyred by foreign Catholics is rare in *The Book of Martyrs*; this scene aligns English nationality unusually neatly with Protestant faith. Here I follow the convention of attributing authorship to Foxe even of posthumous additions to his work.

[61] Ryan Netzley, "The End of Reading: The Practice and Possibility of Reading Foxe's *Actes and Monuments*," *ELH*, 73:1 (2006), 187–214, subjects such claims about Foxe to skeptical scrutiny.

[62] Janel M. Mueller, "Pain, Persecution, and the Construction of Selfhood," in *Religion and Culture in Renaissance England*, ed. Claire McEachern and Deborah Shuger (Cambridge: Cambridge University Press, 1997), 161, presents Foxe's accounts as the first exception to Elaine Scarry's transhistorical claims about torture in *The Body in Pain* (New York: Oxford University Press, 1985). See also John R. Knott, *Discourses of Martyrdom in English Literature, 1563–1694* (Cambridge: Cambridge University Press, 1993), 9. Following Foucault's *Discipline and Punish: The Birth of the Prison*, trans. Alan Sheridan (New York: Pantheon, 1978), 7–12 and *passim*, one could argue for a historical disjunction between the spectacular, public tortures Foxe describes and the private, internalized forms analyzed by Scarry; Knott rejects Foucault's applicability to Foxe (*Discourses*, 9); Mueller considers Foucault's applicability in "Pain," 185 n. 3.

[63] *Forms of Nationhood: The Elizabethan Writing of England* (Chicago: University of Chicago Press, 1992), 268, presents this as an aspect of Foxe's Erastian Protestantism. Contrast Knott's suggestion that the spectators' role is "empathizing with the martyrs and reinforcing their faith" (*Discourses*, 16).

However, beginning in the seventeenth century, Foxe's martyrs were presented as models to all English Protestants;[64] the Introduction to the *Martyrologia Alphabetike* (1677), for instance, explains itself as a simple and accessible version of the *Book of Martyrs* which will underwrite the affective training of poor and less educated Protestants without access to, or the time and ability to read, the full version of Foxe's text:

The Chief things in these Volumes desired by the Vulgar (whose instruction is chiefly designed hereby) is the Lives and deaths, the Constancy and Comforts of the Martyrs, which here are briefly contained as to the most remarkable Martyrs ever since Christ's time; which being portable, may serve as a Manual to be oft in our hands to be perused, till we get their experiences on our hearts.[65]

Of course, the precise meaning of getting "their experiences on our hearts" is not obvious, but the suggestion seems to be one of affective modeling or identification. While the privileging of faith over suffering, and of providential expectation over personal action, in this process marks its difference from later eighteenth- and nineteenth-century models of sentimental sympathy and empathy, nonetheless the use of the suffering body as a privileged site for identification anticipates much of later models of sentimentality.

Indeed, in the late sixteenth and seventeenth centuries, Foxean discourse and imagery had already started to inform accounts of the lives, adventures, and deprivations of the English overseas, particularly in the emerging genre of the captivity narrative. Both Barbary and American Indian captivity narratives, like Foxe's martyr narratives, were often presented as confirmations of Protestant faith through extensive testing.[66] Indeed, these narratives, like Foxe's work, often explicitly attacked Catholicism, sometimes by having their subjects suffer more at the hands of Catholic "rescuers" than under "Turkish slavery."[67] Foxe has also been credited with influencing English travel writing from its beginnings.[68] In stories of the colonial

---

[64] Damian Nussbaum, "Appropriating Martyrdom: Fears of Renewed Persecution and the 1632 Edition of *Acts and Monuments*," in Loades, ed., *Foxe*, 184, relates the "unequivocal call to martyrdom" in the new edition's Introduction to the political context of the 1630s. The 1677 *Martyrologia Alphabetike* takes for granted activist identification with the Martyrs.

[65] This is item (2) of "reasons moving the Epitomizing the voluminous works of the Author" on the last unnumbered page of a preface titled "To The Christian Reader"; this page faces page 1.

[66] For the most famous example, see Mary Rowlandson's *The Soveraignty and Goodness of God* (Cambridge, MA: S. Green, 1682).

[67] Snader, *Caught Between Worlds*, 19, indicates the place of the Inquisition in the early captivity narrative. Colley, *Captives*, 122–3, offers examples from eighteenth-century texts in which Englishmen favorably compare the faith of Muslims to the religious practices of captives.

[68] Hannaford, *Race*, 164–5, states that Foxe's historiographic methodology was an important influence on Hakluyt in particular.

violence emanating from slavery or Indian war, however, the situation for the English Protestant reader familiar with such representations of captives and their tortured bodies becomes increasingly complex. In such scenes, the English narrators begin to become, or become affiliated with, the torturers. At the same time, the victims of torture are no longer true believers but heathens. Their stoic performance challenges the meaning of torture in Foxe's work as a validator of true faith.[69] Their stoicism – quite distinct from the faith of the elect in God's grace – then becomes a sign of savagery rather than of deeply felt belief. Such a change in the meaning of victimhood does little to change the meaning of the role of torturer, however, and this role becomes intensely problematic.[70]

I am using the term "stoicism" here to connect these scenes of suffering and identification with Julie Ellison's argument for a dynamic between stoicism and sentiment in the late seventeenth century which she suggests as a point of origin for eighteenth-century masculine sentimentalism.[71] Following Ellison's analysis, "stoic" response to suffering, pain, or sacrifice implies the strong reality, rather than the simple negation, of that suffering. Stoicism in this sense is a public performance of the control of pain or suffering for a larger purpose, as in Ellison's readings of the stoic fathers in Nathaniel Lee's *Lucius Junius Brutus* and Joseph Addison's *Cato* who sacrifice their sentimental sons for the good of the republic, wavering or otherwise expressing the emotional cost of their decision before they commit to it.[72] This stoicism both invites and repels identification, precisely because the external performance does not negate the underlying pain; in other words, the father's pain is available to the audience, but his ultimate decision – sometimes quite explicitly – can be alienating in its rigidity. It is important to note, then, that in the Foxean scene of martyrdom, the outward performance of "endurance" does not function in the same way. For the martyr, faith negates the experience of bodily pain.[73]

---

[69] See John N. King, "Literary Aspects of Foxe's *Acts and Monuments*," in *Critical Apparatus and Additional Material, Foxe's Book of Martyrs Variorum Edition Online (v.1.0)* http://www.hrionline. ac.uk/foxe/apparatus/kingessay.html (accessed May 17 2004) for a discussion of the "joy" of martyrs – often expressed in the form of wit or humor – as a test of the validity of their martyrdom.

[70] Of course, as Helgerson suggests in elaborating a dynamic between the "Apocalyptic" mode of Foxe and the "Apologetic" mode of Hooker, Foxe's stance was never unquestioned even within specifically English Protestantism; see *Forms*, 274.

[71] Julie Ellison, *Cato's Tears and the Making of Anglo-American Emotion* (Chicago: University of Chicago Press, 1999) esp. chapter 2. For a more detailed account of the revival of classical stoicism in the British seventeenth century, see Andrew Shifflett, *Stoicism, Politics and Literature in the Age of Milton* (Cambridge: Cambridge University Press, 1998).

[72] Ellison, *Cato's Tears*, 35–6, 57–8.

[73] For exceptions, see Mueller, "Pain, Persecution," and Netzley, "The End of Reading."

The reader or onlooker can identify with the faith of the martyr, and can perceive the martyr's lack of suffering as evidence of this faith, but cannot identify with suffering that has been negated rather than submerged. Because of this dynamic, stoic suffering – like that of Roman fathers or tortured colonial subjects – is premised on the difference that calls out for identification to transcend it, while the martyrs on the contrary invite others to repeat their experience, to join in a communal faith so strong that it obliterates the individual self.[74]

For the English narrators, a sentimental identification with sufferers – especially an acknowledgment of their humanity – and the invocation of one's own Christianity is offered as compensation for the failure to stop their suffering, or even the tacit complicity in their torture. If these scenes of colonial torture and execution do call to mind Foxean martyrs, then, they both resemble it uncomfortably and also highlight the difference of these victims from martyrs. Despite the discomfort in the English assuming the torturer's role, part of the trouble with torture in Hubbard's scene, and in Behn's *Oroonoko*, is that the stoic acceptance of mutilation comes awkwardly close to parodying the faith of Foxean martyrs. For Hubbard, and others like him, the Indian's stoic performance raises a second awkward question, beyond aligning the English with Catholic persecutors. Whence does the stoic, but benighted, pagan draw his strength?

Behn's description of Oroonoko's execution and death has recently become the most widely discussed of such torture scenes in seventeenth-century literature:

He had learn'd to take Tobaco; and when he was assur'd he should Dye, he desir'd they would give him a Pipe in his Mouth, ready Lighted, which they did; and the Executioner came, and first cut off his Members, and threw them into the Fire; after that, with an ill-favoured Knife, they cut his Ears, and his Nose, and burn'd them; he still Smoak'd on, as if nothing had touch'd him; then they hack'd off one of his Arms, and still he bore up, and held his Pipe; but at the cutting off the other Arm, his Head sunk, and his Pipe drop'd; and he gave up the Ghost, without a Groan, or a Reproach. My Mother and Sister were by him all the while, but not suffer'd to save him; so rude and wild were the Rabble, and so inhumane were the Justices, who stood by to see the Execution, who after paid dearly enough for their Insolence. (237–8)

---

[74] For a similar account, see Cynthia Marshall, "Foxe and the Jouissance of Martyrology," in *The Shattering of the Self: Violence, Subjectivity and Early Modern Texts* (Baltimore: Johns Hopkins University Press, 2002), 85–105.

Oroonoko here replaces claims of the validity of his faith with a physical act: the smoking of a tobacco pipe.[75] Indeed, throughout the story the character Oroonoko heaps scorn on "Christianity," pointing to the obvious moral failings and hypocrisy of the slave dealers who use a pretense of friendship to betray and enslave him. The tobacco pipe as a replacement for the confession of faith may be a grotesque joke by Behn, a royalist often suspected of Catholic sympathies, an intentional play on the Foxean Protestant martyrdom in which religious devotion is replaced by material devotion to one of colonialism's most notorious products. In this way, Oroonoko's death parodies the death of a Foxean martyr, with vague but multiple possible implications: from a Foxean perspective, the pipe could represent an exhortation to leave behind the material acquisitiveness that fuels the Christian hypocrisy pointed to repeatedly by Oroonoko. From a Catholic – or high church Apologetic – perspective, *Oroonoko* could represent an attack on the notion that stoicism under torture reveals true faith; Oroonoko is a pagan devoted, in this scene, only to his pipe.[76]

Behn's scene directly engages with the problems raised when the English become torturers themselves: "My Mother and Sister were by him all the while, but not suffer'd to save him; so rude and wild were the Rabble, and so inhumane were the Justices, who stood by to see the Execution" (238). Behn's narrator announces the complicity of her family in the scene, but only to deny, or qualify, it. Her phrase "weren't suffered" implies that they were prevented, somehow held back from doing as they intended. This seems to exonerate them from blame. And yet, the phrase raises the problem of pain reminding the reader that they, unlike Oroonoko, did not actually "suffer." Their desire to help Oroonoko is limited by their acceptance of the authority of his torturers; they are not allowed to intervene, and they accept this, while their passivity is similar to that of the onlookers in Foxe's scenes, with the exception that they have a closer relationship to the authorities. Left unclear is the "suffering" they do for

---

[75] Contrast Joyce Green MacDonald, "Race, Women and the Sentimental in Thomas Southerne's *Oroonoko*," *Criticism*, 40:4 (1998), 555–70, at 559, which reads Oroonoko's pipe, and his stoicism, as exoticizing.

[76] I borrow the term "Apologetic" from Helgerson, *Forms*; see also his account of parodies of specific martyrs. Falstaff, for instance, is modeled on the martyr Sir John Oldcastle; see Helgerson, *Forms*, 249. For analysis of another execution scene as a parody of Foxe, see Marshall, "Foxe," 104. Complicating the matter further, martyrdom was claimed by both Puritans and Royalists after the Restoration. Two broadsides, for instance, dramatically contrast the "Royal Martyrs" killed resisting the parliamentarians with Puritan "Holy Martyrs": compare the broadsides "A Catalogue of the Names of those Holy Martyrs who were Burned in Queen Maries Reign" (London, 1679) and "The Royal Martyrs or a List of the Lords, Knights, Commanders, and Gentlemen, that were slain in the late Wars, in Defence of Their King and Country" (London, 1660).

Oroonoko in identifying with him; sympathizing with his suffering here appears to imply their recognition of difference from him, as opposed to the function of faith in unifying audience and martyr.[77]

Behn's family distance themselves from the torture through a weak claim of sentimental identification. The account of their inability to save him implies a desire to do so, in contrast to the "inhuman" justices who "stand by" allowing the torture and execution to go forward, and the "rude and wild" "rabble." Still the narrator's sister and mother seem to "stand by" themselves, even if they can be differentiated from the justices in that as women their passivity is more proper. Of course, part of the displacement of responsibility in the scene comes in the narrator's denial of a direct role and her displacement of participation onto relatives who otherwise have no substantial role in the narrative. In blaming these two groups for their failures of civility and feeling, the narrator implies a claim of civility and feeling for herself and her family. Again, as in Hubbard's scene, the narrator explicitly distances herself from the unfeeling proponents of torture, the rabble and the justices, but also from the "unfeeling," perhaps savage stoicism of Oroonoko himself puffing on his pipe. Indeed, he has earlier enacted the stoic and sentimental sacrifice of family that simultaneously repels and attracts when, before his recapture, he stabs Imoinda to save her and his honor.

A Colonel Martin stands in for the narrator in offering a manly, less passive rejection of the mutilation of Oroonoko.[78] He not only gives voice directly to the aristocratic view of Oroonoko's death, but also to a sentimental rejection of torture and mutilation as methods of discipline:

They cut Caesar in Quarters, and sent them to several of the chief plantations: One Quarter was sent to Colonel M[. . .]tin, who refus'd it; and swore, he had rather see the Quarters of Banister, and the Governor himself, than those of Caesar, on his Plantations; and that he cou'd govern his Negroes without Terrifying and Grieving them with frightful Spectacles of a mangl'd King. (238–9)

This passage has quite appropriately been read in relation to the execution of Charles I.[79] But it is also strongly suggestive of the concept of discipline that underlies the grateful slave scenario, anticipating the later move to (in Foucauldian terms) internalized discipline as effective replacement for

---

[77] For a different view of *Oroonoko*'s relation to sentimentality, see G. A. Starr, "Aphra Behn and the Genealogy of the Man of Feeling," *Modern Philology*, 87:4 (1990), 362–72.

[78] This Martin was apparently the father of the eighteenth-century Colonel Martin who advocated ameliorationist reforms, discussed below in chapter 2, pp. 87–8, 93.

[79] Laura Brown makes an influential argument for this connection, (*Ends of Empire*, 56–7).

spectacle as an external mode of control through violence.[80] This passage, then, connects a sentimental identification with an individual slave with improved, internalized, and sentimental modes of discipline that will come to the fore in the eighteenth-century trope of the grateful slave. However, the sentimental connection to the slave here is deceptive; it is not Oroonoko's suffering, but instead his particular aristocratic worth that makes him an object of sympathy.[81] There is no direct connection, in other words, between Martin's sympathy with him and Martin's relative "kindness" to other slaves, except in the implication of sentimental sympathy as a motivation in each case.

Unlike Martin, Snelgrave wavers between sentimental and spectacular modes of discipline. When describing his ability to make slaves grateful, he seems to favor the internal, sentimental approach. But when it comes to enforcing white supremacy on shipboard, he unhesitatingly returns to the external, spectacular mode:

they having also heard the Negroe's Confession, "That he had killed the white Man;" They unanimously advised me to put him to death; arguing, "That Blood required Blood, by all Laws both divine and human . . . Moreover this would in all probability prevent future Mischiefs; for by publickly executing this Person at the Ship's Fore-yard Arm, the Negroes on board their Ships would see it; and as they were very much disposed to mutiny, it might prevent them from attempting it." These Reasons, with my being in the same Circumstances, made me comply. (181–2)[82]

The clearest difference from Hubbard's, Phillip's, and Behn's scenes of torture here is Snelgrave's insistence on the victim's guilt, on "the Negroe's Confession." Still, echoing all of these scenes of colonial torture, Captain Snelgrave is strangely passive here. He reports that his crews' "reasons, with my being in the same circumstances, made me comply." He is made to perform this action. The knowledge of how to employ violence for such effects is displaced from the captain onto the crew who advise him, and the desire to achieve these effects likewise. Snelgrave's passivity, however, is very unlike that of the providential Protestant or the crowd in one of Foxe's narratives, as he undeniably represents the ultimate temporal power on

---

[80] See Foucault, *Discipline and Punish*.

[81] See Anita Pacheco, "Royalism and Honor in Aphra Behn's *Oroonoko*," *SEL*, 34:3 (1994), 491–506; Lore Metzger, "Introduction," in *Oroonoko* (New York: Norton, 1973), ix–xv; and George Guffey, "Aphra Behn's Oroonoko: Occasion and Accomplishment," in *Two English Novelists, Aphra Behn and Anthony Trollope: Papers Read at a Clark Library Seminar, May 11, 1974* (Los Angeles: Clark Library, 1975), 3–41.

[82] This passage appears in Gallagher's Bedford edition of *Oroonoko*, 258. Including this scene without the earlier grateful slave passages makes Snelgrave seem unapologetically violent.

board of the ship he captains, no matter how eagerly he suggests the displacement of his will. And unlike other men in positions of power, for instance Cromwell, he does not bother to excuse his passivity as waiting for providence. Snelgrave can be understood as developing the secularization of the "passivity" trope in this scene.[83]

The condemned slave speaks up to challenge his executioner like a Protestant martyr, but he invokes very different values:

"but he desired me to consider, that if I put him to death, I should lose all the Money I had paid for him." To this I bid the Interpreter reply, "that tho' I knew it was customary in his Country to commute for Murder by a Sum of Money, yet it was not so with us; and he should find that I had no regard to my Profit in this respect." (182)

Unlike a martyr joyfully asserting a faith that his tormentor cannot fathom, the slave does speak in the language his executioner seems best to understand: the language of financial interest. Still, as Snelgrave tells the story, the slaves' failure to move him with this argument suggests that Snelgrave's motives in fact reside elsewhere; as he puts it himself, "I had no regard to my Profit in this respect." Proceeding with the execution, Snelgrave reports that "This struck a sudden Damp upon our Negroe-Men, who thought, that, on account of my Profit, I would not have executed him" (183).

It is the enforcement of racial difference and racial privilege, rather than the considerations of religion, that underwrites, or justifies, Snelgrave's reluctant violence. The emphasis on whiteness in the phrase "he had killed the white Man" suggests this, but Snelgrave uses a post-execution speech to eliminate any ambiguity:

When the Execution was over, I ordered the Linguist to acquaint the Men-Negroes, "that now they might judge, no one that killed a white man should be spared" ... they never gave us the least reason to be jealous of them; which doubtless was owing to the Execution of the white Man's Murderer. (184–5)

Whiteness and discipline onboard the slave ship are intertwined for Snelgrave as justifications for his violence. He also orders the mutilation of the body after execution in a scene that provides a strange echo of, or better, inverts the theological meaning (salvation) of, execution for Foxe's martyrs:

The Body being let down upon the Deck, the Head was cut off and thrown overboard. This last part was done, to let our Negroes see, that all who offended thus, should be served in the same manner. For many of the Blacks believe, that if

---

[83] Gordon analyzes Cromwell's "passive" submission to providence in guiding the country (*Power*, 23–31).

they are put to death and not dismembred, they shall return again to their own Country. (183–4)

Unlike Foxe's representation of Catholic torturers who completely fail to grasp the faith of their Protestant victims – and thereby reveal its power rather than countering it effectively – Snelgrave here seems proud that he uses mutilation to manipulate the slaves through their beliefs rather than in defiance of them. Paradoxically, then, Snelgrave both initiates the discourse of slave gratitude in descriptions of West Africa and the middle passage, and almost defies the cultural logic that underwrites the necessity of the grateful slave in the novel – except for his insistence on his own passivity. Snelgrave moves away from the need to deny a role as a torturer by trumping it as a defender of "the white man" against "the black slave." Here, despite his desire to claim a belief in African humanity and to present himself as sympathetically and sentimentally engaged with Africans, he nonetheless also presents himself unapologetically as a defender of the privileges of whiteness. Unlike Phillips, Snelgrave appears confident that his metropolitan audience can be brought to understand and accept – even if they do not yet take for granted – the practice of race on board slavers and in the plantation colonies, at least with the aid of his passive posture; still, he has already worked to establish his basic "humane" and sentimental credentials.

Aphra Behn's Colonel Martin – who refuses the quarter of Oroonoko's executed body offered to him, opining that "he cou'd govern his Negroes without Terrifying and Grieving them with frightful Spectacles" – is the father of the eighteenth-century grateful slave reformer in more than a metaphorical sense. His son, Colonel Samuel Martin of Antigua, was a celebrated model of the ameliorating planter. He even wrote a guide, *The Essay on Plantership*, which advocated the "kind" treatment of slaves as an economically beneficial practice. His father – as depicted by Behn – illustrates how, in these seventeenth-century images of slavery, sentimentality (or proto-sentimentality) becomes useful as a defense against possible culpability for colonial violence. In other words, when the English represent the mutilation and execution of enslaved Africans, they strive to distance themselves from responsibility for such violence, and to appear humane, sentimental, and passive. To some degree, they enact a Protestant ideal of passivity, of deferring judgment and action to providence rather than originating actions oneself. The English impulse to identify with suffering and to disavow specific acts of colonial violence, thereby glossing over its systematic nature, points to the cultural needs that the trope of the grateful slave will address.

CHAPTER 2

The origin of the grateful slave: Daniel Defoe's Colonel Jack, 1722

The first novel to represent a scheme to reform a plantation by eliciting slave gratitude was Daniel Defoe's 1722 novel *Colonel Jack*.[1] Although this aspect of Defoe's novel has been little noted,[2] it presented a model eerily prescient of, if not influential on, many later examples. *Colonel Jack* is self-consciously set at a moment when racial categories are inchoate and are developing differently in various parts of the British Atlantic world. It is also written thirty years before the beginning of organized criticism of colonial slavery, and fifty years before slavery and its racial implications became central topics of political discussion for the British.[3] Jack, a young English man, is kidnapped and sold as a "slave" after boarding a ship supposedly bound for London. On arrival in Virginia, Jack must, at first, work – and be disciplined – side-by-side with the Africans who will later become his charges. When he becomes an overseer, however, he sets about articulating "racial" differences between "black" and "white" people. While leaving aside the much-debated question of Jack's aspiration to gentility,[4]

---

[1] Daniel Defoe, *Colonel Jack*, ed. Samuel Holt Monk (New York: Oxford University Press, 1989), 119–52. Further citations are given parenthetically in the text.

[2] Hans Andersen, "The Paradox of Trade and Morality in Defoe," *Modern Philology*, 39:1 (1941), 23–46; Patrick Keane, "Slavery and the Slave Trade: Crusoe as Defoe's Representative," in *Critical Essays on Daniel Defoe*, ed. Roger D. Lund (New York: G. K. Hall, 1997), 97–120; and Maximilian Novak, *Economics and the Fiction of Daniel Defoe* (Berkeley: University of California Press, 1962) all briefly consider *Colonel Jack*, concluding that Defoe always sided with economic over ethical considerations.

[3] Slavery was nonetheless controversial; see above pp. 8–9, esp. n. 28.

[4] The question of Jack's pursuit of gentility is central to readings of *Colonel Jack*, beginning with William H. McBurney, "*Colonel Jacque*: Defoe's Definition of the Complete English Gentleman," *SEL*, 2:3 (1962), 321–36. See also Michael Shinagel, *Defoe and Middle Class Gentility* (Cambridge, MA: Harvard University Press, 1968); Novak, *Economics*, 93; Samuel Holt Monk, "Introduction" in Daniel Defoe, *Colonel Jack* (New York: Oxford University Press, 1965), xiv; George A. Starr, *Defoe & Casuistry* (Princeton: Princeton University Press, 1971), 87–8, 93; James Walton, "The Romance of Gentility: Defoe's Heroes and Heroines," *Literary Monographs*, vol. IV, ed. Eric Rothstein (Madison: Wisconsin University Press, 1971), 99–110; Virginia Birdsall, *Defoe's Perpetual Seekers* (Lewisville: Bucknell University Press, 1985), 123, 129; Michael M. Boardman, *Defoe and the Uses of Narrative* (New Brunswick: Rutgers University Press, 1983), 136; and Hal Gladfelder, *Criminality and Narrative*

I will argue that his aspiration to whiteness is entirely successful within the terms of the novel, and thereby subtly communicates the ideas of racial difference and white privilege to a metropolitan audience not yet familiar with these concepts, despite their new status as taken-for-granted practices in the plantation colonies.

Given that Jack, as a "white" Englishman, is not allowed to remain alongside the African slaves for long, one might assume that Defoe, in referring to an Englishman as a "slave," is merely being inaccurate; but I believe this is telling evidence of the place of the novel in the transatlantic history of racial thinking. In 1722 in England, the practice of calling only Africans "slaves" was not yet established.[5] Indeed, the distinction between life-long, heritable chattel slave status for people of African descent and short-term, relatively privileged "indentured servitude" for "white" Europeans was a recent invention even in the plantation colonies. The term "indentured servant" is a retrospective coinage of historians, and overstates how clearly these distinctions of status on plantations were understood in the Metropolis. In Virginia – the case that has been studied in most detail, and of most relevance to Defoe's mainland American plantation setting – this distinction only fully emerged after Bacon's rebellion of 1676. The historian Theodore Allen argues that the distinction between "black" African "slaves" and "white" European "servants" emerged primarily out of the practical need for the Virginia master class to find numerous allies who could help them control their workers. In the earlier seventeenth century, Africans and Europeans had been lumped together as "bond laborers," performing the same tasks, subject to the same rules, and leading intertwined lives. By systematically distinguishing English and European workers from their African counterparts, and rewarding the "whites" with economic, legal, and social privileges, the masters broke

in *Eighteenth-Century England: Beyond the Law* (Baltimore: Johns Hopkins University Press, 2001), 112. By the mid-1970s, however, Jack's gentility was often seen as ironic: John J. Richetti, *Defoe's Narratives* (Oxford: Clarendon, 1975), 151; Everett Zimmerman, *Defoe and the Novel* (Berkeley: University of California Press, 1975), 132, 152; David Blewett, *Defoe's Art of Fiction* (Toronto: Toronto University Press, 1979), 94–5; Katharine Armstrong, "'I was a kind of an Historian': The Productions of History in Defoe's *Colonel Jack*," in *Tradition in Transition: Women Writers, Marginal Texts, and the Eighteenth-Century Canon*, ed. Alvaro Ribeiro, SJ, and James G. Basker (Oxford: Clarendon, 1996), 105. Lincoln Faller, *Crime and Defoe: A New Kind of Writing* (Cambridge: Cambridge University Press, 1993) offers a nuanced and complex reading, seeing the "whole question of Jack's class status" as being left to "peter out" (177) and warning against readings that make the novel seem too coherent (198–9).
[5] For examples see Kimber, *Mr. Anderson*; James Annesley, *Memoirs of an Unfortunate Young Nobleman*, 1743–7; John Thomson's pamphlet *The Travels and Surprising Adventures of John Thomson*, 1761; and James Boswell, *Boswell's London Journal 1762–1763*, ed. Frederick A. Pottle (New York: McGraw-Hill, 1950), 119.

the sympathy and solidarity between their bond laborers. This sympathy had created a threatening coalition among the lower orders during Bacon's rebellion, and such sympathy was never seen again after the imposition of the system of white-skin privilege.[6]

Defoe's novel, then, represents a moment when the still inchoate category of race is being actively theorized. Furthermore it is set at the very moment when slavery is consciously being reorganized on a racial basis. Although Defoe starts with the possibility of "sympathy" between bond laborers, regardless of race, he does not use it to imagine a return to pre-1676 conditions of common cause between bond laborers and slaves, but instead to theorize a justification of the legal and practical differences that were institutionalized at the end of Bacon's rebellion. Indeed, given readings of Defoe's Maryland and Virginia scenes as propaganda for colonization,[7] and his personal involvement in the transportation business in the late seventeenth century,[8] it is hardly surprising that he would present colonial "whiteness" as a ready means to, or replacement for, gentility. It is also unsurprising that Jack would attempt to represent the emerging social practices of racial difference and white privilege in the colonies to a metropolitan audience. In other words, twelve years before Snelgrave, Defoe broaches the question of race in the British transatlantic world, and uses gratitude and reason to stabilize an unfamiliar colonial concept of difference for his metropolitan audience.

Initially, it is the failure to distinguish between "black" and "white" plantation workers, a failure extending beyond names to labor assignments and modes of punishment, that motivates Jack's "sympathy" for slaves. As we shall see below, later novels' reformers claim to have been prompted by sympathy, that is, the "natural" impulses of their sensible souls in reacting to slaves' suffering. Jack's sympathy for – or understanding of – the African slaves on his master's plantation, in sharp contrast, is not presented as "natural," and is instead given a specific genesis: he has been a "slave" himself, and, given his personal experience under "the same lash" (128), he cannot help feeling for the slaves.[9] On hearing Jack's complaint that his

---

[6] This is a summary of Allen, *Invention* vol. II. For detailed discussion of the relevant historiography, see the Introduction, n. 36. Bacon's rebellion was not a utopian moment in racial history; its purpose was attacking the native peoples of Virginia, in opposition to official policy. See Morgan, *American Slavery*, 250–70.

[7] See Paula Backscheider, *Daniel Defoe: His Life* (Baltimore: Johns Hopkins University Press, 1989), 485–9; Novak, *Economics*, 146; and Shinagel, *Middle Class Gentility*, 166.

[8] George Gifford, "Daniel Defoe and Maryland," *Maryland Historical Review*, 52:4 (1957), 307–15.

[9] Here I am disputing argument that *Colonel Jack* is a sentimental novel: see McBurney, "Colonel Jacque," Monk, *Defoe & Casuistry*, and George A. Starr, "'Only a Boy': Notes on Sentimental

indenture was forced and illegal, the master, Smith, reacting sympathetically, promotes Jack from slave to overseer. Jack does receive a special
hearing, perhaps in part because he, like Smith, speaks English.[10] Although
historically many African slaves were – or were believed to be – the victims
of illegal kidnappings, none here get such attention from Smith. But even
this distinction is not entirely clear; Smith makes a policy of avoiding direct
contact with all his slaves to avoid his own inclination to leniency (129).
This suggests, in line with the theories of Allen and Anthony Parent, and
contra Winthrop Jordan, that Smith consciously sets out to deny his
human sympathy with his African slaves; he must avoid contact with
them because he cannot otherwise suppress his feeling of human identification with them. Ignoring their humanity, then, is a conscious act of
policy for Smith, not a "natural" or unconscious reaction to their blackness.
Smith, like Trelawny, is unable to deny that his slaves are human.

   Smith, then, distinguishes Jack (but not transported British convicts)
from the "black" slaves in practice. But Jack has trouble understanding how
to distinguish himself from the Africans on the plantation. Nonetheless, he
will set about making a distinction in no uncertain terms. On assuming his
new position as overseer, Jack cannot forget his own experiences under the
lash, and sees the slaves' experience as equivalent to his own:

the Horse-whip was given me to correct and lash the Slaves and Servants, when
they proved Negligent, or Quarrelsome . . . This part turn'd the very blood within
my Veins, and I could not think of it with any temper; that I, who was but
Yesterday a Servant or Slave like them, and under the authority of the same Lash,
should lift up my hand to the Cruel Work, which was my Terror but the day
before. (127–8)

Jack's sympathy for the slaves is an unwilling reaction to a shared experience, as he recalls the "Lash . . . which was my Terror but the day before."
The emphasis on physical and personal closeness augments the sense that
the connections Jack makes are involuntary. One must take note that
he does not use the distinction between "servants" and "slaves" to imply
a distinction between black and white as had become habitual in the

   Novels," *Genre*, 10 (1977), 501–27, all citing Charles Lamb's praise of Defoe's "feeling" in the novel
   (*Defoe: The Critical Heritage*, ed. Pat Rogers (London: Routledge, 1972), 87). For readings of the
   novel as unsentimental, see Benjamin Boyce, "The Question of Emotion in Defoe," *Studies in
   Philology*, 50:1 (1953), 45–58; and Leslie Stephen, *Hours in the Library*, reprinted in Rogers, *Critical
   Heritage*, 175.
[10] Contrast James Thompson, *Models of Value: Eighteenth-Century Political Economy and the Novel*
   (Durham, NC: Duke University Press, 1996), 109-11, reading this recognition as dependent on the
   bill of exchange Jack holds.

early twenty-first century. The terms themselves are simply interchangeable to him.[11]

Unlike the later sentimental reformer, Jack's sympathy becomes a hindrance to him, not a sought-after source of pleasure or mark of distinction because, in his words "the *Negroes* perceiv'd it, and I had soon so much Contempt upon my Authority, that we were all in Disorder" (128). Jack actually appears as the inversion of the later sentimental hero: his reforms are not a direct response to sympathy, but rather to his fear that his sympathy will undermine discipline, impinging on the plantation's production and the masters' safety. Jack apologizes for his sympathy, saying to Smith, "I beseech you Pardon me, if I have such a Tenderness in my Nature, that tho' I might be fit to be your Servant; I am incapable of being an Executioner, having been an Offender myself." Smith, implying that slavery is a virtual state of war, responds to Jack, wondering, "Well, but how then can my Business be done? And how will this terrible Obstinacy of the *Negroes*, who they tell me, can be no otherwise governed, be kept from Neglect of their Work, or even Insolence and Rebellion?" (133). Jack's frustration with his own sympathy is one of the clearest signs that self-interest trumps sentimentality for Jack, and therefore shows why, despite tears, pity, and gratitude, *Colonel Jack* is different in kind from later full-blown sentimental novels.[12]

Disgusted with the African slaves, Jack introduces the problem of slave gratitude into the story negatively, denouncing "the ingratitude of their Return, for the Compassion I shew'd them" (128). In so doing, Jack again diverges from the later model of the grateful slave reformer: later in the century, the sentimental reformer typically offers the hypothesis that

[11] At first Jack seems to make a distinction, referring to his duty to "correct and lash the servants and slaves." But to read this as distinguishing between white "servants" and black African "slaves" would be a retrospective misreading. Jack, for instance, understands himself as having been a "Servant or Slave like them." For other examples, see 111 and 123.

[12] See Andersen, "Paradox"; Keane, "Slavery"; and Novak, *Economics*, on Defoe's tendency to give economic interests primacy over other considerations. Jack's self-interestedness, which militates against sentimental naiveté, is often remarked on, for instance by Birdsall, *Defoe's Perpetual Seekers*, 122, and Richetti, *Defoe's Narratives*, 155. Many scholars hold that early sentimentalism – or more precisely the moral sense philosophy of Shaftesbury and Hutcheson – was a response to "materialism" and the emphasis on self-interest of Hobbes and Mandeville. See Starr, "Aphra Behn," and Claudia L. Johnson, *Equivocal Beings: Politics, Gender, and Sentimentality in the 1790s: Wollstonecraft, Radcliffe, Burney, Austen* (Chicago: University of Chicago Press, 1995), 12–13. For an analysis of Mandeville's materialist rebuttal to Shaftesbury, see Wendy Motooka, *The Age of Reasons: Quixotism, Sentimentalism and Political Economy in Eighteenth-Century Britain* (New York: Routledge, 1998), 95–7. This was also an issue in theological controversy – see Isabel Rivers, *Reason, Grace, and Sentiment: A Study of the Language of Religion and Ethics in England, 1660–1780*, vol. II (Cambridge: Cambridge University Press, 2000).

Africans are capable of gratitude as a rebuttal to an interlocutor who suggests their lack of such a capacity. Thus the denigrating denial of gratitude is defined as an unfeeling, unsentimental, inhumane position and distanced from the reformer himself; it is usually the position of a colonial opposing the metropolitan reformer.[13] This is further evidence of Jack's lack of a sentimental nature, or, to put it another way, that Defoe presents his character's motivations as practical and intentional rather than emotional and natural. Indeed, Jack's unwelcome sympathy produces only "ingratitude" in the slaves. He is frustrated that his sympathy prevents him from enforcing a difference between himself and the Africans through a regime of sustained violence like that considered necessary by Trelawny. The slaves astutely read his inability to prevent himself from identifying with them, and they turn it against him: "one of them had the Imprudence to say behind my Back, that if he had the Whipping of me, he would show me better how to Whip a *Negro*" (128). Hence it is Jack's sympathetic failure to maintain discipline that leads him to reform, as he attempts to transform the slaves' contempt into an appreciation of his mercy. Unlike later grateful slave reformers, rejection of violence and "humane" sympathy are strategic, rather than natural, for Jack. Notably, at this point Jack's fellow "white" slaves disappear from the narrative, and he begins to use "African" and "black" as synonyms for "slave."

Before Jack turns to reform, however, the African slaves' "ingratitude," their mockery of his "mercy," and of his identification with them, leads him to a bitter outburst of racial theorizing, in which he asserts that African slaves' "nature" makes them responsible for their masters' brutality. Here, Jack develops his contradictory position as a racializing opponent of slaves' capacity for gratitude, before discovering sentimental engagement with Africans as the solution to his problems and becoming (as is typical of the grateful slave scenario) an advocate of gratitude and humanity. Quite clearly, the possibility of "white" slaves has slipped from view at this point. Jack fantasizes about a regime in which absolute difference between black and white is enforced through brutality, the kind of a regime denied him due to his unwelcome sympathy:

now I began indeed to see, that the Cruelty, so much talk'd of, used in *Virginia* and *Barbadoes*, and other Colonies, in Whipping the *Negro* Slaves, was not so much owing to the Tyranny, and Passion, and Cruelty of the *English* as had been

---

[13] See, for instance, Sir George Elison's disagreement with his Creole wife discussed in chapter 3 below, pp. 129–30.

reported; the *English* not being accounted to be of a Cruel Disposition, and really are not so: But that it is owing to the Brutallity, and obstinate Temper of the *Negroes*, who cannot be mannag'd by Kindness, and Courtisy; but must be rul'd with a Rod of Iron, beaten with *Scorpions*, as the Scripture calls it; and must be used as they do use them, or they would Rise and Murther all their Masters, which their Numbers consider'd, would not be hard to do, if they had Arms and Ammunition suitable to the Rage and Cruelty of their Nature. (128)

Unlike others who see violence as necessary to contain slaves' human desire for liberty, Jack appeals to difference – Africans' "Brutallity" – to justify such violence, even though he cannot perform it himself. Jack adduces the same evidence – resistance and desire for liberty – but reads it as "ingratitude" rather than humanity. Jack here states that masters' cruelty is the necessary result of slaves' "nature," a "nature" he suddenly appears to understand as absolutely different from his own.

While Jack does not begin his differentiation from the Africans with a hypothesis of similarity – that comes a bit later – apparently the experience of an unsettlingly powerful, but entirely unintended, identification is enough to trigger this theoretical articulation of difference. This outburst, then, is Jack's first attempt to negate his practical but inadvertent identification with his fellow slaves. To this point, Jack's approach to the problem of colonial torture is opposite to the scenes analyzed in chapter 1: rather than using a weak claim of "identification" or "sympathy" to distance himself personally from torture and subjection, Jack instead offers a theoretical justification of torture and subjection as an (ultimately failed) attempt to control the troublesome effects of his sympathy.

Although this vision of absolute difference appeals to Jack, it is of no practical value to him, given his uncontrollable sympathy with his charges. Casting about for a more practical, and more easily administered, form of discipline, Jack reverses the causation of his essentialist claims. He quickly settles on the opposite point of view, abandoning theoretical essentialism for an environmental view of slaves' behavior that returns to his own experience "under the lash" as its primary inspiration. He now returns to the mainstream view, implying that slaves' brutality results from, rather than causing, their brutalization by masters and that they therefore have the potential to respond to kindness, even to become fully affective beings:

BUT I began to see at the same time, that this Brutal temper of the *Negroes* was not rightly manag'd; that they did not take the best Course with them, to make them sensible, either of Mercy, or Punishment; and it was Evident to me, that even the worst of those tempers might be brought to a Compliance, without the lash, or at least without so much of it, as they generally Inflicted. (128–9)

Jack's recantation is thorough. He began by suggesting that slaves are
ingrates who are too brutal to be managed with kindness; he now suggests
that genuine kindness – "mercy" – hasn't been tried.[14] Still referring
to their "brutal temper," Jack demonstrates a characteristic eighteenth-
century failure to take the distinction between culture and essence
seriously, now suggesting, without acknowledging his change, that this
"temper" actually results from their treatment. At this moment, Defoe
narrates what could be called the invention of slave-owner paternalism, the
moment in which a policy of unashamed cruelty is abandoned from the
suspicion that gentler ways might produce more efficacious results. His
briefly assayed theory of fundamental African depravity, apparently abandoned, nonetheless allows Jack to treat his slaves' humanity as a hypothesis,
rather than a fundamental truth. Seeking to test this hypothetical humanity, Jack comes to imagine a new system of management that promises a
more effective solution to his problems as an overseer.

Jack's rapid adoption and abandonment of avowed racial difference as a
solution to his management problem suggests the rhetorical situation of
this idea in early eighteenth-century British culture. Defoe does not expect
it to have much resonance with his audience, proceeding as if his readers
will either gloss over or dismiss Jack's suggestion and reversal, rather than
expecting them to wonder how he could engage such an obvious truth only
to abandon it. And while race thus appears to be a weak concept to his
audience here, Defoe must be credited for making Jack's sympathy more
real, more concrete, precisely by presenting it as a problem. By yearning for
torture as a solution, but finding it unavailable due to an unwanted but
troubling sympathy, Defoe paradoxically makes Colonel Jack's sympathy
more believable – and certainly more concrete – than the sympathy that
Hubbard, Behn, and Snelgrave claim even as it fails to prevent the torture
they describe.

Jack's final scheme for circumventing the problem of his sympathy
without decreasing his master's production, arrived at after a few blind
alleys, is ingenious, if distastefully cynical. Again, unlike later grateful slave
reformers, Jack never intends to do away with whipping or other forms of
"discipline," instead setting out to make them less harsh – for tactical
purposes. As he brags to Smith,

---

[14] I am reading Jack as contradictory rather than ironic; Defoe's deployment of irony has long been the
subject of contentious debate: see Wayne Booth, *The Rhetoric of Fiction* (Chicago: University of
Chicago Press, 1961), 316–28; Ian Watt, *The Rise of the Novel* (Berkeley: University of California
Press, 1957), 125; and Maximilian Novak, "Defoe's Use of Irony," in *The Uses of Irony* (Berkeley:
University of California Press, 1966), 7–38.

I have found out that happy Secret, to have good Order kept, the Business of the Plantation done, and that with Diligence, and Dispatch, and that the *Negroes* are kept in Awe, the natural Temper of them Subjected, and the Safety and Peace of your Family secur'd, as well by gentle Means, as by Rough, by moderate Correction, as by Torture, and Barbarity; by due Awe of just Discipline, as by the Horror of unsufferable Torments. (134)

Jack misrepresents his "happy secret" which is indeed based on a fear "of unsufferable torments." His system of reform is this: he will bring the slaves to accept, even to contract for, a lifetime of slavery by threatening them with terrible, deadly punishments, and then showing them "mercy" to elicit their "gratitude."

As Jack explains to Smith, he has already taken the liberty of testing his method on an African slave:

I had him brought into the usual Place, and ty'd him by the Thumbs for Correction, and he was told that he should be Whipp'd and Pickl'd in a dreadful manner.

AFTER I had made proper Impressions on his Mind, of the Terror of his Punishment, and found that he was sufficiently humbled by it, I went into the House, and caus'd him to be brought out, just as they do when they go to Correct the *Negroes* on such Occasions. (135–6)

Here, Jack secularizes the disciplinary aspect of the fire and brimstone Protestantism for his pagan charges, extracting labor-management benefits without the bother of articulating a theology – or of conversion. The negro is "humbled" by "proper impressions" of "the terror of his punishment." Indeed, Jack's vocabulary only becomes more suggestive as he continues, soliciting a promise in exchange for relenting on the torture: "what will you say, or do, *said I*, if I should prevail with the Great Master to Pardon you?" Apparently, Jack gets just the response he was angling for; he brings the slave to accept the state of slavery in exchange for "mercy": "He told me he would lye down, let me kill him, me will, *says he*, run go, fetch, bring for you as long as me live" (136).[15]

Jack's work on the slave, named Mouchat, does not end with this extorted promise. He sees it as part of an experiment in assessing Africans' nature. Jack takes a scientific-experimental tone, seeing if he can elicit a certain response given the right conditions.[16] His language suggests a scientific

---

[15] Compare Jack here to Robinson Crusoe posing as both the governor and the governor's emissary in *Robinson Crusoe*; see *Robinson Crusoe*, 271, and John Bender, *Imagining the Penitentiary: Fiction and the Architecture of Mind in Eighteenth-Century England* (Chicago: University of Chicago Press, 1989), 55–6.

[16] On Defoe's scientific empiricism, see Ilse Vickers, *Defoe and the New Sciences* (Cambridge: Cambridge University Press, 1996), and Backscheider, *Daniel Defoe: His Life*, 15–20.

suspension of judgment as he allows his experiment to verify or disprove his hypothesis; he explains "this was the opportunity I had a mind to have, to trye whether as *Negroes* have all the other Faculties of reasonable Creatures they had not also some Sense of Kindness, some Principles of natural Generosity, which in short is the Foundation of Gratitude" (136). Earlier, in a frustrated outburst, Jack had claimed that the "obstinate Temper of the *Negroes*, who cannot be mannag'd by Kindness, and Courtisy; but must be rul'd with a Rod of Iron" (128) prevented "kindness" and "mercy" from being effective ways to manage them. Here, he instead claims to grant himself nothing, awaiting the results of the trial. Unlike Jack's unwilling sympathy, treating African humanity as a hypothesis to be tested is central to the grateful slave trope in fiction, travel writing, and ameliorationist writings. At this early date – 1722 – it is also noteworthy for departing from the uncomplicated assumption of African humanity.

Jack explains his system to Smith by relating an interview with Mouchat, his experimental subject. He now discovers that African slaves *do not* despise the actual practice of mercy. The problem, as suggested by his earlier equivocations about management, is that the slaves never *experience* real mercy, however much they hear about it: "Master, me speakee de true, they never give Mercièè, they always Whipee, Lashee, Knockee down, all Cruel: *Negroe* be muchee better Man do muchee better work" (137). Prompted by Jack's questions, Mouchat goes on to explain that "when they makee de Mercy, then *Negroe* tell de great Tankee, and love to Worke, and do muchee Work" (138). Jack takes this testimony as a guarantee not of the truth of Mouchat's claims, but of the worthiness of an experiment in a new method of slave management.

Jack's experiment stems from the hypothesis that African slaves are human, and therefore can be managed as he himself would best be managed. But Jack is uninterested in the implications of Africans' "humanity" for the morality of slavery as an institution.[17] Typical of a Defoe character, Jack treats this hypothesis only as a piece of practically useful information; it will make his work as an overseer easier and more effective. However, like other hypotheses about African humanity, from Captain Phillips' to Sir George Ellison's (chapter 3, below), the very posing of the question makes difference into a serious possibility. This points to the function of Jack's essentialist outburst: between that extreme and the "hypothesis" of humanity, there is plenty of

---

[17] Michael Seidel puts it well: Defoe's "humanitarian impulses on the issue of slavery are akin to being against the treatment of the cocks in cock fighting but not against the activity itself" (*Robinson Crusoe: Island Myths and the Novel* (Boston: Twayne, 1991), 106).

room left for difference within the category of the human. On the basis of their hypothetical "humanity," then, Jack sets about manipulating the slaves. He not only ensures that all the slaves will hear that he condemned a slave to be whipped to death, and that the slave was rescued only by the master's supposed leniency, but he also uses the pardoned Mouchat to disseminate the moral of the drama he has staged, that "negroes" need to belie the reputation that "they regard nothing but the whip," because this is, according to Jack, "the reason, why the white man shews them no mercy" (140).

To see if the slave's gratitude is real, he spreads another rumor: that Jack himself has offended the "Great Master," and will be hanged for it. The experiment is a complete success when Mouchat begs to die in Jack's place: "YES, yes," he says to another overseer, "me be hang, for de poor Master that begeé for me [i.e., Jack], *Mouchat* shall hang, the great Master shall hangeé mee, whippeé mee, any thing to save the poor Master that begeé mee" (142). Jack finally ends his experiment when Mouchat "cry'd most pitifully, and there was no room to Question his being in earnest" (142). Jack's initial question – whether "negroes" were *capable* of gratitude – could be answered without going to the extreme of having Mouchat offer to die for Jack. Mouchat's "gratitude" here stands in for something that is less obvious in later novels' plantation reform scenes, but is important to them nonetheless: making the slave feel that he literally owes his life to his master. This goes well beyond gratitude, and instead resembles philosophical imaginings of contracted slavery in the state of nature. In such scenes, a conquered man offers devoted service in exchange for preservation of his life.[18] In *Colonel Jack*, the initial pardoning scene, in which Mouchat offers to "lye down" and be killed in Jack's place, enacts that moment.

Jack's plan is thoroughly successful. As he claims to Smith, it is quite simple, even when extended from his test cases to the whole plantation. As he explains of two other slaves awaiting punishment, his method of discipline is

first to put them into the utmost Horror and Apprehensions of the Cruelest Punishment that they ever had heard of, and thereby enhaunce the Value of their Pardon . . . Then I was to argue with them, and Work upon their Reason, to make the Mercy that was shew'd them sink deep into their Minds, and give them lasting Impressions; explaining the Meaning of Gratitude to them, and the Nature of an Obligation. (144)

---

[18] See the Introduction, n. 18; Jack is unconcerned whether the slave, in Locke's terms, "deserves death." Novak, *Defoe and the Nature of Man* (New York: Oxford University Press, 1963), 119, describes Jack's own "gratitude" to the king for the pardon of his Jacobite activities as similarly Hobbesian.

Jack's conflation of "gratitude" and "obligation" here is telling: the effectiveness of his system lies in convincing the disciplined slaves that they are
under a virtually contractual obligation to devote themselves wholeheartedly to their "merciful" master and overseer, despite the intentionally
deceptive nature of that "mercy." Strikingly, Jack's words here could
describe a preacher reminding his flock of God's mercy to sinners – and
the consequences of failing to repent.

Pragmatic as always, Jack doesn't expect his system to be a universal success: It may
be true, Sir, that there may be found here and there a *Negro* of a senceless, stupid,
sordid Disposition . . . incapable of the Generosity of principle which I am
speaking of . . . But, Sir, if such a Refractory, undocible Fellow comes in our
way, he must be dealt with, first, by the smooth ways, to Try him; then by the
Violent way to Break his Temper, as they Break a Horse; and if nothing will do,
such a Wretch should be Sold off, and others Brought in his Room. (145)

Jack, apparently, has never intended his solution to change the nature of
slavery. Slaves will only be grateful for "mercy" when they know that the
alternative is extreme violence. And violence need not be renounced
altogether – it actually needs to be maintained as a convincing threat,
and employed in certain circumstances. Jack's ultimate goal is to make
slaves docile and increase their production; treating them better, even
conceiving of them as "human," is merely a means to that end.[19] As Jack
explains to Smith, if his recommendations are adopted, "I doubt not, but
you should have all your Plantation carried on, and your Work done, and
not a *Negro* or a Servant upon it, but what would not only Work for you,
but even Die for you" (146).

Selling off the "intractable" slaves is the most successful part of Jack's
plan, through the implied threat of a more violent master:

they would Torment themselves at the Apprehensions of being turn'd away, more
by a great deal, than if they had to be whipp'd, for then they were only Sullen and
Heavy; nay, at length we found the fear of being turn'd out of the Plantation, had
as much Effect to Reform them, *that is to say*, make them more diligent, than any
Torture would have done; and the Reason was Evident, namely, because in our
Plantation, they were us'd like Men, in the other like Dogs. (150)

---

[19] Several critics have expressed mild distaste for Jack's reforms: Novak, *Defoe and the Nature of Man*,
118; James Sutherland, *Daniel Defoe: A Critical Study* (Cambridge, MA: Harvard University Press,
1971), *Defoe's Narratives*, 16; Richetti, 167–8. Only Zimmerman calls his method one of "terror,"
Defoe and the Novel, 135. Many others see his reforms as "moral" or "humanitarian," including
Martin Price, *To the Palace of Wisdom* (New York: Doubleday, 1964), 272; Andersen, "Paradox," 29;
Armstrong, "Productions of History," 99; Birdsall, *Defoe's Perpetual Seekers*, 132; Blewett, *Art of
Fiction*, 101; Monk, "Introduction," xv; and Starr, *Defoe*, 91.

Jack, like George Ellison and other novelistic reformers, uses sale off the plantation as his ultimate sanction. Once again, Jack's discussion of the effect of bringing slaves to "Torment themselves" with "Apprehensions" resonates with the Christian fear of damnation.

Jack's system is intended first and foremost to get the most out of slaves – to maximize production – through a system of internalized discipline that leads slaves to have a strong self-interest in producing for their master. Jack's system is not too far from the purely negative self-interest of avoiding a whipping; such a threat, although distanced, is still the basis of his discipline. The cleverness of the system is in making the slaves wish to *remain* on the plantation, to have a sense that they control their own fates, even as they relinquish that control more than ever. Under the old system, they would be beaten one way or the other; under his, they can avoid being beaten by choosing to obey. In this sense, the function of Jack's mercy is to make the slaves understand themselves as *choosing* mercy or whipping, staying, or being sold, through their own behavior. As Jack notes, other plantations tried to adopt his reforms, but did not succeed with them (149). Crucially, Jack needs the other plantations to remain brutal. If every master became merciful the threat of being sold would no longer be as frightening, and slaves could choose to be "intractable" without fear of being dehumanized, treated as "Dogs," by their next master. However, even Jack's own system is also intended to mark the difference between black and white, between ruled and ruler, between inferior and superior.

Laid bare in *Colonel Jack*, and more cleverly disguised in later grateful slave texts, is the manner in which deploying a strategic play of similarity and difference between Europeans and enslaved Africans allows a pseudo-empirical articulation of racial difference. Clearly, one should not see a mere acknowledgment of shared humanity as an admission of equality. Colonel Samuel Martin, a planter writing a handbook on "plantership," says of slaves, "rational beings they are, and ought to be treated accordingly; that is with humanity and benevolence." But in the next sentence, Martin goes on to claim that "the subordination of men to each other in society is essentially necessary to the good of the whole; and is a just reason for the benevolence of superiors to their inferiors," indicating that while slaves may be "rational" they are nonetheless "inferior," if only in a hierarchical sense.[20] Interestingly, Martin's own slaves were implicated in a 1736 slave conspiracy, giving the lie to the grateful slave trope as a solution to the

---

[20] Martin, *Essay on Plantership*.

conflict at the heart of slavery.[21] Given that Jack's story unfolds in a
moment when racial categories are unstable, it may seem that he rejects
"racism" when he rejects his own theory of Africans' nature as absolutely
different from his own. But it is crucial to recognize that he rejects this
theory only to set his self-interested reforms in motion. Like Colonel
Martin giving advice to his fellow planters, Jack is not much interested in
the implications of slaves' humanity; he is only interested in succeeding as
an overseer. Jack's reforms, far from challenging exploitation, define and
enforce "the racial contract" that excludes non-whites from the polity,
treating them as non-persons who should be exploited for the benefit of
"whites."[22] Indeed, in the reform scene, the recognition of a certain
"human" similarity, a shared emotional capacity, is only the basis of an
articulation of practical superiority. This functions in much the same way
as the anthropological trope of assigning "primitives" to a moment in a
general human past.[23] In recognizing a shared humanity, but describing
another group as "primitive," anthropologists actually grant themselves
authority over those they place in a "common" past. What could be more
laudable than helping "primitives" by exerting a benevolent authority over
them from "our" position in a fully developed present? In each case, the
initial acknowledgment of similarity only serves to authorize a practical
claim of present superiority.

The claim that Africans could easily be manipulated into being "grateful" for slavery is the counterpoint to the increasingly dominant belief that
the English, Irish, and Scottish poor would be best left to their own devices,
by which means they would be converted into more productive workers.[24]
Gratitude itself is not rejected for whites in the novel – indeed, Jack himself
claims to be deeply grateful at several points.[25] However, the difference in
the meaning of gratitude, in the standard for producing it, is pronounced.
Jack is grateful to a Spanish captor for treating him justly and even
helping him with a profitable (if illegal) trade;[26] to his master, Smith, for

---

[21] Gaspar, *Bondmen and Rebels*, 19.

[22] For the "racial contract," see Charles W. Mills, *The Racial Contract* (Ithaca: Cornell University Press, 1997).

[23] See Johannes Fabian, *Time and the Other* (New York: Columbia University Press, 1983), 16–18 and *passim*.

[24] See Andrew, "Poverty and the Attack on Dependency," in *Philanthropy and Police*, 135–62; Charles Tilly on the "proletarianization" of the British labor force, *Popular Contention in Great Britain, 1758–1834* (Cambridge, MA: Harvard University Press, 1995); and J. Jean Hecht, *The Domestic Servant Class in Eighteenth-Century England* (London: RKP, 1956), 73–5 and *passim*.

[25] See Faller's analysis of gratitude as providing coherence to the entire novel through the Virginia episode, but later falling apart (*Crime and Defoe*, 180).

[26] See Faller's analysis of Jack's illegal trading (*ibid.*, 182, 184–5).

elevating him out of slavery altogether; and to God for creating him and for allowing him to find his way to gentility.[27] In each case, the wily Jack does not let gratitude get in the way of his unfettered pursuit of self-interest. African slaves, on the other hand, are expected to forgo self-interest entirely, out of gratitude – and their gratitude is caused by a master merely refraining from beating them severely on a specific occasion! Their gratitude, unlike Jack's, is extreme and irrational.

Indeed, Jack's master Smith tests Jack's gratitude – as Jack had done to Mouchat and the other African slaves – but he does so to opposite effect. Jack, however, is unsure of the meaning of the test. "Will you Buy your Liberty of me, and go to Planting," asks Smith, after Jack's experiment in slave management has proved a smashing success. Jack reads this as a test of loyalty and responds, after an aside to the reader asserting that "I was too cunning for him," with a display of devotion:

> I knew that when he ask'd me if I would Buy my Liberty and go to Planting, it was to try if I would leave him; so, I said, as to buying my Liberty, Sir, *that is to say,* going out of your Service, I had much rather Buy more time in your Service, and am only unhappy that I have but two Year to serve. (148)

Smith's first response is to deny the psychological possibility of such selfless devotion to a master: "come, come, Col., *says he*, don't flatter me, I love plain Dealing, Liberty is precious to every Body." As their conversation develops, the question of whom Smith means to include in the group "every body" becomes pointed. Jack links his "cunning" stance of devotion explicitly to his management of the African slaves – which, after all, was based on his decision to understand them as similar to himself, and to manipulate them based on the psychological possibilities opened up by this assumption of similarity. Indeed, Jack replies to Smith's invocation of "liberty" by insisting "I hop'd he cou'd not believe but I had as much Gratitude as a *Negro*." Jack's attempt at cunning manipulation again fails, as Smith dismisses the proffered parallel with gentle irony: "He smil'd, and said, he would not be serv'd upon those Terms" (148). Jack offers to apply the obligations of grateful slavery to himself, while acknowledging his discomfort with doing so, and his insincerity, to the reader. Smith, lets him off the hook, however, hinting – as he did before in singling out Jack for attention, sympathy, and patronage – that his English servants will not be held to the same expectations as his African slaves.

---

[27] See Novak, *Defoe and the Nature of Man*, 118–21.

Smith's reply is ironic on two conflicting levels. On one level, Smith sees through, exposes, and ironizes the role that Jack is attempting to play. But on another level that neither Jack or Smith acknowledges, they have just suggested that there is something terribly wrong with Jack's system of reforms through gratitude.[28] If Smith will "not be serv'd upon those Terms," how can he continue to accept the devoted labor of his African slaves? Grateful devotion is not, for Smith, a plausible – or even an acceptable – reason for Jack to forgo his "precious" liberty and pursuit of self-interest. This suggests that the African slaves are either putting on a cunning mask, as Jack attempted to do, or that they are not truly parallel to him, indeed that they cannot be included in the category of "every body," at least in relation to Smith's mooted desire for liberty.

Earlier on, Jack, like Colonel Martin, invokes the Renaissance ideal of gratitude as a reciprocal relationship, perhaps in an effort to head off this contradiction. Jack reports of Smith, "as he was so engag'd, by seeing the *Negroes* Grateful, he shew'd the same Principle of Gratitude to those that serv'd him, as he look'd for in those that he serv'd" (150). This does indeed seem to describe accurately Smith's treatment of Jack himself, although Smith willfully continues to maintain his distance from the African slaves. Still, conceiving of their relationship as reciprocal does not immunize Jack from feeling oppressed by the weight of his obligation to Smith. After he rescues Jack from a financial crisis precipitated by investment in a lost ship, Jack notes that "I thank'd him, and did it with more Ceremony and Respect than ever; because I thought my self more under the Hatches than I was before. But he was as good as his Word, for he did not Baulk me in the least of any thing I wanted" (155). Again, for Jack, gratitude is a form of dissimulation, a mask to cover threatening feelings of powerlessness and obligation. Yet he never allows the idea that his African slaves feel them-selves "under the hatches" to intrude on his presentation of his reforms and their success. Jack's choice of the phrase "under the hatches" calls to mind the origins of Jack's own enslavement, as he and his criminal companions were denied their liberty by an unscrupulous ship captain.

This previous experience of captivity appears to have offered a model to Jack for the management of slaves, even those who openly desire their liberty.[29] In fact, as Jack's companions struggle to reclaim their liberty, the

---

[28] Faller suggests viewing the Virginia episode in terms of the Renaissance model of mutual obligation (*Crime and Defoe*, 180), but then points out that slavery "taints the whole equation" (*ibid.*, 189).

[29] John J. Richetti sees Jack's disciplinary system as emerging from his experiences of the English penal system in *The English Novel in History, 1700–1780* (New York: Routledge, 1999), 58.

scene becomes strikingly similar to the shipboard scenes discussed above in chapter 1. The scene starts with a confrontation, as one of Jack's cohorts challenges the ship's captain to take responsibility for his role in their plight: "it was he the Captain that carryed us away, and that whatever Rogue Trappan'd us on Board, now he knew it, he ought no more to carry us away, than Murther us" (114).[30] Much like Captains Phillips and Snelgrave discussed above, this captain invokes the bloody-mindedness of his crew to illustrate his own contrasting "sensible" kindness and restraint to his captives:

> I bear with you the more, because I am sensible your Case is very hard, and yet, I cannot allow your Threatning me neither; and you oblige me by that, to be severer with you than I intended; however, I will do nothing to you, but what your Threatning my Life makes necessary: The Boatswain call'd out to have him to the Geers, as they call'd it, and to have him Tast the *Cat-a-nine-tales*; all which were Terms we did not understand till afterwards, we were told he should have been Whipp'd and Pickl'd, for they said it was not to be suffer'd; but the Captain said, no, no, the young man has been really injured and has Reason to be very much provok'd. (113–14)

Drawing on the credential of this rather theatrical display of merciful restraint, this captain offers his captives a bargain that they are unable to refuse: "do you be quiet, and behave Civilly as you should do, and you shall be us'd as kindly both here, and there too as I can" (115).

Colonel Jack and his friends understand that they have no choice but to acquiesce to this bargain, and yet they (unlike Jack's future African charges) cannot, even if they wish to, believe this captain's protestations of sensibility and sympathy once he acknowledges that he will sell them as slaves:

> the Captain still told them they must submit; And will you then carry us to *Virginia*? *Yes*, says the Captain, and will we be sold says the *Scotsman*, when we come there? Yes, *says the Captain*; Why, then, Sir, says the *Scotsman* the Devil will have you at the hinder end of the Bargain; *say you so*, says the Captain smiling, well, well, *let the Devil and I alone to agree about that*. (115)

Bowing to the reality of his power over them, Jack and his cohorts finally submit to this captain, but they discount his protestations of sympathy, instead insisting on his guilt and relishing the prospect of his ultimate damnation: "we saw there was no Remedy, but to leave the Devil, and the Captain to agree among themselves" (115). This captain provides Jack a model by offering his captives a choice between (patently hollow) sympathy and violent punishment. Even aware as they are of the falsehood of his

---

[30] The cohort is named "Captain Jack." To avoid confusion I will not identify him by name below.

"kindness," they accept the bargain. Still, Jack does not seem to expect his African charges to understand sensibility as the window-dressing of power, or to desire revenge, as he and his cohorts do. Part of the difference seems to come from the attitude toward liberty invoked by Smith. Jack protests to the corrupt ship captain that "[we] were not People to be sold for Slaves" (114). In the immediate context, Jack's claim is to class status and financial well-being, not to white privilege. But in retrospect, after Smith and Jack reveal their assumption that Jack's liberty is too precious to be constrained by gratitude, but never extend this principle to their treatment of the Africans, it comes to seem the very essence of white privilege in the text, as it had in historical reality.

This inequality of conception extends beyond gratitude and obligation, sentiment and reason, liberty and slavery, to the fate of eternal souls. Jack's secularization of the disciplinary dynamics of Christianity creates the clearest distinction between Africans and Europeans. Jack broaches the topic with another articulation of the weight of gratitude on him: "THIS Article of Gratitude struck deep, and lay heavy upon my Mind," he says, ruminating on his relationship to Smith: "I remembered that I was Grateful to the last degree to my old Master, who had rais'd me from my low Condition, and that I lov'd the very name of him, or as might be said, the very Ground he trod on." The invocation of idolatry is not inadvertent, and Jack, like Okeley, clarifies that an important part of the weight of gratitude is due to its tendency to misdirect such worship: "but I had not so much as once thought of any higher obligation; no, nor, so much as like the Pharisee had said, one *God I thank thee*, to him, for all the Influence which his Providence must have had in my whole Affair" (170). In light of these reflections, Jack's gratitude to God becomes a sign that he is on the path to salvation; by contrast, the Africans' gratitude to Jack (as the medium of the "Great Master") would seem to cut them off from God, as Jack himself had been cut off, misdirected, by his gratitude to Smith.[31] In failing to correct this problem Jack appears not to view the Africans as his fellow humans. Not only is he willing to put himself above them as God is above him, but furthermore, he appears unconcerned with their attaining the access to the salvation that he values so highly for himself.[32]

---

[31] Faller sees the hints of the great master as God, Jack as Christ, and the slaves as sinners needing redemption as "heady stuff" but also holding "open the door to terrible blasphemies" (*Crime and Defoe*, 191).

[32] Leopold Damrosch, in *God's Plot and Man's Stories: Studies in the Fictional Imagination from Milton to Fielding* (Chicago: University of Chicago Press, 1985), 5, suggests that, as a novelist, Defoe is already in a sense putting himself in the place of God – inventing God's plot.

Defoe's representations of slave gratitude, although early and possibly without any direct influence on the later century,[33] were, as we shall see below, proleptic of both later representations and later plantation management practices. A few pamphlets, written by slave owners for the guidance of their peers, also urged the deployment of "kindness" as a tool of discipline.[34] Colonel Martin in his *Essay on Plantership* sums up his comments on slave management by remarking that "thus then ought every planter to treat his negroes with tenderness and generosity, that they may be induced to love him out of mere gratitude."[35] Clearly, an interest in eliciting "gratitude" from slaves is by no means an indicator of anti-slavery, or even non-racist positions. Colonel Martin provides an excellent illustration of the self-interested nature of amelioration.[36] He argued for "humane" reforms, admitting that brutality was simply too expensive.[37] He once left his plantation briefly, returning to "find that fourteen Negroes had died as a result of gross mismanagement." As his biographer Richard Sheridan observes, in perhaps too practical-minded a manner, "when it is considered that 28.5 per cent of the capitalized value of Martin's plantation was represented by Negro slaves, it is not surprising that the quality and preservation of the labor force were matters of importance."[38] And, as Defoe and Colonel Martin reveal, "amelioration" was intended primarily to benefit the master, through better discipline, increased production, and

---

[33] The novel was reprinted and apparently widely read in the later eighteenth century, although, unlike Sarah Scott's *Sir George Ellison*, it was not mentioned in the literature of anti-slavery.

[34] In addition to Martin's, the notable planter manual is Sir Philip Gibbes, *Instructions for the Treatment of Negroes* (London: Shepperson and Reynolds, 1786 and reprinted with additions in 1797). Gibbes recommends working slaves under maximum capacity and allowing marriage to promote both happiness and natural population growth. Martin's *Essay* went through seven editions in the century, the first was 1750. An initial ameliorationist section was added to the fifth edition of 1773. According to Richard B. Sheridan, "Samuel Martin, Innovating Sugar Planter of Antigua," *Agricultural History*, 34:3 (1960), 126–39, this section was "motivated in part by a desire to justify the institution of slavery" (129). See also William Belgrove, *A Treatise Upon Husbandry or Planting* (Boston: Fowle, 1755) which includes a second planter treatise by Henry Drax as an unmarked appendix.

[35] Martin, "Innovating," 3.

[36] Martin and his family were often invoked as exemplary slave owners. See Janet Schaw, *Journal of a Lady of Quality; Being the Narrative of a Journey from Scotland to the West Indies, North Carolina, and Portugal, in the years 1774 to 1776*, ed. Evangeline Walker Andrews with Charles McLean Andrews (New Haven: Yale University Press, 1923), 103–9 and 259–73. For a reading of Schaw's idealization of Martin, see Sandiford, *Cultural Politics*, 114–17.

[37] Martin also organized a planter's school and inspired agricultural innovation in late eighteenth-century Antigua: see David Watts, *The West Indies: Patterns of Development, Culture and Environmental Change Since 1492* (Cambridge: Cambridge University Press, 1987), 391–2.

[38] Sheridan, "Samuel Martin," 129.

higher profits.[39] It also always involved a veiled threat of violence; in Defoe's novel, Jack goes so far as to brag that his reforms are based on "Apprehensions of the Cruelest Punishment" (144). Amelioration may have been based on a rhetoric of shared humanity, but, as *Colonel Jack* demonstrates, a rhetorical acceptance of similarity, deployed to articulate "whiteness," could ultimately promote a complex and lasting conception of racial difference.

[39] Some masters even instituted lowered daily work quotas in order to increase efficiency by giving slaves an incentive to work quickly. See Craton, *Testing the Chains*, 50; and J. R. Ward, *British West Indian Slavery, 1750–1834: The Process of Amelioration* (Oxford: Clarendon, 1988), 18, 109, 201.

CHAPTER 3

The evolution of the grateful slave 1754–1777: the emergence of racial difference in the slavery debate and the novel

Eric Williams has famously and influentially argued that slavery produced race. In recent decades, this argument has been developed to show that the racialization of colonial plantation slavery produced "race" as a side effect of, and a justification for, the violence on which it depends.[1] In such arguments, "race" has two intertwined meanings. On the one hand, it refers to the system of white supremacy that grants privileges to "whites," denies them to "blacks," and enforces the distinction with violence; this I shall call the "practice" of race. On the other, "race" also refers to the conceptualization of race, the ascription of essential difference, and inferiority in key capacities, to "blacks." The "dehumanization" of slavery, in this account, leads to the conceptualization of blacks as less than fully human; this I will term the "theory" of race. Each of these aspects of race has been studied intensely, but usually through very different disciplinary approaches. The racialization of plantation slavery and the emergence of a system of white supremacy have been the domain of social historians, and particularly of Marxist-inflected historians, including Edmund Morgan and Theodore Allen, all following the lead of Eric Williams, concentrating on the colonies, and building models of race in legal, social, and economic terms. The theoretical side of race, on the other hand, had been treated by intellectual historians and historians of science, concentrating on intellectual debates, and centering on metropolitan publications.[2]

Literary scholars, when they have engaged with the historiography on the construction of the white race, have assumed that the link between these two strands is a simple, causal connection. The assumption has been that the institution of "white supremacy" and racialized slavery of necessity brought into being theories to justify them. The flaw in this linkage, however, is that it does not reflect the rhetorical self-positioning of the

---

[1] Williams' initial concern was to debunk the idea that racial slavery was natural by showing it to have been an economic decision; for relevant historiography, see the Introduction, n. 36.
[2] This characterizes the works cited in the Introduction, n. 24, with the exception of Fredrickson and Wheeler.

texts that brought these issues before the public. For the first three-quarters of the eighteenth century, the default rhetorical position of British writers – whether colonial or metropolitan – was to deny the reality of significant or essential difference between white and black, and even to regret slavery. The greatest difference between colonial and metropolitan approaches to slavery is in the depiction of violence. Colonial writers, or writers entering into the colonial perspective, accept a great degree of violence as necessary to control and subjugate slaves. Often, as with Trelawny, this is explicitly connected to acknowledgment of slaves' humanity and desire for liberty. The prodigious diarist Thomas Thistlewood – an English immigrant to Jamaica, who after arriving in 1750, parlayed a successful career as an overseer into ownership of his own "slave pen" by 1766, and died in Jamaica in 1786, illustrates the mentality in play.[3] On arriving in Jamaica, Thistlewood was initially disturbed by the callousness Jamaican whites showed toward black life. He quickly assimilated to the system, however, and even became proud of having invented some particularly disgusting and sadistic punishments.[4] Nonetheless, according to his biographer, Trevor Burnard, he never adopted explicitly racist views. Indeed, the love of his life was a Mulatto slave woman, although she appears to have been the only black slave for whom he felt any sympathy. Thistlewood justified his horrific abuse of his enslaved charges not by denying their humanity, but by becoming callous to it and more crucially, by imagining himself as in a state of war with his slaves and all of Jamaica's African-descended population.[5] While Thistlewood is a useful illustration of this mentality, he is hardly unique, nor was his attitude confined to Jamaica or to island colonies. Indeed, such a stance was not confined even to planters themselves. William Moraley, a white indentured servant in the northern colonies, and Edward Kimber, a British journalist traveling southward from New York to Georgia, reflect similar perspectives.[6] Indeed, colonists' acknowledgment of their slaves' humanity is not entirely surprising.

---

[3] See Trevor Burnard, *Mastery, Tyranny, and Desire: Thomas Thistlewood and his Slaves in the Anglo-Jamaican World* (Chapel Hill: University of North Carolina Press, 2004), 2–13.

[4] Burnard, *Mastery, Tyranny, and Desire*, 104, and Philip Morgan, "Three Planters and Their Slaves: Perspectives on Slavery in Virginia, South Carolina, and Jamaica, 1750–1790," in *Race and Family in the Colonial South*, ed. Winthrop D. Jordan and Sheila L. Skemp (Jackson: University Press of Mississippi, 1987), 74.

[5] Burnard, *Mastery, Tyranny, and Desire*, 140–1.

[6] Edward Kimber, *Itinerant Observations in America, 1745–46*, ed. Kevin J. Hayes (Newark, DE: University of Delaware Press, 1998); William Moraley, *The Infortunate: The Voyage and Adventures of William Moraley, an Indentured Servant*, ed. Susan E. Klepp and Billy G. Smith (University Park, PA: Pennsylvania State University Press, 1992).

Institutionalized "racial" oppression of Africans, therefore, preceded the construction of theoretical justification of such oppression by about a century. As discussed above, the watershed event in the emergence of the legal and social system of white supremacy has been dated by several historians to Bacon's Rebellion of 1676 in Virginia. I will argue here, however, that the idea of concrete racial difference of a recognizably modern sort was first put forward in British writing in the early 1770s, in the pamphlet debates about the trial to determine whether or not ex-slave James Somerset could be reclaimed by his master in England under British law. The pressure that led to this theorization of race was the coalescence of attention to the legal status, and the possible illegitimacy, of slavery within England (and then Scotland), and the threat that the same logic could be applied to the colonies themselves. Thus, racial difference was put forward by colonists as a justification of slavery and racial oppression to their metropolitan critics. Crucially, however, the account of racial differences put forward by the supporters of the West Indian interests in response to the hubbub surrounding the Somerset case had already been closely anticipated by the metropolitan fictions imagining plantation reform. Following Defoe's model of reform through gratitude, Edward Kimber (1754), Sarah Scott (1766), and Henry Mackenzie (1777) offered their own visions of the solution to the problem presented by colonial slavery. The last two writers, especially, imply differences between black and white in response to a different pressure. Rather than introducing difference as a political defense in response to a legal challenge, they imagine a difference that "improves" and stabilizes slavery in response to both sentimental charges of cruelty and the threat presented by the emergent ideology of free labor.

Before turning to the ameliorationist fictions that are the center of this chapter I will trace the debates on slavery from 1750 to 1775, culminating in the fall-out over Lord Mansfield's decision in the Somerset case. The readings of these pamphlets will demonstrate that, during this entire period, the rhetorical norm was to affirm that Africans fully shared the same human status as Europeans. The need for such affirmation suggests that this status was unstable or in question. However, very few writers – whatever their stance on slavery – are willing to claim a belief in racial difference as their own. Instead, most writers who discuss racial difference in this period attribute the belief in inferiority to their opponents as a means of discrediting them. Generally, critics of slavery argue that planters must believe their slaves are inferior to be willing to treat them so cruelly. But in at least one case, an apologist for slavery, perhaps sarcastically, accuses a critic of slavery (John Wesley) of implicitly subscribing to racial difference, because he does not seem to extend his view of man's sinful nature to Africans. Placing a remarkably virulent pamphlet – *Personal Slavery Established* (1773) – in this context establishes that it satirizes pro-slavery arguments. Although it is sometimes read as a key document of pro-slavery racism, its suggestion that Africans and monkeys are interrelated is offered in the same spirit as its threat that the West Indies could do without pork imports from the mainland colonies by salting, pickling, and eating all the Africans who die on the middle passage.

In metropolitan discourse, expressions of distaste for slavery and rejection of "race" in both theory and practice were mainstream through the first three-quarters of the century. A 1705 legal manuscript notes that English law "looks on Negroes & Polacks as on the rest of mankind – Negroes are inheritance in Barbadoes. And bringing 'em into England don't make 'em chattels."[7] This legal jotting demonstrates not just differences in law, but in broader cultural tendencies between England and its colonies: it demonstrates the transatlantic gap in legal and social practices of race.[8] In England, the norm in the early eighteenth century was to reject slavery, and furthermore to assume a fundamental similarity between all human groups, based on Christian orthodoxy. At just the same time this remark was scribbled, laws were being codified in Virginia and other colonies defining not only slaves, but all blacks, as an inferior caste, thereby institutionalizing white supremacy and racialized slavery.[9] Marking Africans as an inferior caste, it should be noted, took place at the level of practical and legal social policy. While these practices led to the concept of racial superiority and inferiority, the path was a more circuitous one than has been widely noted.

The central argument of this chapter is that novels representing the amelioration of plantation slavery through the sentimental manipulation

---

[7] James Oldham, "New Light on Mansfield and Slavery," *Journal of British Studies*, 27:1 (1988), 47. The precise dating is Michaelmas 1705–Trinity 1706.

[8] Edward Long, *Candid Reflections Upon the Judgement Lately Awarded by the Court of King's Bench in Westminster-Hall on What Is Commonly Called the Negroe-Cause* (London: T. Lowndes, 1772), 13, takes the similar phrase "the law takes no notice of negroes" to exclude them from the protection of the law. Granville Sharp, *A Representation of the Injustice and Dangerous Tendency of Tolerating Slavery* (London: Benjamin White, 1769), 34, 38–9, sees it as ambiguous. However, Chief Justice Holt in 1707 in Smith vs. Gould, 92 Eng Rep 338, wrote, more clearly, "the law takes no notice of negros being different from other men." See Steven M. Wise, *Though the Heavens May Fall: The Landmark Trial that Led to the End of Human Slavery* (Cambridge, MA: Da Capo, 2005), 28–9, for discussion of the relevant cases.

[9] See Allen, *Invention*; Parent *Foul Means*; and Cheryl Harris, "Whiteness as Property," *Harvard Law Review*, 106:8 (1993), 1717–21.

of African slaves played a crucial role in closing this transatlantic gap in practices of race. When placed alongside texts from the slavery debate, the role of these novels in bridging the gap between colony and metropole becomes clear. Indeed, such texts not only develop a meaningful concept of racial difference in metropolitan discourse, but aid colonials in conceptualizing a theory to defend their practices, buttressing the well-established practice of white supremacy with a theory of white superiority. Furthermore, these texts, seemingly critical of slavery, actually help to lessen the rhetorical resistance to both slavery and racial difference, and anticipate the positions taken by slavery's apologists on both issues at the close of the century.

As Thistlewood indicates, the writings of slave masters from the first three-quarters of the eighteenth century show their strong belief in and commitment to a patriarchal worldview, to hierarchy and subordination, and to the understanding of black and white as engaged in an ongoing state of war, but reveal little evidence of theories of racial inferiority.[10] On another track, those scholars most interested in the institution and operation of white supremacy have seen it as a cynical policy meant to enable a very small number of masters to dominate large numbers of slaves and lower-class whites, rather than as a deeply held belief in racial difference.[11] Indeed, as a number of scholars have suggested, the relationship between master and slave in many ways entails an unavoidable confirmation, if not recognition, of the slave's humanity.[12] Even the colonial practice of racial domination was not a clear indicator of articulated or consistent beliefs in the reality of racial difference. It is quite possible, then, that the articulation of difference in metropolitan debates represents the beginning of conscious theoretical racism not just for the metropole, but even for the colonies themselves. That is, defending colonial practices – rather than simply engaging in them – entailed the development of a theory for their justification.

This chapter describes the conceptions of race underlying discussions of slavery up to 1775 in order to establish the context for the racial meaning of ameliorationist fiction. If we date the beginnings of such fiction to Defoe's 1722 *Colonel Jack*, it preceded the more theoretical ameliorationism of the slavery debate by half a century. The story of the effects of amelioration will continue in chapter 6 below, which will show that amelioration, by the late 1780s, had become a point of consensus for both anti-slavery forces and the

---

[10] Morgan, *Slave Counterpoint*, 263–7, 296–300; Morgan, "Three Planters and Their Slaves"; Burnard, *Mastery, Tyranny, and Desire*; Rhys Isaac, *Landon Carter's Uneasy Kingdom: Revolution and Rebellion on a Virginia Plantation* (New York: Oxford University Press, 2004), 196.

[11] Edmund S. Morgan, *American Slavery*; Allen, *Invention*, vols. I and II; Parent, *Foul Means*.

[12] See the Introduction, n. 2, above.

West Indian interest. Amelioration helped metropolitan observers, for the first time, imagine an acceptable form of slavery. Furthermore, many specific visions of amelioration, certainly including those of the ameliorationist fictions, made slavery acceptable precisely by implying that it could be made suitable to blacks in particular; and this idea of suitable slavery introduced racial difference into the discussion without overtly challenging the conventional wisdom.

HUMANITY AND THE RHETORIC OF RACE IN SLAVERY PAMPHLETS TO 1775

The Somerset case of 1772, arguably the opening salvo of the abolition debate, shows that the transatlantic gap on practices of race had not narrowed significantly since 1705. Counsel for both sides, and the judge, Lord Mansfield, characterized slavery as inherently "odious." Somerset's lawyers' arguments invoked parallels between African slaves in Virginia, East European serfs, Protestant "galley slaves" held by Catholic nations, and Christian slaves held by Muslims.[13] Indeed, Somerset's advocates, following the lead of Granville Sharp, successfully defined colonial laws of slavery as "foreign" laws, establishing the basis of Mansfield's decision that such laws could not be enforced within England itself.[14] No one in the case appears to have suggested that distinct laws could conceivably apply to blacks and whites within England. And these positions were not narrowly legal, but reflected broader cultural trends, as suggested in the observation that English commentators agreed in expecting a decision favorable to Somerset.[15]

   Granville Sharp captured the cultural high ground with his 1769 pamphlet *A Representation of the Injustice and Dangerous Tendency of Tolerating Slavery*, exploiting the rhetorical and cultural norms of rejecting race and slavery. Sharp boldly insisted, in defense of the rights of enslaved blacks to claim the protection of the crown, that colonial masters in England

---

[13] Shyllon, *Black Slaves*, 92–3.

[14] Sharp set the terms of the debate with his pamphlet *A Representation of the Injustice* discussed below. My account of the Somerset case follows Shyllon, *Black Slaves in Britain*, 76–140, and Oldham, "New Light," Most accounts of the case, including Wise, *Though the Heavens May Fall*; Hochschild, *Bury the Chains*, 44–53; Gretchen Gerzina, *Black London: Life before Emancipation* (New Brunswick: Rutgers University Press, 1995), 90–132; and Peter Fryer, *Staying Power: The History of Black People in Britain* (London: Pluto, 1984), 113–26, follow Shyllon closely. Oldham challenges Shyllon's interpretation of Judge Mansfield, and adds new information from the archives to the discussion.

[15] Shyllon, *Black Slaves*, 112, makes this point, but does not draw this implication out in "Public Opinion and the Somerset Case," *ibid.*, 141–64.

"cannot be justified" in "seizing, and detaining" such slaves, "unless they shall be able to prove, that a Negro Slave is neither man, woman, nor child" (15). The wording here shows Sharp's assumption that his audience, including his colonial legal antagonists, will be unable to produce a plausible position, at least as judged in the courts of law and of public opinion, denying the humanity of Africans. Sharp generalizes the point, contending that "the Negro must be divested of his humanity, and rendered incapable of the King's protection, before such an action can lawfully take place" (15–16). While pamphleteers writing for the planter interest conceded that slavery was inherently objectionable, and that blacks were commonly viewed as fully human, this did not dissuade them from eventually, after some awkward groping, taking up Sharp's challenge and attempting to divest "the Negro ... of his humanity." Indeed, in this respect, the Somerset debate can be taken as an example of the problem of unintended consequences, as criticism of the dehumanizing effects of slavery led slavery's apologists to deny explicitly African humanity before it led to political gains and practical reforms. Sharp's formulation of the legal implications of African humanity for slavery and the slave trade, in other words, stimulated the planter interest to challenge the consensus on African humanity, knowing as they mounted their challenge, that they were opposing a cultural norm.

Samuel Estwick published his pamphlet, *Considerations on the Negro Cause, Commonly So Called*, in 1772, hoping to influence Mansfield's decision on behalf of the planter interest, and then revised it in 1773 to question the decision that had been rendered. Estwick, like Mansfield himself, shows that the English investment in "liberty" was normally extended to Africans in concept if not in practice, conceding that the very concept of slavery is "odious."[16] Indeed, even Edward Long, the eighteenth century's most notorious apologist for slavery, expresses in his contribution to this skirmish the implausible hope that "I shall not be misunderstood to stand forth a champion for *slavery*."[17] Estwick's initial strategy in his pamphlet is curious: he simply redefines colonial slaves as "property" and attempts to substitute the word "Negro" for "slave,"

---

[16] Samuel Estwick, *Considerations on the Negroe Cause Commonly So Called*, 2nd edn (London: J. Dodsley, 1773), xi. Interestingly, the concession that the state of slavery is "odious" is added to the second edition. In the first edition, only the *word* slavery is termed "odious," Estwick, *Considerations on the Negroe Cause Commonly So Called* (London: J. Dodsley, 1772), 10. Citations to Estwick are from the much expanded 2nd edition.

[17] Long, *Candid Reflections*, 73.

implying that they should have a different legal status than other humans.[18] This, of course, only serves to reveal the conflict between colonial and metropolitan practices of race, especially when contrasted with the many examples of the enslavement of non-Africans in the eighteenth century offered by Somerset's attorneys. Estwick attempts, quite unsuccessfully, to render African slavery unproblematic by importing linguistically the very colonial practices that Mansfield had found to be legally inapplicable in England.

Estwick bows to the received opinion that denying African humanity is implausible: "seeing that Negroes are human creatures," he remarks, "it would seemingly follow that they should be allowed the privileges of their nature" (64). Instead of directly challenging black humanity, then, Estwick proposes significant and meaningful difference within the category of the human, carefully keeping within the conceptual boundaries of the dominant theory of monogenesis: "May it not be more perfective of the system to say," he writes, "that human nature is a class, comprehending an order of beings, of which man is the genus, divided into distinct and separate species of men?" (74). To distinguish between these distinct species within the genus, Estwick invokes Locke on the differences between men and beasts – both possess forms of reason, but in Estwick's words, "man's superiority over beasts consists in the power of exerting that faculty, and in the compound ratio of its exertion" (75).[19] Similarly, "the *moral sense* being a faculty of the human mind common to all men" (75), it is "the power of exercising that faculty, and the compound ratio of its exercise . . . which makes the grand difference and distinction between man and man" (75–6).[20] In other words, there are profound and concrete differences between the various species of the human genus. These differences are located in the extent and usage of shared capacities. Notably, the key "faculty" revealing difference is Francis Hutcheson's new, controversial, and fashionable faculty of the "moral sense," the faculty at the heart of the philosophical discourse of sentiment and sympathy.[21] Further, Estwick's

---

[18] Estwick, *Considerations*, 30. Long, in *Candid Reflections*, pursues the same strategy, and Burnard shows that Thistlewood prefers the word "Negro" to "slave" even in his private diary (*Mastery*, 131).

[19] Whether Estwick captures Locke's meaning here is debatable; Locke does not entirely exclude animals from having a form of reason but he could be taken to make a clearer distinction than Estwick suggests. See John Locke, *An Essay Concerning Human Understanding*, 1670, vol I, ed. Alexander Campbell Fraser (New York: Dover, 1959), 207–8.

[20] Estwick here imitates Locke's language in the terms "compound ratio" and his concern with "faculties."

[21] Geoffrey Sill, *The Cure of the Passions and the Origins of the English Novel* (Cambridge: Cambridge University Press, 2001), 10, 155–60; Albert O. Hirschman, *The Passions and the Interests: Political Arguments for Capitalism before its Triumph* (Princeton: Princeton University Press, 1977).

use of the natural history term "species" seems to function just as the term "race" would later, despite his theoretical retention of a common genus. Almost as striking as Estwick's theoretical radicalism here is his caution in articulating it.

Estwick himself was not, of course, advocating amelioration. He was challenging Sharp's position, and its apparent acceptance by the courts, in an effort to justify slavery. Estwick offers an account of human difference which he himself presents as both innovative and marginal in 1772: "now, My Lord, it is an opinion *universally* received, that human nature is *universally* the same; but I should apprehend that this was a proposition rather taken for granted, than admitted to be proved" (72). His account of human difference, however, is virtually identical to that of ameliorationist fictions envisioning slave gratitude as a method of plantation reform. Remarkably, Estwick's position, marginal when he presented it as a last ditch defense of slavery in 1772, would become culturally central by the end of the 1780s.

My argument for the cultural centrality of recognition of African humanity runs counter to the most influential histories. In discussing the rhetoric of advocates of the conversion of slaves to Christianity – the issue around which eighteenth-century criticism of colonial slavery first coalesced – Winthrop Jordan finds evidence of an established colonial belief in racism in the very frequency of denials of racial difference (especially of differences in spiritual and mental capacities):

Proponents of conversion would never have felt compelled to declare that the Negro was inherently as intelligent as the European unless they had encountered insinuations to the contrary. To affirm positively that the Negro was the mental equal of the white man was to affirm by indirection that some people thought the Negro was not.[22]

Jordan is undeniably right that the assertion of Africans' basic intelligence would not take place if their intelligence were unequivocally taken for granted. However, he takes this insight rather too far, overlooking the crucial fact that African inferiority is discussed far more often by those who deny it than by those who assert it. This is suggestive of the rhetorical state of play, and therefore of underlying cultural norms.

Were such denials the only evidence we had for assertions of inferiority in the period, the difficulty would be in locating the assertions, and speculation or reconstruction would be our only resources. Jordan does

---

[22] Jordan, *White Over Black*, 189.

speculate for this purpose, as we shall see, but the "defenses" of Africans often specify to what they respond; and quite often, it is to the *treatment* of slaves, rather than to explicit statements. By reviewing a number of the pamphlets involved in this controversy below, I will show that they make the assertion aggressively, in order to claim a cultural high ground and a cultural norm for their own rhetorical purposes, and not at all defensively as Jordan here implies.

Before offering his speculative reconstruction of "racist" attitudes, Jordan stops to discuss, and to decry, the lack of a concept of intellectual ability as precise as "IQ" in the eighteenth century, linking this imprecision to the ease with which a variety of mental and spiritual capacities could be conflated due to the characteristic eighteenth-century failure to distinguish effectively between essential and environmentally determined qualities.[23] Jordan's point here is salutary; when evaluating evidence of racial thinking in the eighteenth century, twentieth- and twenty-first-century scholars are hampered because their subjects do not take for granted the same set of concepts, definitions, and distinctions they do, including such fundamental distinctions as that between environmental and essential characteristics.[24] However, Jordan introduces the problem of the lack of precision in eighteenth-century thought to a very specific purpose, one which seems to contradict this very point. He imagines the colonists views of Africans in terms of familiar prejudices:

The cultural gulf between the two peoples was enormous, and Negroes fresh from Africa and even their children must have seemed very stupid indeed. As with any quality in other people which seems extreme, the Negro's stupidity must at times have seemed downright irredeemable, as hopelessly rooted in his essential character; from there it was no step at all to calling him casually a naturally stupid brute. And because there existed no clear demarcation between inborn and acquired characteristics, it became easy enough to slip into thinking that the Negro's natural and inveterate stupidity was "innate," without however imparting much precision or meaning to the notion. (190)

This passage is contradictory. On the one hand, the colonists do not have the conceptual framework to discriminate between natural and cultural

[23] Jordan's faith in the precision of IQ and the clarity of the concept underlying it now seems difficult to fathom, perhaps partly as a result of the reaction to *The Bell Curve*. For a history of debates about the value of tests of inherent intelligence throughout the twentieth century, see Nicholas Lemann, *The Big Test: The Secret History of the American Meritocracy* (New York: FSG, 1999). Lemann documents charges of socio-economic bias in both SAT and IQ tests as early as 1948 (*Ibid.*, 66).
[24] This problem is explored by Joyce E. Chaplin, "Race," in *The British Atlantic World 1500–1800*, ed. David Armitage and Michael J. Braddick (New York: Palgrave, 2001), 154–73.

qualities. On the other, it is significant if they see "stupidity" as "innate" or "essential." More disturbingly, as the passage moves along, Jordan begins treating "the Negro's natural and inveterate stupidity" as a cause of its perception by the colonists. Indeed, the phrase "thinking the Negro's natural and inveterate stupidity was 'innate'" is at best tautological. Furthermore, the only concrete evidence underlying Jordan's imaginative speculation is writings *defending* blacks' intelligence.

One of the conversionist critics of slavery, George Whitefield, challenges the very possibility of such thoughts, apparently expecting that putting them into words will be enough to dispel them. Whitefield admonishes planters that black slaves need to be taught Christianity just as much as their own children do. "Think you," he asks, "they are in any way better by nature than the poor Negroes? No, in no wise. Blacks are just as much, and no more, conceived and born in Sin, as White men are. Both, if born and bred up here, are equally capable of the same Improvement."[25] Here, Whitefield opposes not actively articulated ideas of inferiority, but practices that seem to imply the possibility of such ideas. And he seems to expect that his audience – in this case, the planters themselves – will disavow such ideas once they have been articulated.

Jordan's thought experiment crucially deviates from the implications of the evidence he considers to set it in motion. One central issue he sidesteps, in the phrase "and even their children" is the widely accepted eighteenth-century distinction between "Africans" and "Creoles." Whitefield invokes this crucial distinction in the words "if born and bred up here." Even such an outspoken theorist of the "stupidity" of the negro as Edward Long – often cited as a preeminent racist for his insistence on the close relationship between Africans and monkeys – insisted on the great superiority of Creole children to their African parents.[26] Despite Long's rhetorical adoption of a scientific persona, allowing him to advance startling hypotheses, he is undeniably an unsystematic thinker. In defiance of his own caveat about the lack of precise distinctions in eighteenth-century thought about intellect, Jordan's need to find essentialism in the slave owners' denigration of their slaves leads to his hypothetical lumping together of slaves and their children. And this misses a point likely to be uppermost in the eighteenth-century pro-slavery mind: conversionists like Whitefield and virulent pro-slavers like

---

[25] George Whitefield, *Three Letters from the Reverend Mr. G. Whitefield* (Philadelphia: D. Franklin, 1740), 15.

[26] See for instance Edward Long, *The History of Jamaica*, vol. II (London: T. Lowndes, 1774), 477; as usual, Long both repeats and contradicts this point elsewhere; for instance, see 410–14.

Long both take a relatively positive view of Creoles, although they often couch it in terms of wonderment. An "improvement" from the first to the second generation of slaves supports the Snelgravian argument for slavery as a positive, humane, improving institution through the insistent point that Creoles are superior to their African parents. This contention also points to the lack of a clear concept of essential race in these early debates on slavery, even among slavery's boldest apologists.

Jordan's treatment of the cultural place of assertions of the equal capacities of Africans, therefore, is inadequate. While he rightly asserts that arguments for equal capacity would not be made unless someone, somewhere was contending the opposite, he does not take account of the tone and the rhetorical self-positioning of such defenses of African humanity and equality. As we have seen with Long's and Estwick's attempts to counter Sharp – and as we will see in a number of pamphlets below – it is the assertions of difference, not the responses to them, that are defensive and hesitant in tone. Even in the colonies, then, practices of racial subjugation have an unclear relationship to articulated – or even conceptualized – beliefs in racial inferiority.[27]

In the eighteenth century, even before the emergence of a full-blown abolition debate, several writers accused slave owners and slave traders, on the basis of the cruelty of their behavior, of a belief in African inferiority. John Woolman, for instance, in his influential essay published in two parts in 1754 and 1762, describes Europeans who believe in their own "superiority" to Africans as worldly, selfish, ungodly, and self-deceived.[28] The pseudonymous Philmore writes in 1760 that "those, who are concerned in the man-trade" show by their behavior that "they have, some how or other, a kind of confused imagination, or half-formed thought, in their minds, that the blacks are hardly of the same species with the white men."[29] Philmore's description of "a confused imagination, or half-formed thought" captures the hesitancy, indirection, and lack of clarity in most early-century suggestions of difference. For both of these writers, the idea that slavers and slave owners might imagine themselves as beings superior to their captives is damning evidence against them. Such a position appears neither plausible nor defensible, at least in addressing a metropolitan audience. The practices

---

[27] Burnard, *Mastery, Tyranny and Desire*, 129, argues that Thistlewood, despite a willingness to employ terror and brutality against slaves, conceived of them as rational and human, but nonetheless in no sense "equal" with whites.

[28] This is from the first part of the essay "Some Considerations on the Keeping of Negroes" (1754); cited from *Works of John Woolman, Part the Second*, 1775 (Miami: Mnemosyne, 1969), 253–74.

[29] Philmore, *Two Dialogues on the Man-Trade* (London: J. Waugh, 1760), 12.

of the colonies, they insist, do imply such beliefs, but even in the colonies the expression of such beliefs remains outré.

Two polemical exchanges in the early 1770s, begun in the wake of the Somerset case, show the continuing dominance of the non-racial view of humanity. In the first, Philadelphia's Benjamin Rush dismisses those who seek to denigrate Africans in racial terms: "I need hardly say any thing in favour of the Intellects of the Negroes, or of their capacities for virtue and happiness, although these have been supposed, by some, to be inferior to those of the inhabitants of Europe."[30] Of course, he does go on for a few pages to rebut specific charges, apparently those made by Edward Long in his 1772 Somerset pamphlet *Candid Reflections*: "All the vices which are charged upon the Negroes in the southern colonies and the West-Indies, such as Idleness, Treachery, Theft, and the like, are the genuine offspring of slavery, and serve as an argument to prove that they were not intended for it" (2). So convinced is Rush (himself, of course, a colonial) that "race" is a self-justifying pretext that he comes to define it in terms resonant with twenty-first-century critical race studies. Rush demands that laws be changed in the colonies in order to "extend the privileges we enjoy, to every human creature born amongst us, and let not the Journals of our Assemblies be disgraced with the records of laws, which allow exclusive privileges to men of one color in preference to another" (25). If there is no essential racial difference, and no genuine belief in it, the social fact of discrimination is simply a matter of the cynical, intentional enforcement of social and legal privileges.[31] Here Rush alters the charges made by Philmore and Woolman. While they accused slave owners of acting in ways that implied a belief in inferiority, Rush now accuses slavery's apologists of consciously using racial difference – a doctrine they know to be false – to shield their iniquity.

In the two rebuttals published in 1773, Rush's antagonists respond by insisting on the reality of racial difference. The first response, Richard Nisbet's *Slavery Not Forbidden By Scripture* (1773), is concerned to defend slavery as humane, on the grounds, for instance, that self-interest and the inherent humanity of the British will protect slaves (16), arguments that will become more prominent as the debate unfolds. Nisbet eventually

---

[30] Benjamin Rush, *An Address to the Inhabitants of the British Settlements, on the Slavery of the Negroes in America*, 2nd edn, 1773 (New York: Arno, 1969), 1–2. Further citations are given parenthetically in the text.

[31] Allen, *Invention*, vols. I and II; Mills, *Racial Contract*; for a seminal text on race privilege in contemporary society, see Peggy McIntosh, "White Privilege and Male Privilege: A Personal Account of Coming to See Correspondences through Work in Women's Studies," Wellesley College Center for Research on Women Working Paper no. 189 (1988).

makes the blunt claim that "on the whole, it seems probable, that they are a much inferior race of men to the whites, in every respect" (21) joining the camp of Estwick and Long but undoing some of their careful rhetorical self-positioning. There is an odd imbalance to Nisbet's rhetoric – typical of such "hypotheses" in the eighteenth century – as he opens by hedging with statements like "on the whole" and "it seems probable," and then goes on to the sweeping claims that "they are a much inferior race of men to the whites in every respect" (21). Notably, this statement is supported with a citation to Hume's notorious footnote. Nisbet seems to be developing this theory of essential inferiority as he claims that the "barbarism" and "stupidity" of Africans are due to a "want of genius," rather than the familiar explanations of either "climate" or of the lack of "chances of improving" (23). Nisbet goes on to compare Africans to other groups, arguing, for instance, that the Chinese seem to hold the possibilities of a "nation of whites," and that it is a disgrace even to compare "ancient Britons" to "modern Africans," and that "even the *Aborigines* of *America*, have shown their superiority over the Africans" (24). Nisbet seems to have established himself as a virulent essentialist racist. But his next point is to insist on the superiority of Creoles over Africans: they "have much superior intellects, and are by far more inclinable to work." He offers this as a refutation of the idea that even freshly imported Africans resent slavery ("yet it is endeavoured to make us believe, that negroes pine and degenerate in our part of the world") and to support the Snelgravian scenario of slavery as a form of Christian rescue from the barbarity of Africa: "these creatures, by being sold to the Europeans, are often saved from the most cruel deaths, or more wretched slavery to their fellow Barbarians" (25). Nisbet's seeming commitment to racial difference in essentialist terms is undermined by his strategic differentiation between Africans and Creoles.[32]

Another response to Rush appears to be the most virulent attack on negroes in the eighteenth century. Edward Long's 1774 *History of Jamaica* is often given this dubious distinction, but the anonymous *Personal Slavery Established* (1773) was actually published an entire year earlier. Despite its anticipation of Long's arguments, and despite having been taken as a pro-slavery text by some scholars, *Personal Slavery* is a satire.[33] Drawing

---

[32] Nisbet recanted in his next publication, *Capacity of Negroes for Religious and Moral Improvement Considered* (London: J. Phillips, 1789), which argues for the fully human capacities of blacks.

[33] *Personal Slavery Established* (Philadelphia: John Dunlap, 1773); Davis, *Age of Revolution*, 300 n. 27, and Nancy V. Morrow, "The Problem of Slavery in the Polemic Literature of the American Enlightenment," *Early American Literature*, 20:3 (1985–6), 236–55, read it as a parody. Duncan Rice sees it as parodic but nonetheless representative of defenses of slavery, *The Rise and Fall of Black*

attention to the often polemical usage of travel accounts of Africa, its author dismisses such evidence with the remark that "notwithstanding the accounts of fabulous voyagers, the Negroes on the western coasts of Africa, are the most stupid, beastly race of animals in human shape, of any in the world" (18).[34] He describes Africans as "utterly devoid of reason," and suggests a subdivision of the African, "arranging them in the order as they approach nearest to reason, as 1st, Negroes, 2nd, Ourang Outangs, 3rd, Apes, 4th, Baboons, 5th, Monkeys" (19). This is a watershed moment in racial discourse, the first explicit argument for a direct linkage between Africans and monkeys.[35] The instability of this historical moment is revealed by the fact that this satirical excess was soon put forward by Edward Long, in moderated form, as a serious argument.

Beginning from his previously suggested division of humanity into four groups, the author here proposes abandoning monogenesis by "retracting the word *species* [to] substitute *genus*" (18).[36] This overt adoption of polygenesis parallels the suggestion in the pamphlet's concluding passage that West Indians could replace pork imports with the salted and pickled flesh of Africans who die in the middle passage. This threat to northern critics of slavery, whose colonies provide the pork, appears to signal satire in its blatant violation of taboos.[37] Indeed, the passage echoes the Swiftian critique of imperialists as cannibals, metaphorical consumers of human flesh.[38] The tone of the pamphlet is snide and hyperbolic throughout, with many barbs apparently aimed at the "rhapsodies," "enthusiasm" and self-deception of anti-slavery activists. It is this denigrating approach to

---

Slavery (New York: Harper, 1975), 206. Jordan, *White over Black*, 306, and Larry E. Tise, *Proslavery: A History of the Defense of Slavery in America, 1701–1840* (Athens, GA: University of Georgia Press, 1987), 29, take the pamphlet in earnest.

[34] In *A Forensic Dispute on the Legality of Enslaving Africans* (Boston: Boyle, 1773), each debater depends on one of two mutually exclusive interpretations of the evidence about life in West Africa.

[35] Wahrman, *Making of the Modern Self*, 130–40, offers Long as the originator of the racist linkage of Africans and monkeys. Brown, *Ends of Empire*, 188–98, uses two texts from 1774, Long and Janet Schaw's *Journal*, to establish the racist implications of connecting apes and Africans for her reading of Swift's *Gulliver's Travels*, which was published in 1726.

[36] The wording in *Personal Slavery Established* implies that the term "species" is from Nisbet's pamphlet, but it appears in the pamphlet only in a quotation from Hume. As we will see below, associating opponents with Hume could be used to discredit them.

[37] In this, it would resemble Swift's *Modest Proposal* in using the casual violation of the cannibalism taboo to signal irony. See Wayne Booth, *A Rhetoric of Irony* (Chicago: University of Chicago Press, 1974), 105–20, for a classic discussion of Swift's irony.

[38] For two excellent literary histories of the cannibalism trope in the early modern period, see Carlo Ginzburg, "Making Things Strange: The Prehistory of a Literary Device," *Representations*, 56 (1996), 8–28; and Claude Rawson, "'Indians' and Irish: Montaigne, Swift, and the Cannibal Question," *Modern Language Quarterly*, 53:3 (1992), 299–363.

other anti-slavery writers that seems to have baffled scholars in analyzing this work.[39]

However, only this strange, radical and satirical pamphlet challenges the idea that human groups belong in a single category and differ within it, otherwise unquestioned in the debate around Somerset, until Long rehashes its charges in his *History of Jamaica*, and hence the pamphlet's status as a satire is worth establishing. Internal evidence suggests that the author of *Personal Slavery* expected his assertion of Africans' natural inferiority to be self-evidently absurd and thus satirical.[40] Indeed, he offers as an epigraph the sentiment that "however amiable Justice and Virtue may be in our abstract ideas of them: the policy of Kingdoms and Commercial states ought ever to be regulated by the more important considerations of Necessity and Convenience," cited to an apparently invented text entitled *Machiavelus Americanus* (title-page). Having stated that "the authority of scripture is now generally rejected by men of a liberal way of thinking" (11) – itself likely a satirical hit – the author of *Personal Slavery* goes on to remark that "One author, in attempting to prove the inconsistency of Slavery under a Christian dispensation, is quite blasphemous" (11–12). Indeed, his central point in the paragraph smacks yet more of satire. The unspeci-fied author he critiques, he continues, "would infer that although there is no *express* precept against the slave trade to Africa or keeping Slaves; they are both absolutely repugnant to the very genius and spirit of Christianity. Just as if we were to imagine any evil was intended to be removed that was not expressly forbidden in the New-Testament" (12). If this arrogantly legalistic approach to scripture is not broad enough to make its satirical intention clear, the author returns to Machiavellianism and again invokes "Popish" values:

This would be to suppose that the lawless ambition of Kings sacrificing millions of their fellow creatures, and the little catalogue of other necessary consequences of the imperfection of our nature, before mentioned, are inconsistent with the Christian religion. How absurd is such reasoning? How impious its author! 'Tis well he is not within the reach of the Popish inquisition; he would certainly have made a principle character in an *auto de fe*. (12)

[39] Tise, *Proslavery*, 29, for instance, cites this language as showing that the author takes on "Philadelphia's entire anti-slavery community".
[40] Montesquieu suggested African inferiority, with searing irony, in *The Spirit of the Laws*, 1748, ed. Franz Neumann (New York: Hafner, 1966), 238–9. Estwick understands and attacks Montesquieu (*Considerations*, 84–5). However, Rice, *The Rise and Fall*, 163, documents that, by 1789, Montesquieu's irony required elucidation.

Here, the satire is undeniable, as the author defends what he himself describes as "lawless ambition." Neither side of the slavery debate wished to defend "sacrificing millions" as consistent with Christianity. Indeed, it is precisely this charge against African kings that underlies Snelgrave's influential concept of slavery as a form of rescue, a concept the author of *Personal Slavery* himself invokes for parodic purposes.[41] Furthermore, offending Catholic authorities (due to their appetite for political machinations) would hardly count against him with a British audience – whether metropolitan or colonial – in the 1770s. *Personal Slavery Established* is an uneven production; sometimes the ironies are laid on thick, sometimes the positions meant to be travestied are merely repeated. But ultimately, the pamphlet's denial of the norm of African humanity appears to be intended as outrageous, as is its support for ignoring scripture, "sacrificing millions," and employing cannibalism as a form of economic protest.

The following year, 1774, another exchange of pamphlets sheds more light on race within the burgeoning slavery debate and reaffirms the rhetorical norm of African humanity. John Wesley, in his pamphlet "Thoughts on Slavery," takes a strongly moral and religious stand against slavery and the slave trade, pushing aside practical objections as worldly, as epitomized in the remark "Better no Trade, than trade procured by villainy."[42] Wesley also takes a relentlessly positive view of Africa, citing the travelers André Brue and Michel Adanson to argue that Europeans have corrupted Africans and Africa, and indeed that Europeans could learn a good deal about honesty from Africans.[43] Wesley insists that the perception of Africans' "stupidity" in the colonies is simply the result of the circumstances of slavery. In the pamphlet's climax, Wesley addresses slavers and slaveholders in the second person, accusing them of deliberate deception in offering difference as an excuse for slavery: "you keep them stupid and wicked," he contends, and then use that as an excuse "for using them worse than brute beasts" (43). Here, Wesley repeats Rush's charges that planters mistreat slaves despite knowing them to be fully human, and try to justify themselves by creating a perception of the slaves' incapacity. Both Olaudah Equiano and James Ramsay will later present colonial white supremacy in similar terms, as entirely dependent on force, rather than reflecting natural

---

[41] He congratulates the RAC for "rescuing many millions of wretched Africans, *as brands from the fire*" (3).
[42] Wesley, *Thoughts Upon Slavery* (London: Hawes, 1774), 37. Further citations are given parenthetically in the text.
[43] Brue and Adanson were key sources for Benezet's *Some Historical Account*, one of the most influential early anti-slavery texts.

relationships of superiority and inferiority; and like Wesley, both suggest that colonists themselves regard this as an obvious fact of colonial life.

In a seeming contradiction, however, to Wesley's apparent radicalism he praises his acquaintance Hugh Bryan by contending that Bryan's kindness leads his slaves to love and reverence him (41); Wesley uses this example, curiously, to set up the point that "liberty is the right of every human creature" (51). The praise for Bryan does not mesh with Wesley's message about the absolute moral wrong of slavery, based on the human right to liberty. Indeed, Bryan can be seen as representing the same ameliorationist impulse behind the "grateful slave" fictions. Bryan was a convert of George Whitefield's who, despite being a member of a very powerful family of planters, ran into trouble with the authorities of South Carolina and Georgia for working toward the conversion of slaves and even prophesying slave rebellion. But Bryan and his family consciously kept themselves short of a radical challenge to the regime of slavery, eventually bringing Whitefield himself to become a slaveholder and an advocate for the extension of slavery into Georgia.[44] Indeed, while some scholars analyzing his actions have suggested that Bryan might have been more radical on slavery than his mentor Whitefield, his actions against slavery all seem to have been suggested in Whitefield's 1739 letter exhorting "the inhabitants of *Virginia, Maryland, North* and *South Carolina.*"[45]

The angriest response to Wesley, misleadingly entitled "Supplement to Mr. Wesley's Pamphlet" (1774), strikingly accuses *him* of a covert belief in species difference between humans. The writer, typical of early entrants in the debate in the planter interest, begins by distancing himself from slavery: "Let him [Wesley] think not I hold detested Slavery in less abomination than himself – far from it."[46] One of his central concerns, however, is to attack Wesley's positive view of Africans, insisting that they are indeed "barbarians" and even cannibals, and that Wesley works from the wrong sources, insisting most "authorities" agree "that the Negroes are in general stupid, senseless,

---

[44] On Hugh Bryan and Whitefield, see Allan Gallay, "Impassioned Disciples: The Great Awakening, George Whitefield, and the Reform of Slavery," in *The Formation of a Planter Elite: Jonathan Bryan and the Southern Colonial Frontier* (Athens, GA: University of Georgia Press, 1989), 30–54; Harvey H. Jackson, "Hugh Bryan and the Evangelical Movement in South Carolina," *William and Mary Quarterly*, 43:4 (1986), 594–614; and Leigh Eric Schmidt, "'The Grand Prophet': Hugh Bryan: Early Evangelicalism's Challenge to the Establishment and Slavery in the Colonial South," *South Carolina Historical Magazine*, 87:4 (1986), 238–50. Gallay sees Bryan as an originator of slaveholding paternalism, Schmidt as a precursor of anti-slavery. Linebaugh and Rediker (*Hydra*, 198) present Bryan and Whitefield as radicals.

[45] Whitefield, *Three Letters*, 13–16.

[46] *A Supplement to Mr. Wesley's Pamphlet* (London: H. Reynell, 1774), 3. Further citations are given parenthetically in the text.

brutish, lazy Barbarians" (60). Like Arthur Lee, who attacked Africans in revenge for Adam Smith's referring to colonists as the "refuse of the jails of Europe," the author of the *Supplement* seems motivated in his attack on Africans more by a desire to uphold European dignity, or superiority, than by an interest in defending slavery.[47] However, in his efforts to oppose Wesley, the author of the *Supplement* does not consider endorsing racial difference. Instead, he rebukes Wesley for failing to apply his own Methodist tenet of the depravity of human nature to Africans (53), and then sarcastically accuses Wesley of agreeing with Hume on race. Rhetorically, this author wishes to ally himself with the conservative position, the cultural and rhetorical norm, that all people are born of one act of creation while discrediting his opponent with a whiff of radical, even atheistic polygenesis and thereby undermining his position as an influential spokesman for religion. The normativity of acknowledging Africans' full humanity is revealed in the fact that the sermons on the missions of the Society for the Propagation of the Bible (SPG) seem to have invariably emphasized the point, even though African inferiority would have provided a convenient excuse for the mission's decision to own slaves, run a plantation, and take a very slow and limited approach to slave conversion.[48] Despite the more radical stances of Hume, Nisbet, and Long, departures from a belief in the unity of the human could be used to discredit opponents, whatever their stances on equality, liberty, and slavery.

Edward Long, the most vigorous racist of the century, provides evidence for the cultural centrality of belief in Africans' full humanity in his very attempts to attack it. His most definitive public statement of his position, in *History of Jamaica* (1774), never goes quite as far as his unpublished notes, in which he adduces the "evidence" that negroes never catch yellow fever as proof of real, biological difference.[49] It is remarkable that Long kept these thoughts private. Along with their suppression, his excited postscript to *Candid Reflections* on Estwick's pamphlet, and his repeating, in somewhat exaggerated form, of its central arguments suggests that Long, despite his brashness and hyperbole, was almost as cautious and as measured

---

[47] See Adam Smith, *The Theory of Moral Sentiments*, 1759, ed. D. D. Raphael and A. L. Macfie (Indianapolis: Liberty Fund, 1982), 206; and Arthur Lee, *An Essay in Vindication of the Continental Colonies, From a Censure of Adam Smith* (London: T. Beckett, 1764); Lee calls Africans "stupid" but concedes this may be partly due to the ill-effects of slavery (38). See Davis, *Western Culture*, 440; Jordan, *White Over Black*, 309–10; and Brown, *Moral Capital*, 115–16, for brief discussions of this exchange.

[48] Eve Stoddard, "A Serious Proposal for Slavery Reform: Sarah Scott's *Sir George Ellison*," *Eighteenth-Century Studies*, 28:4 (1995), 388–93.

[49] George Metcalf, on the eighth page of his unnumbered "New Introduction" to *The History of Jamaica*, vol. I (London: Cass, 1970), cites these private notes of Long's.

in advancing his most radical claims as was Estwick. Burnard suggests that even other Jamaicans Long knew, who were equally committed to the slave system and equally interested in natural history, did not share Long's interest in theories of race; even his closest allies likely reminded him of the radicalism of his arguments.[50]

Strikingly, Long, in *The History of Jamaica*, rehashes the idea of a hierarchy from monkey to white man, via the "negro" first offered in the satirical pamphlet *Personal Slavery Established*: "we observe the like gradations of the intellectual faculty, from the first rudiments perceived in the monkey kind, to the more advanced stages of it in apes, in the *oran-outang*, that type of man, and the Guiney Negroes; and ascending from the varieties of this class to the lighter casts, until we mark its utmost limit of perfection in the pure White."[51] Long adapts the hierarchy of intelligence offered in *Personal Slavery*, hedging his bets by casting it in terms of natural history and by dropping the unprecedented injunction to change "species" to "genus." Indeed, he stays closer to Estwick than *Personal Slavery Established* in choosing to include even Orang-utans in the category of humans rather than attempting to exclude Africans from it, in other words by arguing for such significant difference within the species that the concept of a "species" is rendered almost meaningless.[52] Long is entirely committed to the idea of essential difference in intelligence. He refuses the idea that slavery has degraded Africans, offering the absurd argument that in his observation "they cannot place a dining-table square in the room" and make other errors in the tasks assigned them, as proof of their inherent stupidity, never considering the possibility that such resistance to work could be intentional.[53]

The rhetoric, too, of the most famous pronouncements on race in the early century reflects the dominance of the belief that Africans were fully human. Hume opens his notorious footnote with the words: "I am apt to suspect the negroes to be naturally inferior to the whites."[54] His tone of

[50] Burnard, *Mastery*, 131–2.   [51] Long, *History of Jamaica*, II:374–5.
[52] Long gives an account of the eighteenth-century debate on the status of Orang-utans (*ibid.*, 359–74), following *Personal Slavery Established* in using it to denigrate Africans. For an account of the question of the relation between apes and humans throughout the century, see Richard Nash, *Wild Enlightenment: The Borders of Human Identity in the Eighteenth Century* (Charlottesville: University of Virginia Press, 2003), esp. 15–41 and 131–55. On Lord Monboddo, the primary advocate for the humanity of the Orang-utan (like Long, his work was published in 1774), see Robert Wokler, "Apes and Races in the Scottish Enlightenment: Monboddo and Kames on the Nature of Man," in *Philosophy and Science in the Scottish Enlightenment*, ed. Peter Jones (Edinburgh: John Donald, 1988), 145–68.
[53] *History of Jamaica*, II:408.
[54] David Hume, "Of National Characters," 1742, in *Essays: Moral, Political and Literary*, rev. edn, ed. Eugene F. Miller (Indianapolis: Liberty Fund, 1985), 208.

initial hesitancy – in "apt to suspect," advancing his position as a mere suspicion or hypothesis, even the decision to literally marginalize these remarks by making them a footnote – reflects an awareness that his position is an unlikely or unpopular one, that he is questioning a consensus. Indeed, Hume offers his evidence before returning to a stronger statement of the position: "Such a uniform and constant difference could not happen, in so many counties and ages, if nature had not made an original distinction between these breeds of men" (208). Here, sounding firmer, Hume seems to take a position much closer to outré polygenesis than to orthodox monogenesis; it is this hint of heresy that leads the author of the "Supplement" to attempt to discredit Wesley by linking him to Hume. Still, Hume works within the framework of monogenesis by referring to "races" as "breeds of men." Even for a philosophical thinker, then, the line between these two positions was not clearly drawn.

The author of the "Supplement," had he wished to, might have found another link between Hume and Wesley. Hume offers, *avant la lettre*, the abolitionist position that slaveholding is tyrannical and inherently corrupting. Not only "is domestic slavery more cruel and oppressive than any civil subjection whatsoever," throughout history, but turning to "the remains . . . of domestic slavery" found "in the AMERICAN colonies," Hume contends that "The little humanity, commonly observed in persons, accustomed, from their infancy, to exercise so great authority over their fellow-creatures, and to trample upon human nature, were sufficient alone to disgust us with that unbounded dominion."[55] Interestingly, late in the century, Hume's views on "inferiority" were often cited, but no anti-slavery writers seem to have quoted these words, although the position they outline became an abolitionist commonplace. Perhaps his status as an icon of Enlightenment reason made Hume appealing to the planters interested in defending themselves from accusations of benightedness, while his reputation for atheism made him anathema to the zealous forces of abolition.[56] In any event, for Hume, writing before the explosion of interest in race and slavery in the late century, the two issues are not connected: slavery is inhumane, indeed dangerous, regardless of the hypothetical inferiority of Africans. At least in the realm of intellectual history, then, the Eric William's thesis that "slavery produces race" becomes more complicated in light of the

---

[55] "Of the Populousness of Ancient Nations," 1748, in *Essays: Moral, Political and Literary*, 383–4.
[56] David Brion Davis sees slavery's apologists as claiming Enlightenment reason, while anti-slavery thinkers claimed the religious high-ground, in "The Emergence of Immediatism in British and American Anti-Slavery Thought," *Mississippi Valley Historical Review*, 49:2 (1962), 213.

strangely distinct paths of development for the theory and the practice of race in the eighteenth century.

GRATEFUL SLAVES IN THE NOVEL, 1754–1777

The meaning of sentimental representations of slavery in fiction is still much debated.[57] Markman Ellis has usefully suggested that ameliorationist fictions like Sarah Scott's had more impact in bringing attention to the plight of slaves than in the specific details they offer.[58] Before Ellis, it has often been argued – or simply assumed – that sentimental humanitarianism was a driving force behind England's late eighteenth-century anti-slavery movement, an examination of those novels that bring sentimental strategies to bear on representations of plantation slavery indicates otherwise. Even more importantly, a comparison between these texts and the preliminary stages of the slavery debate – from the early Quaker and Methodist discontent to the beginning of the public debate in regard to the case of James Somerset – reveals that sentimental novelists offer an account of race closer to that of slavery's defenders than its critics.

Daniel Defoe's preference for an instrumental over a sentimental explanation of the motivation for reform suggests one exception to the "humanitarian" interpretation. But even later novels, written in the age of full-blown sentimentality and committed to sentimental values, do not strengthen the case for the historical force of humanitarianism. Between 1750 and 1780 several novels used sentiment to criticize the overt cruelty of plantation slavery, and offered humanitarian reforms. Nonetheless, in these novels, an interest in reform must be distinguished from anti-slavery commitment. In the novels examined here, Edward Kimber's 1754 *History of the Life and Adventures of Mr. Anderson*, Sarah Scott's 1766 *History of Sir George Ellison*, and Henry Mackenzie's 1777 *Julia de Roubigné*, sentimental reforms, and even the extreme step of making a seeming offer of freedom to slaves on a given plantation, are intended not to challenge the institution of slavery, but instead to modernize management techniques and improve slaves' productivity.[59] Indeed, without overstating the case, in these

[57] See Ferguson, *Subject to Others*, 108; Ellis, *Politics of Sensibility*, 49–128; Helena Woodard, *African–British Writings in the Eighteenth Century: The Politics of Race and Reason* (Westport, CT: Greenwood, 1999), 67–98; Rai, *Rule of Sympathy*, 1, 6 and *passim*; and Nussbaum, *Limits of the Human*, 142–50.
[58] Ellis reasserted a more pointed version of this view at the "Slavery and Amelioration" roundtable session at the ASECS conference, Las Vegas 2005.
[59] Lisa Moore, *Dangerous Intimacies: Towards a Sapphic History of the British Novel* (Durham, NC: Duke University Press, 1997) addresses Scott's *Sir George Ellison* in her chapter "Resisting Reform: Sarah Scott's *Millennium Hall*," which was useful to me in formulating my reading of Scott.

representations, reformers improve slaves' lives only in order to enslave them more securely. But their emphasis on modernization, labor discipline and self-interest as a key motivator all invoke the emergent ideology of free labor, leaving a problem for the novels to solve. Why shouldn't African slaves simply be freed and paid for their labor? The novels address this tension by implying that slavery can be reformed by making it particularly suitable to Africans, which then suggests that Africans are suited to slavery; and this, in turn, depends on the idea of racial difference as Estwick would come to define it: a difference in the ability to exercise key capacities.

My argument, then, is that these novelistic representations foreshadow the emergence of sentimental, paternalistic slave management, and work within the rhetorical constraint of a monogenist framework to develop a sense of racial difference. They develop a vision of race and slavery much closer to Estwick's than to Woolman's, Wesley's and Rush's. The reforms they advocate are the very definition of paternalism: masters should take an interest in their slaves, and thereby foster emotional bonds encouraging slaves to identify with their masters. Their complaints about slavery are that relations with slaves were brutal and nakedly exploitative; their suggestion is of another more effective, more profitable, management style. Never do they raise the troubling questions about the slaveholder's regime of racial oppression that come up so often in the pamphlet debate.

Touting what would come to be known as amelioration, all these novels try to show ways to make slavery more pleasant for slaves and, more importantly, more profitable for masters. Each novel poses the question of the difference between "black" and "white," claiming to investigate it empirically. Two of the three also invoke the new theories of labor motivation that will soon coalesce into free labor ideology. In so doing, each subtly develops the implication that Africans are naturally dependent and, when they are shown a modicum of kindness, have an inclination to gratitude that blinds them to their exploitation. Although ameliorationism demands critique, it must be compared to the bizarrely irresponsible sentimentalism of Charlotte Charke in *The History of Henry Dumont* (1756), in which a key character goes along with his associates to a slave auction, although not intending to make purchases himself: "as to slaves, Mr. Jennings never would deal that way, being of too tender a disposition to inflict the heavy grievances and burdens he often saw his fellow creatures undergo."[60] Jennings does buy a slave, however, when he recognizes his cruel Uncle in the lot (226). Here, Charke shows the assumption that white

---

[60] *The History of Henry Dumont and Miss Charlotte Evelyn* (London: H. Slater, 1756), 225–6.

Britons could still be plantation "slaves" at mid-century.[61] Although the cruelty of slavery is represented (226), no real solution is considered; it is apparently enough that Jennings is too sensitive to participate directly in slave punishments. At the close of the novel, we learn that two sons of a Mr. Powel join his trade, and "each marrying two of the greatest fortunes in the colony," both "lived to be the happy instruments of good to several who from their great humanity avoided many sorrows they might have been otherwise exposed to" (256–7). Despite Mr. Jennings' sentimental repulsion from slavery's cruelty, the colonial economy as a whole is accepted without question. Whether or not the Powel sons' humanity extends to the slaves that they must count among their property is left unexplored.

Edward Kimber's *History of the Life and Adventures of Mr. Anderson* (1754) does not delve into the question of labor motivation as will the Sarah Scott and Henry MacKenzie novels treated below. But Kimber's novel – especially when combined with *Itinerant Observations in America*, the published account of the author's travels to the colonies which inspired *Anderson* – provide an excellent case study in the transatlantic representation of practices of racial oppression and its relationship to conceptions of slavery and racial inferiority. Like Defoe's Colonel Jack, the hero of this novel comes to a plantation in Maryland as an indentured servant, although he refers to himself throughout as a "slave." By the beginning of the nineteenth century, and certainly to twenty-first-century historians, Anderson would be considered an indentured servant, as "white" people could not be slaves.[62] Usage in the eighteenth century, even in the colonies, was considerably more ambiguous. For example, William Moraley, a white indentured servant in our terms – whose memoir provides a useful point of comparison for *Anderson* – never described himself as such.[63] Moraley does refer to "indentures," and distinguishes between and "purchased," sometimes "bought," "servants" and "negroes" or "negro slaves" when discussing both groups; at other times, he describes his decision to "sell myself" and also refers to other indentured servants as "voluntary slaves."[64] Until at least

---

[61] Jennings makes this purchase from the estate of a "black planter." I am not convinced by Ferguson's assumption, in *Subject to Others*, 97, that this means a planter of African descent; the term could also refer to a planter using slave labor. For her reading of the novel, see *ibid.*, 94–8.

[62] Although this is the last of several names for the protagonist, I will call him "Anderson" consistently to avoid confusion.

[63] Notably, for the point I am making, in Moraley, *The Infortunate*, the term "indentured servant" is added to the subtitle by the editors of the modern edition.

[64] Further examples include: "indentures," 96; "Servants and Negroes," 86; "purchased servants or Negro Slaves," 93; "the condition of Negroes," 94, compared to "the condition of bought servants," 96; "sell myself," 50; "voluntary slaves," 64.

the mid-eighteenth century the terms "slave" and "servant" could still be used interchangeably for English indentured servants and African slaves in metropolitan discourse, and likely also in the colonies.[65]

Unlike Colonel Jack, who identifies with African slaves only involuntarily, Anderson finds himself naturally inclined to sympathize with slaves; his "kind" treatment of them could be borne of personal identification, especially given that he refers to himself as a "slave," but the narrator instead emphasizes his inherent kindness. Here, Moraley again provides a useful point of comparison. He appears sympathetic to slaves, noting that "the Condition of Negroes is very bad," seeming to view masters as a common oppressor: "the Laws against them are so severe, that being caught after running away, they are unmercifully whipped; and if they dies under the Discipline, their Masters suffer no Punishment, there being no Law against murdering them" (94). Before offering complaints about the similar, if less severe, lot of "bought Servants," however, Moraley unexpectedly offers a justification of the masters, sounding more like Colonel Jack than Anderson. Capturing the Africans' own distaste for their condition and insistence on fully human status, Moraley reports that "I have often heard them say, they did not think God made them Slaves, any more than other Men, and wondered that Christians, especially *Englishmen*, should use them so barbarously" (96).

After having seemingly entered into the slaves' point of view, and suggested the possibility of reversing the usual charges of barbarism, however, Moraley suddenly draws a line of demarcation: "But there is a Necessity of using them hardly, being of an obdurate, stubborn Disposition; and when they have it in their power to rebel, are extremely cruel" (96). Here, Moraley shows the possibility – even for relatively recent British immigrants – of at once charging masters with cruelty, acknowledging Africans' humanity and yet also avowing the necessity of violence to maintain the system of racial slavery and white supremacy. Although Moraley's experience is of the northern mainland colonies, he appears, like Jamaica's Edward Trelawny and Thomas Thistlewood, to see slavery as virtually a state of war between black and white. He does not claim that the slaves are subhuman or inferior, but simply that violence against them is a "necessity"

---

[65] The first examples of the term "indentured servant" listed in the *OED* are from the early nineteenth century; the term "indented slave" appears earlier, cited to Tobias Smollett's 1771 novel *The Expedition of Humphry Clinker*, but is obviously more ambiguous. The distinction in practice appeared earlier than in terminology: see Peter Kolchin, *American Slavery: 1619–1877* (New York: Hill and Wang, 1993), 8–16, and Morgan, *Slave Counterpoint*, 8. See also the works cited in the Introduction n. 36.

in maintaining the upper hand. Such an attitude, I contend, represents a very common colonial position of a commitment to white supremacy quite apart from a theoretical argument for racial superiority. Notably, Moraley, unlike Thistlewood who kept his diary private, unapologetically presents this attitude to a metropolitan audience.

In Kimber's novel, Anderson is exiled by his master to a distant plantation because the master is wary of Anderson's love for his daughter. On that plantation, Anderson becomes a very successful overseer. Kimber describes Anderson's treatment of slaves in a few brief sentences:

> By his sweet treatment of the *Negroes*, he gained their good-will, and shewed that kindness and clemency to those miserable creatures will make them more serviceable than cruelty and brutality; for in the first fortnight, he had more tabacco hoed and housed, and more work of every sort completed, than was ever seen upon that plantation before.[66]

From the very brief treatment given to Anderson's management, one can see that Kimber feels no need to argue for, or to demonstrate, the principle that kindly, paternalistic treatment is more efficacious than cruelty, asserting a principle that was already being established in such planter handbooks as those of Henry Drax and Martin.

Rather than wishing to transform slavery radically, however, Anderson, capturing the essence of ameliorationism *avant la lettre*, wishes to make plantation life more pleasant for the slaves and more profitable for masters: "if you use your servants and dependents with kindness, your work will be done chearfully, and you'll gain as many friends as you purchase" (95). Here, the contrast between the bland optimism of the word "friends" and the inhumanity of "purchase" captures the contradictions of the ameliorationist position. One cannot reasonably expect to keep people as chattel slaves, to conceive of them as mere "creatures," and yet to be accepted by them as a "friend," particularly in the world described by Moraley, in which acknowledgment of the slaves' humanity and desire for freedom amounts to a justification of a more vigilant racial oppression. Nonetheless, ameliorationist novelists expect nothing else.

Alfred Lutz has argued that such slavery reforms in Scott's *Sir George Ellison* – and indeed, its very concept of the reformers' "virtue" – depend on a willful blindness to their own implication in the violence and

---

[66] Edward Kimber, *History of the Life and Adventures of Mr. Anderson* (London: W. Owen, 1754), 73–4. Further citations are given parenthetically in the text. For a reading of *Mr. Anderson* as a textbook example of the sentimental novel, see Gary Ebersole, *Captured by Texts: Puritan to Postmodern Images of Indian Captivity* (Charlottesville: University of Virginia Press, 1995), 109–16.

oppression of slavery and the colonial economy.[67] Does a kind and sentimental reformer like Anderson share Moraley's violent view of the relation between black and white? Can he accept the institution of slavery without accepting a regime of violence and intentional oppression? Or does he depend on willful ignorance? Kimber's novel has long been thought to be a product of his travels to America, and specifically to represent an expansion of certain elements of his account of that journey in his *Itinerant Observations in America*.[68] After analyzing the novel, then, I will contrast it to the accounts of slavery and white supremacy in *Itinerant Observations* to illustrate Kimber's surprising willingness to acknowledge his implication in the violence of the slave system without apparent awareness that it complicates his sentimental and reformist credentials.

Anderson's rather vague – and apparently friendly – reforms are not the most important representations of slavery in the novel. The sentimental recognition of slaves' suffering is made by another character, Fanny, Anderson's beloved. The violence of slavery comes into focus in the interpolated account of her confinement on the plantation of a crass young planter who wishes to marry her against her will. As a prisoner, she sees her own similarity to the slaves, and begins to develop a special sympathy for them, albeit a narcissistic kind of sympathy. She sees the treatment of the slaves as a way of sending messages to her, for instance as she explains that a whipping she witnessed was "a piece of gallantry to me I supposed" (235).[69] And this is not the last such scene that Fanny witnesses: "But this was only the first essay I beheld of their skill, in such usage, and every day afterwards, that I staid, exhibited such acts of unfeeling, obdurate inhumanity to their wretched negroes, that I wonder not the judgment of heaven overtook, at length, the perpetrators of such enormous crimes" (237). Indeed, according to Fanny, the Carters' own brutality is the means through which the judgment on them is brought about: "at the same time it render'd them fear'd, [it] nurs'd up a spirit of hatred and revenge, in the breasts of the slaves, which had hitherto only wanted opportunity to be brought fatally to light" (237).

---

[67] "Commercial Capitalism," esp. 559, 566.

[68] These were first published sporadically in *The London Magazine* in 1745 and 1746; the first book publication of this work is the modern edition cited above in note 6.

[69] Fanny's perception accords with Jacqueline Dowd Hall's understanding of lynching: "Like whipping under slavery, lynching was an instrument of coercion intended to impress not only the immediate victim but all who saw or heard about the event," "'The Mind that Burns in every Body': Women, Rape, and Racial Violence," in *Powers of Desire: The Politics of Sexuality*, ed. Ann Snitow *et al.* (New York: Monthly Review, 1983), 330.

In Fanny's view, then, while kindness may produce "friendship," cruelty causes revolt.

And in a further intertwining of the fates of Fanny and the slaves, a revolt saves her from young Carter just as he is going to rape her. At the crucial moment, he is warned of the uprising and rushes from the room to confront the rebels. Luckily for Fanny, the rebel slaves kill him before he can return. The moment young Carter ceases to threaten her, however, Fanny transfers her fear to the rebels themselves despite her identification with them before the rebellion. Significantly, she is rescued from a burning building not by the rebel slaves, but by white militia men who have come to put down the "mischief doing at *Carter's*" (272). The rebels' only role is to wreak justice on the evil Carters, providing poetic justice for Fanny. Indeed, Kimber stops short of endorsing the slaves' bid for freedom. In this sense the implications of the revolt match the reformers' original scheme: what is needed is humane treatment, sincere paternalism, a "friendly" relation between master and slave, not an end to slavery, and certainly not radical action by the slaves. The revolt suggests that while kindness produces gratitude and loyalty, cruelty produces slave vengeance, a theme that will become dominant after the revolution in Haiti. Kimber does go further in his critique of violence than the other reformers discussed in this chapter: he represents the death of a brutal slave owner as justified, even as divinely ordained. Still, by representing Anderson's kindness as a universally applicable solution to the problems of slavery, Kimber encourages his readers to imagine that violence is the personal choice of cruel slave owners rather than an inherent aspect of plantation slavery.

At another point, Anderson seems to take a stand against slavery. On inheriting his one-time buyer and adoptive father Matthewson's fur-trading business, Anderson sets both the indentured servants and "the *Negroes*" free. He even instructs the men to whom he gives the business to pay the former slaves a "proper wage." Clearly, Kimber conceives this act as purely admirable and good, as Anderson concludes that "All were transported – every one was happy!" (139). Still, several things about this scene remain ambiguous. Firstly, the freed slaves involved were already given much greater freedom than plantation slaves, simply because they work with a backwoods fur-trading business in which extensive supervision would be impossible. Secondly, Anderson's gesture here is part of an outburst of extensive, overwhelming generosity, in which he distributes most of his inheritance to celebrate the memory of his generous adoptive father, Matthewson. Indeed, in another such generous moment, Anderson apparently gives the ability to purchase slaves: for "honest *Duncan Murray*" he bought a pretty plantation, and gave him £100 to stock it" (284). Of course, £100 would not be enough to stock a plantation with many slaves. But at mid-century, slaves in Virginia and the West Indies could be purchased for £35–40, so Anderson could be intending to give the power to buy two or three slaves.[70]

The specific nature of Anderson's reforms always remains vague. Only at one point does Kimber present any details of the type of "kindness" that would make them work; paradoxically, these kindnesses are performed by the brutal Colonel Carter. Fanny explains that Carter is proud of his cruelty, believing that it produces docility: it

was consider'd by the Colonel as a matter of the highest satisfaction, and he us'd to boast that he had the tamest and the most orderly *black stock* in the whole colony. But this tameness proceeded from yet a more generous temper in the negroes; for the policy of their master, as well as his profit, having induced him to provide them wives, or however the greatest number, of their own complexion, the soft tye intimidated them from any revolt or rising, terrify'd with the idea of losing the objects of their care. (261)

Here "kindness" is entirely the result of a calculated attempt to increase profits (although Kimber seems to contradict himself about this), taking the form of an act only incidentally respecting the human and emotional needs of the slaves.

Kimber's vision of slaves as having the same needs and being subject to the same forms of emotional manipulation as British people is typical of his ambiguity about racial difference. Even the Africans' bloody rebellion against the Carters does not reveal an inherently violent or vengeful nature: the slaves are represented as "the agents of heaven" on the one hand, and on the other, their "spirit of hatred and revenge" is "nurs'd up," developed by the "brutal" behavior of their masters. Similarly, when Anderson treats slaves with kindness, the narrator takes their resulting happiness and gratitude for granted, never bothering to explain or examine it. This seemingly positive assessment of the essential shared humanity of Africans leaves Kimber with a glaring logical problem: if there is no natural difference between British servants and African slaves, how can he expect Africans to accept their bondage happily merely in exchange for "kindness"?

The difference between black and white in the novel is dealt with only tangentially and symbolically. At first, Anderson is a slave like the Africans, but he is also unlike them. His slavery is absolutely wrong in the moral

---

[70] See Thomas, *The Slave Trade*, "Appendix Four: Selected Prices of Slaves," 807.

terms of the novel; their slavery is only wrong insofar as their masters are foolishly and excessively cruel. Given the opportunity, Anderson naturally and unproblematically becomes a very effective master. Again, in the revolt, the slaves are justified to lash out against their master, but once they have provided just retribution, they must be defeated by "good" white men. In sum, in *Mr. Anderson*, Kimber appears to believe that Africans are more suited to slavery than Europeans, or at least, like Moraley, to believe that any measures taken to support white supremacy are justified, although he never questions Africans' basic humanity.

Kimber's *Itinerant Observations* confirm and amplify the positions he later took in *Anderson*. He speaks more directly about the wrongfulness of slavery, and shows more clearly his commitment to white supremacy independent of a theory of African inferiority. In his report on a trip to the colonies, published in the mid-1740s in the *London Magazine*, Kimber makes clear his expectation that, at least in rhetorical terms, the slave trade was already understood as unnatural and wrong by his audience: he writes "the Argument, of the Reasonableness and Legality, according to Nature, of the Slave-Trade, has been so well handled on the Negative Side of the Question, that there remains little for an Author to say on that Head" (*Itinerant*, 48). In comments sympathetic to the founding intentions of Georgia, Kimber obliquely suggests his personal objections to slavery, apparently taking the assent of his audience for granted (36).

It is perhaps a bit surprising, then, to hear Kimber suddenly begin to defend slavery:

But allowing some Justice in, or, at least, a great deal of Necessity for, making slaves of this sable Part of the Species; surely, I think, Christianity, Gratitude, or, at least, good Policy, is concern'd in using them well, and in abridging them, instead of giving them Encouragement, of several brutal and scandalous Customs, that are too much practis'd. (48)

Notably, here, "good policy" is distinguished, if not terribly frankly, from "Christianity" and "Gratitude." Perhaps more surprisingly, Kimber appears here to reverse the direction of gratitude established in Defoe, and repeated in all the ameliorationist fictions of the century, insisting on the gratitude of the master to the slave, a movement theoretically entailed by patriarchalism and the moral economy, but rarely seen in practice.[71]

---

[71] Kimber seems to catch the spirit of Hugh Bryan's Whitefieldian reformism here. Kimber's movements through Carolina, Georgia, and Florida suggest that he likely had contact with Whitefieldians, although as a staunch supporter of Oglethorp, and a critic of the extension of slavery into Georgia, he took the other side on local political issues.

Intriguingly, Whitefield uses a similar formula in his pamphlet of 1739, giving it a much more critical cast in addressing planters: "For is it not the highest Ingratitude, as well as Cruelty, not to let your poor slaves enjoy some fruits of their labor" (14). Pushing toward the sentimental reformism of *Anderson*, Kimber spends a moment feeling sympathy for a slave – albeit a hypothetical one: "To be sure, a *new Negro*, if he must be broke, either from Obstinacy, or, which I am more apt to suppose, from Greatness of Soul, will require more hard Discipline than a young Spaniel" (48). But what a strange comment this is: the admiring of "Greatness of Soul" puts Kimber forward as sentimental, as identifying with and striving to understand, in human terms, the plight of the slaves; and yet the comparison to a young spaniel suggests a habit of thinking of Africans as animals, as mere possessions.[72] The significance of such comparisons did not go unremarked in the eighteenth century.[73] And indeed, the point of the exercise is to "break" the imagined slave.

But Kimber in *Itinerant Observations* nonetheless works himself into the state of mind of a grateful slave reformer, more distinctly and effectively than he ever does with Anderson. Part of the effectiveness is his willingness to frankly address racial oppression. Earlier on, he compares the English to the Romans in having "perpetuated a Race of Slaves" (48). Here, he begins envisioning plantation reform by suggesting that "were they not to look upon every white Man as their Tormentor; were a slight Fault to be pardon'd now and then; were their Masters, and those adamantine-hearted *Overseers*, to exercise a little more Persuasion, Complacency, Tenderness and Humanity towards them, it might, perhaps, improve their Tempers to a greater Degree of Tractability" (48–9). Again, Kimber quickly veers from the indictment of the evils of slavery, a possibly sarcastic suggestion of mere decency as an improvement in slave administration ("were a slight fault to be pardon'd now and then") to the practical concerns conceived of above as necessity: he is not imagining a world free of racial oppression or the brutality of slavery, but merely a strategy for increasing "tractability" and discipline for the ultimate benefit of masters. The problem with systemic racial oppression is that it leads slaves "to look upon every white Man as their Tormentor," undermining discipline, not that such a perception reflects reality.

---

[72] Nussbaum, *Limits of the Human*, 137, sees a pattern of such equivalences in the early eighteenth century, although she does not distinguish those meant to highlight slaves' humanity through irony and those meant to occlude it. See also Ellis' analysis of Ellison's wife's Lapdog, *Politics of Sentiment*, 95–6.

[73] See for instance Sharp, *Representations*, 13–16, 69.

Kimber, following this logic, goes on to indict cruel masters, and then makes his strongest statement against slavery: "Slavery, thou worst and greatest of Evils!" (49). He then lists forms of slavery across the world, and the suffering they entail, including "sweating in the mines of *Potosi*," "the Torture of the Whip, inflicted by the Hands, the remorseless Hands of an *American* Planter" and being "trod upon by ermin'd or turban'd Tyrants" (49). Kimber sees slavery in a world continuum, not to deemphasize or relativize the horror of American slavery, but rather to give substance to an invocation of British exceptionalism: "In Britain, and Britain only, thy Name is not heard; thou hast assum'd a new Form, and the heaviest Labours are lightsome under those mild Skies!" (49). Kimber reminds us, as will Somerset's attorneys a quarter of a century later, that "slavery" did not exclusively call to mind African slavery in America; this certainly contributes to the opposition to slavery – because slavery was by no means an unimaginable fate for a white Englishman, even "slavery" in the colonies, as Kimber further reminds in the anecdote that likely inspired the plot of Anderson: the kidnapping of a young English lad into slavery (indeed, both versions of the story hint at sexual abuse). This is the very scenario dreaded by Sharp in the *Representation*: that the illegal kidnapping into slavery of Africans would lead to similar kidnappings of white Englishmen. Oddly Sharp does not invoke any such specific cases, although some were already well known.

Despite his contradictory position on slavery, *Itinerant Observations* confirms Kimber's sympathy for white supremacy, which was suggested in *Anderson* by the ambiguous attitude toward the slave revolt. Indeed, Kimber's overall position regarding slavery makes more sense if we see him as objecting to the impossibility of guaranteeing white supremacy and the exclusion of whites from slavery. His reflexive discounting of black life becomes obvious when he is on a ship which becomes distressed in a storm with six hands, three passengers, and seven Negro slaves (38). Kimber comments tersely that "we forbore to see after the Negroes, but nailed down the Hatches, and left them to the Mercy of Providence" (41). This is the very action, as we will see in chapter 5, that leads Olaudah Equiano to challenge the shipboard regime of white supremacy, and it was likely a typical reaction to a slave cargo during shipboard difficulties.[74] Such action clearly delineates the distinction between those whose lives are valued and those whose lives are not. In the 1781 Zong incident, such actions caused a

---

[74] Notably, Colonel Jack metaphorically describes his discomfort with the obligations of gratitude as being "under the Hatches" (155).

major scandal: 133 living slaves were thrown overboard from a slaver with the intention of collecting insurance for them. This incident, brought to public attention in the metropole by Equiano and Sharp, exposed such dehumanizing attitudes and was an important publicity coup for anti-slavery.[75]

Despite his ambiguous attitude toward slavery and his criticisms of the overt abuse of blacks, however, Kimber appears untroubled by such instances of white supremacy. He reports that the storm continued to batter the ship for three days, and pointedly remarks on "[our] not daring all these last 24 Hours to direct our Eyes to our distemper'd Messmates" (41). When they have come to safety, they return to these men they have had to neglect for twenty-four hours:

We now examin'd our Cabin Associates, and found only the inanimate Remains of three of them. The others had some Signs of Life, and were convey'd on Shore by the Planters who visited us, and were their Neighbors. A thousand Times they lifted their Eyes up with Astonishment at our forlorn Condition. Our Negroes were our next Concern, and here only two were found alive, and such a Stench of Putrefaction in the Hold, as made it necessary to have Recourse to the usual Preservatives from infectious Smells. Ourselves were now to be considered . . . (43)

Here, Kimber denies the slaves even the rhetoric of sentimental identification. The dead and suffering among the cabinmates inspire the "Neighbors" to be astonished at "our forlorn Condition"; the death and suffering of the slaves – already cruelly locked in the hold and denied any attention during the crisis – inspire only a reflection on the resulting smell and the measures to avoid suffering from it. Kimber describes the effects of the colonial practice of white supremacy unblinkingly, and without seeming to notice that it conflicts with his sentimental and humane rhetoric about the state of slavery. Although only a visitor to the colonies, he seems to have entered into the untheorized practice of colonial racial subjugation, and he is able to do so without feeling the need for a dehumanizing theory to justify the practices he relates. In a broad sense, Kimber fits into the pattern of writers like Phillips, Snelgrave, and Defoe, who use sentimental and humane rhetoric to distance themselves from responsibility for colonial violence. And yet Kimber departs from the specific course of their patterns by being less sentimental in his representations of the slaves' death and suffering than in his abstract considerations of their plight. In this, he is like the "indentured servant" William Moraley. Of course, Kimber has the

---

[75] See Shyllon, *Black Slaves*, 184–209; Schama, *Rough Crossings*, 158–69; Carretta, *Equiano, The African*, 237–9.

advantage of being able to present himself as a victim, a sufferer, due to the
deadly storm. Indeed, he uses the fact of the storm and the death of whites
on shipboard to keep the death and suffering of the slaves, and white
responsibility for heightening it, very much in the background.

Sarah Scott's novel *The History of Sir George Ellison* (1766) is the most
frequently noted grateful slave novel. In lamenting the shortcomings of
West Indian slavery, George Ellison presents a rosy picture of what appears
to be the "classless" society of "old" England. He claims that "no subordination exists" in England. Apparent subordination there "is for the benefit
of the lower as well as the higher ranks; all live in a state of reciprocal
services, the great and the poor are linked in compact; each side has its
obligations to perform."[76] Such a description evokes the image of a kind,
just squire who cares for those who live near his estate, considering their
needs alongside, or even before, his own; this is the very image of the
Renaissance model of gratitude.[77] But what might seem a typical nostalgic
account of the harmony of bygone days is intended by Ellison as a
description of present-day agricultural labor in England.[78] He ends his
description by explaining that "if I make use of another man's labour, it is
on condition that I pay him such a price for it, as will enable him to
purchase all the comforts of life, and whenever he finds it eligible to change
his master, he is as free as I am" (17). Ellison is actually describing the "free
market" in labor. Nor was free labor a meaningless abstraction for Sarah
Scott. Her sister, fellow bluestocking, and life-long correspondent Elizabeth
Montagu took great pride in her work overseeing the coalmines owned by her
husband's family and detailed this work in letters to her sister.[79] Montagu saw
herself as "benevolent" to her miners – who she often described as "blacks" or
"quite black."[80] Montagu, however, was committed to free labor, going so far
as to oppose regulations proposed by her fellow mine owners to restrict the
movement of miners between mines, seeing this as a form of "slavery."

---

[76] Sarah Scott, *The History of Sir George Ellison*, 1766, ed. Betty Rizzo (Lexington: University Press of
Kentucky, 1996), 17. Further citations are given parenthetically in the text.
[77] Ellis analyzes this passage in *Politics of Sensibility*, 107.
[78] On the familiarity of such nostalgic accounts of rural labor in the eighteenth century, see Raymond
Williams, *The Country and the City* (New York: Oxford University Press, 1973).
[79] Elizabeth Child, "Elizabeth Montagu, Bluestocking Businesswoman," *Huntington Library Quarterly*,
64: 1–2 (2002), 153–73. This is the special issue *Reconsidering the Bluestockings*, ed. Nicole Pohl and Betty
Schellenberg, which has been reprinted as a book under the same title (San Marino, CA: Huntington
Library, 2003).
[80] Nussbaum, like Child, analyzes the Scott–Montagu correspondence; Nussbaum is specifically
concerned with the light it sheds on *Sir George Ellison* and race (*Limits of the Human*, 143–5).

Despite having invoked the model of English free labor as a guide to solving the problems of slavery, Ellison vacillates about the nature of slaves and their differences from English agricultural laborers. His inspiration for reforming the plantation comes from his insight that slaves' apparent indifference to discipline can be understood as a rational response to the hopelessness of their situation. They are refractory, he argues, because

> they find, however careful [they are], through the weakness of human nature they must sometimes err, and also that by the barbarity and tyranny of their overseers, they shall frequently be punished, even when they are not guilty; and looking upon these sufferings as a misery attending their condition, they do not endeavor to avoid what they cannot prevent. (12)

His insight is that the inevitability, the pervasiveness of violence in the slave system overwhelms or eliminates rational self-interest as a motivation for slaves to work. The assumption here – like that behind Adam Smith's treatment of the problem of motivation for unfree laborers – seems to be that Africans are fully rational. Arguing that free labor benefits masters, Smith explains that, on an estate, free tenants "have a plain interest that the whole produce should be as great as possible, in order that their own proportion may be so," while "a slave, on the contrary, who can acquire nothing but his maintenance, consults his own ease by making the land produce as little as possible."[81] Smith is not the first to make this point in the context of plantation slavery: a pamphlet published four years before *Sir George Ellison* makes the point that "no man in his senses will willingly work, unless he expects a recompense for his labour, which is never the case with slaves."[82] But, by contrast, for Ellison granting rationality to Africans is only incidental; the primary point is to imagine a more efficient system.

This self-interested insight is the fruit of Ellison's sentimental nature. His concern for slaves had been awakened when he stopped the overseer from administering a "most severe punishment." This sparks his desire for reform and reveals to him the irrationality of the old system of punishment. Ellison is spurred on by his sympathetic "extasy" in the "joy of the reprieved wretches" despite the anger of his Creole wife and her overseer. He explains to his wife that, beyond the benefits of increased "obedience," benevolent actions would yield her "a delight nothing in this world can afford but the relieving our fellow creatures from misery, a delight beyond what our weak

---

[81] Adam Smith, *The Wealth of Nations*, 1776, ed. Edwin Cannan (Chicago: University of Chicago Press, 1976), I:413.
[82] The pamphlet, devoted to advocating African colonialism in place of the slave trade, is *A Plan for Improving the Trade at Senegal* (London: R. and J. Dodsley, 1762), 1–2.

senses can well bear" (11). There is a striking resemblance between his vision
of the labor market as a system of mutual obligations, beneficial to rich and
poor, and the vision of a market in feeling, in which relieving the suffering
of the slave "affords" him maximum delight. Ellison's vision of an affective
economy obscures the suffering and inequality necessary to his system: if
workers did not need the money for subsistence, they might not sell their
labor at rates low enough to make their employers rich, despite his talk of
providing workers with "comforts"; if the slaves were not totally subjected
to him, they could not be beaten for minor infractions, and he would not
be able to "rescue" them from such treatment. To Ellison, however, the
exchange of gratitude (on the part of the slave) for sentimental satisfaction
(for the master) creates "a state of reciprocal services," obviating the need to
consider underlying inequalities.

Still, Ellison's "sensibility" draws him into a limited sympathy with, and
a responsibility to, his slaves. His imagining of rational hopelessness as the
cause of their behavior helps him conceive of them as agents, capable of
pursuing self-interest, much like wage laborers. Not only does his savvy as a
manager depend on his sentimental ability to sympathize, but the success
of his reforms also depends on the slaves' ability to make decisions rationally. Indeed, Ellison, unlike his West Indian wife, claims to disavow any
essential difference between himself and the slaves. He turns to Christianity
as a transcendent frame of reference, telling her "when you and I are laid
in the grave, our lowest Black slave will be as great as we are." He then
reframes his point, conflating the order of "nature" with the spiritual order
of the afterlife in remarking that "present difference is merely adventitious,
not natural" (13). But this invocation of the next world is ambiguous.
Despite the expectation of *equality* in the next world, and the suggestion
that such equality is natural, Ellison avoids the possibility that planters will
have to answer for having held their fellow-beings as slaves, a suggestion
explicitly made by Colonel Jack's cohorts when they learn that they will be
sold on reaching Virginia.[83]

George Ellison here seems to disarticulate the cruelty of white supremacy
and racial oppression from the reality of racial difference. The narrator
explains that "the thing which chiefly hurt him during his abode in
Jamaica, was the cruelty exercised on one part of mankind; as if the difference

---

[83] Of course, even the damnation of masters could curiously redound to slavery's credit. In Elizabeth
Bonhote's 1772 novel *Rambles of Mr. Frankly* (Dublin: Sleater, 1773), a West Indian in England
regrets slavery, but concludes that slaves' misery may well benefit their eternal souls (I:73–4). See
Sypher's reference to this scene, *Guinea's Captive Kings*, 269.

of complexion excluded them from the human race" (10).[84] Here, Ellison appears to be invoking the consensus view on African humanity, taking a position like that of pamphleteers from Woolman to Rush. But Ellison continues the statement so as to allow difference much more credence than such writers ever did: "or, indeed, as if their not being human could be an excuse for making them wretched" (10). This is the earliest example of a rhetorical move that became quite common among anti-slavery writers from the late 1780s: pointing out that, if Africans' subhuman status were granted, it still would not justify cruelty. Ellison's combination of these two points is incoherent. The first position is based on the interpretation that cruelty to slaves is a denial of their humanity; the second implies that cruelty reflects on the perpetrator and that the humanity of its victim is irrelevant. Although the concession of African inferiority is here, as later, presented as overtly rhetorical, nonetheless this very move in the last two decades of the century contributes to the erosion of the consensus on Africans' full humanity by shifting away from its centrality as a rhetorical norm.

Indeed, like Colonel Jack and Captain Phillips, Ellison intends his suggestions of Africans' equal humanity only in the manner of a scientist's hypothesis. He sets out "to try whether they deserved good usage" (14). Here, he reframes the question from the moral meaning of cruelty for its perpetrators to what treatment slaves "deserve," implying that kindness must be earned. Ellison remarks to his wife that he would continue to consider slaves "fellow creatures," "till you can prove to me, that the distinguishing marks of humanity lie in the complexion or turn of features" (13). Ellison may seem to be using phrases like "try" and "prove" rhetorically, while already convinced himself. However, his comments about what the slaves "deserve" hint that he is indeed suspending judgment. He approaches his reforms as a test of his slaves, and he observes the results carefully. In other words, he willingly suspends the consensus on Africans' full humanity in order to allow it to be tested. Indeed, Ellison's willingness to test the slaves' humanity can be understood as a willingness to question it.

Even Ellison's apparent denunciations of slavery tend to be slippery, as when he concedes, "this shocking subordination may be necessary in this country, but that necessity makes me hate the country" (16). Remarkably, he chooses to hate the "country" rather than the "shocking subordination" itself; he offers a moral challenge and undermines it by acceding to the "necessity" of the immoral arrangement. Such "necessity" was one of the

---

[84] Nussbaum analyzes this quotation to different effect, *Limits of the Human*, 147.

foremost defenses of slavery throughout the century. Ellison's rhetorical
choice to link the moral failure of slavery to geography and perhaps climate
connects him to a long tradition of fears of "Creole degeneration" that
could be used to explain the immorality of colonial settlers, and that
contributed to the belief in racial difference.[85]

The central test of Ellison's hypothesis comes when he offers his slaves a
new "contract." In presenting the contract, he enumerates the benefits of
being on his plantation under his new system, including safety from
corporal punishment, and pledges that "while you perform your duty . . .
I shall look upon you as free servants, or rather like my children, for whose
well-being I am anxious and watchful" (14). Here, in the phrase "free
servants," Ellison again invokes free labor as the model for his reforms,
but limits the application of this model to slaves. They will only be treated
as "free" while they behave so as to deserve such treatment. The conflation
of "servants" and "children" here is telling, undermining Ellison's earlier
implication that black slaves are rational agents and replacing it with the
implication that they must depend on his guidance. He then lays out the
punitive side of his system:

if gratitude and prudence cannot bind you to good behaviour, the first offence
shall be punished by excluding you from partaking of the next weekly holy-days;
for the second fault you shall not only be deprived of your diversion, but of a day's
food; and if these gentle corrections do not reform you, on the third offence you
shall be sold to the first purchaser, however low the price offered; and this sentence
is irreversible; no prayers, no intreaties shall move me. (15)

Testing the slaves sorts them into two groups: the "grateful" slaves who, in
the role of obedient children, will be "considered free," and the irrational
ingrates who will be removed from his familial plantation and returned to
full slave status. Ellison's system depends on an implicit notion that selling
a slave absolves him for responsibility for that slave's future treatment.
Hence, it also implies the legitimacy of the slave system, at least for the
slaves he sells off, because they have demonstrated their unworthiness in
their failure of both rationality and gratitude. And, for his punishment to
work, the slaves must fear the other plantations, presumably understanding
that their new masters will be violent.[86] Ellison never questions that the

---

[85] For a brief account of the concept of "Creole degeneration," see Wilson, *The Island Race*, 153–4; see
also Wylie Sypher, "The West Indian as 'Character' in the Eighteenth Century," *Studies in Philology*,
36:3 (1939), 503–20.

[86] Nussbaum (*Limits of the Human*, 143) and Lutz ("Commercial Capitalism," 565–6) argue that *Sir
George Ellison* cannot be claimed as anti-slavery due to this failing. Ferguson (*Subject to Others*, 104)

slaves are bound by "duty" to serve him efficiently and well. The slaves are considered "free" only in the very limited case that they cheerfully behave like slaves; once they fail in their "duty," Ellison is no longer bound to "look upon" them as "free servants" or as his children.

In presenting his contract, Ellison draws an analogy to "free workers," but makes sure to circumscribe it. He explains to the slaves that he "did not chuse to consider them as slaves," but he does not free them; instead, he warns that they will regain their slave status if "by ill behaviour they reduced him to the necessity of exerting an absolute power over them" (14), and just as he defers responsibility to the market earlier by selling "unworthy" slaves back into the slave system, he avoids it here through reversing agency in his language, and thereby making them appear to be responsible for any cases in which he exercises his "absolute power." In fact, Ellison refuses to let go of any aspect of the slave system that might benefit him, using the appeal to "necessity" to deny his responsibility, and actually changing only those aspects of the system that he believes will make his workers more productive.

Although Ellison never defines the "duty" that his slaves are bound to, or what the "offences" are that would lead to punishment, he makes clear that the slaves' failure to participate in the affective exchange he has defined shows them as failing his test of their rationality, and justifies their exclusion from the community of fully human, fully sentimental beings. Indeed, those who "force" Ellison to sell them by "offending" three times "shall become the property of some master, whose chastisements may keep within the bounds of duty the actions of that man, whose heart cannot be influenced by gratitude, or his own true interest" (15). Slaves who do not "freely" choose to act like slaves will be forced to, if by another master. Considering Ellison's "hypothesis," one wonders whether those who are guilty of such failures of reason are so "unworthy" that they need not be considered "fellow creatures" any longer. Do such failures of his test prove the reality of racial inferiority to Ellison? Clearly, Ellison is untroubled by keeping those who fail his test enslaved; they have demonstrated to his satisfaction that they do not "deserve" freedom.

A racial and cultural double standard undermines Ellison's claims of humane sympathy. Africans who fail to accept "their duties" are proving

---

more broadly rejects the classification of this text as "antislavery." Ellis (*Politics*, 87) argues that calling attention to the suffering of slaves in the 1760s is enough to classify the text as anti-slavery. Stoddard ("Serious Proposal," 383) reads Scott's concerns with education and conversion as abolitionist because preparatory to emancipation. But Brown (*Moral Capital*, 333–89) argues that the Evangelicals' change from conversionism to abolitionism was not premeditated.

themselves inferior by being "ungrateful" and "irrational," and therefore less than fully human. And yet, any Englishman who accepted the duties they reject would be debasing himself, at least according to Ellison's account of the free market for labor in England, and indeed according to Elizabeth Montagu's understanding of her miners. Here, the contradictory nature of Ellison's test becomes apparent. The very act of determining that Africans must be tested is an assertion of superiority and an assessment that they are lacking, that their humanity cannot be taken for granted. The first slave to fail three times shows that slaves cannot reason and feel (the two have become conflated when "gratitude" measures rationality) as Ellison can. The slave's reaction to his own failure shows the irrationality of his feelings: "when he found that he was really set up to sale, was almost distracted," and his assessment of his own stupidity is overly emotional, driving him out of control: "he was so enraged at his own folly that he was with difficulty restrained from doing violence to himself" (15).

Ellison, unlike this unfortunate slave, can use his reason to control his actions and his emotions. When he resolves to sell the troublesome slave, he finds that "to deny the poor wretch a farther trial grieved him to the soul; and yet he saw that strict adherence to his first declaration was absolutely necessary; he therefore resolved to endure the conflict, though not unmoved" (15). Indeed, he articulates his superiority to the slave in terms of having a greater capability for feeling, and given Scott's conflation of reason and feeling, this comes as no surprise. Although the doomed slave is driven, uncontrollably, to the brink of suicide, Ellison's capacity to be "moved" and yet controlled represents a greater emotional power. Ellison himself explains that "the poor criminal is more outrageous in his expressions, but I question whether he feels more than I do on this occasion" (16).

Ellison's conception of racial difference fills an important gap in the history of eighteenth-century thought about race. He uses the stance of scientific procedure – a hypothesis tested by empirical observation – to grant himself the reality of racial differences in the capacity for reason. The "gratitude" produced by Ellison's testing of his hypothesis marks slaves' need for his control and direction. And, lest the successful reforms accidentally imply that Africans are fully equal to Europeans, the narrator interrupts the narrative to state authoritatively that "negroes are naturally faithful and affectionate, though on great provocation, their resentment is unbounded, and they will indulge their revenge though to their own certain destruction" (17–18). Here, the lesson of the slaves who failed Ellison's test is applied broadly: the narrator assures the reader that all African slaves are irrational and unable to control their own emotions.

On reflection, one sees that the conclusion that Africans have rational and emotional capacities which are more limited (and less under their own control) than those of an English gentleman, is not only workable within, but crucial to Ellison's reforms. The reforms' production of "gratitude" would be untenable if one acknowledged the slaves' ability to recognize their own position, to see that they are indeed being threatened with violence, and, despite Ellison's obfuscation, to see that they are still very much slaves. After all, they are only preserved from the violence of the slave system as long as they keep to the same "duties" they had while enslaved; if they fall away from these "duties," they will be sent to a plantation that does not even have the pretense of freedom and that continues to use violence. Unless one accepts this view of slaves as infantile dupes, Scott's representation of the slaves as ready to "give their lives" in gratitude for Ellison's "kindness" is starkly implausible. Rather than insistently drawing attention to the moral evil of slavery, Ellison's reforms represent a paternalist fantasy: as long as the paternalist can dictate all the terms and be cheerfully obeyed, there will be no problems, including violent punishment, on the plantation. Indeed, as Alessa Johns observes, Scott in other works shows a keen awareness of the power dynamics of gratitude and obligation. Johns characterizes Scott as believing "that when generosity moves in only one direction, the person on whom gifts are lavished is in bondage."[87] And, while Scott's criticism of the brutality of plantation life must be acknowledged, at the same time, the vision of reform she presents depends on a belief in the natural irrationality and servility of Africans. Indeed, it is Scott's invocation of, and commitment to, free labor at home that ultimately demonstrates the difference of her conception of Africans, who can only be considered "free servants" for as long as they behave like happy and dutiful slaves.

Although Mackenzie's *Julia de Roubigné* (1777) was published eleven years after Scott's *History of Sir George Ellison* (1766), the similarity between the representations of slave plantation reform in the two novels is striking. Like Ellison, Mackenzie's central character, Savillon, wants the superior production of free labor and decries the inhumanity of slavery but is unwilling to renounce it. Like Ellison, he attempts to remake slavery in the image of the European system of labor relations. It is in pursuing these goals, then, that

---

[87] *Women's Utopias of the Eighteenth Century* (Urbana: University of Illinois Press, 2003), 106. Johns argues that Scott works to recuperate gratitude and benevolence from the Hobbesian model of submission. See also her overview of the critical debate on slavery in *Sir George Ellison* (*ibid.*, 94–5).

Savillon appears to free his slaves, but despite this appearance, he pulls back from his radical impulse in order to contain its results. Savillon's goal is to have his slaves "choose their work" and thereby improve production. As in the contract scenes in *Colonel Jack* and *Sir George Ellison*, this is quite typical of scenes of slave reform in the novel. All the reforms begin with a sympathetic or sentimental impulse, an impulse subsequently reined in by economic self-interest.

Savillon's reforms are ultimately shaped by the profit motive; Savillon is quite explicit about this, telling a slave that he wants a system of "chuse work" because it is both more efficient and more humane. The slave agrees that choosing work is better than being coerced, calling "chuse work no work at all."[88] In order to induce slaves to choose their work, Savillon has Yambu, who had been a prince in Africa, supervise them; Savillon then declares them free. This would seem like the most radical move possible, a step beyond mere reform, except that Savillon circumscribes this freedom, preferring "the idea of liberty," which encourages productive labor, to its more dangerous and unpredictable reality.

The limit Savillon imposes on this "liberty" is that the "former" slaves are only guaranteed their "freedom" as long as they stay on the plantation and continue to labor as they did before. When Yambu expresses a desire to return to Africa, Savillon dismisses the possibility altogether, remarking "I can not give you back your country, Yambu; but I can make this one better for you" (136). Why such a return would be impossible is unclear; nonetheless, Yambu accepts Savillon's pronouncement without questioning it further.[89] Yambu's case reveals the ambiguity of Savillon's motives for "reforming" his plantation, especially as Savillon describes his initial interest in the slave:

one slave, in particular, had for some time attracted my notice, from that gloomy fortitude with which he bore the hardships of his situation. Upon inquiring of the overseer, he told me that this slave, whom he called Yambu, though, from his youth and appearance of strength, he had been accounted valuable, yet, from the untractable stubbornness of his disposition, was worth less money than almost any other in my uncle's possession – This was a language natural to the overseer.

---

[88] Henry Mackenzie, *The Works of Henry Mackenzie, Esq.*, Vol. II: *Julia de Roubigné* (Edinburgh: R. Sholey, 1815), 136. Further citations are given parenthetically in the text.

[89] For acknowledgment that some Africans were indeed enslaved and then returned to Africa, see Sparks, *Two Princes*, 72–3. In a French novel of the late century, Joseph LaVallée, *The Negro Equalled by Few Europeans*, 4 vols., trans. anon. (London: Robinson, 1790), many African characters, including former slaves, travel between Africa, England, and the West Indies.

I answered him, in his own style, that I hoped to improve his price some hundreds of livres. (134)

Yambu's "gloomy fortitude" appeals to Savillon both sentimentally, in revealing suffering, and practically, in hinting at an ability to endure slavery. Savillon ironically, even parodically, adopts the language of the overseer, discussing Yambu in terms of his cash value. And yet, he sets about doing just what he has ironically said he would: making Yambu far more financially valuable to his uncle.

Savillon tells the slaves that they are free, and that Yambu is to be their only overseer. Nonetheless, he induces them to stay on and work the plantation under the same terms as slavery. They are freed, given shelter, and allotted provision grounds, just like slaves; the difference is that they are allowed the option of "leaving." This is never explored further. However, Savillon shows that he does not see leaving as a viable option for the slaves when he reveals his system of discipline. The only discipline is the same as the ultimate discipline in *Colonel Jack* and *Sir George Ellison*. Savillon explains to the "freed" slaves that "they were at liberty to go; and that if they were found idle or unworthy, they should not be allowed to stay" (138). Savillon reveals the emptiness of the "liberty" he offers by presenting leaving the plantation as both a punishment and proof of liberation in the same sentence. And, in effect, Savillon's system of "chuse work" ultimately only binds the "freed" slaves more tightly to him; as he boasts, "I am under no apprehension of desertion or mutiny; they work with the willingness of freedom, yet are mine with more than the obligation of slavery" (138). Savillon only makes the gesture of "freeing" his slaves in order to allow them to choose their exploitation "freely." Indeed, his statement that "they work with the willingness of freedom, yet are mine with more than the obligation of slavery" could stand as a deconstruction of the trope of the grateful slave.

Adam Smith's use of free labor to critique slavery gives the lie to Savillon's attempt to get the advantages of free labor out of his slaves. As we have seen, Smith attributes rational agency equally to free laborers and slaves regardless of race or origin. Savillon's system of pseudo-freedom, like Ellison's, could not convince rational laborers that they are producing in their own interest; ultimately, the attempt to wed the incentives of freedom with the non-market basis of slavery, in Smith's conception at least, is doomed to failure. Could laborers with no other option really "choose" their work? By presenting this system as effective, Mackenzie implies that slaves are less rational than Europeans, and are therefore capable of being duped through their propensity to gratitude.

Sentimental depictions of slave reform loudly insist that they are recognizing African humanity, but in fact they are carefully circumscribing it. Each
novel insists on the naturalness of Africans' dependence and "gratitude" to
a master, as long as that master is (relatively) kind. Each, then, departs from
the prevailing consensus on the full equality of Africans to imagine meaningful distinctions between human groups. They underwrite the distinction in a form more subtle than slavery's most radical propagandists,
because rather than openly declaring Africans inferior, they merely imply
that the African version of humanity is one which happens to justify
slavery. They elide it by focusing more attention on the reformers' initial
sentimental recognition of shared affective structures than on the ultimate
conception of Africans as naturally inclined to dependence and gratitude.

The reformers' "hypothetical" approach to racial difference is analogous
to those thinkers in the late eighteenth and early nineteenth centuries who
bridged the gap between the "monogenist" idea of a unified human race, and
"polygenist" insistence on absolute difference between races. Thinkers like
Samuel Estwick and Thomas Jefferson, while nominally monogenists,
emphasized difference between groups and claimed empirical authority for
doing so. In 1785 Thomas Jefferson did not attempt to account for the
circularity of observing slaves and then declaring them slavish, paradoxically
insisting that "it would be unfair to follow them to Africa for this investigation." He concluded that Africans lack creative intelligence because,
among slaves, "never yet could I find that a black had uttered a thought
above the level of plain narration."[90] Of course, the illogic of Jefferson's use
of Africa here would not be lost on late eighteenth-century readers, as many
abolitionists made exactly the opposite point, that the situation of slavery,
rather than race or African origin, could explain any observed differences.

These novels, too, articulate a pseudo-empirical claim of racial difference, while making a great show of their monogenist assumptions. Indeed,
the starting point for the articulation of the difference between European
and African workers in these novels representing plantation reform is
paradoxically the moment when the reformer's sympathy seems engaged
with the shared humanity of African slaves. The most paradoxical element
of this assertion of slaves' humanity is that it would be meaningless unless
that humanity were also being called into question. In each representation
of plantation reform, the master (or overseer) begins to see the slaves as

---

[90] *Notes on the State of Virginia*, 1785, ed. Frank Shuffleton (New York: Penguin, 1999), 146–7.

potentially human when he recognizes their suffering. Once this recognition takes place, the slaves' humanity, and their value, can be tested in two ways: by measuring their capacity for sentiment, through their ability to show "gratitude," and their capacity for reason through their ability to act on their self-interest. Each representation of reform conflates these two tests. Masters test their slaves by being kinder, even abolishing corporal punishment. In response, slaves can show gratitude by being good, dutiful, productive workers. If they do so, they also show that they are rational: after all, it is in their self-interest to help the masters maintain their "kinder" regime.

The standards for this test of the slaves' "rationality" are already different than the standards that would apply to Europeans, however. Europeans would be expected to value their freedom too highly – and to need their independence too much – to accept slavery, however "kindly" it was made to seem. Indeed, European workers would be expected to be more productive when left to their own devices to develop "independence."[91] In contrast, within the terms of the reform system, slaves' rationality and their affective ability can be tested simultaneously through "gratitude"; reason and feeling become conflated as the basic measure of humanity. And, in the very act of testing the slaves, the consensus on the full humanity of slaves is undermined, and a sense of almost scientifically verified difference begins to emerge.

So, paradoxically, the moment that a master claims to recognize his slaves' humanity – rather than taking it for granted – is the same moment that the master begins to articulate a difference from – a superiority to – the slaves. Only the master can create the circumstances that allow the slaves to demonstrate their shared humanity. And, of course, the very act of testing the slaves is an articulation of superiority: in that act, the master claims the ability to judge and understand the slaves totally. But the superiority of the judge is not the whole story: once slaves have shown their humanity, they still need masters, so they can continue to demonstrate their humanity by showing their gratitude in the act of serving. Masters comprehend slaves; slaves can only respond to masters. Ultimately, amelioration (at least as represented in the eighteenth-century British novel) becomes an argument not for equality, but for paternalism: it claims to demonstrate that while African slaves are human, with basic affective capacities, they are nonetheless incapable of the "independence" so highly valued in European workers, as suggested by Ellison's conflation of "servants" and "children." Because only gratitude demonstrates slaves' humanity, paradoxically, they must

---

[91] See chapter 2, n. 24 above.

remain slaves, so that they will continue to have masters who can elicit their gratitude. This conception of difference only becomes possible with the emergence of free-labor ideology, which establishes the alternative against which to articulate the system appropriate for African slaves.

These seemingly humanitarian, sentimental representations of plantation slavery, then, were not intended to feed the fires of abolition. Instead of undermining slavery, these representations imagine slavery as a more humane, more productive, and therefore as a more durable institution. Instead of undermining the practical distinctions between black and white that emerged in the late seventeenth century, the apparent sentimental recognition of slaves' humanity actually helps move toward the ossification of those distinctions. This sentimental recognition disguises racial distinctions under the monogenist claim of a common humanity while nonetheless helping to undermine a standing consensus that more fully recognized African humanity. Paradoxically, the reforms stemming from the sentimental recognition ultimately develop into a pseudo-empirical "verification" of practical racial differences, and of the very differences that would justify, even necessitate, the continuation of slavery. Slave reform in the eighteenth-century British novel, then, despite beginning with a sentimental critique of slavery, ends by insisting that slavery must be preserved for the benefit of both masters and slaves, and implying that Africans are somehow less human, less endowed with reason and feeling, than Europeans – but never explicitly confronting or rejecting the doctrine of monogenesis to do so. Unlike Estwick, who was too direct, despite rhetorical posturing, to succeed with his challenge to the consensus on race, these novels are subtle enough, and insistent enough on their sentimental credentials, to communicate their underlying view of race to their metropolitan audience.

CHAPTER 4

The 1780s: transition

The 1780s were a period of transition in approaches to race. The grateful slave fictions of the 1780s, reflecting the sudden ubiquity of slavery as a topic for debate, and the variety of positions on it, were at once ambiguous and adventurous. Grateful slavery became ever more familiar, and inspired tests, variations, even refutations. Its underlying concept of racial difference (nominally contained within monogenesis), however, began to displace the earlier consensus on shared humanity in this decade. The 1780s produced both the apotheosis of grateful slave fictions and the most searching, experimental versions of it. The work of philosopher Raynal, although first published in the 1770s, in his ambiguous and contradictory views of both race and slavery, emphasized in the editions of the 1780s, perhaps best captures the contentious, chaotic, and ultimately transitional views of both slavery and racial difference characteristic of the decade. The emerging philosophical consensus on the reality of racial difference, to which Raynal contributed, did not enter into the mainstream of discourse, even of discourse on slavery, until the 1790s. Two abolitionist thinkers, James Ramsay and his follower Richard Nisbet, show the centrality of the issues raised by the grateful slave to the polemical literature of the 1780s. Both resist the idea that racial difference is a reality, and yet endorse ameliorationism and many aspects of grateful slavery. Both see slaves as needing to be guided toward Christianity and improvement, but argue that their need for guidance is the result of the degrading effects of slavery rather than any essential quality.

PHILOSOPHICAL CONSENSUS

In the 1780s, as the grateful slave began to serve as the basis for polemical variations in fiction, a philosophical consensus on racial difference arose, the terms of which had previously been defined in earlier representations of the grateful slave – that blacks, while sharing in human emotions, are less rational and more emotional than whites. The concept of meaningful differences between races – differences ambiguously contained within the doctrine of monogenesis – although still controversial became culturally familiar. This development is illustrated in the striking similarities in the conceptions of race in key texts by a trio of prominent Enlightenment thinkers: Jefferson's *Notes on the State of Virginia* (1785), Kant's "Was Ist Aufklarung" (1784), and Raynal's *Histoire des Deux Indes*.[1] All three draw different implications for slavery from their quite similar conceptions of race. All also have much in common with Samuel Estwick's suggestion that the difference between black and white can be found in whites' superior ability to exercise the shared capacity of moral sense. Indeed, their clearest difference from Estwick is in their greater willingness to postulate seemingly essential differences.

Raynal is the most outspoken of the three, both in his attacks on slavery and in his articulation of racial difference. And yet while Kant and Jefferson work more indirectly, often by implication, they appear much more deeply committed to racial difference. For Kant, even a "universal" definition of "enlightenment" must exclude some as incapable of it: "Enlightenment is man's emergence from his self-imposed nonage. Nonage is the inability to use one's own understanding with another's guidance. This nonage is self-imposed if its cause lies not in lack of understanding but in indecision and lack of courage to use one's mind without another's guidance."[2] Here, Kant leaves open the possibility that for some an inherent "lack of understanding" could make enlightenment an unreachable goal.[3] Such people must remain forever in a state of nonage, of child-like dependence on their betters.

[1] Raynal's work was first published in 1770, in English translation in 1776 in Edinburgh, and in a more influential English translation of a revised French edition in 1782. I will cite from *A Philosophical and Political History of the Settlements and Trade of the Europeans in the East and West Indies*, 6 vols. (Edinburgh: W. Gordon *et al.*, 1782). All my citations below are from vol. IV. I use the short title *Histoire des Deux Indes* in deference to scholarly convention.

[2] Immanuel Kant, "What is Enlightenment," trans. Peter Gay, in *The Enlightenment: A Comprehensive Anthology*, ed. Peter Gay (New York: Simon and Schuster, 1973), 384.

[3] For the argument that Kant helped disseminate the idea of race as an indicator of serious differences, particularly in intellectual and rational capacities, see Emmanuel Chukwudi Eze, "The Color of Reason: The Idea of 'Race' in Kant's Anthropology," in *Anthropology and the German Enlightenment: Perspectives on Humanity*, ed. Katherine M. Faull (Lewisburg, PA: Bucknell University Press, 1995), 200–41; and Robert Bernasconi, "Who Invented the Concept of Race? Kant's Role in the Enlightenment Construction of Race," in *Race*, ed. Robert Bernasconi (Boston: Blackwell, 2001), 11–36, and "Kant as an Unfamiliar Source of Racism," in *Philosophers on Race*, ed. Julie K. Ward and Tommy L. Lott (Oxford: Blackwell, 2002), 145–66. Sankar Muthu, *Enlightenment Against Empire* (Princeton: Princeton University Press, 2003), 180–4, 312 n. 21, contends that such readings miss the full context of Kant's work, especially his later "anti-imperialism."

In other writings, Kant indicates that the ability to mature fully is not universal: "in the hot countries the human being matures in all aspects earlier, but does not, however, reach the perfection of those in the temperate zones."[4] And this is not merely a question of geography, but becomes essentialized in "racial" terms. Kant claims "the difference between these two races of man" as "fundamental," adding that "it appears to be as great in regard to mental capacities as in color."[5] In sum, then, for Kant, theoretically, Africans' nonage is not merely "self-imposed" due to a failure of will. Unlike Europeans, Africans cannot leave their nonage, because it is their natural limit, and should be understood as permanent. Still, echoing Estwick and grateful slave texts, Kant describes the mental difference in terms of "capacities" rather than faculties. If one resituates this logic in the context of slavery, it parallels, in much blunter terms, the ameliorationist position that Africans benefit from, indeed require, the "guidance" of European masters. If Africans are incapable of emerging from "nonage" by individual acts of will, and they continue to live in the colonies, not only is slavery justifiable, it is necessary. Africans, stuck forever in a state of "nonage," permanently require the guidance of enlightened masters.

Thomas Jefferson, in *Notes on the State of Virginia*, theorizes racial difference through rationality, linking rationality to emotion, and, even more like Estwick and the grateful slave novelists than Kant, discriminating by implication between the capacity to experience emotions and the ability to manage them. Jefferson, like Kant, suggests that blacks are "in reason much inferior" to "whites." In accord with eighteenth-century rhetorical norms, he presents this as a "hypothesis" rather than a fact.[6] According to Jefferson, Africans' emotional (and to some extent, moral) capacities are not as limited as their access to reason: "we find among them numerous instances of the most rigid integrity, and as many as among their better instructed masters, of benevolence, gratitude, and unshaken fidelity" (150). An appearance of greater intrepidity is the deceptive product of their limited capacities: "They are at least as brave, and more adventuresome. But this may perhaps proceed from a want of forethought, which prevents their seeing a danger till it be present. When present, they do not go

[4] Immanuel Kant, from *Physical Geography*, trans. K. M. Faull and E. C. Eze, in *Race and the Enlightenment*, ed. E. C. Eze (Boston: Blackwell, 1997), 63. *Physical Geography* is undated, because it is a posthumous reconstruction from lecture notes. I quote from the anthology because it provides an original English translation.

[5] Immanuel Kant, "Section Four: Of National Characteristics, so Far as They Depend on the Sublime and the Beautiful," in *Observations on the Feeling of the Beautiful and Sublime*, 1763, trans. John T. Goldthwait (Berkeley: University of California Press, 1960), 111.

[6] Jefferson, *Notes on the State of Virginia*, 146.

through it with more coolness or steadiness than the whites" (146). Further-more, Jefferson claims, while "they are more ardent after their female," nonetheless "love seems with them to be more an eager desire, than a tender delicate mixture of sentiment and sensation" (146). In the end, Africans' emotional – and sensual – capacities actually explain their failure to be rational. Jefferson remarks that "their existence appears to participate more of sensation than reflection" (146), suggesting that even such potentially admirable qualities as love of music and intensity of experience are actually products of a physical, as opposed to mental or rational, orientation.

Jefferson links these observations, famously, to two implications: (1) that slavery, though lamentable, cannot be abolished swiftly; and (2) that colonization will be necessary if slavery is to be ended, because resentment and prejudice will make peaceful coexistence between black and white impossible after emancipation.[7] Despite his much more strident position, and tone, on slavery, the Abbé Raynal works from strikingly similar premises about the nature and reality of racial difference. In fact, Raynal likely influenced Jefferson;[8] Raynal begins his section on African slavery in the Americas by opining that Africans are suited to slavery for the same reasons that Jefferson later adduces. Raynal asserts, without even the pretense of offering a hypothesis, that Africans are too passionate to be reasonable: "their intellectual faculties being nearly exhausted, by the excesses of sensual pleasures, they have neither memory nor understanding to supply, by art, the deficiency of their strength" (13). Again, Raynal attributes the same "intellectual faculties" to blacks as to whites, but attempts to account for a difference in the usage of these faculties. Nonetheless, he also

---

[7] Annette Gordon-Reed observes that Jefferson provides quotations which can be used to associate him with any position on slavery and race: see *Thomas Jefferson and Sally Hemings: An American Controversy* (Charlottesville: University of Virginia Press, 1997), 109. For views of Jefferson's equivocations as politically minded, see Davis, *Age of Revolution*, 175–7, and Frank J. Ellis, *American Sphinx: The Character of Thomas Jefferson* (New York: Knopf, 1997), 85–8, 145–9. John Chester Miller, in the classic study, *The Wolf By the Ears: Thomas Jefferson and Slavery*, 1977 (Charlottesville: University of Virginia Press, 1991), sees Jefferson as immersed in the culture of slavery but genuinely desiring to end it. *Jeffersonian Legacies*, ed. Peter Onuf (Charlottesville: University of Virginia Press, 1993) contains three useful essays about Jefferson, slavery, and race: Lucia Stanton, "'The Blessings of Domestic Society': Thomas Jefferson and His Slaves" (147–80), a detailed account of his management and treatment of his slaves; Paul Finkelman, "Jefferson and Slavery: 'Treason Against the Hopes of the World'" (181–221) a skeptical account of his anti-slavery credentials; and Scot A. French and Edward L. Ayers, "The Strange Career of Thomas Jefferson: Race and Slavery in American Memory, 1943–1993" (418–56), a history of scholarly and popular views of Jefferson. See also Ari Helo and Peter Onuf, "Jefferson, Morality, and the Problem of Slavery," *William and Mary Quarterly*, 60:3 (2003), 583–614, and John Saillant, "The American Enlightenment in Africa: Jefferson's Colonizationism and Black Virginians' Migration to Liberia, 1776–1840," *Eighteenth-Century Studies*, 31:3 (1998), 261–82.
[8] See Davis, *Age of Revolution*, 175–7 and 176 n. 18.

offers an early and unusual pseudo-scientific claim for blackness as the basis of difference, claiming that Africans' sperm is black (14). In common with many of the apologists who follow Snelgrave, Raynal contends that in Africa all individuals are held in political slavery by their despots (20, 57–8), but contradicts this point by also echoing Anthony Benezet and commending examples of African "democracy" (17).[9] Raynal also follows the most damning claim of Hume's (a claim repeated by Long and Jefferson, and central to the views of Kant and Hegel) in asserting that "arts are unknown among them" (22).

Raynal's work is riddled with contradictions, and never settles on a single point of view on race or slavery.[10] Indeed, scholars agree that Raynal's authorship was a convenient fiction, fixing credit and responsibility for a work produced by a committee; some prefer to treat Diderot as the author.[11] It is no surprise that such a work is unstable and contradicts itself endlessly; perhaps its importance should be seen in its most original, provocative, and influential statements, rather than in underlying theories that can be teased out with close reading. Raynal, like a surprising number of slavery's apologists, undermines the concept of difference he seems to advocate by arguing that Creole slaves are superior (as does even Edward Long), and builds this toward a point crucial to the late-century ameliorationist consensus: that natural reproduction should be encouraged with imports of women (52). But he then makes a sudden radical move developing this idea in a direction outside the pale for Jefferson and Long by borrowing a principle from agricultural science to contend that cross-breeding the races will strengthen both (77).[12] This embrace of miscegenation (to use an anachronism) is striking in light of the argument that Estwick's and Long's entries in the debate about Somerset were meant to

[9] On the importance of these opposed positions, see my essay "Olaudah Equiano and the Eighteenth-Century Debate on Africa," *Eighteenth-Century Studies*, 40:2 (2007), 241–55.

[10] For varying views of Raynal's contradictions, see Robin Blackburn, *Overthrow of Colonial Slavery 1776–1848* (London: Verso, 1988), 53–4, 243; Srinivas Aravamudan, "Tropicalizing the Enlightenment," in *Tropicopolitans*, 289–331, esp. 297 and 303; Gould, *Barbaric Traffic*, 32. Davis, *Western Culture*, 13–19, treats the text as ultimately coherent.

[11] For accounts of the compositional process, see Davis, *Western Culture*, 13–14 n. 24, and Aravamudan, "Tropicalizing," 293. Muthu, *Enlightenment* 72–3, 295 n. 2, analyzes only those contributions identified as Diderot's; Blackburn sees the radical anti-slavery passages as authored by Jean de Péchmèja (*New World Slavery*, 53–4).

[12] Gordon S. Wood documents Jefferson's "deep fear of racial mixing" in "The Ghosts of Monticello," in *Sally Hemings & Thomas Jefferson: History, Memory and Civic Culture*, ed. Jan Ellen Lewis and Peter S. Onuf (Charlottesville: University of Virginia Press, 1999), 22–3. Gordon-Reed argues that Jefferson viewed Mulattoes as superior to blacks, but only due to their white blood (*American Controversy*, 140).

generate fears of miscegenation.[13] Raynal again repeats conventional anti-slavery wisdom in suggesting that white Creoles are spoiled by having unlimited power over the slaves who must serve them (81).

Oddly enough, Raynal then tacks back to an anti-racist position reminiscent of Equiano and of early critics of slavery such as Woolman and Wesley, suggesting that slavery and white supremacy depend entirely on physical domination figured as "superiority." Raynal deconstructs this notion of "superiority" by assuming the voice of a slave to issue the anti-racist warning that making such "superiority" a justification for slavery in fact authorizes slaves to resist violently. Dominating slaves by sheer force – the basis of slavery and white privilege – is tantamount to begging to be stabbed or poisoned:

> If thou thinkest thyself authorized to oppress me, because thou art stronger and more ingenious than I am; do not complain if my vigorous arm shall plunge a dagger into thy breast; do not complain, when in thy tortured entrails thou shalt feel the pangs of death conveyed by poison into thy food: I am stronger and more ingenious than thou: fall a victim, therefore, in thy turn; and expiate thy crime of having been an oppressor. (55)

The false claim of superiority, supported by force, will inevitably collapse. Not only is the system untenable and ultimately self-destructive, but it is premised on a denial of humanity: "He who supports the system of slavery, is the enemy of the whole human race. He divides it into two societies of legal assassins" (55).

Despite this blazing rhetoric, suggesting that any support for slavery is a crime against humanity, Raynal also contends, like a grateful slave novelist, that "enlightened reason" demands the "reformation" of slavery, that making slavery "easy" is the safer and more profitable course (49). Nonetheless, the memory of such equivocation is obliterated by Raynal's most radical, and influential moments, his prophetic visions of slaves exacting vengeance. He follows a list of acts of slave resistance (massacres, marronage, suicide, poisonings) by announcing: "These enterprises are so many indications of the impending storm; and the Negroes only want a chief, sufficiently courageous, to lead them on to vengeance and slaughter" (61).

Jefferson and Raynal, then, have more in common in their discussions of race and slavery than their reputations would suggest. Both hypothesize meaningful racial difference, and the likelihood of slave rebellion. The difference is primarily in their attitudes toward slaves' vengeance, as Raynal

---

[13] Shyllon, *Black Slaves*, 151–2.

assumes the voice of an oppressed slave and enters a prophetic mode, while Jefferson, perhaps remembering Raynal's prophecies, warns that "ten thousand recollections, by the blacks, of the injuries they have sustained; new provocations; the real distinctions nature has made; and many other circumstances, will divide us into parties, and produce convulsions which will probably never end but in the extermination of one or the other race" (145). Unlike Raynal, of course, Jefferson sees this as evidence not of blacks' humanity but of the impossibility of incorporating them as citizens of Virginia and the United States, not as evidence of the criminal nature of the slave system but as "a powerful obstacle to the emancipation of these people" (151).

Taken together, these Enlightenment thinkers outline a logic of racial difference nearly identical to that implied by novelists' proposed senti-mental reforms of plantation slavery. In the eighteenth-century British novel, African slaves may be "human" and sympathetic, because they are "grateful." Gratitude is initially invoked to demonstrate slaves' emotional faculties but also to suggest that their capacity to manage this faculty, to harness it to reason, is weaker than that of Europeans. Raynal, echoed by Jefferson, adds the warning that slaves' untrammeled vengeance is as likely as gratitude to develop out of the master–slave relationship. Raynal directs his warning to masters, claiming that slaves' very humanity will lead to bloodshed. Jefferson, on the other hand, sees difference as one of the causes of the coming conflict and seems to suggest that emancipation will hasten conflict.

Despite their striking similarities, these philosophers should not be taken as indicating the arrival of a broader cultural consensus on race in the 1780s. Neither should they be seen as originating such ideas. Instead, the philoso-phers' unusually open suggestions of racial difference can be understood as expressions of ideas already available in the culture, if in less overt forms, as seen in the examples of Estwick's pamphlet and the early grateful slave fictions. It is the philosophers' commitment to following taxonomic logic rigorously, and their willingness to ignore the theological implications of their positions, that allows them relative directness of expression. Such approaches, for all the attention paid to "Enlightenment" thought and methods, never became mainstream in the century. Indeed, even these philosophers share with most fiction writers and pamphleteers a tendency to evade overt statements of belief in racial difference. They illuminate other writers, however, by couching their suggestions of difference more directly, even as they invoke scientific language to contain their most radical sugges-tions as mere "hypotheses."

As one might expect, the large increase in attention to slavery in the 1780s brings with it a much greater diversity in approaches and positions. Although the tendency to favor amelioration and the fascination with exploiting slave "gratitude" continues and evolves, new trends emerge. One is a focus on the gratuitous cruelty of masters, often contrasted with the kindness and "humanity" of certain slaves; and another, as might be expected, is the emergence of a more and more thoroughly racialized discourse on the difference between slaves and their masters. In the plantation novels of the 1780s, the theory that "blacks," while fully capable of emotion, are different even in this capacity, because their emotions have a more powerful effect on them, and are less apt to be restrained by reason, is both championed and called into question.

1780S FICTION: APOTHEOSIS AND CRITIQUE

Unsurprisingly, given the philosophical consensus which reveals both the increasing visibility of, and the continuing discomfort caused by, ideas of racial difference in the culture of the time, the grateful slave story reached its apotheosis in the 1780s, in a form that, while still indirect, underlined more firmly than ever before its racial implications. Lucy Peacock's short fiction "The Creole" (1786) represents the relationship between a "good mistress," Mrs. Harriot Sedley, and her slaves as being fundamentally a relationship of "gratitude." Peacock's narrative ultimately draws a clear distinction between the gratitude of slaves and the gratitude of masters. Mrs. Sedley, the narrator of Peacock's tale, sets the scene, suggesting a long-standing familial relationship between the slaves and her parents: "many of the negroes had grown old in my father's service; and though their lives had passed with labour, gentleness and kind treatment had rendered the toil light."[14] Soon enough, this claim is put to the test. Mrs. Sedley's husband drains her resources and flees the island. As a consequence, she must take action that will show just how "grateful" her slaves really are for her family's past "kindness." Mrs. Sedley makes a speech to her slaves, explaining that she will have to sell the plantation. Despite her financial problems, she has decided not to sell them: "my friends, you are from this moment free. Liberty is all your poor mistress has to bestow on you; all she has now left to recompense you for your faithful services" (129). As hard as it is to imagine that slaves would not desire liberty, Peacock's representation gets only less

---

[14] Lucy Peacock, "The Creole," in *The Rambles of Fancy; Or Moral and Interesting Tales*, vol. II (London: T. Bensley, 1786), 111–77, here 127. Further citations are given parenthetically in the text.

plausible, as the slaves themselves seem to share Sedley's implied opinion that they hardly desire freedom at all: "Not a dry eye was seen among them: so far from being elated with the freedom offered them, they seemed desirous of rushing again into slavery, that I might reap the benefit arising from the sale of them" (129–30).

Not only do Mrs. Sedley's slaves wish to deny their freedom, but they even wish for what is often represented as the ultimate punishment on plantation: being sold off and sold apart. Although the emphasis here is on the slaves' collective emotional reaction, the practical result is close to the vision of many slavery pamphleteers who suggest moving from a system of market-based chattel slavery to enserfment.[15] The slaves' display of gratitude paradoxically confirms Mrs. Sedley's desire to free them; as she explains, "this striking instance of their gratitude served only to confirm me in my resolution" (130). Ultimately, Sedley, in need of a caretaker for her infant, bends from this overly harsh determination, "allowing" one young female slave to stay on. However, whatever her intentions, Sedley's insistence on freeing the slaves only serves to increase their gratitude, and their dedication, and even their economic value to her.

On being freed, the ex-slaves immediately become wage-laborers, although the nature of their work is never discussed. However, the ex-slaves' resolution on employing their new wages is represented in detail, as they immediately offer the money to their unfortunate ex-mistress. Mrs. Sedley is unsure how to respond. As she explains, "at first, I absolutely rejected their generous offer; but, finding that my refusal sensibly afflicted them, I consented to accept a third part of the money they offered" (131). Having acquiesced initially, Mrs. Sedley finds the slaves' help increasingly difficult to refuse:

> they constantly persisted in devoting to me the above portion of their wages ... my acceptance of their services seemed to afford them the highest pleasure they were capable of enjoying ... [For] twelve years ... I continued, therefore, entirely supported by the affectionate negroes, by whose assistance I was supplied, not only with the necessaries, but, I may add, even with the comforts of life. This state of dependence was, however, to an ingenuous mind, painful and humiliating. (131–2)

Here, Mrs. Sedley shows that in her understanding the meanings of gratitude for the planter class and the slaves and ex-slaves are crucially different. The slaves enact their "gratitude" for kind treatment with emotional displays, open tears, and financial support of their former mistress.

---

[15] This is a solution proposed by the very influential Dr. James Ramsay, whose central statement, *Essay on the Treatment and Conversion*, will be discussed in more detail below.

Indeed, being able to act on their gratitude demonstrates the upper limits of their capacities, evoking "the highest pleasure they were capable of enjoying." Mrs. Sedley, on the other hand, reacts to their kindness with a "gratitude" that takes the primary form of being painful and shameful to her. Peacock's language here points to the Estwickian concept of differing capacities, especially in the wording of "highest" and "capable." The simultaneous presence of imputed equality (in the presence of feelings) and implication of difference (in the capacities to experience and control them) is clear in this wording.

One reason that the ex-slaves' "gratitude" is not shown as equally painful and humiliating is that none of them becomes a developed character with a psychic interiority investigated by the narrator; we have no access to the ex-slaves' unspoken thoughts in this story. Nonetheless, none of the eighteenth-century novels that do make slaves (or African-descended characters generally) into protagonists ever show their gratitude as anything other than a source of pride and pleasure for them, as we shall see in chapter 6 below. Why is "gratitude" humiliating to Europeans but joyful to slaves? Mrs. Sedley's pain is not simply caused by a change in roles. She was once their master, but now is dependent on them. Of course, even as a master, she was actually dependent on their labor. The substantive change is that she is now dependent on their voluntary support, whereas before, as slaves, they had no choice in the matter. Therefore, Mrs. Sedley's "pain" and "humiliation" point to a surprisingly consistent representation of excessive gratitude as a sign of racial difference. The experience of gratitude is humiliating to Mrs. Sedley because she is white, and because that makes it impossible for her to accept dependence as anything but degradation. On the other hand, gratitude is the "highest pleasure" the slaves are "capable of enjoying."

"Gratitude" is a problem even when whites are not grateful to slaves, but to other whites, as another incident in "The Creole" illustrates. Mrs. Sedley's son falls in love with the daughter of a wealthy captain who has been a benefactor to him and his mother. This gratitude becomes the source of intense misery to him; he explains his dilemma to his mother, saying "No, my mother, rather let me lose her for ever, than, by baseness and ingratitude, cease to deserve her" (138). Sedley's son is tormented by his gratitude. It is a sign of his (prior) dependence on the captain, of his inability to exist as a fully independent being. Being forced to depend on another marks him as socially inferior. Happily for Sedley's son, the captain is kindhearted and unconventional, remarking to Mrs. Sedley, "if they love each other, why, my dear friend . . . should we prevent their happiness?" (139). Still, knowing that he owed the captain a debt of gratitude forces the poor young man to acknowledge the captain's right, if he had chosen to exercise it, to prevent him from marrying his daughter, and this weakness and dependency cause the young man pain.

Thomas Day, writing the novel *Sandford and Merton* during the 1780s (1783–9), offers a reversal of the grateful slave paradigm: Day is concerned to argue that the ill-effects of power (whether one is a slave owner or merely a British gentleman) can be overcome by learning to be grateful. He does not, in the novel, address the questions of the practicalities of power in the colonies or on a plantation, preferring to theorize their effects while his novel is set in London. But he strongly opposes the notion that gratitude is inappropriate for gentlemen, precisely because he believes that "gratitude" can undermine a gentleman's status. The central plot of the novel is the education of a young gentleman, Tommy Merton, out of the arrogance, conceit, prejudice, and ingratitude resulting from his upbringing on a West Indian plantation.[16] The book ends with Tommy making a full acknowledgment of what he owes to a "mere" farmer's son, Harry Sandford:

> Tommy arose, and, with the sincerest gratitude, bade adieu to Harry and all the rest. I shall not be long without you, said he to Harry; to your example I owe most of the little good that I can boast; you have taught me how much better it is to be useful than rich or fine; how much more amiable to be good than great.[17]

Crucially to Day's project, Tommy's ability to experience "sincerest gratitude" – or gratitude that was sincere at all – is premised on his ability to embrace a new system of values, "taught" to him by Harry Sandford, in which "usefulness" becomes the primary value for assessing people, rather than wealth, social position, or race.

Day's central concern in presenting Tommy's education is laying the groundwork for this scene. His goal is to destroy the empty pride of class and replace it with value for manliness, merit, and accomplishment – indeed for "usefulness."[18] Is Day taking the traditional position that the true gentleman is he who can acknowledge gratitude to an inferior without

---

[16] On this trope in eighteenth-century fiction, see Trumpener, *Bardic Nationalism*, 169.

[17] Citations, given below in text, are to the reprint of the first edition: Thomas Day, *The History of Sandford and Merton*, 3 vols., 1783–1789, ed. Isaac Kramnick (New York: Garland, 1977), III:308.

[18] Barker-Benfield agrees that the goal is to undo Tommy's pride of class, and his penchant for effeminizing luxury, but he sees this as a sign of Day's middle-class paternalism (*Culture of Sensibility*, 150–4). See also Mona Scheuermann, *Social Protest in the Eighteenth-Century English Novel* (Columbus: Ohio State University Press, 1985), 60–1. Day, through *Sandford and Merton*, is widely seen as an anti-aristocratic, middle-class propagandist, for instance, by David Cannadine in *The Rise and Fall of Class in Britain* (New York: Columbia University Press, 1999), 34. Anne Chandler challenges such interpretations, seeing Tommy as having been "brought up as a girl"

compromising his own position?[19] I would argue that he is not. Instead, Day rejects the very idea of the gentleman. Day's mouthpiece in the story, the boys' tutor, Rev. Barlow, "instead of widening the distance which fortune has placed between one part of mankind and another, ... was continually intent upon bringing the two classes nearer together" (II:211). Ultimately, then, Day does not dispute the idea that gratitude undermines one's status as a gentleman. Instead, he embraces the notion, and then sets out to undermine gentlemanly status in general, replacing it with the merit-based category of "usefulness." He embraces the socially leveling power of gratitude rather than warning against it, but at the same time, he dissociates gratitude from irrationality.[20] Rather than being irrational, gratitude allows the possibility of transcending one's familiar social position, escaping social prejudice, and learning to judge others by the rational standard of "usefulness."[21]

For Day, "usefulness" and "gratitude" undermine not only class distinctions but also slavery. Day was most famous in the 1780s for his attacks on slavery, especially the poem "The Dying Negro," but in *Sandford and Merton* he folds his questioning of slavery into his larger attack on social and economic distinctions in general.[22] In order to challenge Tommy's belief in the validity of slavery, Barlow asks him "how came these people to be slaves?" Tommy responds "because my father bought them with his money" (I:66). Barlow presses Tommy on the point asking, "if I take you to another country in a ship, I shall have the right to sell you?" and Tommy responds by saying "No but you won't, sir, because I was born a gentleman" (I:67). From this point, Barlow takes the strategy of emptying the idea of the "gentleman" of its social force: "what do you mean by that, Tommy? Why, said Tommy, a little confounded, to have a fine house, and fine cloaths, and a coach, and a great deal of money, as my papa has" (I:67). By accepting this as an adequate definition of "gentleman," Barlow backs

---

and being educated into masculinity; see "Defying 'Development': Thomas Day's Queer Curriculum in *Sandford and Merton*," in *Novel Gazing: Queer Readings in Fiction*, ed. Eve Kosofsky Sedgwick (Durham, NC: Duke University Press, 1997), 205.

[19] See Stewart, "Ingratitude in *Tom Jones*."

[20] Sandra Burr, "Science and Imagination in Anglo-American Children's Books, 1760–1855" (Ph.D. diss., The College of William and Mary, 2005), 92–3, sees Barlow's project of scientific education as premised on making Tommy "aware of, and grateful for, his access to privilege."

[21] Burr argues that Tommy's initial ingratitude represents human nature's lack of firmness and consistency (*ibid.*, 100–101).

[22] Carey reads of Day's use of sentiment to oppose both slavery and racial prejudice (*British Abolitionism*, 68–71). Anne Chandler, "Pedagogical Fantasies: Rousseau, Maleness, and Domesticity in the Fiction of Thomas Day, Maria Edgeworth, and Mary Wollstonecraft" (Ph.D. diss., Duke University, 1995), 62, reads Day as personally identifying with slaves. Burr sees an allusion to the issues of the slave trade in the abuse of horses ("Science and Imagination," 96).

Tommy into a logical corner: "Then if you were no longer to have a fine house, nor fine cloaths, nor a great deal of money, somebody that had all these things might make you a slave, and use you ill, and beat you" (I:67). Tommy, accepting the point that a gentleman is merely a collection of accidental social distinctions, also accepts Barlow's formulation that "no one should use another ill, and making a slave of a person is using him ill, [so] neither ought you to make a slave of any one else" (I:67–8). Barlow's argument convinces Tommy to announce that "for the future I will never use our black William ill; nor pinch him, nor kick him as I used to do" (I:68). Ultimately, Barlow's implication is that being a "gentleman" or a "slave" is merely a social accident, and that neither, therefore, should be accepted as legitimate. Later, once he has introduced the non-arbitrary system of valuing people based on their "usefulness," Day will complete the implication that "gentlemen" are not simply arbitrarily privileged but are in fact pernicious.

Day's attack on Tommy's self-conception as a gentleman is simultaneously an attack on the master–slave relationship. Tommy's character flaws are linked to his history as a "West Indian" lad. He is introduced as a difficult, unruly, spoiled child, and an explanation is offered: "While he lived in Jamaica, he had several black servants to wait upon him, who were forbidden on any account to contradict him" (I:1–2). Indeed, Tommy's arrogant self-conception, his failure to value the "usefulness" so dear to Barlow, stems directly from his arrogant attitude to the slaves on the plantation.[23] Tommy brings one of Barlow's first and most stinging criticisms on himself when he brags about having secretly learned to read:

I am sure, though there are no less than six blacks in our house, that there is not one of them who can read a story like me. Mr. Barlow looked a little grave at this sudden display of vanity, and said rather coolly, Pray, who has attempted to teach them any thing? Nobody, I believe, said Tommy. Where is the great wonder then, if they are ignorant, replied Mr. Barlow? You would probably have never known any thing, had you not been assisted; and even now you know very little. (I:61–2)

Day's insistence that the difference in abilities between a planter's son and an African slave are purely the result of education and circumstances is a

---

[23] In seeing the exposure of this colonial arrogance as part of Day's agenda in the novel, I differ from Jacqueline Rose, who sees *Sandford and Merton* (and possibly all of children's literature) as following *Robinson Crusoe* in disseminating colonialist ideology. See *The Case of Peter Pan or The Impossibility of Children's Fiction* (London: Macmillan, 1984), 51–4.

radical return to the previous consensus on shared humanity, against the
emerging philosophical consensus on racial difference.[24]

Despite Day's resistance to notions of racial difference, *Sandford and
Merton* features both a "grateful slave" and a "grateful black." The slave,
Hamet, appears in an interpolated story entitled "The Grateful Turk," set
in Venice. Like the grateful slave in representations of plantation reform,
Hamet chooses his slavery. But unlike the grateful Africans represented on
plantations, the "Turk" does so at the outset, and also gives a detailed
explanation of his motives to remain a slave, and they could apply to an
European equally well:

when the unfortunate Hamet was taken by your gallies, his aged father shared his
captivity; it was his fate which so often made me shed those tears which first
attracted the notice of your son; and when your unexampled bounty had set me
free, I flew to find the Christian that had purchased him. I represented to him that
I was young and vigorous, while he was aged and infirm; I added too the gold
which I had received from your bounty: in a word I prevailed upon the Christian
to send back my father in that ship which was intended for me . . . since that time I
have staid here to discharge the debt of nature and gratitude, a willing slave. (I:168)

Hamet's gratitude is really on behalf of his father, not himself, and therefore exemplifies filial duty, not irrationality, submissiveness, and inferiority. And, to underline the reciprocity of gratitude in this tale, Hamet later
redeems his Venetian benefactors after their ship has been captured and
they are offered for sale on a Turkish slave market.

The "grateful black" appears as a beggar in England, and enacts his
gratitude to Harry for a few coins by helping Harry Sandford to save
Tommy Merton from an enraged bull. This African character does indeed
embody gratitude, but also self-sufficiency and wisdom. The closest Day's
"grateful black" comes to the irrationality of the grateful slave trope is in
risking his life in thanks for a few coins. The resemblance is passing,
however. Ultimately the character of the "grateful black" is closer to a
Montaignean noble savage than to the typical grateful slave. Rather than
serving as a foil to demonstrate European superiority, he serves as a mouthpiece for Day's criticisms of European society. When Day has the African

---

[24] Hence, Day follows the logic of his anti-slavery pamphlet *Fragment of an Original Letter on the
Slavery of the Negroes; Written in the Year 1776* (London: John Stockdale, 1784) in *Sandford and
Merton*. In it, Day declares that if anyone keeps slaves, "he must be a tyrant and an oppressor whom
it is permitted to destroy by every possible method." Day adds that the only defenses against this are
denying "right and justice altogether" or shewing "some natural distinction by which one part of the
species is entitled to privileges from which the other is excluded" – such a distinction, however, being
"absurd" (*ibid.*, 19–20). For the definitive scholarly account of Day's anti-slavery works, see Carey,
British Abolitionism, 73–84.

observe that "in this country, and many others which I have seen, there are thousands who live like birds in cages upon the food provided by others, without doing any thing for themselves" (III:267), he echoes Montaigne. The essayist's cannibals "noticed that there were among us men full and gorged with all sorts of good things, and their other halves were beggars at their doors, emaciated with hunger and poverty";[25] Rousseau, Day's acknowledged master,[26] also adapts the remark, writing that "a handful of people abound in superfluities while the starving multitude lacks in necessities."[27] This observation is one of Day's strongest statements of his anti-gentleman position, remarkably attributed to the "black" himself. The "black" again speaks frankly and critically of Europeans, using his own example to challenge racial prejudice, in remarking "and considering, how much you white people despise us blacks, I own, I was very much surprized to see so many hundreds of you running away from such an insignificant enemy as a poor tame bull" (III:262). Further, unlike the "grateful slave" trope, far from contributing to the project of redeeming plantation slavery, Day's "grateful black" is never directly associated with slavery.

Indeed, in *Sandford and Merton*, gratitude, far from being confined to the plantation, is to be expected of all members of society, whatever their standing.[28] Gratitude has been established as the normal human response to an act of kindness throughout the novel. In previous examples, Tommy and Harry had assisted a lower-class English family and a brave Highlander soldier, among others (not to mention a variety of animals), and each had returned the favor of invaluable assistance out of gratitude. In the final

---

[25] Montaigne, "Of Cannibals," in *Complete Essays of Montaigne*, trans. Donald Frame (Stanford: Stanford University Press, 1958), 159. See also Ginzburg, "Making Things Strange," and Rawson, "'Indians' and Irish."

[26] See Chandler, "Pedagogical Fantasies," 50–66, and Burr, "Science and Imagination," 37–44.

[27] Rousseau, "Discourse on Inequality," in *The First and Second Discourses and Essay on the Origin of Language*, ed. and trans. Victor Gourevitch (New York: Harper, 1986), 199, and 349 n. 58. For an argument that the "noble savage" is not Rousseau's concept but a retrospective strawman of nineteenth-century racist ethnography, see Ter Ellingson, *The Myth of the Noble Savage* (Berkeley: University of California Press, 2001). Muthu, by contrast, sees Rousseau as critiquing and extending the "noble savage" trope here: "Toward a Subversion of Noble Savagery: From Natural Humans to Cultural Humans," in *Enlightenment Against Empire*, 11–72. Francis Moran III, "Between Primates and Primitives: Natural Man as the Missing Link in Rousseau's *Second Discourse*," in *Philosophers on Race*, 125–44, links Rousseau's essay to the emergence of race.

[28] This suggests that *Sandford and Merton* is not a "middle-class" denunciation of aristocratic values, because it is precisely the new bourgeois contractual view of society which leads to the value on "independence" opposed to "gratitude." Contrast Kramnick's view of Day's novel as a bourgeois parable in his "Preface" to the above-cited edition, vii, and "Children's Literature and Bourgeois Ideology: Observations on Culture and Industrial Capitalism in the Later Eighteenth Century," in *Culture and Politics From Puritanism to the Enlightenment*, ed. Perez Zagorin (Berkeley: University of California Press, 1980), 231–4.

analysis, neither the "grateful black," nor the "grateful slave" in Day's novel undermine his attack on slavery and all other social and racial distinctions.

In *Sandford and Merton*, Day comes at race and slavery more indirectly than do the ameliorationists, through the effect of slavery on Tommy, a planter's son. Nonetheless, Day is willing to challenge both slavery and race in order to sustain his critique of the irrationality of British social hierarchy. Day ultimately implies that gratitude is necessary in teaching gentlemen to throw off their prejudices and evaluate the world rationally. This shows that nothing was inevitable about the ameliorationist linkage of gratitude, irrationality and racial difference. Just as Day attacks slavery in his effort to undermine the idea of the gentlemen, so the ameliorationists are willing to resist gratitude for whites, and argue for racial difference, in their efforts to save the institution of plantation slavery from the possible implications of their own initial critique of its cruelty and inhumanity.

Not all texts that join the philosophical consensus on difference by emphasizing the over-emotional "nature" of African-descended people contrast this with a picture of rational, good-hearted members of the planter class. A few late-century novels depict those masters to whom no one could ever be grateful. One of the new developments in novelistic representations of plantation slavery in the late century is the new, stronger attention to master cruelty (and often, to contrasting slave kindness or sentiment), going well beyond the stimulus to reform of earlier grateful slave fictions. This focus on cruelty tends to come from an active, self-conscious anti-slavery stance that challenges the emerging ameliorationist consensus.

In *Zeluco* (1786), Dr. John Moore denounces the cruelty of slave owners from an anti-slavery point of view, and points out that masters' selfishness can undermine reforms based on economic self-interest. In the previous chapters, master cruelty was important to each representation of plantation slavery as the stimulus for the sentimental response that brought about reform; but in none of the novels discussed there was it the narrative centerpiece. Moore's *Zeluco* is perhaps the most sustained and the most politically self-conscious investigation of such cruelty. His novel is the didactic tale of an anti-hero, Zeluco, whose mistreatment of slaves on a West Indian plantation is only one of many examples of his cruel and immoral behavior.[29] One compelling aspect of Moore's text is that, whether intentionally or not, it throws into relief the flaws of grateful

---

[29] Anna Barbauld, in the Introduction to *Zeluco* for her *British Novelists* series, shows the novelty of its anti-hero: "this work is formed on the singular plan of presenting a hero of the story, if a hero he may be called, who is a finished model of depravity. Zeluco is painted as radically vicious, without the

slave fictions. The writers discussed previously, from Defoe to Peacock, had faith in a key tenet of ameliorationism, that cruelty was opposed to the planter's self-interest, and were therefore optimistic about eliminating it by enlightening the planters.

Moore challenges this facile consensus, suggesting that whatever the "real" bottom line, greed can foment cruelty, and reminding his readers of the complexities of human motivation. "Zeluco having been represented as avaricious as well as cruel," the narrator explains, one might conclude that "the suggestions of self-interest would prevent his pushing cruelty the length of endangering the lives of his own slaves." Moore does not let the inference stand:

let it be remembered, that men who are not naturally compassionate, who are devoid of religious impressions, and in the habit of giving vent to every gust of ill-humour, are apt, in the violence of rage, to become deaf to the voice of common-sense and interest, as well as of justice and mercy. An unfortunate gamester throws the cards into the fire . . . and how often do we see men in absurd rage abuse their most servicable cattle? (I:58)

Moore uses the striking image of the cards, and the disturbingly ambiguous inclusion of slaves in the category of "cattle," to force his reader to enter into the slave-masters' domineering, dehumanizing attitude toward slaves. Indeed, the reader is reminded not only of the human propensity for irrational behavior, but also of masters' view of slaves as the instruments of their fortunes, instruments upon whom they may exercise their anger when disappointed.

Moore also challenges the ameliorationist thesis that self-interest is enough to protect slaves from masters by insisting on the practical difficulty of enlightening planters about their self-interest. The ameliorationists' theory assumes that planters view their investment in their plantation and their slaves in the long term, almost as a gentry family would view their estate. But Moore develops the possibility of a different mode of self-interest. His anti-hero Zeluco never considers that his harshness might have negative consequences:[30] "his view was simply to improve his estates to the utmost; but in the execution of this plan, as *their* exertions did not keep pace with *his* impatience, he found it necessary to quicken them by an

intermixture of one good quality," v, Dr. John Moore, *Zeluco*, 2 vols., *The British Novelists*, vols. xxxiv–xxxv, ed. Mrs. Barbauld (London: Rivington *et al.*, 1820). Further citations are given parenthetically in the text.
[30] Patricia Meyer Spacks, *Desire and Truth: Functions of Plot in Eighteenth-Century English Novels* (Chicago: University of Chicago Press, 1993), 194, sees Zeluco's character as "monotonous" and underdeveloped. Contrast J. M. S. Tompkins's view in *The Popular Novel in England 1770–1800*, 1932 (Lincoln, NB: University of Nebraska Press, 1961), 178–9, 288.

unremitting use of the whip" (I:61). Zeluco is driven by impatience, and never pauses to make long-term calculations.[31]

Given that he views his interests in the short term, Zeluco is not wrong to believe that cruelty will produce optimal results for him, and Moore shows this clearly.[32] Zeluco's goal is certainly not to become a long-term resident of his plantation. Instead, he wants to squeeze maximum profits from it quickly: "he thought it necessary to bring his estate to the highest pitch of improvement; after which he proposed to return to Europe, and there in splendour and magnificence enjoy every pleasure that his heart could desire" (I:56–7). The results of this plan are fatal for Zeluco's slaves, as they in fact often were for real slaves on real plantations: "he laboured with such assiduity and impatience as ... proved fatal to several of his slaves" (I:57). Zeluco's behavior reflects an historical reality. While importing slaves remained easy and legal, many planters were happy to work slaves to death and replace them.[33] Furthermore, as sugar plantation culture was taking shape in the seventeenth century, "headright" land grants for every slave imported actually rewarded such cruel exploitation.[34]

Moore by no means intends to imply that such methods are economically superior; he instead challenges the simplistic, optimistic argument that self-interest will cure slavery's ills and protect individual slaves. He engages the reformers' argument directly, supporting it as showing the most desirable, but certainly not a highly likely, path for a planter to take. After his discussion of Zeluco's management practices, and his relation of the good slave Hanno's story, Moore represents Zeluco as engaged in an extensive debate with an unnamed humanitarian doctor (a character suggestive of Dr. Moore himself).[35] Zeluco himself invites the doctor to argue for amelioration and kind-hearted reforms, asking, "can you really imagine

---

[31] Burnard gives a similar account of Jamaica's white immigrants in *Mastery, Tyranny, and Desire*, 19.

[32] Robin Blackburn, *The Making of New World Slavery: From the Baroque to the Modern 1492–1800* (New York: Verso, 1997), 331 argues that masters took short-term views.

[33] See Barry David Gaspar, "Sugar Cultivation and Slave Life in Antigua Before 1800", in *Cultivation and Culture: Labor and the Shaping of Slave Life in the Americas*, ed. Ira Berlin and Philip D. Morgan (Charlottesville: University of Virginia Press, 1993), 123; Kolchin, *American Slavery*, 37, 39; Blackburn, *Making*, 339. Ward, *British West Indian Slavery*, 29–31, invokes and questions this theory, arguing that masters wished to preserve their valued property, but citing records of masters complaining of excessive mortality at the hands of overseers. Sheridan discusses similar complaints ("Samuel Martin," 129).

[34] Parent, *Foul Means*, documents the use of "headrights" for slaves as a basis of land claims by the "great planters" of Virginia in the seventeenth century. The practice was ended in 1699. Parent (*ibid.*, 44–5) does not link this specifically to the treatment of slaves as disposable.

[35] See Gary Kelly's "Enlightenment and Revolution: The Philosophical Novels of Dr. John Moore," *Eighteenth-Century Fiction*, 1:3 (1989), 224 and 226.

that such treatment as you seem to recommend, would render slaves of equal benefit to the proprietors of West India estates?" (I:77).

The doctor initially responds to Zeluco with a bald, if perhaps ironic, statement of the ameliorationists' position: "Well, considering the business with a view to a man's interest or profit only; long observation on the conduct of others, with my own experience, which has been considerable, convinces me that the master who treats his slaves with humanity and well-directed kindness, reaps more benefit from their labour" (I:77–8). In restating this position, the doctor does not undermine his critique; his remarks are made with an awareness that kindness, although beneficial to masters, is far from universal in practice. Although resonant with the reformers' model he ultimately critiques, the doctor's psychological explanation for the increased efficiency of labor on a kind planter's planta-tion is unusual: "The instant that the eye of the manager is turned from the slave who serves from fear alone, his efforts relax; but the industry of him who serves from attachment is continually prompted by the gratitude, and the regard for his master's interest, which he carries in his breast" (I:78).

The doctor's position here connects gratitude to a tradition of imagining ways to bring about the internalization of discipline.[36] Starting down the same path that led Bentham to imagine the Panopticon, Dr. Moore ultimately follows a different fork. Bentham felt that the way to prevent discipline from flagging when a prisoner was unobserved was to have him internalize the observer, to imagine himself as being watched at all times.[37] Dr. Moore uses instead the reformers' model of the grateful slave to imagine a similar psychological effect: if love and "gratitude" to the master are ever present, an internalized observer already exists.[38] According to this theory, the slave, filled with gratitude, observes himself at each moment and does so from the perspective of his master's interests. Off the planta-tion, however, the solution to labor discipline was far closer to Bentham's than Moore's, perhaps because only irrational, highly emotional workers could fulfill the terms of Moore's plan.[39] Moore dispenses with the assumption of rationality for both master and slave, although, like other

---

[36] On this tradition, see Bender, *Imagining the Penitentiary.*

[37] See the "Panopticism" section of Foucault's *Discipline and Punish*, 195–228, and esp. 201–2. See also Jeremy Bentham, "Panopticon Papers," in *A Bentham Reader*, ed. Mary Peter Mack (New York: Pegasus, 1969), 194–208, esp. 194.

[38] Compare Damrosch's account of Puritan self-scrutiny as preparing the way for the aesthetics of the novel in *God's Plot and Man's Stories*. See also J. Paul Hunter, *Before Novels: The Cultural Contexts of Eighteenth-Century Fiction* (New York: Norton, 1990), 303–37.

[39] Moore did imagine conscience, even in Zeluco, as having a Panopticon-like effect. See Kelly, "Enlightenment," 227.

grateful slave novelists, he positions masters as in control of their choices, while slaves do not have the capacity to control theirs. During the so-called "industrial revolution," English employers gathered their workers into factories in which supervision could be constantly maintained in order to keep up discipline. Testifying to the success of this arrangement, the employers' primary concern with discipline was getting workers into the factory during operating hours, even more than maximizing their efficiency once they were there.[40]

Having shown the limits of rational self-interest as a predictor of planters' actual behavior, Moore, through the character of the good doctor, presents a further argument against cruelty. This argument – that planters must beware of the danger of driving the slaves to desperation and violence – has a more profound effect on Zeluco than the doctor's positive arguments about long-term economic self-interest:

> My advice is this: Alter entirely your conduct towards your slaves; scorn not those who demand justice and mercy; treat them with much more indulgence, and sometimes with kindness; for certainly that man is in a most miserable as well as dangerous situation, who lives among those who rejoice in his sickness, howl with despair at his recovery, and whose only hope of tranquillity lies in their own death or in his. (I:78)

The doctor's advice is particularly pertinent to Zeluco, because when he had previously been in danger of dying (under the care of the same doctor), many of his slaves, who happened to be within his hearing, "burst into a loud and uncontrollable howl of sorrow when his recovery was first announced to them" (I:72). Their sorrow highlights his misunderstanding of them. Indeed, according to Moore, even a master as unapologetically cruel as Zeluco can believe himself the recipient of the gratitude of an individual slave – in this case, a man he has used as his go-between in an affair he is having with his neighbor's wife: "he always employed one particular slave who, he imagined was very cordially attached to him on account of a

---

[40] For an argument that the real Industrial Revolution was in labor discipline, see Stephen A Marglin, "What Do Bosses Do? The Origins and Functions of Hierarchy in Capitalist Production," *The Review of Radical Political Economics*, 6:2 (1974), 33–60, and Maxine Berg's discussion of Marglin, *The Age of Manufactures 1700–1820: Industry, Innovation and Work in Britain*, 2nd edn (New York: Routledge, 1994), 182–207. On workers' resistance to such discipline, see E. P. Thompson, "Time, Work-Discipline and Industrial Capitalism," *Past & Present*, 38 (1968), 56–97, revised and reprinted in *Customs in Common* (New York: New Press, 1993), 352–403; Douglas Reid's articles "The Decline of Saint Monday 1766–1876," *Past & Present*, 71 (1976), 76–101, and "Weddings, Weekdays, Work and Leisure in Urban England, 1791–1911: The Decline of Saint Monday Revisited," *Past & Present*, 153 (1996), 135–63. Finally, John Rule, *The Labouring Classes in Early Industrial England, 1750–1850* (New York: Longman, 1986), 130–8, provides a brief overview of related scholarship.

few indulgences ... In this conjecture, however, Zeluco was greatly mistaken; those slight favors has not eradicated from the man's mind that hatred and thirst for revenge which his master's former treatment had planted there" (I:67–8). Zeluco learns of his mistake when the slave, rather than faithfully acting as his go-between, exposes him to the deceived husband. The vengeful husband subsequently attacks Zeluco, causing the wounds that leave him seemingly on his deathbed. Moore challenges a central tenet of the "grateful slave" tradition in questioning the idea that the slaves would be "grateful" for kindness despite the misery of their overall circumstances.

While other grateful slave novelists imagine irrational, emotional slaves as becoming devoted to either vengeance or gratitude, *Zeluco* is the only novel to represent slave gratitude as a delusive belief of the master, rather than a deeply felt feeling of the slave, at least until Hector MacNeill's *Memoirs of the Life and Travels of Charles MacPherson* (1800), discussed below in chapter 6. Indeed, Moore's comment that Zeluco was "very much mistaken" to "imagine" that a particular slave "was very cordially attached to him on account of a few indulgences," and his exposure of the slave's countervailing conception of "slight favors" that cannot eradicate a "thirst for revenge" make for a reversal of perspective with almost as strongly corrosive an effect on the notion of the grateful slave as Equiano's. Moore can be taken to imply that slave gratitude is more likely to be a slave owner's fantasy than a slave's heartfelt experience. And yet, Moore, by depicting the slave in question as devoted to revenge, does not entirely depart from the consensus view of slaves as overly emotional and irrational.

The doctor's argument that kindness is a necessary preventative to slaves' violence resonates with several other tales, especially Kimber's representation of the Carter's plantation, and Sophia Lee's brief account of a slave revolt in her gothic novel, *The Recess*, in both of which bitterly cruel planters are slaughtered by slaves they have driven to vengeful violence.[41] Of course, as in Kimber's representation, the mere fact that slaves are justified in revolting does not prevent novelists from representing them as bloodthirsty and unnatural in their violence. Still, even the anonymous satirical novel *Jonathan Corncob* (1787), which takes an extremely harsh view of slaves themselves, suggests that planters endanger themselves through cruelty, though neither economic loss nor rebellious slaves are the agents of their punishment. Instead, the depravity of the planters

---

[41] See Sophia Lee, *The Recess, or A Tale of Other Times*, 1783, ed. April Alliston (Lexington: University Press of Kentucky, 2000), 137–8.

(including their sexual liaisons with slaves) is punished by the frequent and destructive hurricanes in the West Indies.[42]

Moore, however, having shown Zeluco's thoughtless character to have been convinced of the dangers and costs of cruelty, by both good advice and harsh personal experience, continues to attend to the gap between rational conclusions and actual behavior. Even the palpable threat of a violent death does not provide enough of a spur to pursuing rational self-interest for Zeluco. Soon enough he returns to his thoughtless and evil ways, even if they are slightly moderated. Zeluco made a "determination to behave with more indulgence to his slaves, being alarmed by what was suggested, and convinced that such conduct in future was highly expedient for his own personal security. Those resolutions were however very imperfectly kept" (I:79).

If Moore had rested content with showing Zeluco's failings and psychological complexities, he would appear to be "moderate," perhaps a reformer urging his fellows to be more realistic, and to hold themselves to a higher standard. However, in the sentimental, didactic tale of the good slave Hanno, he challenges slavery much more strongly. Moore attacks slavery as un-Christian through the character of a slave-martyr, anticipating Stowe's Uncle Tom. Hanno's tale – and troubles – begin when he "allowed symptoms of compassion, perhaps of indignation to escape from him" (I:62) on hearing of an unjust punishment on the plantation. In response, Zeluco orders Hanno to perform the whipping himself. On his refusal, "Zeluco in a transport of rage, ordered him to be lashed severely, and renewed the punishment at *legal* intervals so often, that the poor man was thrown into a languishing disease," a disease which leads to his death (I:62). Moore also anticipates Stowe's point about the immorality of slavery – while, like Stowe, offering an ambiguous message about racial difference.[43]

Hanno's refusal to whip another slave, even at the cost of his own life, is not the only example of his extreme courage and moral fortitude. Earlier, Hanno had also rescued a soldier who was drowning. The soldier's companions, "who were near him, Christians and all, swum away as fast as their legs could carry them, for they were afraid of his catching hold of them" (I:63). Hanno's modeling of true Christian values, and subsequent exposure of the hypocrisy of the Europeans around him who profess to be Christians, does not end with such courageous acts. On his deathbed,

---

[42] *Adventures of Jonathan Corncob, Loyal American Refugee. Written by Himself* (London: The Author, 1787), 128–30, 136.
[43] I will further discuss the connection between *Zeluco* and *Uncle Tom's Cabin* in the Epilogue below.

Hanno hears that Zeluco will suffer eternally in hell; his response is to say "I hope he will not suffer so long" (I:65). Again this appears a model for Uncle Tom's choice to forgive Legree and to pray for the souls of the slaves who cause his death.[44]

Hanno's kindness is more complex than it might first appear. His deathbed wish for God to have mercy on Zeluco's undeserving soul can be read in several ways. First and foremost, it asserts that African slaves – even ones untutored in religion like Hanno – can be better Christians than the educated members of the master class, or than the general run of Europeans, whose moral failings fill the pages of sentimental and satirical novels like Moore's. This possibility of the truly Christian slave could be used both to support and to attack slavery. Much moral fervor – and an important impetus to the anti-slavery movement from its earliest inception – came from the agitation about the *failure* to convert slaves.[45] On the other hand, especially once the conversion of slaves had been accepted, masters could argue that whatever happens to slaves on earth does not hurt their chances of getting into heaven. In fact, the slave-trading and planter interest (following the broad lines of Snelgrave's "rescue" argument) frequently contended that Africans benefited from being taken out of heathen Africa and given the opportunity for salvation.[46] Moore dismisses such arguments by showing the hypocrisy of an established church that turns a blind eye to abuses, and is more concerned to see that Hanno perform the proper rites on his deathbed than to recognize the beauty of his truly moral and courageous behavior, or to acknowledge him as a truly Christian martyr.

Having effectively undermined the key pro-slavery – and ameliorationist – tenet that planter self-interest would ultimately protect slaves, Moore continues to blast away at the limits of amelioration in addressing the problems posed by a systematically violent and tyrannical institution of slavery. The implications of his practical critique become clear when he shows skepticism that even slave codes can effect real change on the plantations. After all, Moore ironically emphasizes that Zeluco manages

---

[44] Harriet Beecher Stowe, *Uncle Tom's Cabin*, ed. Elizabeth Ammons (New York: Norton, 1994), 358–60.

[45] Davis, "The Legitimacy of Enslavement and the Ideal of the Christian Servant: The Failure of Christianization," in *Western Culture*, 197–222; Jordan, "The Souls of Men: The Negro's Spiritual Nature," in *White Over Black*, 179–215; and Brown, *Moral Capital*.

[46] For instance, see *Slave Trade: The Negro and the Free-Born Briton Compared* (London: J. Stockdale: [1789?]), iii; William Innes, *The Slave-Trade Indispensable* (London, W. Richardson *et al.*, 1790), 40; and William Knox, *A Letter from W.K. to W. Wilberforce* (London: J. Debrett, 1790), 10. All of these examples acknowledge the scarcity of actual conversions.

to keep his fatal beating of Hanno within the mandated limits, as he "renewed the punishment at *legal* intervals" (I:62). Hanno's character – unlike other exemplary "kind" slaves designed to be contrasted with their cruel masters – is not one-dimensional, although he is praised for his "gratitude." His foremost characteristics are his insistent morality and his courage; he dies taking a moral stand against the violence of the slave system. In making Hanno heroic for his resistance to the excesses of slavery, and in showing him to be human in his fierce morality, Moore takes a large step away from the patronizing attitude of other reformers who praise slaves for being grateful but who suggest that they are irrational and overly emotional. Notably, however, in so doing, he also comes up with the eighteenth-century character most proleptic of Uncle Tom.

Perhaps unsurprisingly, given the other ways in which he anticipates Stowe, Moore never takes a stand on the damaging effects of the emerging discourse of racial difference. Zeluco comes closest to scoring a point in his debate with the doctor when he challenges the doctor to disagree with his invocation of racial hierarchy: "you will allow, I hope, that they are an inferior race of men?" (I:76). Although the doctor does not exactly allow the point, he sets it aside through irony, paraphrasing Montesquieu: "I will allow, replied the doctor, that their hair is short and ours is long, that their noses are flat and ours are raised, and that their skin is black and ours white; yet after all these concessions, I still have my doubts respecting our right to make them slaves" (I:76). Montesquieu's original lines, first published in *The Spirit of the Laws*, drip with irony, and are meant as a devastating satire, dependent on an expected consensus view rejecting racial difference.[47] Despite being quite demanding of Zeluco throughout the debate, here he allows Zeluco's beliefs to stand (if with an ironic wink to his reader), merely pointing out that he believes that "inferiority" is not the central issue, and that, instead, he rejects slavery as immoral whatever the relative positions of the "races" involved might be in the great hierarchy of life. Moore gropes toward an argument that resonates with the later "Romantic Racialism" of Stowe and other antebellum abolitionists, an argument that accepts racial difference as the basis of a claim that Africans are particularly suited, not to slavery, but to Christianity.[48]

[47] See chapter 3 n. 40.
[48] For the classic instance of this argument, see George M. Fredrickson, "Uncle Tom and the Anglo-Saxons: Romantic Racialism in the North," in *The Black Image*, 97–129. For a reading of Stowe's *Dred* as responding to the limits of the racial views of *Uncle Tom*, see Susan M. Ryan, "Charity

POLEMICAL COMPLEXITIES

The dominant voice of the anti-slavery debate in the 1780s belonged to Dr. James Ramsay.[49] His key work, *Essay on the Treatment and Conversion of African Slaves in the British Sugar Colonies* (1784), shares the central concerns of all three novelists analyzed in this section: with Peacock, Ramsay shares a faith in the efficacy of gratitude as a means of controlling slaves; with Thomas Day, Ramsay shares the conviction that racial difference is not a reality, but the product of environment; and with Dr. Moore, he shares a defining desire to convert the slaves to Christianity.[50] Despite these positions, and despite being viewed by planters as the bogeyman of anti-slavery, Ramsay frequently enters into the slave owners' point of view. Indeed, he takes for granted that the regime of colonial slavery and racial oppression must be maintained. Ramsay was a doctor and minister who had spent time in the British West Indies and was frustrated by the impediments the planters put in the way of his efforts to convert and minister to slaves.[51] His primary issue – conversion – was an old one, and his stance was self-consciously short of being radical: his central plans for reform were divided between two problems, the need to interest slaves in Christianity (disciplining them more generally is an important part of this concept); and the need to convince masters to support, or at least allow, the effort at conversion. In other words, like the novelists of the 1780s, Ramsay's work engages with the central issues of the grateful slave – ameliorationism and racial difference – while ultimately taking ambiguous positions on both.

Ramsay, invoking the consensus position of the 1770s and earlier on Africans' full share of humanity, attacks the idea of meaningful racial difference, while maintaining that slavery has so degraded African slaves that it has rendered them unfit for freedom (244–5). This position diminishes the importance of the distinction between essence and environment: explaining the roots of Africans' incapacity is of less moment than acknowledging their dependence on whites. Here Ramsay perfectly captures the cultural status of race in his moment. Theoretically, mooting genuine difference is an abomination, a heresy, and not admissible as part of the conversation (202–3). In practice, however, race – white supremacy and

---

Begins at Home: Stowe's Antislavery Novels and the Forms of Benevolent Citizenship," in *The Grammar of Good Intentions: Race and the Antebellum Culture of Benevolence* (Ithaca: Cornell University Press, 2003), 143–62.

[49] See Folarin Shyllon, *James Ramsay: The Unknown Abolitionist* (Edinburgh: Canongate, 1977).

[50] (London: James Phillips, 1784). Further citations are given parenthetically in the text.

[51] Shyllon, *James Ramsay*, 7–13.

black oppression in the colonies – is a reality demanding deference and accommodation.[52]

While Ramsay does not dwell extensively on gratitude, or present it as proving African humanity, he does, in a brief and odd passage, make it a key element of his scheme of conversion, or more precisely of a scheme to empower the clergy as key figures in the lives of slaves for disciplinary purposes:

> Whenever there is room for shewing mercy, it should be done at the minister's intercession, that he may be considered as a mediator between the slave on one side, and the master and the law on the other. He should never appear in any other light among them than that of their instructor and benefactor, praying with them, interceding for them, or doing some good office to them; that their esteem for his person, and gratitude for his kindness, may stand to them in place of a law, may produce in them a love for his doctrine, and be a pledge of their good behaviour to the community. (270–1)

Ramsay wishes to restrict the benefits of using gratitude to manipulate slaves to the clergy, and therefore to utilize it for the cause of conversion rather than simply to bind slaves to their masters. Indeed, the concept that the minister "may stand to them in place of a law" suggests a regime like that of the fictional grateful slave, in that it removes slaves from rational engagement with their own world, even from the need to internalize discipline, replacing their need for rationality with external guidance. Given Ramsay's sometime scathing attitude toward the exploitation of slavery and race, it is surprising that he takes for granted that the dynamic of slave gratitude will be an effective means of discipline. Further, his phrasing is disturbing, "whenever there is room for mercy" suggesting that mercy is a luxury not to be lightly employed under slavery. In envisioning "gratitude" inducing the slaves "good behavior," Ramsay enters into the mindset of a grateful slave novelist, tacitly accepting the ongoing reality of slavery, and even bringing slaves to accept their subjugation.

Despite this apparent endorsement of the grateful slave paradigm, Ramsay, in another section, attacks difference in language reminiscent of earlier conversionist Christian critics of slavery, for instance scornfully characterizing Edward Long as having the "same opinion of Hume's, of the negroes being a distinct race" (231). This, Ramsay explains "will not immediately affect our arguments for their humane treatment and mental improvement," and here he anticipates the ameliorationists of the later

---

[52] Burnard sees Ramsay as opposing "herrenvolk egalitarianism," his term for the system of white privilege in Jamaica (*Mastery, Tyranny and Desire*, 85).

1780s and 1790s accommodating themselves to racism by saying that black inferiority is no excuse for the abuses of slavery. But Ramsay also argues of Long's view that "the consequences usually drawn from it shock humanity, and check every hope of their advancement: for, if allowed to be a *distinct* race, European pride immediately concludes them an *inferior* race, and then it follows, of course, that nature formed them to be slaves to their superiors" (231). Here, in his deconstruction of the knowingly false self-justifications of racial privilege, he sounds very much like Wesley – or Equiano. He is also like Raynal in offering tips on the best methods of slave management while asserting that anyone who supports the slave system has blood on their hands; Ramsay offers his experiences as a slaveholder as evidence in support of his arguments. Indeed, Ramsay's opponents attempted to dismiss him as nothing more than a failed slave owner embittered by his own incompetence.[53] Ramsay, like other activists of the early 1780s, was no doubt inspired by the Somerset decision of 1772. But his position respects the compromise enshrined in that judicial ruling: race is unacceptable in Britain but an unshakeable reality in the colonies.

Ramsay again shows his tendency to take up the slaveholders' point of view when he imagines a way to use mulattoes as a buffer class to help ensure white dominance. The historian Theodore Allen has argued that practices of race developed to create a "buffer" class that would support, and identify with, the ruling classes and thus serve as a bulwark against slave rebellion.[54] In Virginia, this group would be poor whites, who would be rewarded for their co-operation with white privilege. In the islands, however, it would be the "colored" class. Ramsay himself envisions this arrangement and uses it to argue for the (eventual) freeing of all mulattoes, contending that "a new rank of citizens, placed between the black and the white races, would be established. They would naturally attach themselves to the white race, as the more honourable relation, and so become a barrier against the designs of the blacks" (289). This moment of total identification with the systems of slavery and race is unsettling in a text that often launches uncompromising attacks on both. Indeed, in his section of anecdotes offered as demonstrating the humanity, the rational and emotional, capacity of slaves, Ramsay celebrates a free black for his cleverness in defying the rules of white supremacy. The black man, a

---

[53] "Some Gentlemen" suggest that he punished his slaves harshly and could never successfully discipline them, 82. James Tobin, *Cursory Remarks upon the Reverend Mr. Ramsay's Essay* (London: G. and T. Wilkie, 1785), 6, wonders sarcastically at Ramsay's failure to object to slavery while he was on the island himself.
[54] Allen, *Invention*, vols. I and II.

shopkeeper, outwits a white colonel who exploits him by demanding endless free samples of cocoa without ever making a purchase. The shopkeeper hires a white clerk and enforces his demand for payment by threatening to have the white clerk provide testimony. The colonel, although enraged, realizes he has been outwitted and pays up (258–9).

Some of the complexity of Ramsay's position – the result of the strangeness of his thinking as a slave owner and yet opposing essentialism – is captured in an anecdote he offers about a slave of his own:

I had a young fellow, who was a notorious gambler, idler, liar, and man of pleasure; yet so well did he lay his schemes, so plausibly did he on all occasions account for his time and conduct, that I, who could not punish unless I could convince the culprit that I had undoubted proof of his guilt, was hardly ever able to find an opportunity of correcting him. This lad, when he came a boy from Africa, shewed marks of sentiment, and of a training above the common run of negroes. But slavery, even in the mildest degree, and his accompanying with slaves, gave him so worthless, dissipated a turn, that I was obliged to send him out of the family, and have him taught a trade in hopes of his reformation. By this he insensibly acquired a little application, and has since attached himself to a wife. (246–7)

Here Ramsay comes close to the position of the grateful slave reformer, as sentimental slaveholder "obliged" to take disciplinary action against a slave, but he is firm in his dismissal of racial difference, and appears genuine in his efforts to help remedy the ill-effects of slavery on the boy in his charge. He appears untroubled by what appear to us as the obvious contradictions of his position. Slavery makes slaves vicious and utterly dependent. The total authority of the slaveholder is at once the cause of the slaves' depravity and the only means to lift them above it.

Ramsay comes very close to joining the consensus on the grateful slave as both the solution to the problems of slavery, and the image that implies the difference between the races. Despite his occasional identification with the slave owners' point of view, however, Ramsay is clear in holding slaveholders responsible for their cruelty to their charges, and in his skepticism toward accounts of racial difference. Taken together, these views differentiate him from Peacock's novel and the views of Raynal, Kant, and Jefferson. He does share with them the belief that slaves are genuinely unequipped to handle freedom, not because they are Africans but because their slavery has made them unfit for independent life (244–5). Here, Ramsay points to the coming convergence of slave trade abolitionists and planters advocating the policy of amelioration in the 1790s. In a striking oddity, Ramsay proposes the solution of enserfing slaves.

Ramsay's emphasis on master cruelty, pointing to it as a problem to be solved through legislation and social engineering, is also suggestive of amelioration. Nonetheless, he claims that masters owe slaves as much "ease" and "indulgence" as possible, noting critically that these "are not deemed matter of right, but of kindness or favour" (87). Like Moore, if in different terms, Ramsay suggests that individual "kindness" is no solution to the problems of slavery. He contends that slavery is dangerously under-regulated in the British colonies, and, in a politically ill-advised rhetorical choice, contrasts the British islands unfavorably with the French. One of his central ideas is that with property and families slaves will come to have a stake in society and will begin improving – that is, overcoming the effects of slavery. But Ramsay insists that his plan must be instituted very gradually.

Ramsay's work, however balanced it appears, however deeply compromised and ameliorationist it may seem in retrospect, had a distinctly polarizing affect on the debate. He inspired some virulent attacks – and ardent articulations of the reality of racial difference. He also inspired zealous adherents. He was often taken as a radical, and attributed positions more radical than those he set forth. In fact, Ramsay himself joined in this game, hinting that his real intentions were much farther reaching then he had let on – but that he had been convinced that the world was not ready for the truth.[55] Nonetheless, he also stated in a reply to pro-slavery critics "I have ever declared myself against the indiscriminate freeing of slaves."[56]

A follower of Ramsay offers the most extended consideration in polemical writing of the concepts underlying the grateful slave trope. Rather than consolidating the racial meaning of the grateful slave with a very cautious ameliorationist politics on slavery, as do grateful slave novelists up to Peacock, Richard Nisbet's *Capacity of Negroes for Religious and Moral Improvement Considered* (1789) instead includes not only the concept of the grateful slave as a solution to the ills of slavery, but also most of the major critiques of the paradigm offered in the 1780s. As discussed in chapter 3 above, Nisbet offered one of the most openly racialist pamphlets of the 1770s during the Somerset controversy. However, returning to the issue in 1789, he took an opposite position, heartily endorsing grateful slave reforms as the perfect solution to the problem of slavery and dedicating his work to Ramsay (76). Nisbet's racial politics appear to move in the opposite direction from those of the broader society, a fact which has

---

[55] James Ramsay, *An Inquiry into the Effects of Putting a Stop to the African Slave Trade* (London: J. Phillips, 1784), 3–5.
[56] *A Letter to James Tobin, Esq.* (London: J. Phillips, 1787), 22.

been darkly associated with his confinement in a Philadelphia mental asylum.[57] However, I would argue that he, like Moore, Day, and Ramsay, in fact captures the ambiguity of the 1780s, the decade's truly transitional status.

Nisbet offers an inspirational example that could be taken from Scott's *History of Sir George Ellison* of a slave owner the result of whose careful "attention to his duty as a master is, that he has a tribe of cheerful, contented, and laborious slaves, who are at all times willing to exert themselves in his service; among whom the lash of the whip is very rarely applied, and such a character as a runaway has not been known in years" (41–2). Indeed, asks Nisbet, commenting on the "general good behaviour of the slaves" in this instance, is "any thing more fair and reasonable to attribute it in a great degree, to a sense of their master's consideration for their welfare, which has established an impression of duty on their part, exciting an adequate return of their gratitude?" (42). But despite this view so like the grateful slave trope, Nisbet offers a number of caveats and reservations that resonate with Day and Moore's critiques. Decrying slave owners' unthinking "prejudice" against blacks, Nisbet admits to having himself previously felt "the force of evil custom upon the mind" (iv).

Nisbet, no longer living permanently in Nevis, but only making "occasional visits to his native country" (iii) presents the very views he formerly held as evidence of a transatlantic gap in conceptions of race: "it will probably appear somewhat extraordinary to the reader who has never visited the sugar colonies, that any reasoning should be enforced, to prove what seems so evident as 'the capacity of negroes for religious and moral improvement in common with the rest of mankind'" (iv). Nisbet returns to the view that held sway in the metropole up to the time of Somerset, echoing Woolman, Wesley and the other early conversionist critics of slavery in arguing that "every prejudice against this unfortunate people is a mere illusion, proceeding from the errors of the human passions, and the natural but pernicious abuses which follow an unlimited power of tyrannizing over our fellow-creatures" (v). Nisbet joins with those anti-slavery advocates who see difference and degradation as a product of the slave system, but he also mounts an implicit defense of slaveholders who believe in race, as he did formerly himself. They are not conscious hypocrites, as Woolman, Wesley and Equiano suggest, but instead are the unconscious victims of their own power and the errors of passion it inspires.

---

[57] Jordan, *White Over Black*, 306.

And yet Nisbet himself continued to own slaves, and he makes his status as a slaveholder clear in offering a section of "Discourses to Negroes" suitable for the use of other slave masters who wish to at once introduce their slaves to religion and preach obedience. Although he insists that a belief in "superiority" is the effect of "evil culture" or "prejudice," he also clearly believes, along with grateful slave novelists and Ramsay, that slaves are in no condition to take on the project of independence and must be carefully mentored and educated before any such possibility will arise. Indeed, he repeatedly insists on the need for a radically simple form of religious instruction for slaves, and his "discourses" for slaves clearly enact such a model. Nisbet marks an important shift, from the assumption that because African humanity is obvious and undeniable, those who deny it are conscious hypocrites, to the newly central argument of the 1780s and 1790s, touched on by both Day and Moore, that even slave masters are victims of, and degraded by, the system of slavery. Perhaps unsurprisingly, this rhetorical change to the baleful effects of slavery on masters comes at just the moment when race is beginning to take on the aura of an undeniable reality.

In addition to his complex view of race, Nisbet also shares Moore's central critiques of amelioration. To begin with he insists, unlike authors of grateful slave fictions, that genuine kindness on the part of masters is rare, and therefore, one may infer, unlikely to spread throughout the slave system:

It is not in our sugar colonies, where there is so seldom any principled relation between master and slave, or any essential benefit conferred by the former, that instances of gratitude, attachment, and rectitude among negroes, are to be frequently expected. These are such as the master does not look for, and indeed he must be sensible, upon an impartial review of the present system of slavery, that he has no title to claim them. (46–7)

Furthermore, like Moore, Nisbet is very skeptical of the motivations of most masters. Responding to the position of apologists for slavery that slaves, as valuable property, will be protected by self-interest, Nisbet articulates one of the lessons of *Zeluco*: "it is one of our infirmities of our nature, and the causes of our misery in this probationary state of existence, that, however we may be capable of discerning, we certainly do not follow our true interest" (56). He does envision "reformation" as a cure for the ills of the system, but he seems to see this reformation being imposed by the government rather than resulting from the natural spread of an advantageous system; nonetheless, he ultimately belongs to the ranks of the ameliorationists (62).

Nisbet, even more so than Ramsay, gives us perspective on the politics of Day and Moore as the dissenting "grateful slave" novelists of the late 1780s. On the one hand, they share with him an approval of the positive possibilities of ameliorationism as a source of immediate improvements to the lives and opportunities of slaves. Putting the spiritual welfare of the slaves at the center of the discussion de-emphasizes the importance of racial difference and allows a return to the scripture-based anti-racial consensus of the period up to the Somerset trial; it makes ameliorationism appealing despite its long-term effect in sustaining slavery as an institution or its underlying implications about race. Furthermore, Nisbet provides a key example of the ways in which the relationship between race and reform in visions of slave gratitude grew more complex in the 1780s, before the philosophical consensus on racial difference finally arrived in the cultural mainstream at the close of the 1790s.

CHAPTER 5

Gratitude in the black Atlantic: Equiano writes back, 1789

Black Atlantic writers' responses to the grateful slave trope demonstrate their awareness of its significance in eighteenth-century culture, and particularly its stakes for racial ideology. This chapter begins by surveying the works of Ignatius Sancho, Ottobah Cugoano, and Olaudah Equiano, establishing their sensitivity to, and interest in, the issue of gratitude. It then turns to a more detailed analysis of Equiano's resistance in *The Interesting Narrative* to his master's demands for gratitude, and through these demands to colonial practices of racial privilege. Equiano's resistance to racial oppression takes the primary form of exposing the transatlantic gap between colonial practices and metropolitan understandings of race, and invoking metropolitan ideals of shared humanity and impartial justice against white privilege in the colonies.

EVADING GRATITUDE

Ignatius Sancho comments on the possibility of a raced meaning for gratitude by treating gratitude in the context of his complex, playful sentimentalism; unlike Equiano and Cugoano, Sancho, more fully assimilated into English culture, does not address gratitude primarily in relation to slavery, but as a part of his experience of a raced identity in the metropolitan context.[1] Sancho was celebrated as the author of a collection of letters published posthumously in 1782; his letters were noted particularly for their highly stylized sentimentalism after the manner of Laurence

---

[1] For studies addressing the uneven development of race in the eighteenth-century transatlantic world, see Philip D. Morgan, "British Encounters With Africans and African Americans, circa 1600–1780," in *Strangers Within the Realm: Cultural Margins of the First British Empire* (Chapel Hill: University of North Carolina Press, 1991), 157–219; Allen, *Invention*, vols. I and II; Thornton, *Africa and Africans*; Wheeler, *Complexion*; Linebaugh and Rediker, *Many-Headed Hydra*; Sparks, *Two Princes*; and W. Jeffrey Bolster, *Black Jacks: African American Seamen in the Age of Sail* (Cambridge, MA: Harvard University Press, 1998).

173

Sterne.[2] He was acknowledged as an important figure in his culture for negotiating the relationship between race and sentiment. His writings and reputation inspired several sentimental African characters in late-century novels, and a number of comments on the phenomenon of an African of refined feeling.[3]

Sancho's use of gratitude in his letters is richly complex. Keith Sandiford, applying a DuBoisian model of black experience in a white world to the eighteenth century,[4] has argued that Sancho's letters have a "double edge": "on the one side, a structure of accommodation intended to appease the myths of his white audience, on the other a structure of sarcasm designed to resist them."[5] Despite, in Sandiford's account, being aware of arguments that his letters could help rebut – that Africans were incapable of writing, or of refined feelings – the letters were published posthumously, and Sancho appears not to have intended, or expected, their collection and publication.[6] Sancho may have written to individuals with the intention of altering their views on slavery, race, and colonialism, he did not write his letters, as a group, with a clear and stable polemical agenda.

Thomas Jefferson in *Notes on the State of Virginia* (1785) momentarily praises Sancho, only to set him up for later dismissal as a highly emotional and ultimately irrational African. Jefferson, then, adduces Sancho as an example of racial difference. Dispensing with obvious counterexamples, Jefferson dismisses Phyllis Wheatley as "below the dignity of criticism" before turning to Sancho, whom he treats more seriously. Still, Jefferson concludes that Sancho's "letters do more honour to the heart than the head," casting him as being, like a grateful slave, at the mercy of his excessive emotions.[7]

---

[2] See Ellis, *Politics*, 60–7, and "Ignatius Sancho's *Letters*: Sentimental Libertinism and the Politics of Form," in *Genius in Bondage: Literature of the Early Black Atlantic*, ed. Vincent Carretta and Philip Gould (Lexington: University Press of Kentucky, 2001), 199–217; Helena Woodard, "Ignatius Sancho and Laurence Sterne: The Measure of Benevolence and the 'Cult of Sensibility'," in *African–British Writings*, 67–98; Nussbaum, *Limits of the Human*, 210; and Carey, *British Abolitionism*, 57–63.

[3] See Vincent Carretta's "Introduction" to Ignatius Sancho, *Letters of the Late Ignatius Sancho, an African*, 1782, ed. Vincent Carretta (New York: Penguin, 1998), xvii–xix. Further citations are given parenthetically in the text. Sancho was the model for Shirna Cambo in *The Memoirs and Opinions of Mr. Blenfield* (London: W. Lane, 1790) and for Sancho in *Berkeley Hall; or the Pupil of Experience* (London: Tindal, 1791).

[4] Sandiford, *Measuring the Moment: Strategies of Protest in Eighteenth-Century Afro-English Writing* (Selinsgrove, PA: Susquehanna University Press, 1988), cites neither Dubois' *Souls of Black Folks* nor Gates' *Signifying Monkey* although he draws on the concepts of "double consciousness" and "signifyin'."

[5] Sandiford, *Measuring the Moment*, 84.   [6] *Ibid.*, 74.

[7] Jefferson, *Notes on the State of Virginia*, 147–8.

At times, Sancho himself seems to endorse the novelistic trope of the grateful slave. He praises Sarah Scott's grateful slave novel *The History of Sir George Ellison* (1766), famously writing to Sterne, "of all my favorite authors, not one has drawn a tear in favour of my miserable black brethren – excepting yourself, and the humane author of Sir George Ellison."[8] He also endorses the idea of using kindness to elicit gratitude from slaves. Writing to a Mr. B – :

> I thank you for your kindness to my poor black brethren – I flatter myself you will find them not ungrateful – they act commonly from their feelings: – I have observed a dog will love those who use him kindly – and surely so, negroes – in their state of ignorance and bondage will not act less generously, if I may judge them by myself – I should suppose kindness would do any thing with them; – my soul melts at kindness – but the contrary – I own with shame – makes me almost a savage. (45)

The phrase "makes me almost a savage" enacts a "double edge" yet more complex than that Sandiford describes, at once drawing on the degrading image of the African as a primitive, bestial "savage" and yet making that image into a threat against those planters who abuse slaves.[9] Indeed, this comment would seem to undermine those critics who see Sancho's sentimentalism as a "failure of masculinity"[10] and to support those who see him as consciously manipulating degrading, polemical representations of Africans. Sancho never explicitly endorses gratitude as a justification of slavery here; he only asserts that Africans will react well to kindness and defend themselves against its opposite.[11]

Some of Sancho's comments do imply a response to one of the most crucial issues in the abolition debate. By insisting both that slaves "act commonly from their feelings" and that they are kept in a state of "ignorance and bondage," Sancho, like Equiano, refuses the claim that slaves are a reliable index of the capacities of Africans, instead asserting the abolitionist

---

[8] Sancho, *Letters of the Late Ignatius Sancho*, 74.

[9] Nussbaum, *Limits*, 209, invokes this phrase to argue that Sancho's "self-presentation as a man of sentiment is perhaps a kind of social reaching."

[10] Paul Edwards, "Introduction," in *The Letters of Ignatius Sancho*, ed. Paul Edwards and Polly Rewt (Edinburgh: Edinburgh University Press, 1994), 1–22; Vince Carretta's above-cited Introduction, and "Three West Indian Writers of the 1780s Revisited and Revised," *Research in African Literatures*, 29:4 (1998), 73–86; and Sandiford, *Measuring the Moment*. Such charges are rejected in Nussbaum, *Limits of the Human*, 209; Ellis, "Ignatius Sancho," 200; and Sukhdev Sandhu, "Ignatius Sancho and Laurence Sterne," *Research in African Literatures*, 29:4 (1998), 88, 89.

[11] Woodard sees Sancho as favoring the proper display of gratitude to benefactors (*African–British Writings*, 74, 91), arguing that "he internalizes the philosophy of racial subordination embedded in the Chain of Being" (*ibid.*, 85).

point that slaves' degradation is a result of their condition.[12] In some
tension with this point, however, is Sancho's implication that he himself
may be an index of the mentality of slaves; here he seems to accept a notion
of shared characteristics, despite his strong acculturation, which contradicts the notion that slaves' degradation points only to slavery's brutality
and not to some essential racial character.

Does Sancho really judge the African slaves by his own example, and his
own reactions to kindness, based on acceptance of the validity of shared
racial characteristics? This is far from clear. As Sandiford argues, Sancho's
irony and subversiveness coalesce around gratitude.[13] Writing to thank a
Mr. J. Spink for an act of generosity, Sancho playfully reverses the obligation conferred:

But I have been well informed that there is a Mr. S[pink] at Bury – and I think I
have seen the gentleman – who lives in a constant course of doing beneficent
actions – and, upon these occasions – the pleasure he feels – constitutes him the
obliged party. – You good Sir, ought of course to thank me – for adding one more
to the number you are pleased to be kind to – so pray remember, good Sir, that my
thanks – (however due in the eyes of gratitude) I conceive to be an act of super-
erogation – and expect that henceforth you will look upon the Sancho's – as a
family that have a rightful call upon your notice. (110)

The reversal is spelled out: "You good Sir, ought of course to thank me."
And this is not the only letter in which Sancho plays such games. In a letter
to a Mr. Meheux, Sancho again rejects the feeling of obligation, knowing
that his correspondent "has a satisfaction in giving pleasure to his friends
which more than repays him" (78). In a final example, Sancho sends wishes
to a Mr. Browne that "the blessings of the season attend you – may you
have the pleasure and exercise of finding out want – and relieving it – and
may you feel more pleasure than the benefited" (197).

But what is most remarkable about the first two instances is that Sancho
cheerily usurps the privilege of the benefactor from the position of the
"benefited." In the sentimental novels from which he draws the notion, it is
the benefactor who makes a point of relishing the deliciousness of his own
benevolence. Far from lessening the gratitude of the beneficiary, the
genuine relish – the sincerity – of the sentimental gentleman seems only
to increase the obligation conferred. Take the example of Sir George
Ellison, whose adventures Sancho had evidently read with attention.
Despite experiencing "delight nothing in this world can afford but the
relieving our fellow creatures from misery, a delight beyond what our weak

---

[12] See Equiano, *Interesting Narrative*, III.   [13] Sandiford, *Measuring the Moment*, 78–9.

senses can well bear" (11) in relieving the slaves, Ellison felt comfortable with the concept that they owed him a lifetime of obligation.

The most significant aspect of these letters, for our purposes, is the awareness they demonstrate of the stakes of "gratitude." Sancho chooses to be playful about – and thereby to resist – even standard expressions of obligation. Is Sancho really willing to endorse the novelists' policy of developing and exploiting gratitude in slaves, as he suggests in his remarks on Sarah Scott and on his reactions to kindness? Or does he merely endorse her to remind Sterne of slaves' suffering? In making the complexities of sentimental gratification his own, Sancho claims an equality of sophistication with his correspondents, even in the act of acknowledging their social and financial superiority to him. Furthermore, his resistance to, and his discomfort with, expressions of gratitude, while playful in tone, show a recognition that gratitude – when unrestricted, taken to the extreme – can imply submission and inferiority.

Ottobah Cugoano's stance is more assertively radical than Sancho's.[14] Rather than endorsing masters' "kindness," Cugoano, in his 1787 *Thoughts and Sentiments on the Evil of Slavery*, denounces those planters who would shield their iniquity behind claims of humanity. He offers a logical refutation of the principle of slave gratitude:

And should any of the best of them plead . . . and tell of their humanity and charity to those whom they have captured and enslaved, their tribute of thanks is but small; for what is it, but a little restored to the wretched and miserable who they have robbed of their all.[15]

Here, Cugoano could be referring directly to William Snelgrave's claims to have elicited gratitude even from slaves in his cargo on the middle passage. Still, the phrase "captured and enslaved" is capacious enough to apply to both slave traders and slaveholders; in any event, his rejection of their claims to "humanity" apply just as fully to the grateful slave reformers in the novel, who were after all much more likely to trumpet their "humanity" in 1787 than were slave traders.

Cugoano goes on to denounce the philosophical justification of slavery stemming from Hobbes' scene of the conquered man offering himself as a slave to his conqueror in exchange for being allowed to live. Treating men

---

[14] See Vincent Carretta, "Introduction," in Quobna Ottobah Cugoano, *Thoughts and Sentiments on the Evil of Slavery*, ed. Vincent Carretta (New York: Penguin, 1999), xxv; and Wheeler, "'Betrayed by Some of My Own Complexion': Cugoano, Abolition, and the Contemporary Language of Racialism," in *Genius in Bondage*, 17–38.

[15] Cugoano, *Thoughts and Sentiments*, 90–1.

"like the spoil of those taken in the field of battle, where the wretched fugitives must submit to what they please" (91) undermines any claim to humanity or justice. Such a refusal of the calculus that allows even Sancho and Equiano sometimes to speak well of "humane" slaveholders follows logically from Cugoano's demands for "total abolition of slavery" and "universal emancipation of slaves" (98); he rejects slavery altogether, refusing to follow the abolitionist party line and defer to political expediency by pursuing the abolition of the trade before attacking the institution of slaveholding itself.[16] This allows Cugoano, almost alone among abolitionists, to refuse to make distinctions between better and worse forms of slavery.[17] Indeed, Cugoano also refuses the subtle implication that independence, personal agency, and liberty (as well as patriotism) are somehow more natural to the British than to West Africans: "those people annually brought away from Guinea, are born as free, and are brought up with as great a predilection for their own country, freedom and liberty, as the sons and daughters of fair Britain" (27). Equiano may well have helped Cugoano write his tract, but Cugoano's politics are distinctly more radical.[18]

But Cugoano does indulge in one strain of fantasy, of hope for the future, resonating with the pernicious logic of the grateful slave:

Were the Africans to be dealt with in a friendly manner, and kind instruction to be administered unto them, as by degrees they became to love learning, there would be nothing in their power, but what they would wish to render their service in return for the means of improving their understanding; and the present British factories, and other settlements, might be enlarged by a very great extent. (100)

Although it accords with the colonialist vision of more orthodox abolitionists like Anthony Benezet and Equiano, Cugoano's scenario of kind Britons and devoted Africans differs dramatically from the scenario of the grateful slave, although of course retaining the assumption that the English will instruct Africans.[19] It is premised on the rationality, and the improved

---

[16] Hochschild, *Bury the Chains*, 135–6.
[17] Dwight McBride, *Impossible Witnesses: Truth, Abolitionism, and Slave Testimony* (New York: New York University Press, 2001), 121, contends that Equiano does not relativize slavery, positioning slavery as Equiano's foremost concern. See n. 26 below for critics who see Equiano as inconsistent on slavery.
[18] Carretta contrasts Cugoano's politics to Equiano's in his Introduction to Cugoano, xvii, xxi, xxv. Paul Edwards suggests that Equiano may have assisted Cugoano in the Introduction to his facsimile edition of *Thoughts and Sentiments* (London: Dawson's, 1969), vii–xi; see also Sandiford, *Measuring the Moment*, 96.
[19] Key eighteenth-century texts arguing for colonialism as a solution to the problem of slavery include Benezet, *Some Historical Account*; James Ramsay, *Inquiry into the Effects of Putting a Stop to the African Slave Trade and of Granting Liberty to the Slaves in the British Sugar Colonies* (London. James

learning, of Africans, not on their emotional excess or rational deficiency, and hence implies that difference is purely circumstantial. The result of Cugoano's vision of colonial harmony would be "Africans ... refined and established in light and knowledge" (100). Cugoano insists that, if the British would treat Africans as rational and independent agents, they would find them to be economically productive as both free laborers in the New World and as trading partners in Africa. Such anti-slavery colonialism was quite common in the late eighteenth century.[20]

The other major departure is in Cugoano's conception of the meaning of an African political identity. His assertion of political freedom as the natural state of Africans departs from the much cagier, more complicated responses of Equiano and Benezet (among others) to contentious accounts of Africa.[21] In the late 1780s, followers of Snelgrave dominated this debate with images of Africa as always, and even as willingly, enslaved to their kings; their opponents, like Benezet, responded with images of Africans as innocent primitives. Cugoano, then, seems to be opposing a collective "raced" identity with a collective political identity for Africans.[22] Nonetheless, Cugoano, like Equiano, does play into the overlapping of abolition and colonialism in late eighteenth-century British culture exemplified by the Sierra Leone colonization plan and by the travel writer Mungo Park and the ambiguous goals of Joseph Bank's African Association, which recruited and outfitted Park and other travelers.[23]

Of the three eighteenth-century black Atlantic authors under discussion here, only Equiano directly engages with the issue of slaves' "gratitude" as an aspect of plantation discipline, and of the colonial regime of race more

Phillips, 1784); Thomas Clarkson, *An Essay on the Impolicy of the African Slave Trade* (London: J. Phillips, 1788); for Equiano see *Interesting Narrative*, 232–6. Further citations are given parenthetically in the text. Even before Benezet, pamphlet writers suggested colonialism as a preferable alternative to the slave trade: see for instance "Plan for Improving the Trade at Senegal."

[20] Philip D. Curtin, "New Jerusalems," in *The Image of Africa: British Ideas and Action, 1780–1850*, vol I (Madison: University of Wisconsin Press, 1964), 88–113; R. A. Austen and W. D. Smith, "Images of Africa and British Slave Trade Abolition: The Transition to an Imperialist Ideology, 1787–1807," *African Historical Studies*, 2:1 (1969), 69–83; Christopher L. Brown, "Empire without Slaves: British Concepts of Emancipation in the Age of the American Revolution," *William and Mary Quarterly*, 56:2 (1999), 273–306, and *Moral Capital*; and Coleman, *Romantic Colonization*. On colonialist egalitarianism, see Schama, *Rough Crossings*, 189–90, and Brown, *Moral Capital*, 314–21.

[21] See my "Olaudah Equiano."

[22] Regarding Equiano, Aravamudan raises the possibility of "separatist nationalism" for British Africans (*Tropicopolitans*, 283). See also C. L. Innes, "Eighteenth-Century Letters and Narratives: Ignatius Sancho, Olaudah Equiano, and Dean Mahomed," in *A History of Black and Asian Writing in Britain, 1700–2000* (Cambridge: Cambridge University Press, 2002), 37.

[23] See Mungo Park, *Travels in the Interior Districts of Africa*, 1799, ed. Kate Ferguson Marsters (Durham, NC Duke University Press, 2000), esp. Marster's Introduction, 9–16.

broadly, describing ways that actual masters deployed "kindness" to produce "thankfulness" in their slaves for disciplinary purposes. Equiano
confirms the effectiveness of one master's management strategy of backing
up relative kindness with the threat of being sold off for "bad" behavior: "If
any of his slaves behaved amiss, he did not beat or use them ill, but parted
with them. This made them afraid of disobliging him; and as he treated his
slaves better than any other man on the island, so he was better served by
them in return" (100). Providing the slaves' perspective, Equiano redefines
what the novelists call "gratitude" as fear, and furthermore, as a rational
response to a thoroughly justified fear. He also shows that even "kind"
masters depend on, and are implicated in, the systemic violence of plantation slavery. The threat that the slaves must obey or face being sold away
from friends and family to a new master who would, most likely, be crueler,
is, in their experience, highly credible, and they do what they can to avoid
such punishment. Equiano's comment that "It is not uncommon, after a
flogging, to make slaves go on their knees, and thank their owners" (107),
shows that expressions of "gratitude" could, on the plantation, be a
humiliating demonstration of slaves' powerlessness over even their own
expressions of feeling, and a demonstration of the hollowness of their
owners' sentimental postures.

Despite these powerful deconstructions of the grateful slave trope, later
in his narrative, Equiano himself becomes the overseer for a plantation on
the Mosquito coast owned by Dr. Charles Irving, a man Equiano admired
after having served him as a hairdresser in London and accompanied him
on an expedition to the North Pole. Himself sounding like a sentimental
reformer in a grateful slave novel, Equiano insists of his slaves that he
"always treated them with care and affection, and did every thing I could to
comfort the poor creatures, and render their condition easy" (211). But he
does not claim that such treatment obviates their condition as slaves. He
does not record using the threat of sale to a harsher master to motivate the
slaves – which would hardly "render their condition easy."[24] After he ceases
to work as their overseer, however, he reports that his former slaves are
horribly abused by his successor ("a white overseer") and, as a result,
ultimately driven to their collective doom: "this man, through inhumanity
and ill-judged avarice, beat and cut the poor slaves most unmercifully; and
the consequence was, that every one got into a large Puriogua canoe, and

---

[24] This scene seems to undermine McBride's argument that the positive representations of slavery in
The Interesting Narrative are ironized in the distinction between Equiano as narrator and Equiano as
character (*Impossible Witnesses*, 121).

endeavored to escape; but, not knowing where to go, or how to manage the canoe, they were all drowned" (217–18). While Equiano here reveals a need to defend and explain his participation in British colonial slavery, particularly in his emphasis on the white man's "inhumanity" and "avarice," nonetheless he here emphasizes precisely the problem that the grateful slave novels are designed to obfuscate.[25] Without explicit comment, the facts Equiano presents suggest that goodness, the intentions, of individual owners or overseers are no match for the systemic violence of slavery, and that benevolent individuals exert at best a transitory influence.

When Equiano leaves the position as overseer, not only does his influence on the plantation cease, but he quickly finds himself battling to maintain his own liberty, as he is beaten and treated as a virtual slave by the captain who has promised to transport him to Jamaica. Dr. Irving appears to be kind and caring; Equiano never questions his personal integrity or goodness; and nonetheless, even Irving is capable of hiring an overseer who drives slaves to their deaths. Indeed, the anecdote ends with Equiano's remark that Irving was "now returning to Jamaica to purchase more slaves" in order to "stock" his plantation once again (218). Equiano does not offer a judgment on Irving, but the context reveals Irving's implication in a system he cannot personally control or change for the better.[26] Harriet Beecher Stowe, more than half a century later, in *Uncle Tom's Cabin*, designs a plot emphasizing that intentions are no match for the nature of the slave system, as caring slave owners like Mrs. Shelby and Augustine St. Claire only, in the end, serve to move Uncle Tom through the system until he falls into the brutal clutches of Simon Legree. Equiano (although he places far less emphasis on this lesson than does Stowe) could be said to anticipate her point with this anecdote, showing quite early that no slave is protected from falling into the hands of a greedy, selfish brute like Sir John Moore's anti-hero Zeluco, no matter the kind intentions of an Equiano-like overseer, or a Sir George Ellison-like owner, momentarily in

---

[25] Here I disagree with S. E. Ogude's claim in "Olaudah Equiano and the Tradition of Defoe," *African Literature Today*, 14 (1982), 77–90, that Equiano's work as an overseer is modeled on Defoe's *Colonel Jack* and that *The Interesting Narrative* largely derives from fiction.

[26] This reading responds to those critics who see Equiano as accepting or endorsing some forms of slavery: see Victor C. D. Mtubani, "The Black Voice in Eighteenth-Century Britain: African Writers Against Slavery and the Slave Trade," *Phylon*, 45:2 (1984), 85–97; Paul Edwards, *Unreconciled Strivings and Ironic Strategies: Three Afro-British Authors of the Georgian Era: Ignatius Sancho, Olaudah Equiano, Robert Wedderburn* (Edinburgh: Edinburgh University Press, 1992). In contrast Gary Gautier, "Slavery and the Fashioning of Race in *Oroonoko, Robinson Crusoe*, and Equiano's *Life*," *The Eighteenth Century: Theory and Interpretation*, 42:2 (2001), 161–79, suggests that Equiano's primary concern with race explains inconsistencies about slavery.

control of his fate. In fact, Equiano himself was betrayed into plantation slavery by the seemingly kindly Captain Pascal.[27] Equiano does make an exception to his discomfort with gratitude in repeatedly expressing his gratitude to the anti-slavery public in his correspondence.[28]

All three of the primary black Atlantic writers of the period, then, reject the charges of insensibility and irrationality made against Africans by their contemporaries. Indeed, all three show an awareness of gratitude as a measure of racial difference. Sancho, the only one writing without an explicitly polemical intent, nonetheless shows a discomfort with "gratitude" and a mastery of what might be called playful sentimental one-upmanship. All three black Atlantic writers, then, point out, and undermine, the assumed irrationality of the grateful slave. Cugoano does this by challenging the very idea of a humane form of slavery; Equiano does so by redefining what the novelists term "gratitude" on the plantation as rationally assessed fear, and by reminding his readers that individual kindness is not a solution to systemic exploitation; Sancho does it by insisting on contextualizing "gratitude," and never allowing obligation to be taken to irrational extremes. In representations of the grateful slave, novelists treat Africans as isolated individuals, who can be manipulated emotionally, but who have no past or future, and no psychological depth. In most grateful slave novels, only one slave is named, individuated, and successfully manipulated; all the other faceless, nameless slaves merely follow suit. To introduce the slave's perspective, as Equiano does, to conceive of Africans as possessing a natural freedom, as Cugoano does, or to show an African as a master of the sophisticated game of metropolitan sentimentality, as Sancho does, begins to call into question the flattened, decontextualized emotions of the grateful slave.

Black Atlantic writers endorse one form of gratitude – gratitude to God – but even this can be used critically, as they reject the pro-slavery argument that Christian conversion justifies the enslavement of Africans, shaping Christian conversion into a position of resistance and a basis for claiming a positive African American (or African British) identity.[29] Indeed, black Atlantic writers reminded white interlocutors that slaveholding may be a

---

[27] Carretta, in *Equiano, The African*, 71–2, 90, 121, sees Equiano as devoted to Pascal; but Equiano's stated eagerness to see Pascal appears ironic (Equiano, *Interesting Narrative*, 138), as he challenges Pascal about prize money on seeing him (Equiano, *Interesting Narrative*, 165).

[28] See his letters reprinted in Carretta, *Equiano, The African*, 342, 349.

[29] This is the argument of Brooks in *American Lazarus*. Brooks draws on Gauri Viswanathan, *Outside the Fold: Conversion, Modernity, and Belief* (Princeton: Princeton University Press, 1998) for the model of conversion as a potential site of resistance.

violation of the gratitude any sincere Christian owes to God. Benjamin Banneker challenged Thomas Jefferson in 1791, reminding him that as a leader of the young nation (at that moment, George Washington's Secretary of State), "you cannot but be led to a serious and grateful sense of your miraculous and providential preservation," opposing this expected gratitude to providence with the "detaining by fraud and violence so numerous a part of my brethren."[30]

Banneker's altering the frame of reference from relations between master and slave to those between God and man reveals that the expectation of slaves' binding themselves out of gratitude to their masters could be seen at the time as fraudulent and irreligious. Indeed, *Colonel Jack*, the first grateful slave fiction, uncomfortably conflated "master" and "God" for the slaves.[31] At the time Banneker wrote to Jefferson, of course, Jefferson's *Notes on the State of Virginia* was still fresh with its hypothesis of racial difference and admission that slavery made him "tremble for my country when I reflect that God is just" (169).

Similarly, despite their joy and pride in embracing Christianity, black Atlantic writers did not allow the conflation of gratitude to God for their conversion with gratitude to their enslavers. This was a sensitive issue, as slavery's apologists insisted that Africans should be grateful for their rescue from African savagery to civilization and Christianity. Equiano, for instance, expresses gratitude to God and even to those who served as the agents of his final, sincere conversion. But, after this conversion, he also makes it extremely clear that whites in general do more to keep him from Christ than to sustain his faith, for instance when he is foiled in attempts to convert Indians, and when he expresses discomfort at being surrounded on shipboard by blasphemers, or, on the Mosquito coast, by whites who refuse to keep the sabbath.[32]

Equiano goes so far as to depict himself as enduring Christ-like suffering for his faith at the hands of white Englishmen. He challenges an abusive captain by remarking to him that "I had been twice amongst the Turks, yet had never seen any such usage with them, and much less could I have expected anything of the kind among the Christians." The captain replies "Christians! Damn you, you are one of St. Paul's men; but, by G –, except you have St. Paul's or St. Peter's faith, and walk upon the water to the

[30] Banneker's letter to Jefferson is quoted in Scot French, *The Rebellious Slave: Nat Turner in American Memory* (Boston: Houghton Mifflin, 2004), 13, from an archival document.

[31] See 92 above.

[32] See Carretta's excellent account of Equiano's conversion and of these situations, *Equiano, The African* 171–5, 182–3, 186–90.

shore, you shall not go out of the vessel," ironically confirming Equiano's charges with his swearing and blaspheming (211). This captain then goes on to test Equiano's faith, as promised, through a kind of nautical parody of a crucifixion, having Equiano hanged up by his wrists and ankles (212). Although he suffers, Equiano passes the test of faith, not by walking on water but by maintaining his faith and his Christian conduct throughout the ordeal: "Whilst I remained in this condition, till between five and six o'clock in the morning, I trusted & prayed to God to forgive this blasphemer, who cared not what he did" (212). Indeed, beyond the fact that most Englishmen and whites he encounters do not count as Christians, Equiano's need to seek out religious education, true conversion, and religious community as a free man in London represents an implicit rebuke to the English, and specifically to his "kind" masters Robert King and Captain Pascal in their failure to attend seriously to his spiritual development.

The black Atlantic writers' demonstration of the flaws of the grateful slave paradigm represents not only a response to a pernicious literary trope, and a contribution to the anti-slavery effort, but also a rejection of an increasing powerful conception of race.[33] The idea of Africans sharing the emotional capacity of Europeans, but differing in rational capacities, is part of the development from the eighteenth-century monogenist notion of a single human race in the direction of, but not all the way to, the firmly racist mid-nineteenth-century polygenist position that the races are entirely separate and must have had separate origins.[34] The black Atlantic writers, however, appeal to the still dominant monogenist consensus, drawing on the abuses of colonial racial practice, and the hypocrisy of the colonists, to demonstrate the urgency of a full return to the consensus. By opposing the ascription of irrationality to Africans, and offering a transatlantic African perspective, then, the black Atlantic writers go much further than even the most radical, the most skeptical of amelioration, of the novelists. In opposing this irrationality, which, in the guise of gratitude initially seems intended as a confirmation of African humanity, the black Atlantic writers demonstrate the absurd unreality of the new conception of racial difference under formation in the late eighteenth-century British Atlantic world.

---

[33] Michael A. Gomez, *Exchanging Our Country Marks: The Transformation of African Identities in the Colonial and Antebellum South* (Chapel Hill: University of North Carolina Press, 1998) contends that positive racial identity was not available to American slaves until the early nineteenth century. Brooks argues, by contrast, that such identities were in formation, particularly through religion, in the eighteenth century (*American Lazarus* 45–6 and *passim*).

[34] See the Introduction, n. 24 above.

"GRATITUDE BOWED ME DOWN": EQUIANO'S RESISTANCE TO WHITENESS

In *The Interesting Narrative*, Equiano describes himself as "resisting oppression" (120). Critics who engage with this statement tend to see Equiano as an abolitionist concerned with fighting slavery, or as defender of African culture, resisting European domination.[35] Equiano is concerned centrally neither with the oppression of slavery, nor with European cultural imperialism. Instead, Equiano devotes himself to opposing the practices of racial oppression in the British colonies of the New World.[36] Equiano emphasizes the transatlantic gap to challenge the emergence of racial difference in the British Atlantic culture of the late eighteenth century, to expose the colonial practice of race to a metropolitan audience, and furthermore, to argue that white colonists themselves consciously recognize the humanity and capacity of blacks but nonetheless conspire to support white supremacy for material benefits.

---

[35] Key readings of Equiano as resisting Western identity and values from an African perspective include Chinosole, "Tryin' to Get Over: Narrative Posture in Equiano's Autobiography," in *The Art of Slave Narrative: Original Essays in Criticism and Theory*, ed. John Sekora and Darwin T. Turner (Macomb, IL: Western Illinois University Press, 1982), 45–54; Wilfred Samuels, "Disguised Voice in The Interesting Narrative of Olaudah Equiano, or Gustavus Vassa, the African," *Black American Literature Forum*, 19 (1985), 64–9; and Robin Sabino and Jennifer Hall, in "The Path Not Taken: Cultural Identity in the Interesting Life of Olaudah Equiano," *MELUS*, 24:1 (1999), 5–19. Other readings position Equiano as more "European" or "Christian" than African, including S. E. Ogude, "Facts into Fiction: Equiano's Narrative Reconsidered," *Research in African Literatures*, 13 (1982), 31–43; Adam Potkay, "Olaudah Equiano and the Art of Spiritual Autobiography," *Eighteenth-Century Studies*, 27:4 (1994), 677–92; Katalin Orban, "Dominant and Submerged Discourses in *The Life of Olaudah Equiano (or Gustavus Vassa?)*," *African American Review*, 27:4 (1993), 655–64; and Tanya Caldwell, "'Talking Too Much English': Languages of Economy and Politics in Equiano's *The Interesting Narrative*," *Early American Literature*, 34 (1999), 263–82. I prefer the critical view of Equiano's identity as hybrid and complex: see Houston A. Baker, Jr., "Figurations for a New American Literary History: Section V," in *Blues, Ideology, and Afro-American Literature: A Vernacular Theory* (Chicago: University of Chicago Press, 1984), 31–50; Henry Louis Gates, Jr., "Trope of the Talking Book," in *The Signifying Monkey: A Theory of African American Literary Criticism* (New York: Oxford University Press, 1986), 152–8; Sandiford *Measuring the Moment*; Marion Rust, "The Subaltern as Imperialist: Speaking of Olaudah Equiano," in *Passing and the Fictions of Identity*, ed. Elaine K. Ginsberg (Durham, NC: Duke University Press, 1996), 21–36; Susan Marren, "Between Slavery and Freedom: The Transgressive Self in Olaudah Equiano's Autobiography," *PMLA*, 108:1 (1993), 94–105; and Carretta, "Introduction" to Equiano's *Interesting Narrative*, ix–xxviii, and "Defining a Gentleman: The Status of Olaudah Equiano or Gustavus Vassa," *Language Sciences*, 22 (2000), 385–99; Helen Thomas, *Romanticism and Slave Narratives: Transatlantic Testimonies* (Cambridge: Cambridge University Press, 2000), 226–54; and Eileen Razzari Elrod, "Moses and the Egyptian: Religious Authority in Olaudah Equiano's *Interesting Narrative*," *African American Review*, 35:3 (2001), 409–25.

[36] Most critics do not see race as a primary concern of Equiano's. Exceptions are Gautier, "Slavery," and Wheeler, *Complexion*, 260–87.

Equiano's formative early experiences on British naval ships – which follow English rather than colonial norms and practices – leave him bewildered by the institutionalized white privilege he encounters in the colonies.[37] His shipboard friend Daniel Queen, for instance, makes him feel like an equal: "he used to say, that he and I should never part; and that when our ship was paid off, as I was as free as himself or any other man on board, he would instruct me in his business, by which I might gain a good livelihood" (92). Another shipboard friend, Richard Baker, although in fact a slave-owning American, typifies these early experiences. Equiano explains that Dick had "a mind superior to prejudice"; and "was not ashamed to notice, to associate with, and to be the friend and instructor of one who was ignorant, a stranger, of a different complexion, and a slave" (65). Indeed, Equiano offers Dick as a model to his white readers; he constantly reminds them of the failure of colonial justice to be race-blind, and emphasizes not only that there are people like Dick, but places in which their values dominate. Equiano, indeed, attributes this unprejudiced, race-blind, or non-racial, attitude to England itself, no doubt meaning to challenge his white readers to live up to this idealization. Thus he can, in moments that have inspired much critical consternation, describe the English as "men superior to us" (78), consider himself "almost an Englishman" (77), and describe his desire to return to "England, where my heart has always been" (147).[38]

In idealizing England and the English, however, Equiano does not merely play to his metropolitan audience, but also points to the uneven development of racial consciousness in eighteenth-century British Atlantic culture. Equiano thoroughly documents his own fruitless attempts in the colonies to get effective redress – legal or social – against whites in the colonies who use their privileged status to abuse him, to rob him of money or commodities, or to force other Africans back into slavery: each such example draws attention to the unevenness of justice in the eighteenth-century Atlantic world, to the failure to uphold freedom of exchange in the colonies, to the transatlantic gap in conceptions and practices of race.[39] Equiano makes explicit the link between economic exploitation and the

---

[37] See N. A. M. Rodger, *The Wooden World: An Anatomy of the Georgian Navy* (Annapolis, MD: Naval Institute, 1986), 160; and Carretta, *Equiano, The African*, 74–5, 86–7.

[38] For examples see Chinosole, "Tryin' to Get Over," 45; Samuels, "Disguised Voice"; Marren, "Between Slavery"; Rust, "Subaltern"; Sabino and Hall, "Path Not Taken"; and William Mottolese, "'Almost an Englishman': Olaudah Equiano and the Colonial Gift of Language," *Bucknell Review*, 41:2 (1998), 160–71.

[39] See Elizabeth Jane Wall Hinds, "The Spirit of Trade: Olaudah Equiano's Conversion, Legalism, and the Merchant's *Life*," *African American Review*, 32:4 (1998), 639–45, and McBride, *Impossible*

racial system, remarking "nor is there any greater regard shewn to the little property than there is to the persons and lives of the negroes" (108). By insisting on recourse to the law, Equiano forces the colonial legal system to articulate, if not to confront, its inequities and injustice.[40]

Equiano's resistance to racial oppression takes precedence even over his concern with slavery.[41] As has often been noted, he does endorse – or at least fails to condemn – some versions of slavery. Equiano goes so far as to argue that slavery seems acceptable when compared with the worse plight of free blacks:

> Hitherto I had thought only slavery dreadful; but the state of a free negro appeared to me now equally so at least, and in some respects even worse, for they live in constant alarm for their liberty, which is but nominal, for they are universally insulted and plundered without the possibility of redress; for such is the equity of the West Indian laws, that no free negro's evidence will be admitted in their courts of justice. In this situation, is it surprising that slaves, when mildly treated, should prefer even the misery of slavery to such a mockery of freedom? (122)

Here, Equiano gives a clear, detailed account of the legal, social, and economic oppression of free blacks in the West Indies authorized by the system of whiteness;[42] he does not, however, bring racial difference into the discussion. The final sentence, invoking the possibility of "preferring slavery," if taken out of context, could sound much like the arguments of slavery's apologists that African slaves would be unable to benefit from freedom;[43] but here, the discussion begins from the understanding of slavery as a "dreadful" state of degradation. Equiano makes notable efforts to distance himself from identity as a slave.[44] This, however, is part of his larger strategy of refusing definition as "black," or more precisely, as excluded from the privileges of whiteness. According to Equiano, the lamentable situation of the "free Negro" has

Witnesses, 138, for an account of Equiano's almost obsessive recourse to the law, and his documenta-tion of the economic exploitation of blacks in the colonies. Mindie Lazarus-Black, in "Slaves, Masters, and Magistrates: Law and the Politics of Resistance in the English Speaking Caribbean, 1736–1834," American Bar Foundation Working Paper no. 9124, contends that slaves did use the law in the colonies more than scholars have realized, despite the restrictions on their access.

[40] For the differing legal regimes in play, see Eliga H. Gould, "Zones of Law, Zones of Violence: The Legal Geography of the British Atlantic, circa 1772," *William and Mary Quarterly*, 60:3 (2003), 471–510.

[41] Larry E. Tise, *The American Counterrevolution: A Retreat from Liberty, 1783–1800* (Mechanicsburg, PA: Stackpole, 1998), 102–3, also sees Equiano as primarily a campaigner for the rights of free blacks.

[42] Gaspar cites this passage as an accurate account of the freedman's lot in Antigua (*Bondmen and Rebels*, 162–3).

[43] See for instance Bryan Edwards, *History, Civil and Commercial, of the British Colonies in the West Indies*, 2 vols. (London: John Stockdale, 1793), II:35–6. This passage is quoted and analyzed in chapter 6 below.

[44] See Carretta, "Defining a Gentleman," 389, and McBride, *Impossible Witnesses*, 140.

nothing to do with blacks' supposedly limited capacities. Instead, it is due to
the colonial regime of race, which paradoxically provides slaves more redress
than freedmen, because a master can bring suit to protect his property. The
free black does not have even such compromised and arbitrary protection.
Equiano's objections to the institution of slavery may have to do more with
the impossibility of escaping its stigma in a racialized society than with the
inherent injustice of slavery itself.

In one of the strangest scenes of the *Interesting Narrative*, Equiano, at
this point a newly freed sailor in Savannah, Georgia, beats the slave of a
Mr. Read. Equiano uses the incident to illustrate his own oppression as
a free black and to insist on an identity – and a physical appearance –
distinguishing him from slaves. Equiano's account of his decision to strike
the slave is complex, and hinges on the relation of slave and master:

> I entreated him, with all the patience I was master of, to desist, as I knew there was
> little or no law for a free negro here; but the fellow, instead of taking my advice,
> persevered in his insults, and even struck me. At this I lost all temper, and fell on
> him and beat him soundly. (139)

Equiano is aware that there is "no law" for free blacks in this colony.
Although he does not say it directly, he shows his awareness that there is a
"law" for slaves, one that reduces them to being their master's property, but
gives them status in that aspect. Equiano echoes this perversity of the law by
refusing to identify the slave except with his master's name. Equiano
presents his rational attempt to persuade the slave "to desist," with "all
the patience I was master of," as a form of "mastery," which, symbolically,
should give him the power to control a mere slave. However, rather than
relating his "advice" to the slave, Equiano discloses only his own primary
desideratum, that "there was little or no law for a free negro here." Equiano
suggests that if he were in a place with an effective system of justice, he
likely would have beaten the slave earlier. The slave's failure to acknowledge Equiano's superior status, his freedom and his self-mastery, overrides
these concerns, causing Equiano to lash out: "instead of taking my advice . . .
[he] even struck me." As a slave could not risk striking a free white man –
the punishment in some colonies for such an act was death – by striking
Equiano, the slave tauntingly exposes his free status as a sham.

When first confronted by Read, Equiano takes the high road: "I told
him that he [the slave] had insulted me, and had given the provocation by
first striking me," (139) insisting on race-blind, rational justice. But
Equiano also contemplates the anecdote of "a free black man, a carpenter,
that I knew, who, for asking a gentleman that he had worked for, for the

money that he had earned, was put in goal" (139), showing his awareness that being in the right is not of great practical value for a "free negro" in Georgia. Equiano's key white ally in this situation, Thomas Farmer, the captain of his ship, offers an initial response to the situation that is certainly better than craven submission to white supremacy – "when Mr. Read came and applied to him to deliver me up, he said he knew nothing of the matter, I was a free man" – but Equiano does not find it reassuring. Indeed, he remarks "I was astonished and frightened at this" (139); Equiano knows all too well that the captain's appeal to his free status is useless and that an effective defense will require sterner measures.

Equiano's free status, due to colonial racial oppression, paradoxically increases the threat that his body will be permanently, humiliatingly, marked as a slave's:

I dreaded, of all things, the thoughts of being stripped, as I never in my life had the marks of any violence of that kind. At that instant a rage seized my soul, and for a while I determined to resist the first man that should attempt to lay violent hands on me, or basely use me without a trial; for I would sooner die like a free man, than suffer myself to be scourged by the hands of ruffians, and my blood drawn like a slave. (139–40)

If he were a slave, anyone else whipping him would have to answer to his master, who would have legal standing to sue for the damage to his property. Absent this protection, the threat of being "stripped" like a slave at first goads Equiano to a posture of defiant insistence on his freedom, even to a resolution to use violence. But it also (although this remains unsaid) exerts pressure on him not to resist openly, because open defiance is the course mostly likely to result in a flogging. As a result, Equiano ultimately accedes to advice to hide rather than to resist.

While in hiding, Equiano manages to network with potential white protectors, parlaying Captain Farmer's recommendation into enough social pressure on the captain to force him into a vigorous and effective stance. Equiano explains that "the good character which my Captain always gave me, as well as some other gentlemen, who also knew me, procured me some friends" (140). These friends

told my Captain that he did not use me well, in suffering me thus to be imposed upon, and said they would see me redressed, and get me on board some other vessel. My captain, on this, immediately went to Mr. Read, and told him, that ever since I had eloped from the vessel, his work had been neglected. (140)

Appealing to Equiano's free status, in essence, leaves the matter up to Read's goodwill. On the other hand, the argument that Read is causing economic damage to another white man is persuasive, carrying as it does the implicit threat of social and even legal retribution.

Several critics, following Houston Baker, have noted Equiano's insistence on his own economic success.[45] The slave has legal and social standing – but only as the property of his master. Equiano, similarly, only has the power to get whites to act strongly on his behalf when the abuse he suffers impacts their financial interests. So Equiano's economic value to the captain is the bottom line that insures a modicum of decent treatment for him, gives him legal status, via his patron, to equal that the slave has through his master. But it also does a bit more. It reveals the truth that the whites cannot deny: that it is Equiano's intelligence, ability, and humanity that ultimately make him valuable.

The dependent state of ex-slaves most clearly illustrates Equiano's experience of racial oppression. Orlando Patterson, in *Slavery and Social Death*, explains that emancipation in most slave societies is accompanied by ritual expressions of gratitude to the master for freedom; this "gratitude" initiates a patronage relationship.[46] Under British colonial slavery, these rituals may have been attenuated, but the importance of the patronage relationship was, if anything, heightened.[47] Equiano provides an instance of the validity of Patterson's description for the British eighteenth century, as he depends on white patronage to achieve manumission. Equiano's master, Robert King, makes a verbal contract to sell him back his liberty. Once Equiano collects the money, however, he still needs another white ally, Captain Farmer, to convince King to follow through: "Come, Robert," Farmer cajoles King, "I think you must let him have his freedom; – you have laid your money out very well; you have received good interest for it all this time, and here is now the principal at last . . . and he will still save you money, as he will not leave you" (135). Farmer enables Equiano to

---

[45] See Hinds, "Spirit of Trade"; Joseph Fichtelberg, "Word Between Worlds: The Economy of Equiano's *Narrative*," *American Literary History*, 5:3 (1993), 459–80; Sonia Hofkosh, "Tradition and the *Interesting Narrative*: Capitalism, Abolitionism, and the Romantic Individual," in *Romanticism, Race, and Imperial Culture, 1780–1834*, ed. Alan Richardson and Sonia Hofkosh (Bloomington: Indiana University Press, 1996), 330–43; and Terry S. Bozeman, "Interstices, Hybridity, and Identity: Olaudah Equiano and the Discourse of the African Slave Trade," *Studies in the Literary Imagination*, 36:2 (2003), 61–70.

[46] "Manumission: Its Meanings and Modes," in *Slavery and Social Death*, 209–39, esp. 211, on gratitude for manumission, and "The Status of Freed Persons," 240–61, on patronage relationship for ex-slaves.

[47] Patterson suggests that the "ritual" conferring of obligation on freed slaves was "premodern," but nonetheless, "In modern capitalistic slave systems, even though slaves paid dearly in one way or another for their freedom, that freedom itself was still regarded as a gift from the master or mistress" (*Slavery and Social Death*, 217).

claim his freedom, but at the same time he circumscribes it, promising on Equiano's behalf that he will not leave. In intervening, as it turns out, Farmer also saddles Equiano with a second patron who can demand his "gratitude."

Such a patronage relationship hardly constitutes the freedom Equiano desires for himself. Equiano unironically describes his ecstasy on obtaining freedom, his fantasy of having obtained complete power over his fate: "I who had been a slave in the morning, trembling at the will of another, now became my own master, and compleatly free" (137). However, when Farmer and King ask him to continue working for them, Equiano has no choice but to submit. He delicately remarks that "gratitude bowed me down; and none but the generous mind can judge of my feelings, struggling between inclination and duty" (138). Even this description overstates Equiano's control over himself as a freed West Indian slave. "Gratitude" and "duty" are not simply feelings he must weigh, but are structural components of his emancipation. Equiano later reveals that even a free black with legitimate papers could not ship out of a West Indian port without being advertised, a process which effectively gives any white the power to stop him from departing, unless a powerful patron intervenes (162).

And indeed, Equiano also shows his seemingly heartfelt gratitude to Farmer as produced by racial oppression. After striking the deal to buy himself from King, Equiano "used every honest means" to earn the money, and was soon "master of a few pounds" (119). Equiano remarks that "my friendly captain knew very well" of the money, and "this occasioned him sometimes to take liberties with me; but whenever he treated me waspishly, I used plainly to tell him my mind, and that I would die before I would be imposed open as other negroes were, and that to me, life had lost its relish when liberty was gone" (120). Despite this moment of confrontation, Equiano ultimately suppresses his anger at Farmer for pragmatic reasons, qualifying his threat of suicide: "This I said, although I foresaw my then well-being or future hopes of freedom (humanly speaking) depended on this man" (120). It is here that Equiano directly invokes "oppression": "I thus went on, filled with the thoughts of my freedom and resisting oppression as well as I was able" (120). Hence, the phrase specifically refers to the racial oppression of white supremacy, in the form of the economic exploitation and burdensome patronage relationships, rather than to slavery itself.

The patronage system as detailed by Patterson, made visible in King and Farmer's demand that Equiano perform his "gratitude," becomes a restraint on his freedom; it allows masters to extend a slave-like control over those ex-slaves nominally granted their freedom. After purchasing his freedom, even after Farmer's death, Equiano is still constrained to serve King out of "gratitude."[48] Remarking that Farmer's death has deprived him of a "great benefactor and friend," Equiano considers that: "I had little inducement to remain longer in the West Indies, except my gratitude to Mr. King, which I thought I had pretty well discharged" (147). Equiano then expresses his wish "of returning to England, where my heart has always been" (147). Evidently, however, the measure of whether or not Equiano's gratitude to King has been discharged is not Equiano's own feelings on the matter. Equiano reports that "Mr. King still pressed me very much to stay with his vessel; and he had done so much for me, that I found myself unable to refuse his requests" (147). Equiano subtly and yet insistently shows this "gratitude" to be coercive, much closer to a legally enforceable debt (something to be "fully discharged") than to a sentimental sensation. Indeed, neither Equiano nor King seems to be indulging in, or savoring, sentimental roles like those relished by Sir George Ellison and playfully described by Sancho. Equiano makes it quite clear that he no longer *feels* the gratitude himself, but that King nonetheless demands that he continue to perform the obligations of this gratitude. The situation is close to that of a fictional grateful slave, but Equiano shows that he feels the demand for the performance of his obligation not as a pleasure worth devoting his life to, but instead as an oppressive and socially enforceable debt.

Even in discussing the ways that whites exploit the chattel status of slaves to rob them with near-impunity, Equiano develops the ways that racial oppression and the patronage system could be seen as imposing a yet greater burden on freedmen. Equiano relates the tale of "a poor Creole negro I knew well" (110). The slave relates to Equiano the problems that arise whenever he goes fishing:

"Sometimes when a white man take away my fish, I go to my master, and he gets me my right; and when my master, by strength, take away my fishes, what must me do? I can't go to any body to be righted . . . I must look up to God Mighty in the top for right." (110)

This anecdote, in Equiano's retelling, makes the denial of property rights a complaint on behalf of slaves, and yet also reinforces the point that slaves actually have more recourse than free blacks. The fisherman, after all, can appeal to his master for help – whenever, that is, the master is not

---

[48] Here I differ from Carretta in *Equiano, The African*, 127, who sees Equiano's gratitude to King as sincere.

personally exploiting him. The many incidents in which Equiano tries and fails to get legal recourse against whites who have robbed him imply that, almost perversely, slaves' status as white property gives them more "rights" than black freedmen have in the raced world of the colonies.

Equiano's commentary on the slave fisherman's plight, in his biblical allusion, can be read as implying the righteousness of resistance to slavery, race, and gratitude. As Eileen Razzari Elrod has observed, Equiano here seems to endorse Christian quietism for slaves, via the suggestion that prayer and the next world are their only hopes for redress: "this artless tale moved me much, and I could not help feeling the just cause Moses had in redressing his brother against the Egyptian. I exhorted the man to look up still to God on the top, since there was no redress below" (110–11). But, Elrod reminds us, in the biblical passage in question, Moses in fact slays an Egyptian for abusing a Hebrew slave.[49] In light of this, she points out, the passage could be taken to support violent resistance to slavery.[50] This raises some intriguing interpretive issues. If Equiano makes his point "indirectly," it is unclear to whom he is communicating his indirect, but more heartfelt message. His audience would have to be his fellow Africans, or those who know their Bible well enough that they would instantly discern the embedded point, or indeed both. If the message is for his fellow Christians and abolitionists – the groups to whom his book is most explicitly directed – why does Equiano make the point covertly rather than explicitly?

Further, Equiano's repetition of the word "redress" leaves his point ambiguous. He seems to insist that there is "no redress below," making the quietist point that God's justice awaits in the afterlife. And yet he does so only moments after characterizing Moses as, precisely, having offered "redress." Moses' slaying of the Egyptian is only indirectly inspired by God. Equiano leaves unresolved whether or not he views similar acts of "redress" in this world as divinely sanctioned, and if he believes in the possibility of a black Atlantic Moses – perhaps embodied in himself. After all, his book acts as a plea for redress of injuries in this world.

While the reference to Exodus opens up the possibility of a subtle endorsement of violent resistance, an investigation of eighteenth-century biblical commentaries known to be owned (or consulted) by Equiano suggests another complex linkage between gratitude, slavery, and race in

---

[49] The allusion is to Exodus 2:11–12.
[50] Potkay explicitly rules out such an interpretation of this passage, although he wrote before Elrod ("Equiano," 681–2, 688).

his thinking.[51] The commentators suggest that Moses, in this very episode, is called by God to an awareness of his brotherhood with the Hebrews, and that this sense of brotherhood motivates and justifies the slaying (although the story in Exodus provides no concrete indication of such a moment of enlightenment).[52] They do, however, try to explain away the violence of the passage and its seeming endorsement of direct resistance to worldly oppression.[53] Matthew Henry's commentary, however, adds the further point that Moses "was obliged in gratitude as well as interest to Pharaoh's daughter, and yet he obtained a glorious victory by faith over this temptation" in order to embrace his divinely revealed brotherhood with the Hebrews.[54] Presumably, he would be tempted by gratitude because she had saved his life as an infant, raised him in the royal household, and thereby allowed him to lead a life infinitely more attractive than that of his Hebrew brethren.

The idea of gratitude as a temptation to be resisted strengthens Elrod's case that there is a biblical version of signifying underlying Equiano's choice of this passage as a reference. If Equiano did indeed have such resonances of the passage in mind – and of course, however compelling they seem, this must remain a matter of speculation – it is nonetheless striking that he hides them under the overt quietism of the "God on the top" remark. If we are indeed being invited to read enslaved Africans as a modern version of the Israelites in Egypt, Equiano could be implying that no African should allow himself to act on "gratitude" for being allowed a role, or a fate, more appealing than that of his brethren. In a sense, this would imply that the difference between a relatively successful denizen of the black Atlantic, like Equiano, and an oppressed slave like the fisherman,

---

[51] Equiano cites John Gill, *An Exposition of the Old Testament*, 1788 (46) and John Brown, *A Dictionary of the Holy Bible*, 1788 (246 n. 70). Carretta notes that Equiano owned Matthew Henry, *An Exposition of the Old and New Testament* (1772) (*Interesting Narrative*, 246, n. 70).

[52] Gill, *An Exposition of the Old Testament* (London: The Author, 1763), I:298; John Brown, *A Dictionary of the Holy Bible* (Edinburgh: John Gray, 1769), II:188. Matthew Henry, *An Exposition of the Old and New Testament* (London: J. Stratford, [1793]), vol I, Exodus 2:11 (unpaginated) says "he boldly owns and espouses the cause of *God's people*" and that "he found himself (no doubt) under a divine direction and impulse."

[53] Henry specifies that Moses acted "by special warrant from Heaven (which makes not a precedent in ordinary cases)," noting the Jewish tradition that Moses slew the Egyptian with words rather than a weapon; Gill registers discomfort by noting that Moses buried the body (as described in Exodus 2:12) "not from any consciousness of guilt" (I:298); Brown interpolates the fact that the Egyptian was murdering the Hebrew into his retelling of the tale (*Dictionary*, 188).

[54] Henry, *Exposition*, vol. I, Exodus 2:11 (unpaginated); the same wording appears in the 3rd edn, which carries the slightly different title *An Exposition of All the Books the Old and New Testament* (London: J. Clark *et al.*, 1725), I: 155. I was unable to locate the 1772 edition, but there is no reason to expect this comment would have been lacking from that edition.

ought not to be seen as offering any defense of the slave system itself: Moses' life in the royal palace provides no justification of the Egyptians, but is properly construed only as giving Moses a precious opportunity to strike a blow for freedom. Hence, grateful slaves – or even "grateful" freedmen, like Equiano – are not merely mistaken, but tempted into sin, if they act, or constrain themselves, out of gratitude to benefactors.[55]

Interestingly, then, these commentaries, in their contention that God makes Moses come to an awareness of himself as a "Hebrew," also point to a concept of identity as at once real – even God-given – and yet also as a strategic necessity in the immediate struggle against slavery. This same dynamic applies to Equiano: he rejects the "blackness" that the colonial system of whiteness would impose on him, and yet he makes common cause with his "countrymen" the slaves and ex-slaves – and, of course, he often did this, for instance as a spokesman and leader of London's black community and a participant in the Sierra Leone project.[56] He identifies with enslaved and oppressed Africans in the Atlantic world to make common cause against oppression – perhaps even seeing this as a divine mission – while nonetheless refusing the terms of "raced" identity as practiced in the colonies. If it is true that Equiano was born in South Carolina, then his claim to have been born in Benin becomes striking evidence of his self-consciously adopting an African identity for political purposes.[57]

Equiano's rejection of "whiteness," however, is not merely a matter of speculative reconstructions of his signifying on the Bible. Indeed, he confronts white privilege directly in the text, depicting himself as heroically opposing and exposing it. After Captain Farmer's death, when Equiano finds himself incapable of resisting King's insistence on his debt of gratitude, Equiano begins sailing with a new captain, William Phillips, who is more unrelentingly committed to white privilege than was the relatively humane, if nonetheless exploitative, Farmer.

---

[55] Brooks shows that the Exodus story was appropriated to African-American uses in the eighteenth century (*American Lazarus*, 26, 49, 94–5, 105). For the importance of Moses and Exodus in nineteenth-century black religion, see Albert J. Raboteau, "African-Americans, Exodus, and the American Israel," in *African-American Christianity: Essays in History*, ed. Paul E. Johnson (Berkeley: University California Press, 1994), 1–17, and Genovese, *Roll Jordan Roll*, 252–5.

[56] See Carretta, *Equiano, The African*, 223–35; James Walvin, "Back to Africa," in *An African's Life: The Life and Times of Olaudah Equiano, 1745–1797* (London: Cassell, 1998), 137–50; and Schama, *Rough Crossings*, 193–4, 198–200.

[57] For the evidence about Equiano's birthplace, see Vincent Carretta, "Olaudah Equiano or Gustavus Vassa? New Light on an Eighteenth-century Question of Identity," *Slavery and Abolition*, 20:3 (1999), 96–105.

Navigation has already been marked as a form of knowledge reserved for whites during Equiano's service with Farmer. Equiano pays a mate of Farmer's to instruct him in navigation. When apprised of the situation, Farmer "rebukes" the mate, because, Equiano reports, "it was a shame for him to take any money from me" (123). Farmer promises Equiano free instruction (time permitting), but his offer is quickly overturned by social pressure: as Equiano relates, "some of our passengers, and others, seeing this, found much fault with him for it, saying, it was a very dangerous thing to let a negro know navigation" (123). On his deathbed and unable to navigate the ship himself, Farmer realizes that he has sacrificed the safety of his ship and crew to white privilege: "the Captain was now very sorry that he had not taught me navigation, and protested, if ever he should get well again, he would not fail to do so" (142).[58] Farmer never does recover; but Equiano successfully brings Farmer's ship into port, navigating "by mere dint of reason" (142). Celebrated for this in the port, Equiano playfully remarks "the sable captain lost no fame" (144).

Neither Captain Farmer, nor the anonymous whites who prevent Equiano's instruction suggest that Equiano, or blacks in general, are incapable of learning navigation. Nonetheless, Equiano's satisfaction in relating the story of his success as "the sable captain" derives at least in part from its demonstration that white privilege is only an alliance for material purposes, unable to suppress or deny Equiano's superior talents. And indeed, Equiano's success as an untrained navigator, depending only on his reason, seems to goad Captain Phillips into a self-defeating attempt to display his superior abilities as a trained navigator, and ultimately into a shipwreck.

Equiano begins the tale of his voyage with Phillips with the remark that "our new captain boasted strangely of his skill in navigating and conducting a vessel; and in consequence of this, he steered a new course" (147). When one of the men on overnight watch reports to Equiano that he sees a "grampus" (or killer whale) near the ship, Equiano checks, and quickly deduces that it is instead a serious danger: "when I saw the sea wash up against it again and again, I said it was not a fish but a rock" (148). He immediately reports to Captain Phillips. The captain will not take Equiano seriously, at first indifferently assuring him that "it was very well," then promising, but failing, to come up on deck and take command of the situation. The captain simply refuses to accept Equiano's reasoned

---

[58] Equiano explains that he wished to learn navigation in order to escape to England if he was unable to obtain his liberty by other means (122).

deductions that the ship is doomed, and the implied challenge to his navigation – despite the life-or-death implications.

Not until Equiano demands an immediate response – and it is too late to avoid the rocks – does Phillips finally respond: "The captain immediately ordered the hatches to be nailed on the slaves in the hold, where there were above twenty, all of whom must unavoidably have perished if he had been obeyed" (149). Phillips's response is bizarre, securing privilege for a few rather than even attempting to mitigate the approaching danger. The crew begins to follow this cruel order, but Equiano overrules the captain, exposing his motives: "I desired them to stop. The captain then said it must be done; I asked him why? He said, that every one would endeavour to get into the boat, which was but small, and thereby we should be drowned for it would not have carried above ten at most . . ." (149–50). Here the captain plainly states that his priority is defending the privileges of the crew – all but two of whom are apparently white – against the possibility that the black slaves would struggle to save their lives.

Equiano, finding himself in a liminal position between the black slaves and the white crew, wins the support of the entire crew, and succeeds in preventing Phillips' murderous plan by challenging his competence and holding him, as captain, responsible for the wreck: "I could no longer restrain my emotion, and I told him he deserved drowning for not knowing how to navigate the vessel; and I believe the people would have tossed him overboard if I had given the least hint of it. However, the hatches were not nailed down" (150). In his anger, Equiano seizes on the issue of navigation, accusing his captain of "not knowing how to navigate," and thereby finally naming the as yet unspoken crux of the struggle between the two men.

Equiano's assertion of his power onboard ship is complex. Although he has clearly supplanted the captain for the duration of the emergency, at the same time, he carefully maneuvers to deny the obvious implication of mutiny. The sailors do not protect the privileges of "whiteness," because they are more concerned with the immediate threat to their own lives and need Equiano as a leader. Equiano's challenge to Phillips, and the crew's decision to side with him, may be explained by an awareness that privileges denied to slaves are almost always also denied to free blacks, and hence Equiano himself – whose talents and determination are necessary to the survival of the group – is at risk once the hatches get nailed down. Indeed, this moment can be taken as one of the strongest examples of Equiano's persistent implications that colonial whites themselves understand white supremacy as a matter of maintaining material advantages by force, rather than a reflection of essential differences between black and white.

The overturned decision to nail down the hatches does not end the illustration of racial privilege in the narrative of the boat wreck. Equiano, along with "three black men and a Dutch creole sailor," desperately ply the lifeboat oars to save their white companions from drowning. The whites do nothing to aid the effort: "not one of the white men did anything to preserve their lives; and indeed they soon got so drunk that they were not able, but lay about the deck like swine, so that we were at last obliged to lift them into the boat, and carry them on shore by force" (151). Perhaps the whites, familiar with a society in which black labor sustains white life, take for granted that this will happen. Or, perhaps, they expect the blacks to save them out of gratitude for not having been sacrificed during the wreck. Again without mentioning the idea of racial difference, Equiano underlines the point that the blacks are diligent and responsible, while the whites exhibit the bestial behavior attributed to Africans in pro-slavery literature. Equiano, then, can be taken to show that race privilege makes whites, not blacks, lazy and indolent. Here, he extends the well-established anti-slavery point about the corrupting effects of power on slave owners – so central to abolitionist discourse in the 1780s and 1790s – to the effect of race privilege on all colonial whites. Furthermore, like the exploited slaves who sustain the lives and wealth of white colonists, the consequences of his effort are dire for Equiano: "This want of assistance made our labour intolerably severe; insomuch that, by putting them on shore so often that day, the skin was partly stript off my hands" (151).

In challenging the captain's order to nail down the hatches, Equiano argues that Captain Phillips (and by extension, Phillips' anxiety to validate his white privilege) is responsible for the wreck. But Equiano offers also another, more bewildering explanation for the accident. Equiano sees the ultimate cause of the accident an "oath" – "damn the vessel's bottom out" (148) – that he thoughtlessly uttered. He explains: "All my sins stared me in the face; and especially I thought that God had hurled his direful vengeance on my guilty head for cursing the vessel on which my life depended" (149). Indeed, before he rescues the slaves from the certain death of being nailed under the hatches, he feels that even Phillips' cruel order stems from his own sinful actions: "when he desired the men to nail down the hatches I thought that my sin was the cause of this, and that God would charge me with these people's blood" (149). This explanation sits uneasily with Equiano's presentation of his challenge to the captain, but it also echoes his earlier belief that Captain Pascal's decision to sell him from a naval ship into colonial slavery is a punishment from God for uttering a similar curse. In both instances, Equiano interprets the acts of individuals enforcing the regime of racial difference as providential acts of God. It is almost as if Equiano cannot accept the idea that God allows the systematic exploitation of Africans, so he reframes these traumatic events as a matter of individual sin, rather than of race as an institution – despite also consciously protesting against the institution. At the same time, of course, Equiano's belief implies that he is closer to God than are his white shipmates, whose lives are endangered to test him and teach him a lesson. His sense of being closer to God than his impious white shipmates again undermines the pro-slavery argument that slaves are brought to Christianity by being brought to the New World. Equiano consistently shows slavery and practices of racial difference as obstacles to his true conversion. Indeed, he also suggests that they pose obstacles to the true conversion of the whites who surround him.

Equiano approaches this contradictory tangle with a clear head, at least in the analysis of his own motivations:

I could not help thinking that if any of these people had been lost, God would charge me with their lives, which, perhaps, was one cause of my labouring so hard for their preservation, and indeed every one of them afterwards seemed so sensible of the service I had rendered them, that while we were on the key, I was a kind of chieftain amongst them. (151)

If the wreck and the incident in which Equiano rescues the slaves from being nailed into the ship's hold are produced by his sin, they also provide the grounds for him to redeem himself, both in the eyes of God and in the eyes of English readers who, unlike colonists, do not yet have a fully developed sense of racial difference as either a theory or a practice.

Equiano's sin leads to the providential punishment of the wreck; but the wreck also offers providential occasion for Equiano's vindication, and the demonstration of the absurdity of the racial system that attempts to suppress and deny his merits. The wreck, in creating a struggle to survive, suspends social rules. Under these conditions, the white captain, despite the advantages of training and privilege, is unable to match Equiano as a navigator, a chieftain, or a Christian. The whites in general, become, in Equiano's description, "sensible of the service I had rendered them," even selecting him as a "kind of chieftain." Being sensible of service rendered is exactly what the regime of race normally prevents. Whites are legally entitled to any advantage, any service, they can wrest from blacks, and are socially bound to pursue this advantage. In other words, God intervenes here providentially, not just to rebuke Equiano for a small failing, but also to demonstrate that, even for colonial whites, racial difference is merely a shallow cover for economic exploitation. In this situation offering no opportunity for profit, the whites do not even pretend to believe in racial difference, especially if it would mean depending on Captain Phillips, rather than Equiano, to preserve their lives.

The section on Captain Phillips and the boat wreck shows Equiano directly confronting the problem of "white privilege," exposing both its fundamental irrationality and whites' failure to justify their exploitation with a sincere belief in racial difference. The biblical commentaries that Equiano is known to have consulted may have deepened his sense of Moses as a model for his experience, not least in presenting "gratitude" as a temptation, a sinful betrayal of God's designs for Equiano in particular, and perhaps for free blacks in the English colonies more generally. While Equiano approached this problem indirectly through allusion, he makes clear to his reader that his "gratitude" to his white patrons is a painful constraint. He explains, for instance, that after obtaining his freedom "I began to think of leaving this part of the world, of which I had long been tired, and returning to England, where my heart had always been"; but, he relates, "I found myself unable to refuse" his former owners' requests for continued service (147). An even more dramatic illustration of the injustice and illogic of colonial racial practices, and his resistance to them, comes in the almost allegorical tale of the shipwreck that is caused by white privilege and which ultimately confirms his superiority to his white shipmates. Equiano demonstrates that even as a free man he is bound by the chains of "gratitude" under the colonial system of racialized slavery. Ultimately, his indignation about these injustices, and their distortion of human relationships, is meant to remind his metropolitan readers of their values of humanity and justice – and to expose colonial practices of race as a betrayal of those values.

CHAPTER 6

The 1790s: ameliorationist convergence

The 1790s saw the end of hopes like Equiano's for leveraging the humane values, the insistence on human similarity, of earlier metropolitan discourse against colonial practices of racial oppression. Instead of ushering in an emphatic return to this earlier view, the flowering of the abolition movement was accompanied by an increasing investment in racial difference, not only in the colonies, but also in metropolitan and even anti-slavery writing. In 1787, the central London Committee for the Abolition of the slave trade was formed, and, over the principled objections of Granville Sharp, set as its top priority the political goal of abolishing the slave trade, leaving the question of emancipation aside as politically unfeasible.[1] This led to the amelioration of West Indian plantation slavery becoming the goal, rhetorically at least, of both planters and anti-slavery activists.[2] Abolitionists argued that the parliamentary abolition of the slave trade would leave planters no choice but to treat their slaves with care and kindness. Once imports were eliminated, and slaves who died from abuse and overwork could no longer be replaced, they held, economic necessity would force planters to care for their slaves, and even to encourage them to raise proper families in order to maintain slave population through "natural reproduction."[3] Thomas Clarkson even envisioned slaves "being bound to their masters by gratitude" after the amelioration forced by

---

[1] See James Walvin, *England, Slaves and Freedom 1776–1838* (Jackson: University Press of Mississippi, 1986), 106–9, and Hochschild, *Bury the Chains*, 110.

[2] This convergence has not been widely discussed by historians. For a call for scholars to attend to it, see Matt D. Childs, review of *The Sugar Industry and the Abolition of the Slave Trade, 1774–1810* by Selwyn H. H. Carrington, H-Net reviews in the Humanities and Social Sciences, 2004, http://www.h-net.org/reviews/showpdf.cgi?path=162771080787028 (accessed January 3, 2006).

[3] See Thomas Clarkson's account of the meeting, and the thinking behind the decision, *History of the Rise, Progress and Accomplishment of the Abolition of the Slave Trade* (Philadelphia: James P. Parke, 1808), 229. Clarkson develops the vision of post-abolition amelioration in great detail in *An Essay on the Impolicy of the African Slave Trade*, 1788 (Freeport, NY: Books for Libraries, 1971), 89–111. See also the testimony of Mr. Botham in John Ranby, *Observations on the Evidence . . . In Support of the Bill for Abolishing the Slave Trade* (London: J. Stockdale, 1791), 33.

abolishing the trade.[4] Such visions of ameliorated slavery, however, would remain troubling if Africans were sincerely thought of as the equals of Europeans. As a result, difference received increasing emphasis, as did the possibility that Africans were particularly suited to slavery, and could even be brought to embrace it in a gentler, more humane form.

Slavery's apologists presented their own version of amelioration.[5] They argued that they were already passing new laws to protect their slaves, that they were already encouraging natural reproduction, that they already recognized the benefits of amelioration and were practicing it.[6] Some went so far as to criticize the slave trade as cruel and to distance themselves from it (without actually calling for its abolition), in particular Bryan Edwards, the "moderate" planter whose very well-received work, *History, Civil and Commercial, of the British Colonies in the West Indies* (1793) captured the dominant attitude toward slavery in the 1790s.[7] Given this convergence – if not consensus – amelioration became an almost universally touted solution to the ills of West Indian slavery in the 1790s.[8] Who could oppose the idea of taking immediate, practical measures to improve the lot of slaves, slaves who had undoubtedly been suffering under harsh conditions? Even those who privately preferred the goal of emancipation had to publicly accede to such moderate desires. As we have seen, even the black Atlantic writers Sancho and Equiano (but not Cugoano) lent their support to the idea that amelioration was desirable, even as they resisted its racial implications.

In the 1790s, with a working agreement in place that the immediate future of slavery should be defined by the pursuit of amelioration, while the future of the African slave trade remained contentious, the terms of the philosophical consensus of the 1780s on racial difference rose for the first time in British history into the cultural mainstream. Overt expressions of

---

[4] He imagined this gratitude being expressed in the terms of "a firm and faithful protection to the islands in the time of war" (131), although elsewhere he sees similar developments in labor relations.

[5] This claim is based on my own reading of numerous polemical works on slavery of the 1790s; see also Jeff D. Bass, "An Efficient Humanitarianism: The British Slave Trade Debates, 1791–2," *Quarterly Journal of Speech*, 75 (1989), 152–65.

[6] See Ward, *West Indian Slavery*, 2 and *passim*, and Gaspar, "Sugar Cultivation," 122.

[7] While not uncontroversial, Edwards was successful at appearing "moderate." For an anti-slavery response to his *History*, see William Preston, *A Letter to Bryan Edwards, Esquire* (London: J. Johnson, 1795).

[8] The emphasis on amelioration sets 1790s defenses of slavery apart from Antebellum US pro-slavery. Contrast Tise, *Proslavery*, 75–123. For examples of ameliorative defenses of slavery, see William Innes, *The Slave-Trade Indispensable* (London: W. Richardson *et al.*, 1790); Gilbert Francklyn, *Observations, Occasioned by the Attempts Made in England to Effect the Abolition of the Slave Trade* (London: Logographic, 1789); James Makittrick Adair, *Unanswerable Arguments Against the Abolition of the Slave Trade* (London: J. P. Bateman, [1790?]).

belief in essential difference remained rare, and terms blurring the difference between the cultural and the essential were still greatly preferred.[9] Nonetheless, no longer were those who strayed from monogenic views sure of rebuke or stinging satire, and concessions to the serious possibility of racial difference took on the air of "realism."[10] Anti-slavery activists more and more frequently conceded the possibility of difference, at least rhetorically, as in the argument, "if they are inferior, are not our obligations to protect them all the greater?"[11] Furthermore, the rhetoric of the sugar boycotts protesting slave products was racialized, playing on disgusting images of slaves' bodies.[12]

The slavery fictions of the 1790s, a decade noted for its literary "Jacobins" and the emergence of Romanticism, often give the appearance of radicalism. Particularly notable is the appearance of new types of characters: African narrators, given sub-plots of their own, no doubt influenced by Equiano and the other black Atlantic writers; noble African protagonists, one a rebel leader, no doubt influenced by the events of Haiti; others, functioning as overseers in the reforming vein of grateful slavery. The seeming radicalism of such innovations, however, is belied by the insistent return of these texts to racial difference, exemplified in the intensely emotional irrationalism of these African characters, and by the heavy reliance on exceptional, noble African characters who serve as leaders of their less capable, less exalted countrymen, whether as overseers or rebels. Grateful slaves became so familiar that Royall Tyler has his protagonist, a slave-ship doctor, report of his ship's cargo that "their gratitude was excessive" and that "they were praying to their god for my prosperity" because he had helped convince the captain to land the ship briefly to care for sick slaves.[13]

---

[9] Some anti-slavery writers insisted that seeming differences resulted from slavery itself: see for instance Noah Webster, *Effects of Slavery, on Morals and Industry* (Hartford, CT: Hudson and Goodwin, 1793).

[10] Davis, although he dates this trend all the way back to the 1770s, gives an excellent description of it (*Age of Revolution*, 303).

[11] This phrasing is mine. For expressions of the sentiment, see Thomas Gisborne, *The Principles of Moral Philosophy Investigated*, 2nd edn (London: T. Bensley, 1790), 158; William Belsham, *Essays, Philosophical, Historical, and Literary* (London: C. Dilly, 1789), 439; Zephaniah Swift, *An Oration on Domestic Slavery* (Hartford, CT: Hudson and Goodwin, 1791), 11. Similar rhetoric had appeared earlier, but was followed by a more insistent rejection of difference. See for instance Joseph Woods, *Thoughts on the Slavery of the Negroes*, 2nd edn (London: James Phillips, 1785), 11–15.

[12] See Charlotte Sussman, "Women and the Politics of Sugar, 1792," in *Consuming Anxieties: Consumer Protest, Gender and British Slavery, 1713–1833* (Stanford: Stanford University Press, 2000), 110–29, and Deirdre Coleman, "Conspicuous Consumption: White Abolitionism and English Women's Protest Writing in the 1790s," *ELH*, 61:2 (1994), 341–62.

[13] Royall Tyler, *The Algerine Captive, or the Life and Adventures of Doctor Updike Underhill*, 1797, ed. Caleb Crain (New York: Modern Library, 2002), 100–101.

The most unusual slavery novel of the decade, Hector MacNeill's *Memoirs of The Life and Travels of the Late Charles Macpherson* (1800), begins with a searing critique of the grateful slave model, insisting that it fails to take sufficient account of the depraved sensuality and irrationality of Africans. Nonetheless, its thorough-going view of racial difference established, the novel is at pains to redeem a familial version of amelioration, one presumably useful for "natural reproduction," making this move with the planters' interests firmly in view, although with the caveat that most slaves are incapable of enjoying such reforms. In sum, in the 1790s, the underlying concepts of the grateful slave trope – amelioration and meaningful difference between racial groups – finally became so familiar that they could be taken for granted, and the conflicted, contradictory ambiguity of the 1780s was on the wane. The passionate, irrational nature of Africans, marking their inferiority, became a given. In the realm of the novel, the only debate left was how best to manage racial difference.

In polemical writing, Bryan Edwards reflects the trends of the 1790s primarily in his attempt to move the emphasis of criticism from slavery itself to the slave trade, turning the abolition committee's political decision to good account for planters, and providing a clear parallel to the underlying implications of seemingly "anti-slavery" fictions of the decade. Edwards opines that "nothing is more certain than that the Slave Trade may be very wicked, and the planters in general very innocent," extending this argument with the claim that the planters themselves "neither introduced, nor, as I shall hereafter shew, have been wanting in their best endeavors to correct and remedy many of the evils" of slavery.[14] Whatever the guilt of slave traders, planters are left to deal with the reality of slavery, and their efforts at amelioration show their properly moral approach.[15] Edwards twice touches on the question of grateful slavery, first seeming to endorse it in telling the anecdote of "an overseer of singular tenderness and humanity" whose "life was spared from respect to his virtues" during Tacky's revolt of 1760 by slave "Insurgents" who knew of his reputation (II:64).[16] But then, in his discussion of the characteristics of

---

[14] *History, Civil and Commercial, of the British Colonies in the West Indies*, 2 vols. (London: John Stockdale, 1793), II:35. Further citations are given parenthetically in the text.

[15] Edwards had reservations about the slave trade – particularly because of his fear of rebellions led by "African" (as opposed to Creole) slaves – but he still opposed abolition. See Olwyn M. Bloquet, "Bryan Edwards and the Haitian Revolution," in *The Impact of the Haitian Revolution in the Atlantic World*, ed. David P. Geggus (Columbia: University of South Carolina Press, 2001), 44–57.

[16] Bloquet argues that Tacky's revolt was the formative experience that taught Edwards to fear "African" slaves ("Bryan Edwards," 44). For narrative history of Tacky's revolt, skeptical of Edward's account, see Hart, *Slaves Who Abolished*, 130–56. See also Craton, *Testing the Chains*, 125–39.

"Eboes" (that is, Igbos) Edwards seems more skeptical of slave gratitude than almost any novelist. He remarks that "Eboes" require "the gentlest and mildest treatment to reconcile them to their situation; but if their confidence be once obtained, they manifest as great fidelity, affection, and gratitude, as can reasonably be expected from men in a state of slavery" (II:74). Although Edwards, for all his apologetics for slavery, here distinguishes himself from most grateful slave novelists merely by asking the question of whether gratitude can be "reasonably expected" of slaves, still he leaves the question unanswered. He might be taken to suggest that very little gratitude is reasonable to expect, given that he laments slavery in general, remarking on "the sad prospect of 450,000 reasonable beings (in the English Islands only) in a state of barbarity and slavery" (II:34).

But it becomes clear as Edwards' discussion develops that "barbarity" and "slavery" are conditions with separate causes, and, in fact, "slavery" may be a welcome cure for "barbarity." Edwards suggests that the African population of the West Indies is not ready for freedom, that emancipation is a visionary error, telling of those in England who come into the possession of plantations: "some of these gentlemen, unacquainted with local circumstances, and misled by the popular outcry, have humanely given orders to emancipate all their slaves, at whatever expense; but are convinced that their benevolent purposes cannot be carried into effect consistently with even the happiness of the Negroes themselves" (II:35). Edwards develops this rather cryptic claim by invoking the fact that the Society for the Propagation of the Gospel (SPG) has chosen to continue running, and even restocking, its plantations. The SPG becomes a model for considering the problem of slavery:

They well know that moderate labour, unaccompanied with that wretched anxiety to which the poor of England are subject, in making provision for the day that is passing over them, is a state of comparative felicity: and they know also, that men in savage life have no incentive to emulation: persuasion is lost on such men, and compulsion, to a certain degree, is humanity and charity. (II:36)

For "such men" – those in "savage life" – slavery, properly moderated and ameliorated, is not only justified, but even a form of "humanity and charity." It can even be compared favorably to the "wretched anxiety" of free labor. Planters, following the model of the SPG, far from committing the crime of inhumanity, are merely doing their Christian duty. Here we see established the form of racial difference, lightly disguised in "cultural" terms, on which the grateful slave novelists of the 1790s consistently drew.

Edwards here, like many a grateful slave novelist, endorses the notion
that the difference of Africans from Europeans suits them to slavery, but he
is uncomfortable with delving into the nature of such difference. His key
terms – "savage life" or "barbarity" – blur the border between cultural and
essential difference. Edwards, though, happily gives detailed accounts of
the nature and character of West African sub-groups (Mandingos, Eboes,
Coromantiens). In these sections, his faith in deep-seated human differences is clear. But it remains obscure whether he sees such difference as
primarily cultural or essential. He distances himself from the emergent
scientific discourse of race, although in doing so he also invokes it:

> I believe indeed there is, in most of the nations of Africa, a greater elongation of the
> lower jaw, than among the people of Europe; but this distinction I think is more
> visible among the Eboes, than in any other Africans. I mean not however to draw
> any conclusion of natural inferiority in these people to the rest of the human race,
> from a circumstance which perhaps is purely accidental, and no more to be
> considered a proof of degradation, than the red hair and high cheek bones of
> the Natives of the North of Europe. (II:74)

Here, Edwards melds a far milder version of Jefferson's "hypothesizing"
racism with Ramsay's practical-minded dismissal of the question of difference. The exact source of difference is less important than its implications
for slavery – which are, to Edwards, and to the grateful slave novelists of the
1790s, that slavery, properly ameliorated, is the best practical solution to
the situation of West Indian slaves – and perhaps even a solution to be
praised as humane, charitable, and particularly suitable to them.

Given the popularity of ameliorationism in the 1790s, it is unsurprising to
find that the novel representations of kindly masters whose grateful slaves are
highly productive for them are more abundant than ever. The most notable
differences from the earliest examples of the grateful slave scenario, and from
the complex demurrals of the 1780s, are trends toward having Africans, both
slaves and ex-slaves, featured as narrators and protagonists, representing the
irrational cruelty of the bad master, and toward offering two new supreme
tests of gratitude: slave revolts (if slaves refuse to rebel against a given master,
it proves his true goodness) and, as anticipated by Peacock, offers of freedom
(slaves are so devoted that they insist on staying with, even working to
support, their masters). Both of these, trends, notably, went on to become
staples of the pro-slavery plantation fiction of the Antebellum US.[17]

---

[17] See Jean Fagan Yellin, *The Intricate Knot: Black Figures in American Literature, 1776–1863* (New York:
New York University Press, 1972), 15–81; Susan J. Tracy, *In The Master's Eye: Representations of Women,
Blacks and Poor Whites in Antebellum Southern Literature* (Amherst, MA: University of Massachusetts

An emerging opposition between gratitude and vengeance suggests one reason that gratitude becomes more appealing not only to slavery's apologists, but even to its opponents, at the close of the century. From 1792 to 1798 Toussaint L'Ouverture's successful war effort against, at various times, the French, the Spanish, and the British in St. Domingue (Haiti) moved the possibility of military revenge by ex-slaves, for Europeans, from the realm of fearful fantasy to an established, and frightening, reality.[18] Having accepted – or fearing – emancipation's eventual likelihood raised the question of how ex-slaves would react to freedom.[19] Thus, those on both sides of the slavery debate turned back to the question of slaves' gratitude with renewed interest as it represented a potential model for preventing post-emancipation troubles. Mary Pilkington's resetting of a "grateful slave" story to London suggests this interest. Alternatively, as shown in MacNeill's *Macpherson*, slave gratitude offers a way to imagine Europeans, rather than Africans, as responsible for the violence in Haiti. *Macpherson* insists that masters who deviate from stern measures are misunderstanding the nature of Africans, indulging in a mistaken and self-defeating sentimentalism, and thereby dooming themselves. Haiti, in this light, becomes a failure of management on a grand scale rather than a confirmation of blacks' abilities and desire for freedom. Indeed, the unusually conservative *MacPherson* shares this feature with seemingly radical novels, which are willing to go so far as to praise slave rebellions, as long as the rebels stay within the bounds of grateful slavery.

NOBLE NEGROES OF THE 1790S: ''WE FIGHT *FOR* MASSA; HE SO GOOD''

The convergence of the racial politics of the texts in this section is perhaps best indicated by the fact that the vision of race does not differ between the

Press, 1995), 141–74; Joy Jordan-Lake, *Whitewashing Uncle Tom's Cabin: Nineteenth-Century Women Novelists Respond to Stowe* (Nashville: Vanderbilt University Press, 2005), 1–24; Sarah Meer, *Uncle Tom Mania: Slavery, Minstrelsy and Transatlantic Culture in the 1860s* (Athens, GA: University of Georgia Press, 2005), 75–101; and Sarah Nelson Roth, "Rebels and Martyrs: The Debate Over Slavery in American Popular Culture, 1822–1865" (Ph.D. diss., University of Virginia 2002), 59–109, 148–80.

[18] For the classic history of Toussaint and the revolution, see C. L. R. James, *The Black Jacobins: Toussaint L'Ouverture and the San Domingo Revolution*, 1938, 2nd edn (New York: Vintage, 1963). For an updated history, see David P. Geggus, *Haitian Revolutionary Studies* (Bloomington: Indiana University Press, 2002); for the reaction to the revolution outside Haiti, see Geggus, ed., *The Impact of the Haitian Revolution*; for considerations of the impact of the image of Toussaint as revolutionary leader, see Susan Buck-Morss, "Hegel and Haiti," *Critical Inquiry*, 26 (2000), 821–65, and Aravamudan, *Tropicopolitans*, 289–325.

[19] See Davis, *Age of Revolution*, 255–342, and Joanne Pope Melish, *Disowning Slavery: Gradual Emancipation and Race in New England 1780–1860* (Ithaca: Cornell University Press, 1998), 84–162.

one – *Zimao* (1800) – featuring a rebel slave hero and the two – Anna Maria Mackenzie's *Slavery: or The Times* (1792) and *The Negro Equalled by Few Europeans* (1790) – whose protagonists thwart rebellions and serve as reforming overseers. Despite their seeming radicalism in using African protagonists and even depicting an uprising sympathetically, none of these novels succeed at distancing themselves from the racial implications of the grateful slave. Perhaps this is because their primary concern has become the fear of slave vengeance. Vengeance was already an aspect of the emergent consensus on the irrational, passionate nature of Africans in Abbé Raynal's predictions of vengeful violence and Jefferson's worries about a post-emancipation race war, and, of course, was a worry much heightened by the unfolding events in Haiti throughout the decade.

 Zimao shares with *The Negro Equalled by Few Europeans* and *Slavery: or The Times* the appearance of being unusually radical. And yet, in all three cases, the radical moves made by the text are countered by reactionary ones. *Zimao* does celebrate as a hero the titular character, an African rebel who leads his fellow slaves on a bloody course of rebellion. Nonetheless, the portrait of the African-descended characters in *Zimao* is thoughtless and clichéd. Zimao speechifies in his own justification, announcing that "I have vindicated my race and lineage . . . Shun me not for the crimson that defiles me! Tis of the blood of tyrants" and "ye men of peace! abhor not the unfortunate Zimao. The thunder of my wrath was just."[20] The narrator of the novella, a white man visiting a friend who is a benevolent planter, verifies Zimao's self-portrait (Zimao is known to the whites by his slave name, John): "we learned that John slew men, women, and children, indiscriminately, in plantations where the negroes had been maltreated; that in others, he contented himself with simply liberating the slaves" (22). This representation of rebellion, then, serves the purpose of defining amelioration as a magic cloak of invulnerability for "humane" planters, rather than of engaging with the slaves' humanity and considering their grievances.

 Despite his vindication as a crusader for the oppressed African, Zimao (much like Aphra Behn's Oroonoko) is described as exemplifying an European, even classical, ideal of beauty: "The celebrated statues of Apollo and of Antinoüs possessed not more regular features, or more exact proportions. I was particularly struck with his noble and commanding aspect" (23).

---

[20] [J. F. de St. Lambert], *Zimao, The African*, trans. Rev. Weeden Butler (Dublin: Brett Smith, 1800), 24 and 25. Further citations are given parenthetically in the text. Sypher, *Guinea's Captive Kings*, 315, sees this novel as "arriving at the outposts of negrophile savagery."

As was not yet the case for *Oroonoko* in the late seventeenth century, because of the unfamiliarity of race in that era, the resonance for readers of *Zimao*, given the stability of belief in difference in the 1790s, is that he is an African who transcends expected African limitations to become almost like a white European man.[21] As Wylie Sypher argues, Zimao and Oroonoko both represent a "noble savagery" different in kind from that of Montaigne and Rousseau.[22] Sypher's disgust with the unrealistic representation of such "noble Negroes," however, is very much a product of nineteenth-century essentialist views of race.[23] Rather than seeing "the primitive" or "savage" as purer, more essential, and more honest than European man, *Zimao* and other "noble Negro" fictions of the 1790s present naturally exceptional Africans as capable of almost – but not quite – transcending African limitations to attain to a European version of nobility.

Most slaves in *Zimao* are quite unlike this image of the avenging classical warrior. The narrator's planter friend Wilmot is such a good master that his slaves are utterly, devotedly grateful to him, his family, and even his friends. His goodness is established, in part, by his policy that "Every negro who behaved well for the space of ten years, was sure of obtaining his liberty" (6). When Zimao and his rebels approach the plantation, Wilmot arms the slaves: "'My lads!' Cried Wilmot, 'here are arms for you. If I have been a hard task-master, kill me: I deserve to die. But, if you have found me an indulgent father, join now in protecting my wife and little ones'" (11). This act of trust, no doubt, is intended to illustrate the self-confidence born of Wilmot's goodness and his sincere rejection of cruelty. In the event, arming the slaves allows them to lavish grateful devotion on their good master. The slaves "solemnly swore they would all shed the last drop of blood in our defense. Some inflicted deep gashes in their flesh with knives, to evince their sovereign contempt of wounds and pain" (12). Even the friends of the good master, it seems, are worth dying for in the eyes of these devoted slaves.

Zimao, however, averts the need for these grateful slaves to demonstrate the extent of their devotion by shedding their blood. Zimao, too, acknowledges Wilmot's goodness, refusing to attack him. Afterwards, rather than attaching themselves to this noble, avenging African hero, the slaves take

---

[21] See my discussion of such interpretations of *Oroonoko* above, pp. 51–3, esp. n. 30.
[22] For further discussion see pp. 154–5, esp. n. 27 in chapter 4 above.
[23] See Sypher, *Guinea's Captive Kings*, 258, 313–15 and *passim*. Sypher's persistent disgust with "noble Negroes" seems to exemplify Ellingson's contention that the "noble savage" is a retrospective strawman of racist nineteenth-century ethnography. However, Ellis, *Politics of Sensibility*, 121, contends that "the noble slave is a genuine anti-slavery trope."

the opportunity to express their devotion to Wilmot (and his friend who happens to be visiting): "They swore they would sooner die than leave us. They faultered in their speech, and wept. All seemed afraid they could not sufficiently demonstrate their strong sense of gratitude, respect, and love" (26). Zimao himself is drawn into the sentimental maelstrom: "'Henceforth,' said he, 'I shall love two *whites*'" (28). Then, without any compelling narrative reason, Zimao goes on to articulate the grateful slave trope's underlying theory of racial difference: "Your white men are cold and phlegmatic; they neither love nor hate; they pant only for gold. Whereas our passions are all broad awake; impetuous, permanent, over-bearing. Souls of the complexion of ours, cannot be broken by hardship," concluding that "an unoffended negro is harmless and sweet-tempered" (31). Despite seeming to endorse a slave rebellion, *Zimao* is far more committed to racial difference than emancipation. Of course, the rebellion is only endorsed because Zimao and the rebels stay within the bounds of grateful slavery, refusing to attack "humane" masters; only bad, inhumane masters who refuse to ameliorate get the punishment they deserve.

Adolphus, the protagonist of Anna Maria Mackenzie's *Slavery: or The Times*, like Zimao is an African from a noble family who is explicitly praised for his resemblance to a European, while common slaves are contrasted with him, and their gratitude is constantly invoked.[24] One Englishwoman praises the hero, calling Adolphus "amost [sic] as white as a christian."[25] Adolphus eventually is put in charge of a plantation, and he reforms it just as Scott's Sir George Ellison would. A grateful slave offers Adolphus his devotion:

> Oh! massa, (said he,) we be all good. We serve you willing, you be so kind. Some bad people, great ways off, be lazy, sulky – no work, no speak. – They be much much beat. – Then they rise, kill, fight, burn plantation – Oh! We be so sorry. – We fight too; but we fight *for* massa; he so good, – so – so very good. – We defend him house, him plantation, him life, him every thing. (217)

Adolphus, like the rebel Zimao, himself sounds just like an ameliorationist defending the institution of slavery as he remarks that "you see ... *one* instance at least of gentle government, and also of the fruits of it. – Do not doubt then but there are many more ... I tell you, *all* planters are not alike" (217). Like Ellison, Savillon, and even Colonel Jack, Adolphus inspires devoted and highly productive labor: "Their master had the pleasure of

---

[24] Sypher sees *Slavery: or The Times* as the "apotheosis of the noble negro" (287); Ferguson mentions it as a "racist, anti-Semitic novel" (*Subject to Others*, 221).

[25] Anna Maria Mackenzie, *Slavery: or The Times* (Dublin: P. Wogan, 1793), 62. The comment appears intended as gauche. Further citations are given parenthetically in the text.

beholding them renew their labours with an alacrity that the whip could not inspire" (218). The one part of the tale intended as disturbing is the enslavement and excessive punishment of Adolphus' father. But even this (as in *Oroonoko*) seems to depend on the horror of a nobleman – indeed a king – being abused, rather than on anything inherent to slavery.

The Negro Equalled by Few Europeans also follows the formula of *Zimao* and *Slavery: or The Times*. The central character, Itanoko, is of African noble ancestry, but becomes a slave within Africa after fighting on the losing side of a battle. Eventually, he winds up on a European slave ship where he strikes up a deeply sentimental relationship with a slave-owner's son, Ferdinand.[26] Out of love for Ferdinand, he betrays a shipboard revolt, which is presented as an admirable act.[27] In the early scenes, set in Africa, Itanoko describes his own character in Jeffersonian terms, remarking that "my sensibility often wandered from my prudence,"[28] and that "my judgement was a slave to the ardour of my character" (I:36). The phrasing of the second declaration carries the ideological freight of the grateful slave paradigm, suggesting that Africans are inherent slaves, if not to Europeans then to their own uncontrollable impulsiveness. However there is another African warrior who is the opposite of the sentimental Itanoko: Otorou was "always calm, always peaceable" (I:36).[29]

Despite this one deviation from the Jeffersonian position, Itanoko's story ultimately stays as close as all these seemingly radical novels to the ameliorationist consensus. Having saved the life of a master, Itanoko is freed and made an overseer. Like a conflation of Henry Mackenzie's reformer Savillon and the African slave prince, Yambu, that Savillon uses to manipulate his slaves, Itanoko declares his slaves free only to find them more devoted and productive than ever. On becoming overseer, Itanoko declares: "They tell me that I am your master! Ah, I am your friend! *Liberty*! This shall be the first exercise of my power!" (III:112). The slaves' reaction is

---

[26] John Saillant, "The Black Body Erotic and the Republican Body Politic, 1790–1820," in *Sentimental Men: Masculinity and the Politics of Affect in American Culture*, ed. Mary Chapman and Glenn Hendler (Berkeley: University of California Press, 1999), 89–111, offers an extensive reading of *The Negro Equalled* as drenched in homoeroticism and as a paradigmatic text for later American representations of slavery (esp. 96).

[27] Sypher sees this as undermining Itanoko's claims to nobility (*Guinea's Captive Kings*, 284), and sees the novel as "wrong-headed" (*ibid.*, 285).

[28] LaVallée, *The Negro Equalled*, I:11. Further citations are given parenthetically in the text.

[29] Despite this aspect of the text, Mary Wollstonecraft wrote a review in 1790 recommending it to "young people" to combat "prejudice." See *The Works of Mary Wollstonecraft*, vol. VII, ed. Janet Todd and Marilyn Butler (New York: New York University Press, 1989), 282. See discussion in Virginia Sapiro, *A Vindication of Political Virtue: The Political Theory of Mary Wollstonecraft* (Chicago: University of Chicago Press, 1992), 110–11.

pure grateful slavery: "Receive our oath – cried they. Never will we quit you. On this land will we pay our debt to you. We will render it tenfold fertile" (III:113). Itanoko, despite having personally freed the slaves, denies any credit and instead tries to turn the slaves' gratitude in another direction: "Thank your real benefactors. The generous Europeans, to whom we owe the happiness that penetrates all our minds" (III:113). In case the ameliorationist resonance of this scene is lost on the reader, Itanoko clarifies its implications: "give to all Europeans the goodness of our deliverers, and negroes will perish for them with joy!" (III:114). Otorou's status as an exception from the rule of African's uncontrolled sensibility never amounts to much in the narrative, given that the entire plantation of slaves (in essence) refuse their freedom out of instant devotion to Itanoko for freeing them. Strikingly, then, the noble negro protagonist who leads a rebellion is intent on teaching the same lessons about amelioration and Africans' irrational, passionate nature as his two noble peers who become overseers rather than rebels. The ultimate suggestion is that slave rebellions are accidents created by European mismanagement, by the failure to pursue amelioration and humane slave management; by no means do they confirm Africans' humanity and desire for liberty. Furthermore, the "noble" protagonists are closer to European standards of humanity than are the average, faceless slaves, but even the protagonists are marked as different by their irrational, uncontrollable passions.

SLAVE NARRATORS: "LIVE WHITE MAN; LIVE TO CONQUER BLACK MAN BY HUMANITY"

The second group of novels to be investigated in this chapter offer short, interpolated tales narrated by ex-slaves themselves: Robert Bage's *Man As He Is* (1792) and Elizabeth Helme's *The Farmer of Inglewood Forest* (1796). Coming in the wake of the popular success of Equiano's *Interesting Narrative* (1789), they appear to have been inspired by the black Atlantic writers. But, like the "noble African" tales treated above, their substance is pure grateful slavery, amelioration justified by Africans' passionate irrationality. Both novels attempt to exploit the rhetorical power of the slave narrative, but put it in the service of a simplistic, reassuring ameliorationist agenda. Notably, this pair of novels in their similarity confirm the cultural centrality of grateful slavery in the 1790s; the two authors are, on the one hand, a reforming radical (Bage) and, on the other, a reactionary anti-Jacobin (Helme). Oddly, it is the radical, Bage, who insists on having his African character speak in an infantilizing dialect, while the conservative writer, Helme, has her African character speak in elegant, polished English; in this they differ from their Antebellum US successors, for whom dialect represented a comic insistence on difference, even a reference to the minstrel tradition, while elegant speech represented an abolitionist insistence on the educability of blacks.[30]

In Bage's *Man As He Is* (1792), an interpolated tale narrated by the ex-slave Fidel both endorses the notion that slaves are naturally grateful, and yet also emphasizes the extent of arbitrary cruelty by masters, after the manner of Ramsay's *Essay* and Moore's *Zeluco*. Here, Bage has Fidel satirically suggest that in the context of plantation slavery, even arbitrary whippings could be seen as relatively kind:

We were so good we did not want de whip; so we had it only once a week, I could not ver tell why; but masser was a good man and did not insist upon these whippings being bloody. Masser was a Creole to be sure, and I do tink the groans and shrieks of we de poor negroes under de whip, be the finest music in de vorld to dem; but masser was kind hearted; I do ver believe he would not have take the pleasure in de whip, if he did know a better vay to send a profitable cargo of the sugar into dis England.[31]

The effect of putting this parodic vision in Fidel's mouth is odd. His "innocence," and his reluctance to condemn his master, heighten the ironic effect. And yet, these same elements make Fidel seem ignorant and even Samboish in his uncomprehending acceptance of arbitrary violence. Similarly paradoxical effects are produced by the decision to represent Fidel as speaking in dialect. The arbitrary intrusion of non-dialect phrases – "profitable cargo" – does not help matters.

A commitment to the idea of slave gratitude further warps Bage's narrative. Fidel (as his name suggests) seems born to the role of the faithful, grateful slave. Fidel desires a grateful relationship and at first seems to be developing one with his master's young son, but the young master, devoted to cruelty, becomes his nemesis instead:

I did love him much, and it did grieve me to see dat he did love cruelty for cruelty's sake; and de poor negro was used worse and worse. So I did ask him why? He said, to make de dogs work. And I said, if you did use dem as well as dogs they would be great deal better of. He did look angry at me, and said, dogs were a superior species of animal to negroes, and had better understandings. (205)

---

[30] See Yellin, *Intricate Knot*, 87–120, and Meer, *Uncle Tom Mania*, 75–101.
[31] Robert Bage, *Man As He Is*, 4 vols., 2nd edn (London: Minerva, 1792), IV: 203–4. Further citations, given parenthetically in the text, are to this volume.

Fidel exhibits an unusual degree of daring and intelligence when he throws the young master's racist claims back in his face, saying "if God did give de white men more understanding, it was de tousand pities dey could not see how to make de better use of it." This, however, brings trouble to Fidel, because the young master reacts by hitting him, and then Fidel chases after him to exact revenge. Despite the opinion of the local planters that "such monstrous behavior ought to have punishment little short of death" (206), Fidel, implausibly, is rescued from this impending fate by "Massa Colerain's" rousing speech on the immorality of slavery, in the first of two incidents in which Bage invokes the effects of white supremacy only to show them as overcome by the planters' moral qualms. The results of this rescue are doubly beneficial to Fidel. Not only does he live, but he is united with Colerain, the master to whom he is finally able to feel grateful. There is a notable imbalance in *Man As He Is*; Fidel is defined by his gratitude, while his having saved the lives of each of his masters does not similarly transform them.

Bage, a self-conscious radical and opponent of slavery, doubtlessly means for Fidel's touching nature to throw the masters' cruelty into relief, in much the same way that Dr. Moore employed the contrast between Hanno and Zeluco.[32] Nonetheless, another incident attributes an unrealistic level of justice and good intentions to West Indian planters. At one point, Fidel has to leave for the continent. He reluctantly leaves his beloved, Flowney, behind in the power of his old master. When the old master dies, his young son seduces Flowney and then turns her over to his overseer to be raped and beaten.[33] When Fidel returns, he kills the overseer in "honorable circumstances" and then is rescued by Colerain's timely arrival and the agreement of a group of white men to punish the "Young Master" for his crimes against Flowney. As Fidel explains,

Dey spread de news; dey told de trute; for they were white men, and durst speak trute. So my story flew. Every body did pity me; did detest Benfield ... de evidence of de rape of my poor Flowney was strong enough to enduce many gentlemen at Kingston to enter into de subscription for de prosecution of Massa Benfield. (219)

[32] Eleanor Ty, *Unsex'd Revolutionaries: Five Women Novelists of the 1790s* (Toronto: University of Toronto Press, 1993), 12, 162 n. 52 and 165 n. 80, reviews the debate on Bage's radicalism. Paul Flynn, in "*Man As He Is* and Romanticism as It Ought to Be," *Critical Survey*, 4:1 (1992), 28–35, insists on Bage's radicalism; Peter Faulkner, "*Man As He Is*: The Establishment Challenged," in *Robert Bage* (Boston: G. K. Hall, 1979), 102–21, esp. 117, detects signs of a moderate outlook.
[33] Sypher, *Guinea's Captive Kings*, 293, sees the representation of this rape as extreme and sensational.

The jarring inconsistency of the dialect aside, this passage is notable for its depiction of plantation justice. Although slave owners sometimes prosecuted one another for cruelty, the idea that they would back an ex-slave who had killed a white man because of evidence that a slave woman had been raped is inconceivable.[34] In the English anti-slavery debate, the sexual exploitation of slave women was often ignored, or discussed in prudish terms, blaming the women themselves for being "harlots."[35] When directly mentioned, it was a volatile issue.[36] Bage either misunderstood the extent to which white men took their access to slave women for granted, or was aiming at poetic justice for Fidel and Flowney over accurate representation of plantation life.[37] Bage's decision to represent planters as pursuing justice, however, was a familiar one, if not in anti-slavery writing. Bryan Edwards, for instance, was particularly insistent on the progress being made in legal protection for slaves in the political process of amelioration in the colonies, and this was a general strategy of the planters.[38] Thus, whether through ignorance or conscious choice, Bage here endorses the planter's public self-presentation as progressive.[39] Fidel is an odd character, at once forthright, self-assertive, active and yet also predisposed to devotion and gratitude.

In *The Farmer of Inglewood Forest*, Helme's ex-slave, Felix, is much like Bage's Fidel, despite Helme's politics being opposite to Bage's.[40] Felix refuses an independent fortune to stay with Mrs. Palmer, a relative of his beloved master. And as a young slave, he manages to develop the kind of sentimental bond of friendship and gratitude with his young master that Bage's Fidel seemed to crave. After a childhood in which his young master, Henry Walters, is consistently kind to, and protective of, him, Felix

[34] Flynn avoids mention of these equivocations, presenting Bage as an outspoken critic of slavery's brutality (*Man As He Is*, 34–5).
[35] See p. 228 below for a related moment in *MacPherson*.
[36] See Barbara Bush, *Slave Women in Caribbean Society 1650–1838* (Bloomington: Indiana University Press, 1990), 110–19, and Clare Midgley, *Women Against Slavery: The British Campaigns, 1780–1870* (New York: Routledge, 1992), 20–2, 90–1. Maaja Stewart, "The Shadow Behind the Country House: West Indian Slavery and Female Virtue in *Mansfield Park*," in *Domestic Realities and Imperial Fictions: Jane Austen's Novels in Eighteenth-Century Contexts* (Athens, GA: University of Georgia Press, 1993), 105–36, argues for the impact of knowledge of the sexual exploitation of slave women on several British novels.
[37] For examples of the pervasiveness, and casualness, of white men's sexual exploitation of slave women, see Douglas Hall, *In Miserable Slavery: Thomas Thistlewood in Jamaica, 1750–86* (London: MacMillan, 1989), 50, 74, 118.
[38] Edwards, for instance, includes the new consolidated slave act of Jamaica of 1792 as an appendix, to demonstrate the commitment of planters to amelioration (*History*, II:150).
[39] Clearly, Edwards, who published his *History* a year after Bage's novel, was not a direct influence.
[40] M. O. Grenby relates Helme's representation of slave revolt to the anti-Jacobin project of showing the horrors of revolution: *The Anti-Jacobin Novel: British Conservatism and the French Revolution* (Cambridge: Cambridge University Press, 2001), 49.

remarks that "by this time I was about fourteen, and perfectly understood my situation, which I considered as fixed for life, yet cannot say the thought on my own account gave me much pain; so true it is, that kindness and humanity may make even bondage bearable."[41]

Later, when the other slaves revolt and kill the young master's mother and father, Felix protects him. The rebels demand the young master in order to kill him, but Felix offers his own life instead, proclaiming that "Ingratitude is not a negro vice" (111). Felix opens the doors of their hiding place, challenging the rebels: "if your hearts will let you, kill the truest friend you have among the Christian men, and stab the bosom who would willingly bleed to give you liberty and happiness; for I will not survive him; we will die together" (111). When the young master fearlessly offers his bared breast to them, saying "I am prepared, strike," the rebel slaves are "conquered" sentimentally: "My countrymen, at these words, set up a loud cry, exclaiming, 'live white man; live to conquer black man by humanity'" (111).[42] Although the novel casts slavery in a grim light, nonetheless it shows the emotional conquest of Africans by white kindness – or by the sentimental displays of grateful slaves themselves – as more desirable than the excessive revenge that Africans are otherwise inclined to pursue.[43]

For a novelist, using an ex-slave as a narrator certainly adds a sense of authenticity, and emotional power, to representations of slavery. In Helme's novel, a statement like "I was born on the coast of Guinea, and kidnapped from thence when about twelve years old, and brought to Jamaica, where I was exposed to sale" (107), especially in its plain-spokenness, brings out the human cost of slavery with an immediacy unattainable for a third-person narrator. It also allows the novelist to attribute the concept of slave gratitude to slaves themselves, as in Felix's account of his sale: the planter judged him incapable of labor, but the planter's "son, who was about my own age . . . looked upon me with such compassion, that, sensible of my situation, I could not avoid saying, 'if I must be a slave, I had rather be so to you than any other'" (107). Here, indeed, the sentimentalized master–slave relationship takes on a wistfulness, a sense of the oppression of slavery. The resignation to a fate of slavery is made explicit rather than being assumed

---

[41] Elizabeth Helme, *The Farmer of Inglewood Forest*, 1796, reprinted in *The New Novelists Magazine*, vol. II, (New York: T. Kinnersly, 1836), 108. Further citations are given parenthetically in the text.

[42] Sypher, *Guinea's Captive Kings*, 298–9, reading this scene as the absurd height of eighteenth-century "negro eloquence," is dismissive of Helme's "crudity."

[43] Ferguson, *Subject to Others*, 231, reads *The Farmer of Inglewood Forest* as a response to Haiti, generally presenting slaves as brutal, but in this scene hinting that slaves have the capacity to become Christian, and thereby contesting "the old plantocratic chestnut that slaves cannot feel."

or ignored as it is in most grateful slave fictions, but nonetheless, gratitude becomes normalized after this moment, and other slaves are assumed to be primed for gratitude with no consideration of their need for "resignation." Felix not only comes to fully accept his own bonds of gratitude, but he goes on to fashion more such bonds for his fellow slaves.

Felix himself puts to use the lessons in kindness and gratitude that Henry Walters has taught him after the two devoted friends are separated when his young master abandons Jamaica in disgust. Walters, interestingly, does not foreswear slaveholding, instead keeping his plantation and insisting that Felix stay on it to implement his vision of amelioration. Felix explains, "I was very unwilling to be left behind; but my dear master so clearly pointed out that my stay nearly concerned his interest and the quiet of the plantation, that I consented" (111). Walters makes Felix his overseer and, in the tradition of grateful slave reformers before him, Felix achieves very profitable results:

for twenty years I fulfilled the duty he enjoined me with great satisfaction to him, and also to those over whom he had given me command; and if I have any thing in the world to boast of, it is that, by mild measures, fifty negroes on our plantation did as much labour as double that number on most others. (111)

Ultimately, then, Felix is not only inherently grateful, but is willing to use what he has learned about African gratitude from his own example to increase his beloved masters' profits.

From 1790 to 1800, then, the novels that centered on Africans, whether free or ex-slaves, treated the African protagonist or hero as an exceptional figure, deserving to be set apart from the mass of his "countrymen" due to an Oroonoko-like inherent nobility, with "whitening" effects, both mentally and physically. The mass of slaves are represented as so grateful to reformers (who may happen to be exceptional Africans) that they refuse the consequences of emancipation, and refuse to participate in violence against "good," "humane" masters. As emancipation loomed ahead as a serious possibility, this scenario represented an unrealizable fantasy soothing to the anxieties of both slavery's opponents and supporters. Not only had Haiti's slaves secured their own freedom, but France abolished slavery (from 1793 to 1803), and several US states had enacted gradual emancipation statutes. The idea that excessive African vengeance could be countered by equally excessive gratitude seems particularly untenable, implying that Africans would acknowledge certain forms of slavery as acceptable, even good, while rejecting only the cruelest instances. Of course, their unreality does not mean that such fantasies were without consequence.

NEW DIRECTIONS

All the novels considered in this chapter, despite representing conflicting views on slavery, contribute to the ameliorationist consensus and bolster emerging ideas of racial difference. The last two stories to be considered push in different directions. Mary Pilkington's "The Faithful Slave," despite explicit protestations against ideas of racial difference, turns the irrational, excessive nature of the grateful slave to the purpose of imagining the willing submission of free blacks to whites. MacNeill's *Memoirs of The Life and Travels of the Late Charles Macpherson* (1800), by contrast, questions the possibility of reforms based on slaves' gratitude from an explicitly racist point of view, arguing that slaves are incapable of the minimal capacity for reason required for the reforms to succeed, and ultimately that slavery – in an unflinchingly brutal form – could be mutually beneficial for both slaves and masters.[44]

Mary Pilkington's story for children, "The Faithful Negro" (1798), was printed in two editions in both England and the USA before the end of the eighteenth century, and continued to be reprinted often in the nineteenth century. Its most significant move is to reset the standard grateful slave story from a plantation to London; in so doing it combines it with a *Sandford and Merton*-like contrast between a good, feeling English boy and his domineering Creole counterpart.[45] Julius Godfrey asks his father, Mr. Godfrey, to buy him a black boy to play with because his Creole friend Charles Henley has one. Mr. Godfrey lectures Julius, explaining that slavery is not legal in England and denouncing the racist ideas – such as "black people have no feeling" – that Charles has taught Julius (190). A nearly starved black boy named Yanko – the very one Julius had hoped to buy – comes to the Godfreys' door to beg for food and is taken into the family as a quasi-servant. Mr. Godfrey charges Julius with teaching Yanko and, particularly, with developing his feelings of "fidelity and attachment" (193). The plan works well. Julius and Mr. Godfrey also attempt – with unclear results – to convince the cruel Charles to treat his black boy, Peter, more kindly. Julius insists that hearing genuine expressions of Yanko's "attachment to himself" give him far more pleasure than he ever got from forcing Peter to amuse the white boys (205).

---

[44] Sypher sees *Macpherson* as offering "plausible remedies" to slavery, because "the fire of the crusade has dimmed" when it was written (*Guinea's Captive Kings*, 312).

[45] Further citatations, given parenthetically in the text, are from Mary Pilkington, "The Faithful Negro," in *Tales of the Hermitage; Written for the Instruction and Amusement of the Rising Generation*, 1798 (London: J. D. Dewick, 1800), 188–209.

The averted slave rebellion of the standard grateful slave tale is not possible given the English setting, but Yanko, having overheard his fellow servant Robert planning to rob and assassinate the Godfrey family, nonetheless finds occasion to demonstrate his devotion, and even to swear "Yanko *die for Massar! Yanko die for Massar!*" (207). The story ends as Yanko further proves his gratitude to the Godfreys by refusing the offer of a monetary reward for his extraordinary services. Although the story explicitly rejects racial difference, especially the dehumanizing abuse meted out by West Indian Creoles to their black dependents, it still reasserts the need of blacks for white guidance, and indeed their willingness to devote themselves to subservient roles, even to risk their lives, for a less abusive master. Yanko sings an impromptu song about his happiness – delighting Mr. Godfrey and Julius when they overhear it – which concludes with the lines "Yanko *love* his massar dear / Love, because he can no *fear*, / When no *cat-o-nine-tails near*" (198). Although Mr. Godfrey insists there is no such thing as slavery in England, Yanko himself seems to understand the Godfreys as kind slave masters rather than insurers of his freedom. Indeed, the use of the word "slave" in the title highlights this perspective. This story, in other words, is not strictly speaking "ameliorationist," but nonetheless adapts the vision of race underlying grateful slave tales to the nineteenth-century purpose of offering reassurances that the racial order of slavery will be maintained even after emancipation. The frontispiece to *Tales from the Hermitage* (Figure 4) is one of the most striking eighteenth-century visual images of black submission and gratitude.

MacNeill's *Macpherson*, after a seemingly standard beginning – the pronouncements and endeavors of an idealistic young planter bent on reform – unexpectedly departs from the established pattern: the reforms fail, causing a revolt and ending in complete disaster. The reformer Beaumarché at first appears much like his novelistic peers: "Being a man of universal benevolence and humanity, his chief attention was directed to the comfort and happiness of those wretched sons and daughters of adversity, whom misfortune had doomed to perpetual slavery."[46] His motivations, however, are not the typical sentimental ones, but are contained in his upbringing: "Accustomed to scenes where festivity and freedom had brightened the pastimes of those with whom he had spent his early days on the continent of Europe, he could not behold the sun of liberty set on thousands around him, without sighing for calamity, and

---

[46] *Memoirs of the Life and Travels of the Late Charles Macpherson, Esq.* (Edinburgh: Arch. Constable. 1800), 180. Further citations are given parenthetically in the text.

4. Detail from the frontispiece to Mary Pilkington's *Tales from the Hermitage* illustrating "The Faithful Slave." No artist credit given. London: Vernor and Hood, 1798. Courtesy of the Cambridge University Library.

endeavouring, by every indulgence, to meliorate their condition" (180). MacNeill hints at a conservative, anti-Jacobin suspicion of sentimentality in draining Beaumarché's feelings for the slaves of any real moral significance, even of real sympathy, beyond his love of "festivity."

And Beaumarché differs from his peers among sentimental overseers in at least one other crucial respect – he is much less successful than they are: "In vain did his managers and neighbours represent the impropriety and danger annexed to a suddenly relaxed system . . . [Which] might otherwise lead to a want of due subordination among the slaves" (180). The reaction of Beaumarché's "managers and neighbours" also marks a significant difference from other narratives of plantation reform. Here, for the first time, MacNeill does not blithely assume that other planters would be untroubled by – even enthusiastic about – one of their fellows trying to improve their system on the basis of a moral critique; instead, he anticipates a negative, even fearful reaction.[47] The event demonstrates, however, that this is due to the planters' clear-headed view of African inferiority, not from a pig-headed resistance to progress or resentment of challenges to their own morality.

MacNeill's Beaumarché is a parody of the sentimental reformer in the mode of Sarah Scott's Sir George Ellison. Like Ellison, Beaumarché initially appears in the passage as a "man of universal benevolence and humanity," a man who "could not behold the sun of liberty set on thousands" without being impelled to action "to meliorate their condition." However, MacNeill does not distinguish this seemingly benevolent impulse from Beaumarché's status as a playful man of leisure. We get the odd biographical detail that he was "accustomed to scenes" of "festivity and freedom." Freedom and "festivity" are made equivalents as "brightening pastimes." Freedom is not a necessary component of the citizen's identity here, or even the opposite of "captivity" or "slavery"; it is merely the opposite of industry and labor, the essence of leisure and "festivity."

Laxness causes Beaumarché's failure as a reformer. According to Macpherson, his system, rather than being kinder, more humane, or more rational, is merely "more relaxed" than the normal plantation system. Beaumarché's "chief attention was directed to the comfort and happiness" of slaves, instead of to the improvement of their condition (or of his estate). Instead of studying ways to increase slaves' efficiency through carefully orchestrated disciplinary uses of kindness, he employs "every indulgence." When he spurns the advice of his neighbors to proceed with caution, Beaumarché again revels in his misguidedness, "as he despised suggestions, which he considered in no other light than the sneaking instigations of interest and callous insensibility to the sufferings of the unfortunate," and announced his own principles, exclaiming that "'the love of FREEDOM is implanted in every breast; and comfort, relaxation, and mirth, are privileges particular to no set of men upon earth'" (181). Here, Beaumarché seems to provide nothing more than a parody of the revolutionary rhetoric

---

[47] Charlotte Smith, *The Story of Henrietta*, vol. II of *The Letters of a Solitary Wanderer*, 1800 (New York: Woodstock, 1995), 283, represents attempted plantation reforms defeated by the opposition of other planters. See my article, The Horror of Hybridity: Enlightenment, Anti-slavery and Racial Disgust in Charlotte Smith's *Story of Henrietta Essays and Studies*, 60 (2007), 87–109. (Special volume: *Slavery and The Cultures of Abolition: Essays Marking the Bicentennial of the British Abolition Act*, ed. Brycchan Carey and Peter Kitson.)

of the rights of man, focusing not on "basic" rights such as freedom, but rather on such frivolities as "mirth." Perhaps MacNeill has in mind James Ramsay's indignant suggestion that "ease" and "indulgence" should be considered as rights.[48] In this passage, MacNeill associates Beaumarché with the French Revolution and simultaneously attempts to belittle his reforms by conflating radicalism and frivolity.[49] Furthermore, MacNeill offers a riposte to one of the underlying motive forces of British anti-slavery: the assumption of the moral superiority of metropolitans, the tendency to blame slavery on distant American colonials.[50] This tendency was integrated into the grateful slave trope, as the reforming sentimentalist – despite being modeled on the reform program of West Indians like Colonel Samuel Martin – was most often a metropolitan shocked into action by exposure to the horrors of colonial cruelty. In pointed contrast, Beaumarché's attempts to impose his metropolitan prejudices on the plantation lead him directly to disaster.

In fact, MacNeill takes the frivolity of Beaumarché's concerns to an extreme, using the disastrous results of his failed reforms as a lesson, not only about the proper concerns that one should bring to such a project, but also about the nature and concerns of the slaves themselves. Before Beaumarché can fully institute his reforms, the "negroes" bring him down. As the narrator (Madame Bellanger, the former Madame Beaumarché) explains, Beaumarché's rash insistence on giving the slaves two succeeding days off from work was "the rock he afterwards split upon, and proved the fatal cause of his ruin" (185).[51] As Beaumarché himself explains, he intends this to be "the means of affording the Negro a *complete holiday*," because Sunday, under the prior system, is the only "day of rest and recreation; but pray, how is this accomplished? This is the only day they have to cultivate their grounds, carry their provisions to market, and travel often between twenty and thirty

[48] *Essay on the Treatment and Conversion of African Slaves in the British Sugar Colonies* (London: James Phillips, 1784), 87. See discussion of this remark in chapter 4, p. 169, above.
[49] The association of the Revolution with anti-slavery – France issued an emancipation decree in 1793 – greatly hampered British anti-slavery politics until Napoleon restored slavery and the color line in 1803. See Davis, *Age of Revolution*, 29–31, 115, 117; Ferguson, *Subject to Others* 193–4; and Schama, *Rough Crossings*, 261–5, 371–2. M. M. Bahktin's "carnivalesque," in *Rabelais and His World*, trans. Helene Iswolsky (Bloomington: Indiana University Press, 1984), and applied to the British eighteenth century by Peter Stallybrass and Allon White in *The Politics and Poetics of Transgression* (London: Methuen, 1986), suggests that frivolity can be a form of resistance.
[50] See Brown, *Moral Capital*, 36–7.
[51] The "danger" of consecutive days of rest for slaves is predicted in one of the most virulent responses to Ramsay, which also argues for African inferiority: "Some Gentlemen of St. Christopher," in *An Answer to the Reverend James Ramsay's Essay, on the Treatment and Conversion of Slaves* (Basseterre, St. Christopher: Edward L. Low, 1784), 43. Notably, even they begin with a sentimental claim that they, rather than Ramsay, have the slaves' interests at heart (3).

miles . . . Is this a day of *rest*? can it be called a day of *recreation*?" (184). Here, Beaumarché's insistent conflation of humanity and "recreation" is his fatal error, precisely because the nature of the "negroes" requires severer discipline than would European workers. Embedded in this failure is a critique of sentimentalism: Beaumarché is doomed when he imagines himself in the place of the slaves and acts accordingly. His "sympathy" fails because it leaves him trapped within his own theoretical understanding of himself, with no access to the realities of the slaves' nature or even to their real experiences. Beaumarché's "sympathy" is as mechanical as Colonel Jack's, with the significant exception that rather than aiding him, it misleads him.

MacNeill fully exploits the melodramatic possibilities of Beaumarché's "fatal" misconception of the Africans; as

he listened with rapture to the nightly sound of the *bangah* and the *tom tom* on his estate, and indulged himself in the pleasing reflection that the hapless children of bondage were enjoying comforts arising from a melioration of their condition, and burying recollection of their misfortune in the rustic merriment of their hamlet, a very different train of operations was going on. (188–9)

Beaumarché's pleasure in hearing instruments signifying both festivity and the call to arms emblematizes his fatal misunderstanding of the slaves. Indeed, some of this "train of operations" has already been revealed: just as the love of leisure and "festivity" born of a youth in Europe has misled Beaumarché, so the slaves are led into error by leisure: "a constant participation of indulgence was attended with consequences as natural as fatal among those who neither reason with propriety nor act with discretion. From ease, comfort, and recreation, a love of pleasure became the predominant desire. This led to excess; excess to turbulence; and turbulence to *rebellion*" (189–90). The first signs of trouble convince Beaumarché to take a different approach to his slaves, but his "enlightenment" comes too late. Beaumarché had never totally opposed physical violence against slaves, remarking at the height of his reforms that "Punishment must, and shall be, inflicted for crimes and misdemeanours; but *never* by the wantonness of passion or the caprice of power" (183–4). Resistance quickly brings him to violence. On hearing of trouble, he immediately "determined, by one bold step, to intimidate by terror rather than enforce by precept" (190). Beaumarché's eagerness to adopt the repressive measures of the planters he earlier criticized as self-interested makes his commitment to reform appear dubious. MacNeill seems unable to resist having Beaumarché fall back into the behavior he has critiqued, suggesting that violence is necessary to discipline slaves, and hinting at the hypocrisy of sentimentalists.

Unlike his fellow novelistic reformers, Beaumarché never links the new "advantages" he offers his slaves to their behavior to manipulate them psychologically. Apparently, as suggested by his language of "rights," Beaumarché does not view his reforms as incentives; in practice, he seems to believe only in punishment as a motivation. It is only once their rebellious behavior has begun that he even attempts such a linkage: "Beaumarché, in a firm tone, told them, that, seeing they had made such a bad use of the indulgence and favours granted them, he had determined to reduce them to their former state, until, by their behaviour, they evinced a complete reformation" (191). Here, too, he hardly holds out a carrot, merely demanding that the slaves choose between "complete reformation" or the stick. Indeed, Beaumarché's behavior suggests that he really views the problem with slavery not as a fundamental one of the deprivation of "freedom," but rather as a painful restriction of "festivity," "comfort," and "recreation" that could be remedied with an extra day off a week.

When he is challenged by a rebellious slave leader, a fearless "Coromantee," "Beaumarché, seeing no alternative, laid him instantly dead at his foot" (192). He has no hesitation, no qualms, about killing a slave to preserve discipline. None of the other novelistic reformers are ever faced with such a dilemma; they all view selling a slave off from their plantation as the ultimate sanction. Beaumarché's acceptance and endorsement of the planter's right to kill a slave for disobedience makes him an unlikely critic of the institution of slavery. And, as noted above, he makes little effort to get his slaves to internalize his kindness as a type of discipline and work-motivation; it is only after killing the leader and publicly punishing his compatriots that Beaumarché explains to the slaves that he "left it to their own choice, whether, by their conduct, they were to be treated, in future, as good Negroes, or punished as bad ones" (193–4). His language here conflates "negroes" and "slaves," clearly thinking within the terms of colonial white supremacy.

Beaumarché's failures as a disciplinarian, his misplaced concern with the slaves' "comfort" and "recreation" ultimately led not merely to the failure of his reforms but also to his death. Continuing to develop the sense of Beaumarché as a noble, but betrayed soul, the narrator pursues the melodramatic portrait of him as deceived by his own good intentions: "For some time, however, matters went on in the usual routine; and Beaumarché was at length so much convinced of the thorough reformation of his slaves, that the period was fixed upon, and even promised, for the restoration of all their former indulgences" (194). Apparently changing her evaluation of Beaumarché's work as a reformer to heighten the sense that the rebels are evil, traitorous ingrates, the narrator adds that "these regulations never took place; nor did the period ever arrive, when this kind and benevolent master reaped the rewards which his benevolent and humane system so justly intitled him to" (195). The shift to viewing him as "kind" and "benevolent" is abrupt and unconvincing. MacNeill, having mocked Beaumarché's delusive, self-indulgent sentimental kindness, is now willing to grant it for the rhetorical purpose of heightening the slaves' depravity. MacNeill may intend this as a reminder that the story is narrated by Beaumarché's widow, Madame Bellanger, but that did not restrain criticism of his failures earlier.

Subsequently, the slaves' actual rebellion takes place off-stage, and the violent results are summarized quite briefly: "Suffice it to say, that, after doing every thing which humanity, prudence, and courage, could execute, my dear and ill-fated husband, and all his followers, were massacred, in a manner too shocking for description" (198–9). Despite this change of tone, a last reminder of the failings of Beaumarché's attempt at reform precedes it by only a few pages, arguing that slaves feel nothing but "the desire to extend the unbounded limits of sensuality; while recent establishments of order, restrictions, and punishments, dwelt incessantly on the mind and filled the savage soul with bloody and ungovernable revenge" (195). However, a shift is already underway: it is not Beaumarché's emphasis on "leisure" and "comfort" that causes the downfall of his reforms; it is the way that the slaves transform his ideas – "comfort" and "recreation" become "a desire to extend the unbounded limits of sensuality" – that make them dangerous and even deadly, not only to Beaumarché but also to the slaves themselves.

Beaumarché's attempt at reform brings him up against the double edge of slaves' unreasoning nature. Any kindness or indulgence feeds their infinite capacity for "sensuality": any restriction or discipline merely hurries the "savage soul" along its course to "bloody and ungovernable revenge." In this scheme of things, slaves are not ever "grateful," they are always treasonous ingrates; they are irrational to the point that they cannot identify their own interests. Beaumarché, on the other hand, is a complete failure as a reformer: rather than instilling work-discipline (like all his novelistic predecessors), and consciously working to have the slaves internalize it, Beaumarché undermines discipline without realizing it. His key mistake, it seems, is in assuming that the slaves are like him and therefore share his compelling need for "festivity" and "indulgence." In fact, he is unlike the other grateful slave reformers he parodies in that he does not from the outset assume that Africans are irrational and in need of his attentive guidance.

In this representation, MacNeill turns two central points of the other novelistic reformers on their heads. He never considers "gratitude" as a key part of slaves' motivation; in fact, he totally rejects the notion that slaves will be aware of their own self-interest. The slaves, in his account, are unreasoning "savages" capable only of "sensuality" or "revenge." He therefore rejects "gratitude" in favor of the theory that the slaves' "savage souls" are so compelled by their "sensuality" that nothing short of draconian violence can compel their obedience. He also rejects the notion that "humanitarian" awareness of slaves' suffering and a desire to discipline them can go hand in hand; Beaumarché's initial "humanitarian" concern with the comfort of the slaves blinds him totally to the needs of discipline; on the plantation, MacNeill implies, the planter's first concern has to be with discipline. Furthermore, Beaumarché underestimates the inherently undisciplined inclinations and behavior of his charges. He sees them as human like himself, failing to account for their savage depravity. The uprising of Beaumarché's slaves – like Zimao's rebellion – does not reveal their urgent desire for freedom, but rather his failures of management technique. This was no doubt a reassuring thought for whites in the age of the Haitian revolution and Gabriel's rebellion.

But MacNeill, via Mrs. Bellanger, the narrator of Beaumarché's tale, does not mean to argue that all attempts at amelioration are equally misguided. Indeed, Mrs. Bellanger tells of her own quite successful reforms, very different than Beaumarché's, in scope, in intention, and in results. The key to her reforms is marriage; she makes marriage a tool for improving slaves' morality and discipline. Although her reforms are presented as admirable, Mrs. Bellanger emphasizes that she has carefully delimited them. Mrs. Bellanger has learned the lesson imparted by her first husband's death. She introduces her reforms by showing that they have had the ultimate success, in terms shared by many other novels of plantation slavery. Her slaves "are regular, decent, and orderly, in their conduct; kind to one another; and so attached to me, and pleased with their condition, that they prefer it to absolute *freedom*; an offer which they have repeatedly refused" (212). Given the lack of discipline and the devotion to pleasure that brought about Beaumarché's downfall, this would appear no small accomplishment. Alongside the racism of the Beaumarché tale, Madame Bellanger's reforms complete *Macpherson's* anticipation of Antebellum US pro-slavery fiction: in addition to the insistence on black inferiority, she offers the vision of the caring, familial, paternalist planter.

One must wonder why MacNeill, despite arguing for the legitimacy, even necessity, of violence for controlling slaves' behavior, despite his insistent emphasis on discipline, despite dismissing concern for slaves' "comfort" and "happiness" as misguided frivolity, is nonetheless concerned to represent such a scene of slave "happiness." Why represent certain reforms that produce "happy slaves" who accept their captivity after arguing that reform and happiness are less important than – and possibly detrimental to – slave discipline? After all, as Robert Fogel has compellingly argued, the planters' free hand with violence was what made plantations into the laboratories of capitalist work discipline, the factor that allowed them to create discipline regardless of their workers' inclinations.[52] MacNeill, unlike the 1830s plantation novelists he in many ways anticipates, hardly shies away from the issue of plantation slavery's systemic violence, instead representing planter violence – against the implied backdrop of Haiti – as a justified, even heroic, form of self-defense. Mr. Penguin, a character who is never repudiated (in fact, the final assessment of his dispute with Mrs. Bellanger is that it was an argument "not badly supported on either side" (251)) implies that any concern with slave happiness is detrimental to the planters' interests: "Instead of *feasts*, we must impress *fear*; instead of *indulgencies*, we must attend to *discipline*. Nothing agrees with this infernal turbulent animal so much as strict subordination" (231). If one accepts violence as a necessary part of the slave system, and as fully effective form of discipline, why look for alternate means for disciplining enslaved workers?

One possible answer is that MacNeill is concerned here not just with the situation of plantation slaves, but also with the issue of work-discipline more generally; he is imagining ways, as Fogel's connection suggests, to bring the advantages of plantation discipline back home to the factory. This is an odd but intriguing possibility given the insistent comparison of slaves and free laborers in apologies for slavery. Still, MacNeill hints that he works with a different context in representing Mrs. Bellanger's reforms as admirable but impractical replacements for the violence of the current plantation system. Mrs. Bellanger herself points out these limits, saying "what I have happily accomplished could not be practicable *every where*, but my situation being particularly favorable, I availed myself of the opportunity" (213). Her refusal to present her reforms as a solution to the systemic problems of slavery distinguishes her from grateful slave reformers, and keeps her from lapsing into the "visionary" errors so despised by the anti-Jacobins. Still, her efforts, in their resonance with those of

---

[52] Robert Fogel, *Without Consent or Contract: The Rise and Fall of American Slavery* (New York: Norton, 1989), 25.

European reformers, suggest that planters desire moral reforms, but are hampered from implementing them not by their own recalcitrance but by the depravity of slaves.[53]

Mr. Penguin, Mrs. Bellanger's argumentative adversary, merely has to elaborate on the opening she has provided him to attack her. He calls her system *"impracticable,"* claiming that "this, to every person generally acquainted with the nature of West Indian property, is apparent" (232–3). Mr. Penguin's objections are based on his understanding of "the nature of West Indian property," the "negro character" or, as he puts it here, "this infernal turbulent animal" (231). He condemns all people of African descent for moral failings that he imagines to be inherent to them, and sees as illustrated by the failure of Beaumarché's attempted reforms. Penguin asks rhetorically: "What shall we say of a set of mortals who, in defiance of every inconvenience, and in spite of every punishment, will sacrifice and utterly destroy their own health and future comforts, merely for the gratification of a temporary enjoyment?" (242). To MacNeill's (albeit limited) credit, Mrs. Bellanger responds incisively to Mr. Penguin's question; she reminds him that slave owners are hardly moral exemplars, especially given the planters' sexual exploitation of slave women (239–40). But her response implicitly endorses Mr. Penguin's claim that slaves are morally bankrupt as a group, while at the same time raising the important issue of planter conduct. After all, Madame Bellanger herself takes the position that her reforms cannot be applied to most slaves because of their inherent deficiencies.

Penguin's response, nonetheless, is a haughty and dismissive invocation of essential difference in the capacity to manage "passions": "nor is it easier for a camel to pass through the eye of a needle, than to make *one* Negro wench chaste, or commonly decent, in her conduct. Can passions so inordinate, or dispositions so prone to excess, originate in *slavery?*" (243). Although Mrs. Bellanger does raise interesting questions about planters' behavior, she nonetheless seems to share many of Mr. Penguin's racist assumptions. She does not, for instance, invoke the familiar abolitionist position that the situation of slavery accounts for the slaves' degradation. She echoes Bryan Edwards, explaining that her reforms improve "the condition of the Negro, not only with regard to mere slavery, but to the various miseries annexed to a state of savage and unsocial barbarism" (213),

---

[53] Brown, *Moral Capital*, 333–89, argues that planters' obstruction of efforts to convert slaves was an important factor in galvanizing the anti-slavery movement; pro-slavery writers appear to have acknowledged this mistake by the end of the century.

using Edwards' conflation of the cultural and the essential to accede quietly to Mr. Penguin's view of African slaves as a "racial" group.

Although Madame Bellanger points out these apparently "racial" failings, her solution isolates social issues and in fact could be spoken by English capitalist employers of their concern to improve workers' morality and discipline together:[54] she is "convinced, that the principal source of calamity was a total neglect of institutions, calculated to wean the mind insensibly from habits of *intemperance*, and make it enamoured of *social and domestic peace*" (214). Ultimately, despite her apparent scorn for much of Mr. Penguin's position, she agrees with him on one crucial point. The central problem of slavery and slave reform is not a question of the failings of the slave system; it is a question of the moral failings of slaves, failings that have already been linked to their cultural and racial status. Her solution is to locate those rare slaves who can be saved and, by dint of tremendous effort, turn them from their wicked ways. Her solution is one that would have resonance for English employers. As several factors suggest, marriage likely did help to discipline workers; not only did it raise the minimal amount of wages needed for subsistence by those workers who preferred leisure to labor, but it also brought sometimes vocal allies into workers' homes in the employers' struggle against "St. Monday" and other primarily male traditions that militated against discipline.[55]

The success of Mrs. Bellanger's marriage-based reforms, and of the satire on novelistic reformers in *The Memoirs of Charles Macpherson*, seems to carry a double message for broader considerations of slavery and of work discipline. On the one hand, several of the strands suggest ways to improve the discipline of any workers, slave or free, who present problems because they favor leisure over work. These ideas would seem far more relevant to European workers, who on some level (at least according to their employers' complaints) still had some discretion about whether or not to work on a given day. Her concern for moral improvement and work discipline in

---

[54] Despite the sense of such studies as Armstrong's *Desire and Domestic Fiction*, the moral "reform" of the working class was not simply an imposition of the "bourgeois value" of "domesticity" by the "middle class." See Anna Clark, *The Struggle for the Breeches: Gender and the Making of the British Working Class* (Berkeley: University of California Press, 1995), 61. See also Thomas Laqueur, *Religion and Respectability: Sunday Schools and Working Class Culture 1780–1850* (New Haven: Yale University Press, 1976), 189; and Robert W. Malcolmson, *Popular Recreations in English Society, 1700–1850* (Cambridge: Cambridge University Press, 1973).

[55] Anna Clark states that "Wives dreaded the working man's custom of Saint Monday, celebrated by historians as proletarian resistance to time discipline" (82) primarily because men tended to drink to excess and to stay around the house. Douglas Reid, ironically, reads the plebian habit of getting married on a Monday as a continuation of the "Saint Monday" tradition in "Weddings, Weekdays."

the abstract ally her with the broader moral agenda of many critics of slavery.[56] The other strand, however, suggests that slaves are so different – both racially and culturally – from their masters that they cannot be reformed or improved, but only contained. Even the successes of Mrs. Bellanger point in this direction. After all, she emphasizes that her success rests on the small scale of her enterprise, the isolation of her plantation, and her extreme selectivity about the slaves she chooses to work with. Notably, her reforms do not provoke the opposition that met Beaumarché's efforts.

In the end, then, *Macpherson* shunts aside the complexity of the grateful slave consensus that slaves are inferior precisely because of their capacity for gratitude, and instead insists on the point that slaves and, more specifically, African-descended people, are simply – and universally – inferior. In so doing, *Macpherson* at once harks back to the earlier eighteenth-century concept that slavery, as a state of war, requires violence regardless of difference, and yet also looks forward to the nineteenth-century US fictional defenses of slavery, with their curious insistence on both African inferiority and slave owners' benevolent paternalism.

CONCLUSION: MANAGING SENTIMENTS

The 1790s produced a striking crop of grateful slave fictions, with an increasingly fervent insistence on the possibility that blacks could be brought to devote themselves with irrational fervor to "kind," humane whites. These literary products of a contentious decade, known both for radicals and reactionaries, turn out to fall into a pronounced pattern. Introducing slave narrators and protagonists – even heroic rebels – quickly devolves into an excuse to put in the mouths of blacks sentiments like "we fight *for* massa; he so good." Slaves are regularly depicted as defending "kind" masters during rebellions and refusing freedom with pronouncements like "Never will we quit you. On this land we will pay our debt to you." These ostensibly "anti-slavery" fictions, then, give birth to the tropes that will be repeated endlessly in the pro-slavery plantation fiction of the 1830s United States. And the only novel to take a different direction on plantation slavery – *Macpherson* – does so to insist on an even more explicit account of racial difference and African depravity. The 1790s, in other words, show the emergence of the grateful slave, and its accompanying account of racial difference, into cultural centrality in British discourse for the first time, at the very moment when the abolition movement was at its

---

[56] Brown, *Moral Capital*, 386–8.

zenith. In this sense, it appears that the intense attention to slavery accompanying the abolition movement was also the watershed moment for a habitual belief in racial difference in British culture. The slavery fictions of the 1790s, then, represent the culmination of the grateful slave tradition and perhaps the clearest example of its racial underpinnings.

Indeed, the grateful slave trope could be understood as tradition not just for imagining possible futures for slavery, but as an evolving series of attempts to manage public attitudes toward slavery and race; less an effort at practical reimaginings of plantation management and more an effort at managing the public's sentiments about African slavery. The trope began in the 1720s, at a time when there was no abolitionist movement, but there was nonetheless a strong public dislike of slavery, a time of what Christopher L. Brown has aptly termed "antislavery without abolitionism."[57] Defoe's titular hero, Colonel Jack, invents the grateful slave scenario as a way of solving a specific problem: his own unwilling sympathy with the slaves, born of having been a slave alongside them himself, which undermines his ability to employ violent discipline. In a sense, Jack's dilemma mirrors that of British people of his moment: how can they continue to develop enthusiastically the plantation economy that is making them a major European power for the first time, when doing so requires ruthlessly exploiting Africans whom they imagine to share their humanity? Defoe's effort is followed by William Snelgrave's sentimental account of his slave trading in Africa as an effort to rescue Africans from the barbarity of their kings and even to keep families together. In the decade when John Thomson penned the line "Britons Never, Never, Never Will Be Slaves," Snelgrave offers a vision of racial difference as a justification of slavery by depicting Africans eagerly embracing their enslavement by benevolent whites.

Scott's and MacKenzie's ameliorationist fictions of the 1760s and 1770s are sometimes hailed as "anti-slavery" for bringing attention to the cruelty of slavery. In a sense this is reasonable, but at the same time, it must be understood that these fictions are more intent on making slavery acceptable to an audience that rejected it instinctively than on exposing its problems. Indeed, these fictions coincide with times of great public agitation for liberty and concern about slavery – in the Wilkes affair, the build up to the American Revolution, and the deeply influential decision by Lord Mansfield in the Somerset case. Rather than meaning to challenge slavery, then, these ameliorationist fictions promote the evangelical attitude toward

---

[57] *Ibid.*

slavery before the flowering of the abolitionist movement – a desire to attend to the spiritual condition of slaves, while keeping the slaves contained within the institution of slavery.

Only in the 1780s, in the wake of the loss of the American colonies, and at the beginnings of the abolition movement, do British writers seriously question the key elements of the grateful slave trope. Thomas Day and the black Atlantic writers question racial difference and subordination through gratitude, while Dr. John Moore questions the notion that planters' economic interests will drive them to embrace amelioration. And yet, at the same time, Lucy Peacock puts in place the elements of grateful slavery for the 1790s and the Antebellum US, with a reassuring depiction of blacks rejecting freedom in order to support their kind mistress. The 1790s, as we have seen, close off the questioning of the 1780s to embrace enthusiastically the image of blacks as irrationally passionate, devoted to gratitude or to vengeance. This image proves doubly useful, justifying the newly central goal of amelioration by suggesting that blacks are naturally suited to a gentler form of slavery, and at the same time insinuating that slave insurrections are merely the result of white mismanagement of blacks' essential nature, not the inevitably fatal result of trying to confine human beings to a cruel, relentless and unjustifiable system of labor exploitation, and, as we shall see in the epilogue, sets the terms for the development of the discourse of race in Antebellum America perhaps even more so than in Britain itself.

Epilogue: Grateful slaves, faithful slaves, mammies and martyrs: the transatlantic afterlife of the grateful slave

The slave, a black man with a simple soul, is a good Christian. His master is cruel, relentless, materialistic – and motivated only by his short-term profits. The slave is a faithful, reliable servant, stoic and uncomplaining on his own behalf; his focus is on the next world. Nonetheless, he makes clear his compassion for the suffering of his fellow slaves, and refuses to countenance his master's cruelty. The master, enraged at his calm, principled defiance, has his Christian slave whipped beyond human endurance. Before his death, however, the slave manages to pray, sincerely, for the soul of his cruel master. This scene may be quite familiar to you. Perhaps you have read this affecting scene of sentimental martyrdom yourself. Did you read it in Dr. John Moore's 1789 novel *Zeluco*? Does it call to mind the names Hanno and Zeluco? Perhaps not. Perhaps you thought instead of Uncle Tom and Simon Legree.[1]

Stowe's and Moore's scenes of martyred slaves, of course, are not identical. Hanno protests another slave's whipping as excessive, and then is whipped to death when he refuses to perform it himself. Uncle Tom knows of Cassie and Emmeline's plan of escape and is whipped to death for refusing to divulge it. Still, the broad outlines are shared, as is the specific implication for the slavery debate drawn by the author in each case. In her chapter "The Martyr," Stowe reiterates Moore's central challenge to the economic arguments of slavery's apologists, and of grateful slave novelists, if in far more explicitly religious language, commenting even before Tom's death: "Ye say that the *interest* of the master is a sufficient safe-guard for the slave. In the fury of man's mad will, he will wittingly, and with open eye,

---

[1] Despite extensive scholarly interest in the sources for Uncle Tom, *Zeluco* has not been previously mentioned. For a detailed study of Stowe's sources, see E. Bruce Kirkham, *The Building of* Uncle Tom's Cabin (Knoxville: University of Tennessee Press, 1977). "The Martyrdom" is treated on 72–7; possible sources for Uncle Tom's character on 88–100.

sell his own soul to the devil to gain his ends; and will he be more careful of his neighbor's body?" (355).

Indeed, like Moore implicitly critiquing the grateful slave trope, Stowe herself makes clear that being an ideal slave is itself no guarantee of safety: "Tom was a faithful, valuable servant; and, although Legree hated him the more for that, yet the consideration was still somewhat of a restraint to him" (355). But her language and conception shows that the idea of the devoted slave has shifted between late eighteenth-century England and Antebellum America. Eighteenth-century grateful slaves – although Hanno is himself an exception to this rule – are grateful for specific acts of kindness; they are not simply devoted and faithful. Perhaps this is why, of all eighteenth-century stories about slavery, *Zeluco* was the most useful source for Stowe; it was almost unique in making the slave character faithful to God and Christianity rather than grateful to a master for specific kindnesses; Moore was critiquing the excesses of "grateful slave" and ameliorationism rather than endorsing these culturally central positions of his moment. Equiano, too, used this technique, depicting himself praying for the soul of a blaspheming captain who was abusing him for his faith and planning to sell him back into slavery after he was free.[2]

For Stowe, however, making Tom such a character fits within the stereotypes and the dominant tropes of her time. Slaves with a narrative explanation for their "gratitude" faded from prominence in the Antebellum period, and the essentialized characters of the "happy," "contented," or "faithful" slave took their place, as the pro-slavery ideology of paternalism, depicting black slaves as children in need of the fatherly guidance of white masters was not opposed, but rather adopted into the anti-slavery ideology of "Romantic Racialism," holding that Africans were a meek, childlike, even feminine race particularly well suited to Christian devotion.[3] However, this evolution was not simply the product of the changing politics of slavery. The grateful slave story had become woven into the fabric of Antebellum culture; taking the characteristics of the grateful slave for granted as essential elements of the black personality was an almost inevitable development. While it faded from use in adult fiction, the British version of "the grateful slave" became a staple of children's literature; pro-slavery writers emphasized the slaves' devotion

---

[2] Equiano, *Interesting Narrative*, 211–12; see the discussion of the passage above, p. 184.
[3] Fredrickson, "Romantic Racialism," in *The Black Image*; Yellin, *Intricate Knot*; Roth, "Rebels and Martyrs." For a complex account of the relationship between images of slave docility and happiness and practices of violence against slaves, see Saidiya V. Hartman, *Scenes of Subjection: Terror, Slavery, and Self-Making in Nineteenth-Century America* (New York: Oxford University Press, 1997).

to masters, while anti-slavery writers warned of slaves' vengeful response to cruelty.[4]

As the eighteenth century drew to a close, "grateful slave" stories became more and more closely tied to the problem of revolution. Those slaves whose emotional, irrational nature was not channeled into devotion by masterly kindness were likely to become vengeful and even engage in bloody acts of revolt. Antebellum "faithful slaves," including Uncle Tom himself, do not present this threat. Their grateful devotion has been essentialized into a racial characteristic no longer requiring narrative explanation as it had in earlier British discourse; Stowe's twist, likely borrowed from Dr. Moore, is to make the slave faithful to Christ rather than to a specific kind master. With the end of the slave trade, the promise of amelioration ceased to be a meaningful response to criticism of slavery; slavery had to be represented as already ameliorated, and slaves as already consenting to their condition, rather than as capable of being made to consent through improvements in sympathy and kindness.

The grateful slave, grateful for specific kindnesses, is nonetheless replaced in the 1830s by two characters: the "faithful slave" as a comic sidekick, largely drawn from minstrelsy, who almost inevitably refuses an offer of freedom indignantly, and the beloved "Mammy" who has raised the planter character and is emotionally reunited with him. The faithful slave has no back-story explaining his devotion; the back-story is instead supplied by the "mammy" who legitimates the idea of slavery as familial and as a mutual emotional bond. An obscure novel of 1836, Joseph Ingraham's *Lafitte: Or the Pirate of the Gulf*, known for its depiction of piracy rather than for dealing with slavery, does represent a "grateful slave," devoted to his master for kindness; but this slave does not require a narrative explanation for his devotion due to his essential humanity, but rather because such devotion seems inconsistent with his thorough-going depravity.[5]

Harriet Beecher Stowe never acknowledged direct literary influences on her most famous work.[6] She offered three conflicting explanations for the origins of the famous climactic scene of *Uncle Tom's Cabin*, "The Martyr," in which Uncle Tom dies only after praying for the souls of Simon Legree,

---

[4] Sarah N. Roth, "The Mind of a Child: Images of African Americans in Early Juvenile Fiction," *Journal of the Early Republic*, 25:1 (2005), 79–109.

[5] Reprint, 2 vols. in 1 (Upper Saddle River, NY: Gregg, 1970), II:36.

[6] Most discussions of her influences have followed the lead of Stowe's own *Key to Uncle Tom's Cabin* in looking for specific slaves, specific incidents on Antebellum plantations, or Antebellum anti-slavery documents, as her sources. See Kirkham's account of those claiming to be the "real Uncle Tom" (*Building*, 86–96).

the cruel master who caused his death, and his henchmen. In the most dubiously documented explanation, Stowe is reported to have claimed that she wrote the scene of Uncle Tom's martyrdom long before the rest of the book as an instructive entertainment for her children.[7] In two better-documented and more frequently offered explanations, Stowe recounted specific (although contradictory) moments when the "vision" of the scene had first come to her.[8] In one instance, she again claimed that it had been the first scene of the novel to be written. In another, she presented it as a solution to the inevitable narrative need for Uncle Tom's death: "I knew that he must die from the first, but I did not know *How*."[9] Stowe's primary agenda in the two dominant versions of this story was to present this crucial scene as being rooted in quasi-divine inspiration.[10] She also stressed the strong emotional reaction of her children to hearing the scene as an inspiration to her in writing the full-length novel.

This Epilogue, however, is not centrally concerned with the exact lines of influence between Moore and Stowe. The intention is not to devalue Stowe's work, or even to engage the question of the divinity of her inspiration.[11] Instead, my point here is that Stowe's famous novel had its roots at least sixty years before its publication in a specific eighteenth-century British grateful slave fiction as suggestive of the extent to which the grateful slave trope lived on after the British had abolished the slave trade in 1807 and even emancipated their remaining slaves in 1833. Not only did the trope continue to influence British perceptions of slavery and race, but it became an ingrained part of Antebellum US culture, shaping the American view of blacks' "child-like docility" and deeply influencing "key decisions about black civil rights in the pre-Civil War period."[12]

The image of Uncle Tom as a slave-martyr has also been read as a brilliant solution to the problems of representing slaves in Antebellum

---

[7] Kirkham, *Building*, 73–4.   [8] *Ibid.*, 72–4.

[9] Annie Fields, ed., *Life and Letters of Harriet Beecher Stowe* (Boston: Houghton Mifflin, 1898), 164; quotation discussed in Kirkham, *Building*, 73.

[10] Kirkham, *Building*, 75. Charles Nichols, "The Origins of Uncle Tom's Cabin," *Phylon*, 19:3 (1958), 328–34, esp. 329, views claims of divine inspiration as stemming from the charlatanism of the Beechers.

[11] Indeed, the charge that Stowe's novel was a creation of literary influence – a "derivative piece of hack work" if not "devoid of all originality"–has been made, although in connection to an earlier Antebellum work, Richard Hildreth's *The Slave: or the Memoirs of Archy Moore*. The character suggested as the basis for Uncle Tom, Thomas, does make a speech which Uncle Tom echoes. But far from being a martyr, takes violent revenge and abandons Christianity. See Nichols, "The Origins," 330–1. Kirkham rejects Nichols' argument, *Building*, 96–7. See also Evan Brandstater, "Uncle Tom and Archy Moore: The Antislavery Novel as Ideological Symbol," *American Quarterly*, 26:2 (1974), 160–75.

[12] Roth, "Mind of a Child," 79 and 80.

America, perfectly managing the disturbing possibility of slaves' rebellious violence and therefore as a key element in the phenomenal popularity of Stowe's novel.[13] Stowe must be credited with perfection in timing and managing the trope, however, not with inventing it or even introducing it to anti-slavery fiction. Indeed, it is not unlikely that Stowe was familiar with Dr. Moore's most successful work. *Zeluco* was far less obscure in Antebellum America than it is has since become. It was included in Anna Letitia Barbauld's edition of *The British Novelists* and was likely to be in the collection of any decent circulating library in the USA. Dr. Moore's book was invoked surprisingly often in literary journalism, although most frequently under the rubric of books often mentioned but rarely read.[14] While there is no direct evidence that Stowe owned or read the novel – other than the eerie resemblance of the climactic scene of its slavery sub-plot to the climactic scene of *Uncle Tom's Cabin* – there is evidence that it was a book to pique the curiosity of young women of her generation; Margaret Fuller struck a bargain with her father for the privilege of being allowed to read it.[15] Moore was often invoked by Maria Edgeworth, who exerted a mighty influence on female writers in Antebellum America, especially those interested in morality and reform. Edgeworth included him as a character – Dr. X – in her novel *Belinda*, and referenced the novel throughout her works, even specifically recommending *Zeluco* as reading matter for inculcating morals in young women.[16]

Indeed, Edgeworth is also the key figure in the dissemination of "the grateful slave" in nineteenth-century England and America, well beyond her advocacy of Dr. Moore's bizarre proto-gothic masterpiece. She herself wrote a classic "grateful slave" tale, "The Grateful Negro," included in her volume of *Popular Tales* (1804).[17] The tale drew a parallel between the good, "grateful" slave of a kind master, and the violent, vengeful slave of a neglectful one who allowed his plantation to be run by a cruel overseer. *Popular Tales* was often reprinted in Antebellum America and was recommended by Lydia Maria Child to mothers for the instruction of their

[13] Roth, "Rebels and Martyrs," 110–47.

[14] For discussion of *Zeluco* as a neglected – or deservedly unread – classic, see *The Living Age*, 2:23 (October 19, 1844), 643, and 58:737 (July 10, 1858), 125, and E. A. Duyckinck, "Out-of-the-Way Books and Authors: I. Dr. Jno. Moore," *Putnam's Magazine*, 1:6 (1868), 649–59.

[15] Charles Capper, *Margaret Fuller: An American Romantic Life* (New York: Oxford University Press, 1992), 49.

[16] See for instance her story "The Good French Governess," in *Moral Tales*, 1801 (Philadelphia: Appleton, 1851), 84–5.

[17] Maria Edgeworth, "The Grateful Negro," *Popular Tales* (London: J. Johnson, 1804), 193–240.

children.[18] Although this specific tale, rather strikingly, given Child's anti-slavery commitment, is not among those she specifically recommended, its presence in *Popular Tales* was emphasized in Antebellum reprints of the collection; the frontispieces to several of the nineteenth-century editions illustrated "The Grateful Negro."[19] Indeed, Sarah N. Roth argues that this story was an ur text for the representation of blacks in nineteenth-century US children's fiction, and hence a shaping influence on white Antebellum citizens' concepts of race.[20]

Although I have argued elsewhere that Edgeworth intended her tale as a moderate ameliorationist gesture meant to make the continuation of slavery thinkable, moved into the Antebellum US context, the story could take on a somewhat different resonance.[21] The tale still suggests the irrationality of slaves and their need for white guidance – a position anticipating both the pro-slavery vision of slaves as members of the family, and the anti-slavery Romantic racial view of slaves as docile and feminine – but, if Stowe can be taken to work from Edgeworth's text, she reimagines the scenario of the "good" and "bad" masters and the slave sold off for debt to distinctly anti-slavery effect. Unlike Edgeworth, who presents good masters as a viable solution to the problem of slavery, and only the "bad" master as vulnerable to having to sell off his slaves, Stowe, by making the Shelbys sell Tom for a debt, suggests that "good" masters offer no substantial protection within a system of slavery; as long as slaves are defined as commodities, they cannot be protected from the effects of being sold no matter how good their master's intentions. Interestingly, many pro-slavery plantation fictions make a point of contrasting kind, truly paternal aristocratic masters with cruel, grasping, and exploitative poor whites, not seeming to notice that this renders the image of the contented slave dubious at best. While the primary disciplinary measure of the grateful slave fictions – selling slaves off the plantation – would no longer be acceptable given Antebellum anti-slavery critiques of the destruction of slave families, plantation fictions such as George Tucker's *Valley of the Shenandoah* (1824), John Kirke Paulding's *Westward Ho!* (1832), and William Gilmore Simm's *Woodcraft* (originally entitled *The Sword and*

[18] Child, *The Mother's Book* (Boston: Carter and Hendee, 1831), 105.
[19] Illustrations by William Croome were added to the US 1853 edition, *Popular Tales*: Philadelphia: C. G. Henderson & Co.; New York: D. Appleton & Co. and reprinted many times; in Britain, illustrations by various hands were added to the Edgeworth collection *Tales and Novels*, 18 vols. (London: Baldwin and Cradock, 1832). The "Grateful Negro" frontispiece is in vol. V. See Figures 5 and 6.
[20] Roth, "The Mind of a Child."   [21] Boulukos, "Edgeworth's 'Grateful Negro.'"

the Distaff) (1852) nonetheless represent slaves being sold to pay their masters' debts. Indeed, Edgeworth is much more insistent that good planters are secure from the dangers of debt than are her Antebellum pro-slavery successors. Despite the apparent influence of Edgeworth on Antebellum fiction, Stowe may well have had her pro-slavery rivals more firmly in mind in developing this plot device.

Edgeworth's influential story can be seen as the apotheosis of the late eighteenth-century grateful slave tale in the wake of the Haitian revolution. Not only does it endorse the "moderate" pro-slavery views of Bryan Edwards and explicitly privilege amelioration over emancipation as a desirable solution to slavery's problems, but it also counters its titular "grateful negro," Caesar, with an equally irrational "vengeful" negro, Hector, who participates in a slave conspiracy and uprising. Of course, rebel slaves like Edgeworth's Hector were also an insistent image in Antebellum discussions of slavery; unlike in the eighteenth century, and in Edgeworth's tale, however, "grateful" or happy slaves and rebel slaves were usually held apart in Antebellum America rather than being presented as two sides of the same coin. Most scholars agree that slave rebels were too disturbing, presented too pressing a threat, to be effectively deployed even in anti-slavery propaganda.[22] Pro-slavery southerners did everything they could to suppress evidence of slaves' violent resistance to them and to propagate the image of the happy slave, even if they managed to undermine their own efforts through inconsistency.[23] Anti-slavery activists were also eager to imagine slaves grateful for their efforts and eagerly submitting themselves to the educational and disciplinary efforts of their white "friends."[24] Apparently, the irrationality of Africans, made familiar to an eighteenth-century audience in part through the grateful slave trope, was now taken for granted, and the debate was whether this irrationality tended more to violence or docility. Shockingly, discussions of the "realism" of representations of slavery took the ignorance and contentment of the

[22] French, *The Rebellious Slave*, 1–33, 65–134; Roth, "Rebels and Martyrs"; Eric Sundquist, *To Wake the Nations: Race in the Making of American Literature* (Cambridge, MA: Harvard University Press, 1993), 50–5, 161.

[23] Roth, "Rebels and Martyrs," 59–109; Fredrickson, *The Black Image*, 43–96; Yellin, *Intricate Knot*, 15–81; Meer, *Uncle Tom Mania*, 75–101.

[24] See Ryan, *Grammar of Good Intentions*, esp. 109–42; Lesley Ginsberg, "Of Babies, Beasts, and Bondage: Slavery and the Question of Citizenship in Antebellum American Children's Literature," in *The American Child: A Cultural Studies Reader*. ed. Caroline F. Levander and Carol J. Singley (New Brunswick: Rutgers University Press, 2003), 85–92; and for an example in anti-slavery fiction, see Peter Neilson, *Life and Adventures of Zamba*, 1847 (rpt. Freeport: Books for Libraries, 1970), 186–7.

"slaves" of minstrel performance as a standard in the 1830s, causing digni-
fied and defiant slaves like the titular hero of Richard Hildreth's *Archy
Moore* to be dismissed as unconvincing.[25] Similarly, that blacks were to be
depicted as either docile and loyal or restive and vengeful was so much
taken for granted that anti-slavery writers accused their opponents of
contradicting themselves by invoking both slaves' devotion and their
potential for violence.

The most critically controversial Antebellum representation of a slave
rebellion, Melville's *Benito Cereno*, hangs on just this disjunction – the
difficulty of seeing past the expectation of slave docility – as the narrator is
so committed to notions of black simplicity and the "faithful" slave that he
cannot recognize that the slaves have in fact seized control of the distressed
ship he visits – despite many clues, including the ship's resonant name of
San Dominick.[26] Melville's narrator, Amasa Delano, resolves the problem
of his mistake by quickly moving from the notion of slaves' devotion to
their master to their complete commitment to vengeance. As is revealed in
the effort of critics to make sense of Delano's ability to switch between
these contradictory views of slaves, the two poles of Edgeworth's vision of
slave irrationality – vengeance and devotion – remained dominant, but the
link between them had become radically unstable. For Edgeworth, and for
other grateful slave stories engaging the possibility of rebellion, vengeance or
gratitude were clearly linked. Africans' irrational, highly emotional nature
inevitably lead to one extreme or the other. While this idea of slaves'
irrationality and need for guidance went on to be dominant in the
Antebellum period, the essentialized linkage between vengeance and gratitude disappeared, contented slaves replaced slaves grateful for specific kindness, and as the poles of anti- and pro-slavery replaced amelioration. While
Edgeworth uses the rebellious slave as a threat providing an additional
incentive to be a "good master," the idea of slave rebellion could serve no
such purpose in the Antebellum US. Interestingly, William Croome's frontispiece for the 1852 US edition of Edgeworth's *Popular Tales* – published

---

[25] Meer documents the use of minstrelsy's versions of blackness to rebut anti-slavery accounts (*Uncle
Tom Mania*, 84–7); For the reactions to Hildreth, see Yellin, *Intricate Knot*, 99; Roth, "Rebels and
Martyrs", 118–19. For an argument that abolitionist discourse and slave narratives introduced the
desire for "realism" to the Antebellum literary public, see Augusta Rohrbach, *Truth Stranger than
Fiction: Race, Realism and the U.S. Literary Marketplace* (New York: Palgrave, 2002), 1–50.

[26] The debate on this text is too vast to account for here. For similar readings, see Yellin, *Intricate Knot*,
215–27; Sundquist, *To Wake the Nations*, 135–84; Ryan, *Grammar of Good Intentions*, 69–75; for a
useful overview of the critical debate, see Maggie Montesinos Sale, *The Slumbering Volcano:
American Slave Ship Revolts and the Production of Rebellious Masculinity* (Durham, NC: Duke
University Press, 1997), 146–72.

5. W. Harvey, detail from the frontispiece for Maria Edgeworth's *Popular Tales* illustrating "The Grateful Negro," engraved by F. Engleheart. London: Baldwin and Craddock, 1832. Courtesy of Morris Library, SIUC.

when the Antebellum literary attention to slavery was at its highest pitch – shows the "good master," Edwards, in an ambiguous position, standing over a grateful submissive female slave in a somewhat menacing posture, holding a crop; the British 1832 edition, published right at the moment of emancipation, on the other hand, depicts a far less masculine Edwards in the act of handing his trusted slave a sharp knife (see Figures 5 and 6).

   In the Antebellum period, then, gratitude remained a charged term, even as it sank from view as a primary marker of racial difference. Frederick Douglass challenges the "familial" view of slavery, for instance, by insisting on his master's "base ingratitude to my poor old grandmother."[27] Still, even Douglass' grandmother is not a "grateful slave," but instead a loyal, faithful one. His challenge is less to the "grateful slave" than to the proslavery vision of the plantation Mammy: "She had served my old master faithfully from youth to old age. She had been the source of all his wealth;

[27] Douglass, *Narrative*, 76.

6. William Croome, detail from the frontispiece for Maria Edgeworth's *Popular Tales* illustrating "The Grateful Negro," 1852, Baltimore: Kelly, Piet & Co, 1869. Courtesy of Morris Library, SIUC.

she had peopled his plantation with slaves; she had become a great grandmother in his service" (76). Rather than being rewarded with her master's kindness, according to Douglass, her devotion is repaid only with cruelty, although it nonetheless never seems to wane:

in their hands she saw her children, her grandchildren, and her great-grandchildren, divided, like so many sheep, without being gratified with the small privilege of a single word, as to their or her own destiny. And, to cap the climax of their base ingratitude and fiendish barbarity, my grandmother, who was now very old, having outlived my old master and all his children, having seen the beginning and end of all of them, and her present owners finding she was of but little value, her frame already racked with the pains of old age, and complete helplessness fast stealing over her once active limbs, they took her to the woods, built her a little hut, put up a little mud-chimney, and then made her welcome to the privilege of supporting herself there in perfect loneliness; thus virtually turning her out to die! (76–7)

Douglass here accepts the irrational devotion of the "faithful," rather than the "grateful" slave, in the image of the plantation Mammy, only to turn it to account as an index of slave owners' selfish depravity.

The radical abolitionist T. W. Higginson, who wrote a series for the *Atlantic* on slave rebellions for the express purpose of countering the image of slave contentment and docility, and showing the manly achievements of African Americans, nonetheless offers a sentimental tale of a "faithful slave" (in a report on the aftermath of Nat Turner's uprising) that translates the eighteenth-century "grateful slave" into Antebellum terms:

There is one touching story, in connection with these terrible retaliations, which rests on good authority, that of the Rev. M. B. Cox, a Liberian missionary, then in Virginia. In the hunt which followed the massacre, a slaveholder went into the woods, accompanied by a faithful slave, who had been the means of saving his life during the insurrection. When they had reached a retired place in the forest, the man handed his gun to his master, informing him that he could not live a slave any longer, and requesting him either to free him or shoot him on the spot. The master took the gun, in some trepidation, levelled it at the faithful negro, and shot him through the heart. It is probable that this slaveholder was a Dr. Blunt, – his being the only plantation where the slaves were reported as thus defending their masters. "If this be true," said the "Richmond Enquirer," when it first narrated this instance of loyalty, "great will be the desert of these noble-minded Africans." This "noble-minded African," at least, estimated his own desert at a high standard: he demanded freedom, – and obtained it.[28]

The meaning of this bizarre anecdote is difficult to parse. In many "grateful slave" stories, the slave is "grateful" despite in fact being the one who has saved his master's life. At first blush, Higginson might seem to be parodying the absurdity of such a vision; he is certainly recasting the "faithful slave" of plantation fiction, refusing to depict him as a comic minstrel figure. Higginson seems instead to be genuinely intent on setting up the "faithful slave" as a "noble-minded" martyr. Biographical evidence shows that Higginson, despite his stated agenda in his series on rebellions for the *Atlantic* of countering the image of slave docility, was nonetheless convinced that blacks were disposed to be "devoted" to white leaders, even

---

[28] See *Army Life in a Black Regiment: And Other Writings*, 1870, intro. Robert D. Madison (New York: Penguin, 1997), 259–60. The original article, "Nat Turner's Insurrection," was first published in *The Atlantic*, 8:46 (August 1861), 173–87, and was later collected into Higginson's book, *Black Rebellion*.

bragging about the malleability of the black troops he commanded during the Civil War and boasting that he could induce them to follow any order of his.[29] Like Stowe, despite his series on insurrections, Higginson seems to prefer the sentimental impact of the self-sacrificing slave martyr to the harrowing threat of the determined slave rebel.

"The grateful slave," then was a transformative trope in the eighteenth century, making plausible a sense of serious racial difference within the framework of Christian monogenesis, thereby justifying the continued pursuit of slavery in ameliorated form. Although as George M. Fredrickson argues, "scientific" difference remained marginal throughout the Antebellum period, nonetheless racial difference and meaningful racial characteristics began to be taken for granted, and so the specifics of the grateful slave trope lost their efficacy. But nonetheless, the underlying dynamics of the grateful slave trope became even more central. The idea that slaves consented to their bondage no longer needed narrative explanation, but instead became a cornerstone of the society, in pro-slavery paternalism, anti-slavery "romantic racialism," and even more broadly in widely disseminated texts, often aimed at the education of children, promulgating what Lesley Ellen Ginsberg has termed "the myth of the willing captive," a myth that authorized relations of domination in sentimental terms across a number of relationships by rendering them equivalent, including owner–pet, parent–child, husband–wife, and slave–master.[30]

The grateful slave, then, lives on in the nineteenth century less in direct adaptations and revisions, than in providing a model of sentimentalized views of slavery adaptable for both pro-slavery and anti-slavery writers, and even more crucially in the images of black docility – and black violence – as "racial" characteristics. Jean Fagan Yellin begins *The Intricate Knot*, her study of the tropes of slavery in Antebellum fiction, with Jefferson's *Notes on the States of Virginia*, arguing that it provided inspiration to pro-slavery writers, in its suggestions of racial difference, and to anti-slavery writers in its dark warnings of coming insurrection. I have argued that Jefferson's depiction of blacks as "creatures of sensation rather than reflection" is a philosophical rendition of the racial difference encoded in the grateful slave trope. Several scholars have issued calls for a recognition of the debts of Antebellum sentimentalism to the moral philosophy of the Scottish

---

[29] Fredrickson, *The Black Image*, 169–71.
[30] See "The Willing Captive: Childhood and the Ideology of Love in Hawthorne's *A Wonder Book for Boys and Girls*" in "The Romance of Dependency: Childhood and the Ideology of Love in American Literature, 1825–1870" (Ph.D. diss., Stanford University, 1997), 148–93.

Enlightenment,[31] but despite the association of sentimentalism with depictions of slavery, and the recent renewal of interest in literary and cultural transatlanticism, little work has been done in tracing the evolution of eighteenth-century British tropes of slavery and race into their nineteenth-century US successors. I offer this Epilogue as a tentative step toward understanding these transatlantic connections.

---

[31] See Bruce Burgett, *Sentimental Bodies: Sex, Gender and Citizenship in the Early Republic* (Princeton: Princeton University Press, 1998), 15–16, and June Howard, "What is Sentimentality," *American Literary History*, 11:1 (1999), 69–71.

Bibliography

Adair, James Makittrick. *Unanswerable Arguments Against the Abolition of the Slave Trade*. London: J. P. Bateman, [1790].

Adventures of Jonathan Corncob, Loyal American Refugee. Written by Himself. London: The Author, 1787.

Adventures of a Kidnapped Orphan. London: M. Thrush, 1747.

Africanus, Leo. *The History and Description of Africa*. 1600. 3 vols. Trans. John Pory. Ed. Robert Brown. London: Hakluyt Society, 1896.

Allen, Theodore. *The Invention of The White Race*, Vol. I: *Racial Oppression and Social Control*. London: Verso, 1994.

   The Invention of the White Race, Vol. II: *Origin of Racial Oppression in Anglo-America*. New York: Verso, 1997.

Anderson, Benedict. *Imagined Communities: Reflections on the Rise and Spread of Nationalism*. Rev. edn. London: Verso, 1991.

Andersen, Hans. "The Paradox of Trade and Morality in Defoe." *Modern Philology*, 39:1 (1941), 23–46.

Andrew, Donna T. *Philanthropy and Police: London Charity in the Eighteenth Century*. Princeton: Princeton University Press, 1989.

Annesley, James. *Memoirs of an Unfortunate Young Nobleman*. 3 vols. London: J. Freeman, 1743–7.

Appiah, Anthony. "The Uncompleted Argument: DuBois and the Illusion of Race." In *"Race," Writing, and Difference*. Ed. Henry Louis Gates, Jr. Chicago: University of Chicago Press, 1985. 21–37.

Appiah, Anthony and Amy Gutmann. *Color Conscious: The Political Morality of Race*. Princeton: Princeton University Press, 1996.

Aravamudan, Srinivas. *Tropicopolitans: Colonialism and Agency, 1688–1804*. Durham, NC: Duke University Press, 1999.

Armitage, David. *The Ideological Origins of the British Empire*. Cambridge: Cambridge University Press, 2000.

Armstrong, Katharine. "'I was a Kind of an Historian': The Productions of History in Defoe's *Colonel Jack*." In *Tradition in Transition: Women Writers, Marginal Texts, and the Eighteenth-Century Canon*. Ed. Alvaro Ribeiro, SJ, and James S. Basker. Oxford: Clarendon, 1996. 97–110.

Armstrong, Nancy. *Desire and Domestic Fiction: A Political History of the Novel*. New York: Oxford University Press, 1987.

Atkins, John. *A Voyage to Guinea, Brazil and the West Indies in His Majesty's Ships, the "Swallow" and "Weymouth."* 1735. London: Cass, 1970.

Aubin, Penelope. *Life of Carlotta Du Pont, an English Lady.* London: Bettesworth, 1723.

Augstein, Hannah F. "Introduction." In *Race: The Origins of an Idea.* London: Thoemmes, 1996. ix–xxxiii.

Austen, R. A. and W. D. Smith. "Images of Africa and British Slave Trade Abolition: The Transition to an Imperialist Ideology, 1787–1807." *African Historical Studies*, 2:1 (1969), 69–83.

Backscheider, Paula. *Daniel Defoe: His Life.* Baltimore: Johns Hopkins University Press, 1989.

    Daniel Defoe: Ambition and Innovation. Lexington: University Press of Kentucky, 1986.

Baepler, Paul. "The Barbary Captivity Narrative in Early America." *Early American Literature*, 30 (1995), 95–120.

    White Slaves, African Masters: An Anthology of American Barbary Captivity. Chicago: University of Chicago Press, 1999.

Bage, Robert. *Man As He Is.* 2nd edn. 4 vols. London: Minerva, 1792.

Bailyn, Bernard. *Atlantic History.* Cambridge, MA: Harvard University Press, 2005.

    "The Idea of Atlantic History." *Itinerario*, 20 (1996), 19–44.

Baker, Houston A. Jr. "Figurations for a New American Literary History: Section V." In *Blues, Ideology, and Afro-American Literature: A Vernacular Theory.* Chicago: University of Chicago Press, 1984. 31–50.

Bakhtin, M. M. *Rabelais and His World.* Trans. Helene Iswolsky. Bloomington: Indiana University Press, 1984.

Barker, Anthony J. *The African Link: British Attitudes to the Negro in the Era of the Atlantic Slave Trade, 1550–1807.* London: Cass, 1978.

Barker-Benfield, G. J. *The Culture of Sensibility: Sex and Society in Eighteenth-Century Britain.* Chicago: University of Chicago Press, 1992.

Bartels, Emily C. "Before Imperialism: Richard Hakluyt and the Construction of Africa." *Criticism*, 34 (1992), 517–38.

    "*Othello* and Africa: Postcolonialism Reconsidered." *William and Mary Quarterly*, 54:1 (1997), 45–64.

Barthelemy, Anthony. *Black Face Maligned Race: The Representation of Blacks in English Drama from Shakespeare to Southerne.* Baton Rouge: Lousiana State University Press, 1987.

Basker, James G. "'To the Next Insurrection of the Negroes': Johnson, Race and Rebellion." *The Age of Johnson*, 11 (2000), 37–51.

Basker, James G., ed. *Amazing Grace: An Anthology of Poems about Slavery, 1660–1810.* New Haven: Yale University Press, 2002.

Bass, Jeff D. "An Efficient Humanitarianism: The British Slave Trade Debates, 1791–2." *Quarterly Journal of Speech*, 75 (1989), 152–65.

Behn, Aphra. *Oroonoko, or, The Royal Slave: A True History.* London, 1688.

    Oroonoko: A Bedford Cultural Edition. Ed. Catherine Gallagher. New York: Bedford, 2000.

Belgrove, William. *A Treatise Upon Husbandry or Planting*. Boston: Fowle, 1755.

Belsham, William. *Essays, Philosophical, Historical, and Literary*. London: C. Dilly, 1789.

Bender, John. *Imagining the Penitentiary: Fiction and the Architecture of Mind in Eighteenth-Century England*. Chicago: University of Chicago Press, 1989.

Bender, Thomas, ed. *The Anti-Slavery Debate: Capitalism and Abolitionism as a Problem in Historical Interpretation*. Berkeley: University of California Press, 1992.

Benezet, Anthony. *Some Historical Account of Guinea*. Philadelphia: Crukshank, 1771.

Bentham, Jeremy. "Panopticon Papers." In *A Bentham Reader*. Ed. Mary Peter Mack. New York: Pegasus, 1969. 194–208.

Berlin, Ira. *Many Thousands Gone: The First Two Centuries of Slavery in North America*. Cambridge, MA: Harvard University Press, 1998.

Berg, Maxine. *The Age of Manufactures, 1700–1820: Industry, Innovation, and Work in Britain*. 2nd edn. New York: Routledge, 1994.

Bernasconi, Robert. "Kant as an Unfamiliar Source of Racism." In *Philosophers on Race*. Ed. Julie K. Ward and Tommy L. Lott. Oxford: Blackwell, 2002. 145–66.

"Who Invented the Concept of Race? Kant's Role in the Enlightenment Construction of Race." In *Race*, ed. Robert Bernasconi. Boston: Blackwell, 2001. 11–36.

Birdsall, Virginia. *Defoe's Perpetual Seekers*. Lewisville: Bucknell University Press, 1985.

Blackburn, Robin. *The Making of New World Slavery: From the Baroque to the Modern 1492–1800*. London: Verso, 1997.

Overthrow of Colonial Slavery 1776–1848. London: Verso, 1988.

Blasingame, John. *The Slave Community: Plantation Life in the Antebellum South*. New York: Oxford University Press, 1972.

Blewett, David. *Defoe's Art of Fiction*. Toronto: Toronto University Press, 1979.

Bloquet, Olwyn M. "Bryan Edwards and the Haitian Revolution." In *The Impact of the Haitian Revolution in the Atlantic World*. Ed. David P. Geggus. Columbia: University of South Carolina Press, 2001. 44–57.

Boardman, Michael M. *Defoe and the Uses of Narrative*. New Brunswick: Rutgers University Press, 1983.

Boime, Albert. *The Art of Exclusion: Representing Blacks in the Nineteenth Century*. Washington: Smithsonian Institution, 1990.

Bolster, W. Jeffrey. *Black Jacks: African American Seamen in the Age of Sail*. Cambridge, MA: Harvard University Press, 1998.

Bonhote, Elizabeth. *Rambles of Mr. Frankly*. Dublin: Sleater, 1773.

Boose, Linda. "'The Getting of a Lawful Race': Racial Discourse and the Unrepresentable Black Woman." In *Women, "Race," and Writing in The Early Modern Period*. Ed. Margo Hendricks and Patricia Parker. New York: Routledge, 1994. 35–54.

Booth, Martin. *The Rhetoric of Fiction*. Chicago: University of Chicago Press, 1961.

Boswell, James. *Boswell's London Journal 1762–1763*. Ed. Frederick A. Pottle. New York: McGraw-Hill, 1950.

Boulukos, George. "Maria Edgeworth's 'Grateful Negro' and the Sentimental Argument for Slavery." *Eighteenth-Century Life*, 23 (1999), 12–29.

"Olaudah Equiano and the Eighteenth-Century Debate on Africa." *Eighteenth-Century Studies*, 40:2 (2007), 241–55.

"The Horror of Hybridity: Enlightenment, Anti-slavery and Racial Disgust in Charlotte Smith's *Story of Henrietta* (1800)." *Essays and Studies*, 60 (2007), 87–109. (Special volume *Slavery and the Cultures of Abolition: Essays Making the Bicentennial of the Brition Abolition Act*. Ed. Brycchan Carey and Peter J. Kitson.)

Bowen, Scarlett. " 'A Sawce-Box and Boldface Indeed': Refiguring the Female Servant in the Pamela–Antipamela Debate." *Studies in Eighteenth-Century Culture*, 28 (1999), 257–85.

Boyce, Benjamin. "The Question of Emotion in Defoe." *Studies in Philology*, 50:1 (1953), 45–58.

Bozeman, Terry S. "Interstices, Hybridity, and Identity: Olaudah Equiano and the Discourse of the African Slave Trade." *Studies in the Literary Imagination*, 36:2 (2003), 61–70.

Brandstater, Evan. "Uncle Tom and Archy Moore: The Antislavery Novel as Ideological Symbol." *American Quarterly*, 26:2 (1974), 160–75.

Brantlinger, Patrick. *Rule of Darkness: British Literature and Imperialism, 1830–1914*. Ithaca: Cornell University Press, 1988.

"Victorians and Africans: The Genealogy of the Myth of the Dark Continent." In *"Race," Writing, and Difference*. Ed. Henry Louis Gates, Jr. Chicago: University of Chicago Press, 1985. 185–222.

Braude, Benjamin. "The Sons of Noah and the Construction of Ethnic and Geographical Identities in the Medieval and Early Modern Periods." *William and Mary Quarterly*, 64:1 (1997), 103–42.

Breen, T. H. and Stephen Innes. *"Myne Owne Ground": Race and Freedom on Virginia's Eastern Shore*. New York: Oxford University Press, 1980.

Brooks, Joanna. *American Lazarus: Religion and the Ride of African-American and Native Literatures*. New York: Oxford University Press, 2003.

Brown, Christopher Leslie. "Empire without Slaves: British Concepts of Emancipation in the Age of the American Revolution." *William and Mary Quarterly*, 56:2 (1999), 273–306.

Moral Capital: Foundations of British Abolitionism. Chapel Hill: University of North Carolina Press, 2006.

Brown, John. *A Dictionary of the Holy Bible*. Edinburgh: John Gray, 1769.

Brown, Laura. *Ends of Empire: Women and Ideology in Early Eighteenth-Century Literature*. Ithaca: Cornell University Press, 1993.

Brown, Laura and Felicity Nussbaum, eds. *The New Eighteenth Century*. New York: Methuen, 1987.

Buck-Morss, Susan. "Hegel and Haiti." *Critical Inquiry*, 26 (2000), 821–65.

Burgett, Bruce. *Sentimental Bodies: Sex, Gender and Citizenship in the Early Republic*. Princeton: Princeton University Press, 1998.

Burke, Edmund. *A Letter from the Right Honorable Edmund Burke to a Noble Lord.* London: J. Owen and F. and C. Rivington, 1796.

Burnard, Trevor. *Mastery, Tyranny, and Desire: Thomas Thistlewood and his Slaves in the Anglo-Jamaican World.* Chapel Hill: University of North Carolina Press, 2004.

Burr, Sandra. "Science and Imagination in Anglo-American Children's Books, 1760–1855." Ph.D. diss., The College of William and Mary, 2005.

Bush, Barbara. *Slave Women in Caribbean Society 1650–1838.* Bloomington: Indiana University Press, 1990.

Caldwell, Tanya. " 'Talking Too Much English': Languages of Economy and Politics in Equiano's *The Interesting Narrative.*" *Early American Literature*, 34 (1999), 263–82.

Cannadine, David. *The Rise and Fall of Class in Britain.* New York: Columbia University Press, 1999.

Canup, John. *Out of the Wilderness: The Emergence of an American Identity in Colonial New England.* Middletown, CT: Wesleyan University Press, 1990.

Carey, Brycchan. *British Abolitionism and the Rhetoric of Sensibility: Writing, Sentiment, and Slavery, 1760–1807.* New York: Palgrave, 2005.

Carretta, Vincent. "Defining a Gentleman: The Status of Olaudah Equiano or Gustavus Vassa." *Language Sciences*, 22 (2000), 385–99.

Equiano, The African: Biography of a Self-Made Man. Athens, GA: University of Georgia Press, 2005.

"Olaudah Equiano or Gustavus Vassa? New Light on an Eighteenth-Century Question of Identity." *Slavery and Abolition*, 20:3 (1999), 96–105.

"Three West Indian Writers of the 1780s Revisited and Revised," *Research in African Literatures*, 29:4 (1998), 73–86.

Carretta, Vincent and Philip Gould, eds. *Genius in Bondage: Literature of the Early Black Atlantic.* Lexington: University Press of Kentucky, 2001.

"A Catalogue of the Names of those Holy Martyrs who were Burned in Queen Maries Reign." London, 1679.

Cave, Alfred A. "Canaanites in a Promised Land: The American Indian and the Providential Theory of Empire." *American Indian Quarterly*, 12 (1988), 277–97.

Chandler, Anne. "Defying 'Development': Thomas Day's Queer Curriculum in Sandford and Merton." In *Novel Gazing: Queer Readings in Fiction.* Ed. Eve Kosofsky Sedgwick. Durham, NC: Duke University Press, 1997. 201–26.

"Pedagogical Fantasies: Rousseau, Maleness, and Domesticity in the Fiction of Thomas Day, Maria Edgeworth, and Mary Wollstonecraft." Ph.D. diss., Duke University, 1995.

Chaplin, Joyce E. "Race," In *The British Atlantic World 1500–1800.* Ed. David Armitage and Michael J. Braddick. New York: Palgrave, 2001. 154–73.

Charke, Charlotte. *History of Henry Dumont, esq. and Miss Charlotte Evelyn.* London: H. Slater, 1756.

Cheyfitz, Eric. *The Poetics of Empire: Translation and Colonization from The Tempest to Tarzan.* New York: Oxford University Press, 1991.

Child, Elizabeth. "Elizabeth Montagu, Bluestocking Businesswoman." *Huntington Library Quarterly*, 64:1–2 (2002), 153–73.

Childs, Matt D. Review of *The Sugar Industry and the Abolition of the Slave Trade, 1774–1810* by Selwyn H. H. Carrington. H-Net reviews in the Humanities and Social Sciences, 2004. <http://www.h-net.org/reviews/showpdf.cgi?path_162771080787028>. (accessed January 3, 2006).

Chinosole. "Tryin' to Get Over: Narrative Posture in Equiano's Autobiography." In *The Art of Slave Narrative: Original Essays in Criticism and Theory*. Ed. John Sekora and Darwin T. Turner. Macomb, IL: Western Illinois University Press, 1982. 45–54.

Clark, Anna. *The Struggle for the Breeches: Gender and the Making of the British Working Class*. Berkeley: University of California Press, 1995.

Clark, J. C. D. *The Language of Liberty 1660–1832: Political Discourse and Social Dynamics in the Anglo-American World*. Cambridge: Cambridge University Press, 1994.

Clarkson, Thomas. *An Essay on the Impolicy of the African Slave Trade*. London: J. Phillips, 1788.

History of the Rise, Progress and Accomplishment of the Abolition of the Slave Trade. Philadelphia: James P. Parke, 1808.

Claydon, Tony and Ian McBride, eds. *Protestantism and National Identity: Britain and Ireland, c.1650–c.1850*. Cambridge: Cambridge University Press, 1998.

Coleman, Deirdre. "Conspicuous Consumption: White Abolitionism and English Women's Protest Writing in the 1790s." *ELH*, 61:2 (1994), 341–63.

Romantic Colonization and British Anti-Slavery. Cambridge: Cambridge University Press, 2005.

Colley, Linda. *Britons: Forging the Nation 1707–1837*. New Haven: Yale University Press, 1992.

Captives. New York: Pantheon, 2002.

Constantine, J. Robert. "The African Slave Trade: A Study of Eighteenth-Century Propaganda and Public Controversy." Ph.D. diss., Indiana University, 1953.

Cox, Jeffery N. ed., *Slavery, Abolition and Emancipation: Writings in the British Romantic Period*. Vol. V: *Drama*. London: Pickering and Chatto, 1999.

Cranston, Maurice. *The Noble Savage: Jean-Jacques Rousseau 1754–1762*. Chicago: University of Chicago Press, 1991.

Craton, Michael, *Testing the Chains: Resistance to Slavery in the British West Indies*. Ithaca: Cornell University Press, 1982.

Cugoano, Quobna Ottobah. *Thoughts and Sentiments on the Evil of Slavery*. Ed. Vincent Carretta. New York: Penguin, 1999.

Curtin, Philip D. *The Image of Africa: British Ideas and Action, 1780–1850*. Vol. I. Madison: University Wisconsin Press, 1964. 88–113.

Dabydeen, David. *Hogarth's Blacks: Images of Blacks in Eighteenth-Century English Art*. Athens, GA: University of Georgia Press, 1987.

Damrosch, Leopold. *God's Plot and Man's Stories: Studies in the Fictional Imagination from Milton to Fielding*. Chicago: University of Chicago Press, 1985.

Davidson, Basil. *West Africa Before the Colonial Era: A History to 1850*. New York: Longman, 1998.

Davis, David Brion. *Inhuman Bondage: The Rise and Fall of Slavery in the New World*. New York: Oxford University Press, 2006.

"The Emergence of Immediatism in British and American Anti-Slavery Thought." *Mississippi Valley Historical Review*, 49:2 (1962), 209–30.

The Problem of Slavery in the Age of Revolution, 1770–1828. Ithaca: Cornell University Press, 1975.

The Problem of Slavery in Western Culture. New York: Oxford University Press, 1966.

Day, Thomas. *The Dying Negro*. London, 1773.

Fragment of an Original Letter on the Slavery of the Negroes; Written in the Year 1776. London: John Stockdale, 1784.

The History of Sandford and Merton. 3 Vols. 1783–1789. Ed. Isaac Kramnick. New York: Garland, 1977.

Deal, J. Douglas. *Race and Class in Colonial Virginia: Indians, Englishmen, and Africans on the Eastern Shore During the Seventeenth Century*. New York: Garland, 1993.

Defoe, Daniel. *Colonel Jack*, 1722. Ed. Samuel Holt Monk. New York: Oxford University Press, 1989.

Robinson Crusoe. 1719. Ed. J. Donald Crowley. Oxford: Oxford University Press, 1972.

The Great Law of Subordination Consider'd. London: S. Harding *et al.*, 1726.

Dodsley, Robert. *The Oeconomy of Human Life*. 9th edn. Vol I. London: Dodsley, 1758.

Douglass, Frederick. *Narrative of the Life of Frederick Douglass*. Ed. Benjamin Quarles. Cambridge, MA: Harvard University Press, 1960.

Dykes, Eva Beatrice. *The Negro in English Romantic Thought, Or a Study of Sympathy for the Oppressed*. Washington: Associated Publishers, 1942.

Ebersole, Gary. *Captured by Texts: Puritan to Postmodern Images of Indian Captivity*. Charlottesville: University of Virginia Press, 1995.

Eddy, Donald D. "Dodsley's 'Oeconomy of Human Life,' 1750–1751." *Modern Philology*, 85:4 (1988), 460–79.

Edgeworth, Maria. *Belinda*, 1801. Ed. Eiléan Ni Chuilleanain. London: Dent, 1993.

"The Good Aunt." In *Moral Tales*. London: Routledge, 1801. 200–74.

"The Grateful Negro." In *Popular Tales*. London: J. Johnson, 1804. 193–240.

Edwards, Bryan. *History, Civil and Commercial, of the British Colonies in the West Indies*. 2 vols. London: J. Stockdale, 1793.

Edwards, Jonathan. "The Nature of True Virtue." In *Basic Writings*. Ed. Ola Winslow. New York: Signet, 1966. 241–9.

Edwards, Paul. "Introduction." In Ignatius Sancho. *The Letters Of Ignatius Sancho*. Ed. Paul Edwards and Polly Rewt. Edinburgh: Edinburgh University Press, 1994. 1–22.

"Introduction." In Ottobah Cugoano. *Thoughts and Sentiments*. Reprint edn. London: Dawson's, 1969. vii–xi.

Unreconciled Strivings and Ironic Strategies: Three Afro-British Authors of the Georgian Era: Ignatius Sancho, Olaudah Equiano, Robert Wedderburn. Edinburgh: Edinburgh University Press, 1992.

Elkins, Stanley. *Slavery: A Problem in American Institutional and Intellectual Life.* Chicago: University of Chicago Press, 1959.

Ellingson, Ter. *The Myth of the Noble Savage.* Berkeley: University of California Press, 2001.

Ellis, Frank J. *American Sphinx: The Character of Thomas Jefferson.* New York: Knopf, 1997.

Ellis, Markman. "Ignatius Sancho's *Letters*: Sentimental Libertinism and the Politics of Form." In *Genius in Bondage: Literature of the Early Black Atlantic.* Ed. Vincent Carretta and Philip Gould. Lexington: University Press of Kentucky, 2001. 199–217.

The Politics of Sensibility: Race, Gender and Commerce in the Sentimental Novel. Cambridge: Cambridge University Press, 1996.

Ellison, Julie. *Cato's Tears and the Making of Anglo-American Emotion.* Chicago: University of Chicago Press, 1999.

Elrod, Eileen Razzari. "Moses and the Egyptian: Religious Authority in Olaudah Equiano's *Interesting Narrative.*" *African American Review*, 35:3 (2001), 409–25.

Ennis, Daniel James. *Enter the Press-Gang: Naval Impressment in Eighteenth-Century British Literature.* Cranbury, NJ: University of Delaware Press, 2002.

Equiano, Olaudah. *The Interesting Narrative and Other Writings.* Ed. Vincent Carretta. New York: Penguin, 1995.

Erickson, Peter. "Representations of Blacks and Blackness in the Renaissance." *Criticism*, 35:4 (1993), 499–527.

Estwick, Samuel, *Considerations on the Negroe Cause Commonly So Called.* London: J. Dodsley, 1772.

Considerations on the Negroe Cause Commonly So Called. 2nd edn. London: J. Dodsley, 1773.

Eze, Emmanuel Chukwudi. "The Color of Reason: The Idea of 'Race' in Kant's Anthropology." In *Anthropology and the German Enlightenment: Perspectives on Humanity.* Ed. Katherine M. Faull. Lewisburg, PA: Bucknell University Press, 1995. 200–41.

Eze, Emmanuel Chukwudi. ed. *Race and the Enlightenment.* Boston: Blackwell, 1997.

Fabian, Johannes. *Time and the Other.* New York: Columbia University Press, 1983.

Faller, Lincoln. *Crime and Defoe: A New Kind of Writing.* Cambridge: Cambridge University Press, 1993.

Faulkner, Peter. *Robert Bage.* Boston: G. K. Hall, 1979.

Ferguson, Moira. "Juggling the Categories of Race, Class and Gender." In *Women, "Race," and Writing in The Early Modern Period.* ed. Margo Hendricks and Patricia Parker. New York: Routledge, 1994. 138–59.

"*Mansfield Park*: Slavery, Colonialism, and Gender." *Oxford Literary Review*, 13 (1991), 118–39.

"*Oroonoko*: Birth of a Paradigm." *New Literary History*, 32:2 (1992), 346–7.

Subject to Others: British Women Writers and Colonial Slavery, New York: Routledge, 1992.

Fichtelberg, Joseph. "Word Between Worlds: The Economy of Equiano's Narrative." *American Literary History*, 5:3 (1993), 459–80.

Fields, Barbara J. "Slavery, Race and Ideology in the United States of America." *New Left Review*, 181 (1990), 95–118.

Finkelman, Paul. "Jefferson and Slavery: 'Treason Against the Hopes of the World.'" *Jeffersonian Legacies*. Ed. Peter Onuf. Charlottesville: University of Virginia Press, 1993. 181–221.

Fisher, Phillip. "Making a Thing into a Man: The Sentimental Novel and Slavery." In *Hard Facts: Setting and Form in the American Novel*. New York: Oxford University Press, 1985. 87–127.

Fletcher, Anthony. *Gender, Sex and Subordination in England 1500–1800*. New Haven: Yale University Press, 1995.

Fliegelman, Jay. *Prodigals and Pilgrims: The American Revolution Against Patriarchal Authority 1750–1800*. Cambridge: Cambridge University Press, 1982.

Floyd-Wilson, Mary. *English Ethnicity and Race in Early Modern Drama*. Cambridge: Cambridge University Press, 2003.

Flynn, Paul. "*Man As He Is* and Romanticism as It Ought to Be." *Critical Survey*, 4:1 (1992), 28–35.

Fogel, Robert. *Without Consent or Contract: The Rise and Fall of American Slavery*. New York: Norton, 1989.

A Forensic Dispute on the Legality of Enslaving Africans. Boston: Boyle, 1773.

Foucault, Michel. *Discipline and Punish: The Birth of the Prison*. Trans. Alan Sheridan. New York: Vintage, 1979.

Foxe, John. *Acts and Monuments*. Vol. III. London, 1684.

Fraiman, Susan. "Jane Austen and Edward Said: Gender, Culture, and Imperialism." *Critical Inquiry*, 21:4 (1995), 805–21.

Francklyn, Gilbert. *An Answer to the Rev. Mr. Clarkson's Essay*. London: Logographic, 1789.

Observations, Occasioned by the Attempts Made in England to Effect the Abolition of the Slave Trade. London: Logographic, 1789.

Fredrickson, George M. *The Black Image in the White Mind: The Debate on Afro-American Character and Destiny, 1817–1914*. New York: Harper, 1971.

French, Scot. *The Rebellious Slave: Nat Turner in American Memory*. Boston: Houghton Mifflin, 2004.

French, Scot and Edward L. Ayers. "The Strange Career of Thomas Jefferson: Race and Slavery in American Memory, 1943–1993." In *Jeffersonian Legacies*. Ed. Peter Onuf. Charlottesville: University of Virginia Press, 1993. 418–56.

Froger, François. *A Relation of a Voyage Made in 1695, 1696, and 1697*. London, 1698.

Fryer, Peter. *Staying Power: The History of Black People in Britain*. London: Pluto, 1984.

Gallagher, Catherine. "*Oroonoko's* Blackness." In *Aphra Behn Studies*. Ed. Janet Todd Cambridge: Cambridge University Press, 1994. 235–58.

"Workers and Slaves: The Rhetoric of Freedom in the Debate over Industrialism." In *The Industrial Reformation of English Fiction 1832–1867*. Chicago: Chicago University Press, 1985. 3–35.

Gallay, Allan. *The Formation of a Planter Elite: Jonathan Bryan and the Southern Colonial Frontier*. Athens, GA: University of Georgia Press, 1989.

Garvey, John and Noel Ignatiev, eds. *Race Traitor*. New York: Routledge, 1996.

Gates, Henry Louis, Jr., ed. *"Race," Writing and Difference*. Chicago: University of Chicago Press, 1986.

The Signifying Monkey: A Theory of African American Literary Criticism. New York: Oxford University Press, 1986.

"Writing, 'Race' and the Difference it Makes." In *"Race," Writing and Difference*. Ed. Henry Louis Gates. 1–20.

Gaspar, David Barry. *Bondmen and Rebels: A Study of Master–Slave Relations in Antigua with Implications for Colonial British America*. Baltimore: Johns Hopkins University Press, 1985.

"Sugar Cultivation and Slave Life in Antigua Before 1800." In *Cultivation and Culture: Labor and the Shaping of Slave Life in the Americas*. Ed. Ira Berlin and Philip D. Morgan. Charlottesville: University of Virginia Press, 1993. 101–23.

Gautier, Gary. "Slavery and the Fashioning of Race in Oroonoko, Robinson Crusoe, and Equiano's *Life*." *The Eighteenth Century: Theory and Interpretation*, 42:2 (2001), 161–79.

Geggus, David P. *Haitian Revolutionary Studies*. Bloomington: Indiana University Press, 2002.

Geggus, David P. ed. *The Impact of the Haitian Revolution*. Columbia: University of South Carolina Press, 2001.

Genovese, Eugene. *Roll Jordan Roll: The World the Slaves Made*. New York: Vintage, 1976.

Gerzina, Gretchen. *Black London: Life Before Emancipation*. New Brunswick: Rutgers University Press, 1995.

Gibbes, Sir Philip. *Instructions for the Treatment of Negroes*. London: Shepperson and Reynolds, 1786, reprinted with additions, 1797.

Gifford, George. "Daniel Defoe and Maryland." *Maryland Historical Review*, 52:4 (1957), 307–15.

Gill, John. *An Exposition of the Old Testament*. London: The Author, 1763.

Gilroy, Paul. *Against Race: Imagining Political Culture Past the Color Line*. Cambridge, MA: Harvard University Press, 2000.

The Black Atlantic: Modernity and Double Consciousness. Cambridge, MA: Harvard University Press, 1993.

Ginsberg, Lesley Ellen. "Of Babies, Beasts, and Bondage: Slavery and the Question of Citizenship in Antebellum American Children's Literature." In *The American Child: A Cultural Studies Reader*. Ed. Caroline F. Levander and Carol J. Singley. New Brunswick: Rutgers University Press, 2003. 85–92.

"The Romance of Dependency: Childhood and the Ideology of Love in American Literature, 1825–1870." Ph.D. diss., Stanford University, 1997.

Ginzburg, Carlo. "Making Things Strange: The Prehistory of a Literary Device." *Representations*, 56 (1996), 8–28.

Gisborne, Thomas. *The Principles of Moral Philosophy Investigated*. 2nd edn. London: T. Bensley, 1790.

Gladfelder, Hal. *Criminality and Narrative in Eighteenth-Century England: Beyond the Law*. Baltimore: Johns Hopkins University Press, 2001.

Godwin, William. *Enquiry Concerning Political Justice*. 3 vols. Ed. F. E. L. Priestley. Toronto: University of Toronto Press, 1946.

Godwyn, Morgan. *The Negro's and Indians Advocate*. London: The Author, 1680.

Goldberg, David Theo. *Racist Culture: Philosophy and the Politics of Meaning*. Cambridge: Blackwell, 1993.

Racial Subjects: Writing on Race in America. New York: Routledge, 1997.

Gomez, Michael A. *Exchanging Our Country Marks: The Transformation of African Identities in the Colonial and Antebellum South*. Chapel Hill: University of North Carolina Press, 1998.

Gookin, Daniel. *An Historical Account of the Doings and Sufferings of the Christian Indians in New England in the Years 1675, 1676, 1677. Transactions and Collections of the American Antiquarian Society*, 2 (1836), 423–534.

Gordon, Scott Paul. *The Power of the Passive Self 1640–1770*. Cambridge: Cambridge University Press, 2002.

Gordon-Reed, Annette. *Thomas Jefferson and Sally Hemings: An American Controversy*. Charlottesville: University of Virginia Press, 1997.

Gould, Eliga H. "Zones of Law, Zones of Violence: The Legal Geography of the British Atlantic, circa 1772." *William and Mary Quarterly*, 60:3 (2003), 471–510.

Gould, Philip. *Barbaric Traffic: Commerce and Antislavery in the Eighteenth-Century Atlantic World*. Cambridge, MA: Harvard University Press, 2003.

Gould, Stephen J. *The Mismeasure of Man*. New York: Norton, 1981.

Green, William A. "Race and Slavery: Considerations on the Williams Thesis." In *British Capitalism and Caribbean Slavery: The Legacy of Eric Williams*, ed. Barbara L. Solow and Stanley L. Engerman. Cambridge: Cambridge University Press, 1987. 25–49.

Grenby, M. O. *The Anti-Jacobin Novel: British Conservatism and the French Revolution*. Cambridge: Cambridge University Press, 2001.

Guasco, Michael. "Encounters, Identities, and Human Bondage: The Foundations of Racial Slavery in the Anglo-Atlantic World." Ph.D. diss., College of William and Mary, 2000.

Guffey, George. "Aphra Behn's Oroonoko: Occasion and Accomplishment." In *Two English Novelists, Aphra Behn and Anthony Trollope: Papers Read at a Clark Library Seminar, May 11, 1974*. Los Angeles: Clark Library, 1975. 3–41.

Hair, P. E. H. "Attitudes to Africans in English Primary Sources on Guinea up to 1650." *History in Africa*, 26 (1999), 43–68.

Hair, P. E. H. and Robin Law. "The English in Western Africa to 1700." In *The Origins of Empire: British Oversees Expansion to the Close of the Seventeenth Century*. Ed. Nicholas D. Canny. New York: Oxford University Press, 1998.

Hall, Douglas. *In Miserable Slavery: Thomas Thistlewood in Jamaica, 1750–86*. London: MacMillan, 1989.

Hall, Jacqueline Dowd. " 'The Mind that Burns in every Body': Women, Rape, and Racial Violence." In *Powers of Desire: The Politics of Sexuality*. Ed. Ann Snitow *et al*. New York: Monthly Review, 1983.

Hall, Kim F. *Things of Darkness: Economies of Race and Gender in Early Modern England*. Ithaca: Cornell University Press, 1995.

Hannaford, Ivan. *Race: The History of an Idea in the West*. Baltimore: Johns Hopkins University Press, 1996.

Harris, Cheryl. "Whiteness as Property." *Harvard Law Review*, 106:8 (1993), 1707–91.

Hart, Richard. *Slaves Who Abolished Slavery: Blacks in Rebellion, 1985*. Kingston: University of West Indies Press, 2002.

Hartman, Saidiya V. *Scenes of Subjection: Terror, Slavery, and Self-Making in Nineteenth-Century America*. New York: Oxford University Press, 1997.

Haskell, Thomas L. "Capitalism and the Origins of Humanitarian Sensibility, Part I.& Part II." *American Historical Review*, 90 (1985), 339–61, 547–67.

Hatfield, April Lee. " 'A Very Wary People in their Bargaining' or 'Very Good Marchandise': English Traders' Views of Free and Enslaved Africans, 1550–1650." *Slavery & Abolition*, 23:4 (2004), 1–17.

Haydon, Colin. *Anti-Catholicism in Eighteenth-Century England, c. 1714–80: A Political and Social Study*. Manchester: Manchester University Press, 1993.

Hecht, J. Jean. *The Domestic Servant Class in Eighteenth-Century England*. London: RKP, 1956.

Heilman, R. B. *America in English Fiction: 1760–1800*. Baton Rouge: Louisiana State University Press, 1937.

Helgerson, Richard. *Forms of Nationhood: The Elizabethan Writing of England*. Chicago: University of Chicago Press, 1992.

Helme, Elizabeth. *The Farmer of Inglewood Forest*, 1796. Reprinted in *The New Novelists Magazine*. New York: T. Kinnersly, 1836.

Helo, Ari and Peter Onuf. "Jefferson, Morality, and the Problem of Slavery." *William and Mary Quarterly*, 60:3 (2003), 583–614.

Hendricks, Margo and Patricia Parker, eds. *Women, "Race," and Writing in The Early Modern Period*. New York: Routledge, 1994.

Henry, Matthew. *An Exposition of All the Books the Old and New Testament*. Vol. I. London: J. Clark, *et al.*, 1725.

An Exposition of the Old and New Testament. Vol. I. London: J. Stratford, [1793].

Higginson, T. W. "Nat Turner's Insurrection." *The Atlantic Monthly*, 8:46 (1861).

Hinds, Elizabeth Jane Wall. "The Spirit of Trade: Olaudah Equiano's Conversion, Legalism, and the Merchant's *Life*." *African American Review*, 32:4 (1998), 635–47.

Hirschman, Albert O. *The Passions and the Interests: Political Arguments for Capitalism Before its Triumph*. Princeton: Princeton University Press, 1977.

Hobbes, Thomas. *Leviathan*. 1651. Ed. C. B. MacPherson. Baltimore: Penguin, 1968.

Hochschild, Adam. *Bury the Chains: Prophets and Rebels in the Fight to Free an Empire's Slaves*. Boston: Houghton Mifflin, 2005.

Hofkosh, Sonia. "Tradition and the *Interesting Narrative*: Capitalism, Abolitionism, and the Romantic Individual." In *Romanticism, Race, and Imperial Culture, 1780–1834*. Ed. Alan Richardson and Sonia Hofkosh. Bloomington: Indiana University Press, 1996. 330–43.

Hogg, Peter C. *The African Slave Trade and its Suppression: A Classified and Annotated Bibliography of Books Pamphlets and Periodical Articles*. London: Cass, 1973.

Honour, Hugh. *The Image of the Black in Western Art*. Vol. IV: *From the American Revolution to World War I*. Pt. 1: *Slaves and Liberators*. Cambridge, MA: Harvard University Press, 1989.

Hornback, Robert. "Emblems of Folly in the First Othello: Renaissance Blackface, Moor's Coat, and 'Muckender.'" *Comparative Drama*, 35:1 (2001), 69–99.

Howard, June. "What is Sentimentality?" *American Literary History*, 11:1 (1999), 63–81.

Hubbard, William. *A Narrative of the Troubles with the Indians in New-England*. 1677. Reprinted in *The History of the Indian Wars in New England*, 2 vols. Ed. Samuel Drake. New York: Burt Franklin, 1865.

Hudson, Nicholas. "'Britons Never Will be Slaves'": National Myth, Conservatism, and the Beginnings of British Antislavery." *Eighteenth-Century Studies*, 34 (2001), 559–76.

Hughes, Derek. "Race, Gender, and Scholarly Practice: Aphra Behn's *Oroonoko*." *Essays in Criticism*, 52:1 (2002), 1–22.

Hulme, Peter. *Colonial Encounters: Europe and the Native Caribbean 1492–1797*. New York: Routledge, 1986.

Hume, David. *Essays: Moral, Political and Literary*. Rev edn. Ed. Eugene F. Miller. Indianapolis: Liberty Fund, 1985.

Hunter, J. Paul. *Before Novels: The Cultural Contexts of Eighteenth-Century Fiction*. New York: Norton, 1990.

Hutchinson, William. *The Princess of Zanfara*. London: Wilkie, 1789.

Ignatiev Noel, *How the Irish Became White*. New York: Routledge, 1995.

Inchbald, Elizabeth. *Such Things Are*. London: J. Robinson, 1788.

Innes, C. L. *A History of Black and Asian Writing in Britain, 1700–2000*. Cambridge: Cambridge University Press, 2002.

Innes, William. *The Slave-Trade Indispensable*. London: W. Richardson *et al.*, 1790.

Isaac, Rhys. *Landon Carter's Uneasy Kingdom: Revolution and Rebellion on a Virginia Plantation*. New York: Oxford University Press, 2004.

Jackson, Harvey H. "Hugh Bryan and the Evangelical Movement in South Carolina." *William and Mary Quarterly*, 43:4 (1986), 594–614.

James, C. L. R. *The Black Jacobins: Toussaint L'Ouverture and the San Domingo Revolution*. 2nd edn. New York: Vintage, 1963.

Jefferson, Thomas. *Notes on the State of Virginia*, 1785. Ed. Frank Shuffleton. New York: Penguin, 1999.

Jobson, Richard. *The Golden Trade or A Discovery of the River Gambra and the Golden Trade of the Aethiopians*. 1623. London: Dawsons, 1968.

Johns, Alessa. *Women's Utopias of the Eighteenth Century*. Urbana: University of Illinois Press, 2003.

Johnson, Claudia L. *Equivocal Beings: Politics, Gender, and Sentimentality in the 1790s: Wollstonecraft, Radcliffe, Burney, Austen*. Chicago: University of Chicago Press, 1995.

   Jane Austen: Women, Politics, and the Novel. Chicago: University of Chicago Press, 1988.

Johnson, Samuel. "Taxation No Tyranny." In *The Works of Samuel Johnson, LL. D.: Together with His Life*. Vol. X. Ed. John Hawkins. London: J. Buckland *et al.*, 1787.

Jones, Chris. *Radical Sensibility: Literature and Ideas in the 1790s*. New York: Routledge, 1993.

Jones, Eldred D. *The Elizabethan Image of Africa*. Charlottesville: University of Virginia Press, 1971.

Jordan, Winthrop. "An Antislavery Proslavery Document." *Journal of Negro History*, 47:1 (1962), 54–6.

   White Over Black: American Attitudes Toward the Negro 1550–1812. Baltimore: Penguin, 1969.

Jordan-Lake, Joy. *Whitewashing Uncle Tom's Cabin: Nineteenth-Century Women Novelists Respond to Stowe*. Nashville: Vanderbilt University Press, 2005.

Kant, Immanuel. *Physical Geography* (selections). Trans. K. M. Faull and E. C. Eze. *Race and the Enlightenment*. Ed. E. C. Eze. Boston: Blackwell, 1997.

   "Section Four: Of National Characteristics, so Far as They Depend on the Sublime and the Beautiful." In *Observations on the Feeling of the Beautiful and Sublime*. 1763. Trans. John T. Goldthwait. Berkeley: University of California Press, 1960.

   "What is Enlightenment." Trans. Peter Gay. In *The Enlightenment: A Comprehensive Anthology*. Ed. Peter Gay. New York: Simon and Schuster, 1973. 383–9.

Kaul, Suvir. *Poems of Nation, Anthems of Empire: English Verse in the Long Eighteenth Century*. Charlottesville: University of Virginia Press, 2000.

Keane, Patrick. "Slavery and the Slave Trade: Crusoe as Defoe's Representative." In *Critical Essays on Daniel Defoe*. Ed. Roger D. Lund. New York: G. K. Hall, 1997.

Kelly, Gary. "Enlightenment and Revolution: The Philosophical Novels of Dr. John Moore." *Eighteenth-Century Fiction*, 1:3 (1989), 219–37.

Kimber, Edward. *History of the Life and Adventures of Mr. Anderson*. London: W. Owen, 1754.

   Itinerant Observation in America, 1745–46. Ed. Kevin J. Hayes. Newark, DE: University of Delaware Press, 1998.

King, John N. "Literary Aspects of Foxe's Acts and Monuments." In *Critical Apparatus and Additional Material. Foxe's Book of Martyrs Variorum Edition Online v.1.0*. http://www.hrionline.ac.uk/foxe/apparatus/kingessay.html (accessed May 17, 2004).

Kirkham, E. Bruce. *The Building of* Uncle Tom's Cabin. Knoxville: University of Tennessee Press, 1977.

Knott, John R. *Discourses of Martyrdom in English Literature, 1563–1694*. Cambridge: Cambridge University Press, 1993.

Knox, William. *A Letter from W. K. to W. Wilberforce*. London: J. Debrett, 1790.

Kolchin, Peter. *American Slavery: 1619–1877*. New York: Hill and Wang, 1993.

Kramnick, Isaac. "Children's Literature and Bourgeois Ideology: Observations on Culture and Industrial Capitalism in the Later Eighteenth Century." In *Culture and Politics From Puritanism to the Enlightenment*. Ed. Perez Zagorin. Berkeley: University of California Press, 1980. 203–40.

Kumar, Krishan. *The Making of English National Identity*. Cambridge: Cambridge University Press, 2003.

Kupperman, Karen Ordahl. *Indians & English: Facing off in Early America*. Ithaca: Cornell University Press, 2000.

Lacey, Barbara E. "Visual Images of Blacks in Early American Imprints." *William and Mary Quarterly*, 53:1 (1996), 137–80.

Langford, Paul. *A Polite and Commercial People*. New York: Oxford University Press, 1992.

Laqueur, Thomas. *Religion and Respectability: Sunday Schools and Working Class Culture 1780–1850*. New Haven: Yale University Press, 1976.

LaVallée, Joseph. *The Negro Equalled by Few Europeans*. 4 vols. Trans. anon. London: Robinson, 1790.

Law, Robin. "'Here is No Resisting the Country': The Realities of Power in Afro-European Relations on the West African Slave Coast." *Itinerario*, 18:2 (1994), 50–64.

  The Slave Coast of West Africa 1550–1750: The Impact of the Atlantic Slave Trade on an African Society. Oxford: Clarendon, 1991.

Lawrence, Sir William. *Lectures on Physiology, Zoology, and the Natural History of Man*. London: James Smith, 1822.

Lazarus-Black, Mindie. "Slaves, Masters, and Magistrates: Law and the Politics of Resistance in the English Speaking Caribbean, 1736–1834." American Bar Foundation Working Paper no. 9124.

Lee, Arthur. *An Essay in Vindication of the Continental Colonies, From a Censure of Adam Smith*. London: T. Beckett, 1764.

Lee, Sophia. *The Recess, or A Tale of Other Times*. 1783. Ed. April Alliston. Lexington: University Press of Kentucky, 2000.

Lemann, Nicholas. *The Big Test: The Secret History of the American Meritocracy*. New York: FSG, 1999.

Lepore, Jill. *New York Burning: Liberty, Slavery and Conspiracy in Eighteenth-Century Manhattan*. New York: Knopf, 2005.

The Name of War: King Philip's War and the Origins of American Identity. New York: Knopf, 1998.

Linebaugh, Peter and Marcus Rediker. *The Many-Headed Hydra: Sailors, Slaves, Commoners, and the Hidden History of the Revolutionary Atlantic.* Boston: Beacon, 2000.

Lipking, Joanna. "Confusing Matters: Searching the Backgrounds of *Oroonoko.*" In *Aphra Behn Studies.* Ed. Janet Todd. Cambridge: Cambridge University Press, 1994. 259–81.

Locke, John. *An Essay Concerning Human Understanding.* 1670. 2 vols. Ed. Alexander Campbell Fraser. New York: Dover, 1959.

The Second Treatise of Government, 1690. Ed. Thomas P. Peardon. Indianapolis: Bobbs-Merrill, 1952.

Long, Edward. *Candid Reflections Upon the Judgement Lately Awarded by the Court of King's Bench in Westminster-Hall on What Is Commonly Called the Negroe-Cause.* London: T. Lowndes, 1772.

The History of Jamaica. 3 vols. 1774. Intro. George Metcalf. London: Cass, 1970.

Lovejoy, David S. *Religious Enthusiasm in the New World: Heresy to Revolution.* Cambridge, MA: Harvard University Press, 1985.

Lutz, Alfred. "Commercial Capitalism, Classical Republicanism, and the Man of Sensibility in *The History of Sir George Ellison.*" *SEL*, 39:9 (1999), 557–74.

MacDonald, Joyce Green. "Race, Women and the Sentimental in Thomas Southerne's *Oroonoko.*" *Criticism*, 40:4 (1998), 555–70.

Macfarlane, Alan. *The Origins of English Individualism.* Oxford: Blackwell, 1978.

Mackenzie, Anna Maria. *Slavery: or The Times.* Dublin: P. Wogan, 1793.

Mackenzie, Henry. *Julia de Roubigné.* 1777. In *The Works of Henry Mackenzie, Esq.* Vol. II. Edinburgh: R. Sholey, 1815.

Maclaren, Archibald. *The Negro Slaves.* London, 1799.

[MacNeill, Hector]. *Memoirs of the Life and Travels of the Late Charles Macpherson, Esq.* Edinburgh: Arch. Constable. 1800.

Malcolmson, Robert W. *Popular Recreations in English Society, 1700–1850.* Cambridge: Cambridge University Press, 1973.

Malone, Maggie. "Patriarchy and Slavery in *Mansfield Park.*" *Essays in Poetics*, 18:2 (1993), 28–41.

Marglin, Stephen A. "Understanding Capitalism: Control Versus Efficiency." In *Power and Economic Institutions: Reinterpretations in Economic History.* Ed. Bo Gustafsson. Aldershot: Elgar, 1991. 225–52.

"What Do Bosses Do? The Origins and Functions of Hierarchy in Capitalist Production." *Review of Radical Political Economics*, 6:2 (1974), 33–60.

Marren, Susan. "Between Slavery and Freedom: The Transgressive Self in Olaudah Equiano's Autobiography." *PMLA*, 108:1 (1993), 94–105.

Marshall, Cynthia. "Foxe and the Jouissance of Martyrology." In *The Shattering of the Self: Violence, Subjectivity and Early Modern Texts.* Baltimore: Johns Hopkins University Press, 2002. 85–105.

Martin, Colonel Samuel. *Essay on Plantership*. 1750. 7th edn. Antigua: Robert Mearns, 1785.

Martyrologia Alphabetike. London: R. Butler, 1677.

Matar, Nabil. *Turks, Moors, and Englishmen in the Age of Discovery*. New York: Columbia University Press, 1999.

McBride, Dwight. *Impossible Witnesses: Truth, Abolitionism, and Slave Testimony*. New York: New York University Press, 2001.

McBurney, William H. "*Colonel Jacque*: Defoe's Definition of the Complete English Gentleman," *SEL*, 2:3 (1962), 321–36.

McCann, Andrew. "Conjugal Love and the Enlightenment Subject: The Colonial Context of Non-Identity in Maria Edgeworth's *Belinda*." *Novel*, 30:1 (1996), 56–77.

McIntosh, Peggy. "White Privilege and Male Privilege: A Personal Account of Coming to See Correspondences through Work in Women's Studies." Wellesley College Center for Research on Women Working Paper no. 189. 1988.

Meer, Sarah. *Uncle Tom Mania: Slavery, Minstrelsy and Transatlantic Culture in the 1860s*. Athens, GA: University of Georgia Press, 2005.

Melish, Joanne Pope. *Disowning Slavery: Gradual Emancipation and Race in New England 1780–1860*. Ithaca: Cornell University Press, 1998.

Metzger, Lore. "Introduction." In Aphra Behn. *Oroonoko, or The Royal Slave*. New York: Norton, 1973, ix–xv.

Midgley, Clare. *Women Against Slavery: The British Campaigns, 1780–1870*. New York: Routledge, 1992.

Miller, John Chester. *The Wolf By the Ears: Thomas Jefferson and Slavery*. 1977. Charlottesville: University of Virginia Press, 1991.

Mills, Charles W. *The Racial Contract*. Ithaca: Cornell University Press, 1997.

Montaigne, Michel de. "Of Cannibals." In *Complete Essays of Montaigne*. Trans. Donald Frame. Stanford: Stanford University Press, 1958. 150–9.

Montesquieu, Baron de. *The Spirit of the Laws*. 1748. Ed. Franz Neumann. New York: Hafner, 1966.

Moore, Francis. *Travels into the Inland Parts of Africa*. London: E. Cave, 1738.

Moore, John, Dr. *Zeluco*, 1786. 2 vols. *The British Novelists*. Ed. Mrs. Barbauld. Vols. XXXIV–XXXV. London: Rivington *et al.*, 1820.

Moore, Lisa L. *Dangerous Intimacies: Towards a Sapphic History of the British Novel*. Durham, NC: Duke University Press, 1997.

Moraley, William. *The Infortunate: The Voyage and Adventures of William Moraley, an Indentured Servant*. Ed. Susan E. Klepp and Billy G. Smith. University Park, PA: Pennsylvania State University Press, 1992.

Moran, Francis, III. "Between Primates and Primitives: Natural Man as the Missing Link in Rousseau's *Second Discourse*." In *Philosophers on Race*. Julie K. Ward and Tommy L. Lott. Oxford: Blackwell, 2002. 125–44.

Morgan, Edmund S. *American Slavery, American Freedom: The Ordeal of Colonial Virginia*. New York: Norton, 1975.

Morgan, Philip D. "British Encounters with Africans and African Americans, circa 1600–1780." In *Strangers within the Realm: Cultural Margins of the First British Empire*. Chapel Hill: University of North Carolina Press, 1991. 157–219.

Slave Counterpoint: Black Culture in the Eighteenth-Century Chesapeake and Lowcountry. Chapel Hill: University of North Carolina Press, 1998.

"Three Planters and Their Slaves: Perspectives on Slavery in Virginia, South Carolina, and Jamaica, 1750–1790." In *Race and Family in the Colonial South*. Ed. Winthrop D. Jordan and Sheila L. Skemp. Jackson: University Press of Mississippi, 1987. 37–79.

Morrow, Nancy V. "The Problem of Slavery in the Polemic Literature of the American Enlightenment." *Early American Literature*, 20:3 (1985–6), 236–55.

Motooka, Wendy. *The Age of Reasons: Quixotism, Sentimentalism and Political Economy in Eighteenth-Century Britain*. New York: Routledge, 1998.

Mottolese, William. "'Almost an Englishman': Olaudah Equiano and the Colonial Gift of Language." *Bucknell Review*, 41:2 (1998), 160–71.

Mtubani, Victor C. D. "The Black Voice in Eighteenth-Century Britain: African Writers Against Slavery and the Slave Trade." *Phylon*, 45:2 (1984), 85–97.

Mueller, Janel M. "Pain, Persecution, and the Construction of Selfhood." In *Religion and Culture in Renaissance England*. Ed. Claire McEachern and Deborah Shuger. Cambridge: Cambridge University Press, 1997. 168–87.

Muthu, Sankar. *Enlightenment Against Empire*. Princeton: Princeton University Press, 2003.

Nash, Richard. *Wild Enlightenment: The Borders of Human Identity in the Eighteenth Century*. Charlottesville: University of Virginia Press, 2003.

Netzley, Ryan. "The End of Reading: The Practice and Possibility of Reading Foxe's *Actes and Monuments*." *ELH*, 73:1 (2006), 187–214.

Nichols, Charles. "The Origins of Uncle Tom's Cabin." *Phylon*, 19:3 (1958), 328–34.

Nicholson, Erwin. "Eighteenth-Century Foxe: Evidence for the Impact of the *Acts and Monuments* in the 'Long' Eighteenth Century." In *John Foxe and the English Reformation*. Ed. David Loades. Aldershot: Scolar, 1997. 143–77.

Nisbet, Richard. *Capacity of Negroes for Religious and Moral Improvement Considered*. London: J. Phillips, 1789.

Slavery Not Forbidden By Scripture. Philadelphia, 1773.

Novak, Maximilian. *Defoe and the Nature of Man*. New York: Oxford University Press, 1963.

"Defoe's Use of Irony." in *The Uses of Irony*. Ed. Maximilian Novak. Berkeley: University of California Press, 1966. 7–38.

Economics and the Fiction of Daniel Defoe. Berkeley: University of California Press, 1962.

Nussbaum, Damian. "Appropriating Martyrdom: Fears of Renewed Persecution and the 1632 Edition of *Acts and Monuments*." In *John Foxe and the English Reformation*. Ed. David Loades. Aldershot: Scolar, 1997. 178–91.

Nussbaum, Felicity A. "Being a Man: Olaudah Equiano and Ignatius Sancho." In *Genius in Bondage: Literature of the Early Black Atlantic*. Ed. Vincent Carretta and Philip Gould. Lexington: University Press of Kentucky, 2001. 54–71.

The *Limits of the Human: Fictions of Anomaly, Race, and Gender in the Long Eighteenth Century*. Cambridge: Cambridge University Press, 2003.

Ogude, S. E. "Facts into Fiction: Equiano's Narrative Reconsidered." *Research in African Literatures*, 13 (1982), 31–43.

"Olaudah Equiano and the Tradition of Defoe." *African Literature Today*, 14 (1982), 77–90.

Oldham, James. "New Light on Mansfield and Slavery." *Journal of British Studies*, 27:1 (1988), 45–68.

Olwell, Robert. *Masters, Slaves, and Subjects: The Culture of Power in the South Carolina Low Country, 1740–1790*. Ithaca: Cornell University Press, 1998.

Onuf, Peter, ed. *Jeffersonian Legacies*. Charlottesville: University of Virginia Press, 1993.

Orban, Katalin. "Dominant and Submerged Discourses in *The Life of Olaudah Equiano (or Gustavus Vassa?)*." *African American Review*, 27:4 (1993), 655–64.

Pacheco, Anita. "Royalism and Honor in Aphra Behn's *Oroonoko*." *SEL*, 34:3 (1994), 491–506.

Paine, Thomas. *The Rights of Man*. London: J. Johnson, 1791.

Paley, William. *The Principles of Moral and Political Philosophy*, Foreword by D. L. Le Mahieu. Indianapolis: Liberty Fund, 2002.

Parent, Anthony S., Jr. *Foul Means: The Formation of a Slave Society in Virginia 1660–1740*. Chapel Hill: University of North Carolina Press, 2003.

Park, Mungo. *Travels in the Interior Districts of Africa*. 1799. Ed. Kate Ferguson Marsters. Durham, NC: Duke University Press, 2000.

Pateman, Carole. *The Sexual Contract*. Cambridge: Polity, 1988.

Patterson, Orlando. *Slavery and Social Death: A Comparative Study*. Cambridge, MA: Harvard University Press, 1982.

Peacock, Lucy. "The Creole." *The Rambles of Fancy; Or Moral and Interesting Tales*. Vol. II. London, T. Bensley, 1786. 111–77.

Pearson, Jacqueline. "'Slave Princesses and Lady Monsters': Gender and Ethnic Difference in the Work of Aphra Behn." In *Aphra Behn Studies*. Ed. Janet Todd. Cambridge: Cambridge University Press, 1994. 219–34.

Personal Slavery Established. Philadelphia: John Dunlap, 1773.

Phillips, Thomas. "Journal of a Voyage Made in the Hannibal of London, Ann. 1693, 1694." In *A Collection of Voyages and Travels*. Ed. Awnsham Churchill and John Churchill. Vol. VI. London, 1732. 171–239.

Philmore. *Two Dialogues on the Man-Trade*. London: J. Waugh, 1760.

Pieterse, Jan Nederveen. *White on Black: Images of Africa and Blacks in Western Popular Culture*. New Haven: Yale University Press, 1992.

Pilkington, Mary. "The Faithful Negro." In *Tales of the Hermitage; Written for the Instruction and Amusement of the Rising Generation*. 1798. London: J. D. Dewick, 1800. 188–209.

Pitts, Jennifer. "Edmund Burke's Peculiar Universalism." In *A Turn to Empire: The Rise of Imperial Liberalism in England and France*. Princeton: Princeton University Press, 2005. 59–100.

A Plan for Improving the Trade at Senegal. London: R. and J. Dodsley, 1762.

Pocock, J. G. A. "The Mobility of Property and the Rise of Eighteenth-Century Sociology." In *Virtue, Commerce and History: Essays on Political Thought and History, Particularly in the Eighteenth Century*. Cambridge: Cambridge University Press, 1985. 103–23.

Pohl, Nicole and Betty Schellenberg, eds. *Reconsidering the Bluestockings*. San Marino, CA: Huntington Library, 2003.

Postlethwayt, Malachy. *Selected Works*. Vol. II. Farnborough: Gregg, 1968.

Potkay, Adam. "Olaudah Equiano and the Art of Spiritual Autobiography." *Eighteenth-Century Studies*, 27:4 (1994), 677–92.

Pratt, Mary Louise. *Imperial Eyes: Travel Writing and Transculturation*. New York: Routledge, 1992.

Preston, William. *A Letter to Bryan Edwards, Esquire*. London: J. Johnson, 1795.

Price, Martin. *To The Palace of Wisdom*. New York: Doubleday, 1964.

Raboteau, Albert J. "African-Americans, Exodus, and the American Israel." In *African-American Christianity: Essays in History*. Ed. Paul E. Johnson. Berkeley: University of California Press, 1994. 1–17.

Radcliffe, Ann. *The Italian, Or The Confessional of the Black Penitents: A Romance*. 1796. Ed. Robert Miles. London: Penguin, 2000.

Rai, Amit S. *Rule of Sympathy: Sentiment, Race and Power 1750–1850*. New York: Palgrave, 2002.

Ramsay, James. *Essay on the Treatment and Conversion of African Slaves in the British Sugar Colonies*. London: James Phillips, 1784.

An Inquiry into the Effects of Putting a Stop to the African Slave Trade. London: J. Phillips, 1784.

A Letter to James Tobin, Esq. London: J. Phillips, 1787.

Ranby, John. *Observations on the Evidence . . . In Support of the Bill for Abolishing the Slave Trade*. London: J. Stockdale, 1791.

Rawson, Claude. "'Indians' and Irish: Montaigne, Swift, and the Cannibal Question," *Modern Language Quarterly*, 53:3 (1992), 299–363.

Raynal, Guillaume, Abbé. *A Philosophical and Political History of the Settlements and Trade of the Europeans in the East and West Indies*. 6 vols. Edinburgh: W. Gordon *et al.*, 1782.

Reid, Douglas. "The Decline of St. Monday 1766–1876." *Past and Present*, 71 (1976), 76–101.

"Weddings, Weekdays, Work and Leisure in Urban England, 1791–1911: The Decline of Saint Monday Revisited." *Past & Present*, 153 (1996), 135–63.

Rice, Duncan. *The Rise and Fall of Black Slavery*. New York: Harper, 1975.

Richardson, John. *Slavery and Augustan Literature: Swift, Pope, Gay*. New York: Routledge, 2004.

Richetti, John J. *Defoe's Narratives*. Oxford: Clarendon, 1975.

The English Novel in History, 1700–1780. London: Routledge, 1999.

Rivero, Alberto J. "Aphra Behn's *Oroonoko* and the 'Blank Spaces' of Colonial Fictions." *SEL*, 39:3 (1999), 443–62.

Rivers, Isabel. *Reason, Grace, and Sentiment: A Study of the Language of Religion and Ethics in England, 1660–1780.* Vol. II. Cambridge: Cambridge University Press, 2000.

Rodger, N. A. M. *The Wooden World: An Anatomy of the Georgian Navy.* Annapolis, MD: Naval Institute, 1986.

Roediger, David. *The Wages of Whiteness: Race and the Making of the American Working Class.* New York: Verso, 1991.

Rogers, Nicholas. "Vagrancy, Impressment and the Regulation of Labour in Eighteenth-Century Britain." *Slavery & Abolition*, 15:2 (1994), 102–13.

Rogers, Pat, ed. *Defoe: The Critical Heritage.* London: Routledge, 1972.

Rohrbach, Augusta. *Truth Stranger than Fiction: Race, Realism and the US Literary Marketplace.* New York: Palgrave, 2002.

Rose, Jacqueline. *The Case of Peter Pan or the Impossibility of Children's Fiction.* London: Macmillan, 1984.

Roth Sarah Nelson. "Rebels and Martyrs: The Debate Over Slavery in American Popular Culture, 1822–1865." Ph.D. diss., University of Virginia, 2002.

"The Mind of a Child: Images of African Americans in Early Juvenile Fiction," *Journal of the Early Republic*, 25:1 (2005), 79–109.

Rousseau, J. J. "Discourse on Inequality." In *The First and Second Discourses and Essay on the Origin of Language.* Ed. and trans. Victor Gourevitch. New York: Harper, 1986.

Emile: Or On Education. Ed. and trans. Allan Bloom. New York: Basic, 1979.

Rowlandson, Mary. *The Sovereignty and Goodness of God.* Cambridge, MA: S. Green, 1682.

"The Royal Martyrs or a List of the Lords, Knights, Commanders, and Gentlemen, that were Slain in the Late Wars, in Defence of Their King and Country." London: Newcomb, 1660.

Rozbicki, Michael J. "To Save Them From Themselves: Proposals to Enslave the British Poor; 1698–1755." *Slavery & Abolition*, 22:2 (2001), 29–50.

Rule, John. *The Labouring Classes in Early Industrial England 1750–1850.* New York: Longman, 1986.

Rush, Benjamin. *An Address to the Inhabitants of the British Settlements, on the Slavery of the Negroes in America.* 2nd edn. 1773. New York: Arno, 1969.

Rust, Marion. "The Subaltern as Imperialist: Speaking of Olaudah Equiano." In *Passing and the Fictions of Identity.* Ed. Elaine K. Ginsberg. Durham, NC: Duke University Press, 1996. 21–36.

Ryan, Susan M. *The Grammar of Good Intentions: Race and the Antebellum Culture of Benevolence.* Ithaca: Cornell University Press, 2003.

Sabino, Robin and Jennifer Hall. "The Path Not Taken: Cultural Identity in the Interesting Life of Olaudah Equiano." *MELUS*, 24:1 (1999), 5–19.

Said, Edward. *Culture and Imperialism.* New York: Knopf, 1993.

Saillant, John. "The American Enlightenment in Africa: Jefferson's Colonizationism and Black Virginians' Migration to Liberia, 1776–1840." *Eighteenth-Century Studies*, 31:3 (1998), 261–82.

"The Black Body Erotic and the Republican Body Politic, 1790–1820." In *Sentimental Men: Masculinity and the Politics of Affect in American Culture*. Ed. Mary Chapman and Glenn Hendler. Berkeley: University of California Press, 1999. 89–111.

Sale, Maggie Montesinos. *The Slumbering Volcano: American Slave Ship Revolts and the Production of Rebellious Masculinity*. Durham, NC: Duke University Press, 1997.

Samuels, Wilfred. "Disguised Voice in the Interesting Narrative of Olaudah Equiano, or Gustavus Vassa, the African." *Black American Literature Forum*, 19 (1985), 64–9.

Sancho, Ignatius. *Letters of the Late Ignatius Sancho, an African*. 1782. Ed. Vincent Carretta. New York: Penguin, 1998.

Sandiford, Keith A. *The Cultural Politics of Sugar: Caribbean Slavery and Narratives of Colonialism*. Cambridge: Cambridge University Press, 2000.

Measuring the Moment: Strategies of Protest in Eighteenth-Century Afro-English Writing. Selinsgrove, PA: Susquehanna University Press, 1988.

Sandhu, Sukhdev. "Ignatius Sancho and Laurence Sterne." *Research in African Literatures*, 29:4 (1998), 88–105.

Sapiro, Virginia. *A Vindication of Political Virtue: The Political Theory of Mary Wollstonecraft*. Chicago: University of Chicago Press, 1992.

Sayres, William Gosnell. "Compounding the Crime: Ingratitude and the Murder Conviction of Justine Moritz in Frankenstein." *English Language Notes*, 31:4 (1994), 48–54.

"The Discourse of Gratitude in the Novels of Jane Austen." Ph.D. diss., University of New Hampshire, 1995.

Scarry, Elaine. *The Body in Pain*. New York: Oxford University Press, 1985.

Schama, Simon. *Rough Crossings: Britain, the Slaves, and the American Revolution*. New York: Ecco, 2006.

Schaw, Janet. *Journal of a Lady of Quality; Being the Narrative of a Journey from Scotland to the West Indies, North Carolina, and Portugal, in the years 1774 to 1776*. Ed. Evangeline Walker Andrews with Charles McLean Andrews. New Haven: Yale University Press, 1923.

Scheuermann, Mona. *Social Protest in the Eighteenth-Century English Novel*. Columbus: Ohio State University Press, 1985.

Schiebinger, Londa. *Nature's Body: Gender in the Making of Modern Science*. Boston: Beacon, 1993.

Schmidt, Leigh Eric. "'The Grand Prophet': Hugh Bryan: Early Evangelicalism's Challenge to the Establishment and Slavery in the Colonial South." *South Carolina Historical Magazine*, 87:4 (1986), 238–50.

Schochet, Gordon J. *The Authoritarian Family and Political Attitudes in 17th-Century England: Patriarchalism in Political Thought*, 1975. New Brunswick: Transaction, 1988.

Scott, Sarah. *The History of Sir George Ellison*, 1766. Ed. Betty Rizzo. Lexington: University Press of Kentucky, 1996.

Seidel, Michael. *Robinson Crusoe: Island Myths and the Novel*. Boston: Twayne, 1991.

Sharp, Granville. *A Representation of the Injustice and Dangerous Tendency of Tolerating Slavery*. London: Benjamin White, 1769.

Sheridan, Richard B. "Samuel Martin, Innovating Sugar Planter of Antigua." *Agricultural History*, 34:3 (1960), 126–39.

Shifflett, Andrew. *Stoicism, Politics and Literature in the Age of Milton*. Cambridge: Cambridge University Press, 1998.

Shinagel, Michael. *Defoe and Middle Class Gentility*. Cambridge, MA: Harvard University Press, 1968.

Shyllon, F. O. *Black Slaves in Britain*. London: Oxford University Press, 1974.

James Ramsay: The Unknown Abolitionist. Edinburgh: Canongate, 1977.

Sidbury, James. *Ploughshares into Swords: Race, Rebellion, and Identity in Gabriel's Virginia, 1730–1810*. Cambridge: Cambridge University Press, 1997.

Sill, Geoffrey. *The Cure of the Passions and the Origins of the English Novel*. Cambridge: Cambridge University Press, 2001.

Skinner, Gillian. *Sensibility and Economics in the Novel, 1740–1800: The Price of a Tear*. New York: St. Martins, 1998.

Slave Trade: The Negro and the Free-Born Briton Compared. London: J. Stockdale, [1789].

Smith, Adam. *The Theory of Moral Sentiments*. 1759. Ed. D. D. Raphael and A. L. Macfie. Indianapolis: Liberty Fund, 1982.

The Wealth of Nations, 1776. Ed. Edwin Cannan. Chicago: University of Chicago Press, 1976.

Smith, Charlotte. *The Story of Henrietta*. In *The Letters of a Solitary Wanderer*. Vol. II. 1800. New York: Woodstock, 1995.

The Wanderings of Warwick. London: J. Bell, 1794.

Smith, Johanna M. "'Cooped Up': Feminine Domesticity in Frankenstein." In *Frankenstein*. E. Johanna Smith. 2nd edn. Boston: Bedford, 2000. 313–34.

Snader, Joe. *Caught Between Worlds: British Captivity Narratives in Fact and Fiction*. Lexington: University Press of Kentucky, 2000.

Snelgrave, William. *New Account of Some Parts of Guinea and the Slave Trade*. 1734. London: Cass, 1971.

Solomon, Harry M. *The Rise of Robert Dodsley: Creating the New Age of Print*. Carbondale, IL: Southern Illinois University Carbondale Press, 1996.

Some Gentlemen of St. Christopher. *An Answer to the Reverend James Ramsay's Essay, on the Treatment and Conversion of Slaves*. Basseterre, St. Christopher: Edward L. Low, 1784.

Spacks, Patricia Meyer. *Desire and Truth: Functions of Plot in Eighteenth-Century English Novels*. Chicago: University of Chicago Press, 1993.

Sparks, Randy J. *The Two Princes of Calabar: An Eighteenth-Century Atlantic Journey*. Cambridge, MA: Harvard University Press, 2004.

Stallybrass, Peter and Allon White. *The Politics and Poetics of Transgression*. London: Methuen, 1986.

Stanton, Lucia. "'The Blessings of Domestic Society': Thomas Jefferson and His Slaves." In *Jeffersonian Legacies*. Ed. Peter Onuf. Charlottesville: University of Virginia Press, 1993. 147–80.

Starr, G. A. "Aphra Behn and the Genealogy of the Man of Feeling." *Modern Philology*, 87:4 (1990), 362–72.

"'Only a Boy': Notes on Sentimental Novels." *Genre*, 10 (1977), 501–27.

Stepan, Nancy. *The Idea of Race in Science: Great Britain, 1800–1960*. Hamden, CT: Archon Books, 1982.

Stevens, Laura. *The Poor Indians: British Missionaries, Native Americans, and Colonial Sensibility*. Philadelphia: University of Pennsylvania Press, 2004.

Stewart, Maaja. "Ingratitude in *Tom Jones*." *Journal of English and Germanic Philology*, 89 (1990), 512–32.

"The Shadow Behind the Country House: West Indian Slavery and Female Virtue in *Mansfield Park*." In *Domestic Realities and Imperial Fictions: Jane Austen's Novels in Eighteenth-century Contexts*. Athens, GA: University of Georgia Press, 1993. 105–36.

[St. Lambert, J. F. de]. *Zimao. The African*. Trans. Rev. Weeden Butler. Dublin: Brett Smith, 1800.

Stoddard, Eve. "A Serious Proposal for Slavery Reform: Sarah Scott's *Sir George Ellison*," *Eighteenth-Century Studies*, 28:4 (1995), 379–98.

Stowe, Harriet Beecher. *Uncle Tom's Cabin*. Ed. Elizabeth Ammons. New York: Norton, 1994.

Straus, Ralph. *Robert Dodsley: Poet, Publisher, and Playwright*, 1910. New York: Burt Franklin, 1968.

Sundquist, Eric. *To Wake the Nations: Race in the Making of American Literature*. Cambridge, MA: Harvard University Press, 1993.

A Supplement to Mr. Wesley's Pamphlet. London: H. Reynell, 1774.

Sussman, Charlotte. *Consuming Anxieties: Consumer Protest, Gender, and British Slavery, 1713–1833*. Stanford: Stanford University Press, 2000.

Sutherland, James. *Daniel Defoe: A Critical Study*. Cambridge, MA: Harvard University Press, 1971.

Sweet, James H. "The Iberian Roots of American Racist Thought." *William and Mary Quarterly*, 54:1 (1997), 143–66.

Swift, Zephaniah. *An Oration on Domestic Slavery*. Hartford, CT: Hudson and Goodwin, 1791.

Sypher, Wylie. *Guinea's Captive Kings: British Anti-Slavery Literature of the XVIIIth Century*. 1942. New York: Octagon, 1969.

"The West Indian as a 'Character' in the Eighteenth Century." *Studies in Philology* 36 (1939), 503–20.

Thomas, Helen. *Romanticism and Slave Narratives: Transatlantic Testimonies*. Cambridge: Cambridge University Press, 2000.

Thomas, Hugh. *The Slave Trade*. New York: Simon & Schuster, 1997.

Thompson, E. P. *Customs in Common*. New York: New Press, 1993.

"Time, Work-Discipline and Industrial Capitalism." *Past & Present*, 38 (1968), 56–97.

Thompson, James. *Models of Value: Eighteenth-Century Political Economy and the Novel*. Durham, NC: Duke University Press, 1996.

Thomson, John. *The Travels and Surprising Adventures of John Thomson*. Edinburgh, 1761.

Thornton, John. *Africa and Africans in the Making of the Atlantic World*. 2nd edn. Cambridge: Cambridge University Press, 1998.

Tilly, Charles. *Popular Contention in Great Britain, 1758–1834*. Cambridge, MA: Harvard University Press, 1995.

Tise, Larry E. *The American Counterrevolution: A Retreat from Liberty, 1783–1800*. Mechanicsburg, PA: Stackpole, 1998.

　Proslavery: A History of the Defense of Slavery in America, 1701–1840. Athens, GA: University of Georgia Press, 1987.

Tobin, James. *Cursory Remarks upon the Reverend Mr. Ramsay's Essay*. London: G. and T. Wilkie, 1785.

Tokson, Elliot. *Popular Image of the Black Man in English Drama, 1550–1688*. Boston: G. K. Hall, 1982.

Tompkins, J. M. S. *The Popular Novel in England 1770–1800*. 1932. Lincoln, NB: University of Nebraska Press, 1961.

Tracy, Susan J. *In The Master's Eye: Representations of Women, Blacks and Poor Whites in Antebellum Southern Literature*. Amherst, MA: University of Massachusetts Press, 1995.

Trelawny, Edward. *Essay Concerning Slavery*. London: Charles Corbett, [1746].

Trumpener, Katie. *Bardic Nationalism: The Romantic Novel and the British Empire*. Princeton: Princeton University Press, 1997.

Ty, Eleanor. *Unsex'd Revolutionaries: Five Women Novelists of the 1790s*. Toronto: University of Toronto Press, 1993.

Tyler, Royall. *The Algerine Captive, or the Life and Adventures of Doctor Updike Underhill*. 1797. Ed. Caleb Crain. New York: Modern Library, 2002.

Unsworth, Barry. *Sacred Hunger*. New York: Doubleday, 1992.

Uring, Nathaniel. *A History of the Voyages and Travels of Capt. Nathaniel Uring*. London, 1726.

Vaughan, Alden T. *Roots of American Racism: Essays on the Colonial Experience*. New York: Oxford University Press, 1995.

Vaughan, Alden T. and Virginia Mason Vaughan, "Before Othello: Elizabethan Representations of Sub-Saharan Africa." *William and Mary Quarterly*, 54:1 (1997), 19–44.

Vickers, Ilse. *Defoe and the New Sciences*. Cambridge: Cambridge University Press, 1996.

Viswanathan, Gauri. *Outside the Fold: Conversion, Modernity, and Belief*. Princeton: Princeton University Press, 1998.

Vitkus, Daniel J. ed. *Piracy, Slavery, and Redemption: Barbary Captivity Narratives from Early Modern England*. New York: Columbia University Press, 2001.

Wahrman, Dror. *The Making of the Modern Self: Identity and Culture in Eighteenth-Century England*. New Haven: Yale University Press, 2004.

Walton, James. "The Romance of Gentility: Defoe's Heroes and Heroines." In *Literary Monographs* Vol. IV. Ed. Eric Rothstein. Madison: Wisconsin University Press, 1971. 99–110.

Walvin, James. *An African's Life: The Life and Times of Olaudah Equiano, 1745–1797*. London: Cassell, 1998.

England, Slaves and Freedom. Jackson: University Press of Mississippi, 1986.

Ward, J. R. *British West Indian Slavery, 1750–1834: The Process of Amelioration*. Oxford: Clarendon, 1988.

Watts, David. *The West Indies: Patterns of Development, Culture and Environmental Change Since 1492*. Cambridge: Cambridge University Press, 1987.

Wesley, John. *Thoughts Upon Slavery*. London: Hawes, 1774.

West, Cornel. *Race Matters*. New York: Vintage, 1994.

Wheeler, Roxann. "'Betrayed by Some of My Own Complexion': Cugoano, Abolition, and the Contemporary Language of Racialism." In *Genius in Bondage: Literature of the Early Black Atlantic*. Ed. Vincent Carretta and Philip Gould. Lexington: University Press of Kentucky, 2001. 17–38.

The Complexion of Race: Categories of Difference in Eighteenth-Century British Culture. Philadelphia: University of Pennsylvania Press, 2000.

Whitefield, George. *Three Letters from the Reverend Mr. G. Whitefield*. Philadelphia: D. Franklin, 1740.

Williams, Eric. *Capitalism and Slavery*. Chapel Hill: University of North Carolina Press, 1944.

Williams, Raymond. *The Country and the City*. New York: Oxford University Press, 1973.

Wilson, Kathleen. *The Island Race: Englishness, Empire and Gender in the Eighteenth Century*. New York: Routledge, 2003.

The Sense of the People: Politics, Culture, and Imperialism in England, 1715–1785. Cambridge: Cambridge University Press, 1995.

Wise, Steven M. *Though the Heavens May Fall: The Landmark Trial that Led to the End of Human Slavery*. Cambridge, MA: Da Capo, 2005.

Wokler, Robert. "Apes and Races in the Scottish Enlightenment: Monboddo and Kames on the Nature of Man." In *Philosophy and Science in the Scottish Enlightenment*. Ed. Peter Jones. Edinburgh: John Donald, 1988. 144–68.

Wollstonecraft, Mary. *A Vindication of the Rights of Men*. London: J. Johnson, 1791.

Wood, Gordon S. "The Ghosts of Monticello." In *Sally Hemings & Thomas Jefferson: History, Memory and Civic Culture*. Ed. Jan Ellen Lewis and Peter S. Onuf. Charlottesville: University of Virginia Press, 1999. 19–34.

Wood, Marcus. *Blind Memory: Visual Representations of Slavery in England and America 1780–1865*. New York: Routledge, 2000.

Slavery, Empathy and Pornography. Oxford: Oxford University Press, 2002.

Woodard, Helena. *African–British Writings in the Eighteenth Century: The Politics of Race and Reason*. Westport, CT: Greenwood, 1999.

Woolman, John. "Some Considerations on the Keeping of Negroes." 1754. In *Works of John Woolman, Part the Second*. 1775. Miami: Mnemosyne, 1969. 253–74.

Yellin, Jean Fagan. *The Intricate Knot: Black Figures in American Literature, 1776–1863*. New York: New York University Press, 1972.

Index

273